Minnesota
Land of 10,000 Lakes

Minnesota

Land of 10,000 Lakes

Amy C. Rea

with photographs by the author

The Countryman Press ✳ Woodstock, Vermont

FIRST EDITION

Copyright © 2008 by Amy C. Rea

First Edition

All rights reserved. No part of this book may be reproduced in any way by electronic or mechanical means, including information storage and retrieval systems, without permission in writing from the publisher, except by a reviewer, who may quote brief passages.

ISBN 978-0-88150-727-0

Cover photo © Bob Splichal, RS Photography
Interior photos by the author unless otherwise specified
Book design by Bodenweber Design
Page composition by PerfecType
Maps by Mapping Specialists Ltd., © 2008 The Countryman Press

Published by The Countryman Press, P.O. Box 748, Woodstock, Vermont 05091

Distributed by W.W. Norton & Company, Inc., 500 Fifth Avenue, New York, NY 10110

Printed in the United States of America

10 9 8 7 6 5 4 3 2 1

DEDICATION

To the "boys": Jim, Mitchell, and Michael, for their support, love, and laughter.
To my parents, for their support, love, and *lefse*.

EXPLORE WITH US!

Welcome to the first edition of a comprehensive guide to the Land of 10,000 Lakes: the state of Minnesota. Certainly there are lakes, and actually there are far more than 10,000, but Minnesota offers much more than just water. This guide is a friendly welcome to the state, filled with ideas to pique the interest of all kinds of visitors.

Minnesota: An Explorer's Guide is designed to be easy to read and simple to use. With this book in hand, you'll be ready to discover this state in all its glory: from remote wilderness, to charming small towns, to bustling metro areas with wide-ranging food and entertainment options. And contrary to popular opinion, the state doesn't close down for the winter—far from it. What follows is a quick guide to what's included in the chapters.

WHAT'S WHERE

Located at the beginning of this book, "What's Where" is an alphabetical listing of special highlights and important information that you can reference quickly. You'll find advice on everything from the upscale boutique hotels and fine dining of the Twin Cities to the best maps for navigating the Boundary Waters.

LODGING

The lodgings included in this guide were chosen on their merits; none of the innkeepers listed was charged for inclusion.

Prices: Please don't hold us or the respective innkeepers responsible for the rates listed as of press time. Changes are inevitable. As of press time in 2008, the state and local room tax can vary from 6 to 13 percent, and it is not included in rates listed in this guide.

RESTAURANTS

In most sections, please note the distinction between *Dining Out* and *Eating Out*. Restaurants listed under *Eating Out* are generally less expensive and more casual than those found in *Dining Out*. Beginning entrée prices are given for each restaurant.

SMOKING

Some communities, including the city of Minneapolis, have implemented no-smoking policies in all public places, including restaurants and bars. The issue is up for debate in other communities. Before lighting up at a restaurant or bar, check to make sure it's allowed.

KEY TO SYMBOLS

🐾 **Pets**. The dog-paw icon denotes lodgings that accept pets, which is not standard. Accommodations that accept pets usually charge extra fees and may have restrictions on types or sizes of pets allowed; they may also require advance notice.

✎ **Child-friendly**. The crayon represents a place or activity appropriate for young children. Most B&Bs prohibit children under 12.

♿ **Handicapped accessible**. The wheelchair symbol represents lodgings and restaurants that are handicapped accessible.

🍸 **Bar on premises**. The martini glass indicates a restaurant or hotel with a bar on site.

Please visit my blog (www.flyover-land.com) for up-to-the-minute reviews and news and to share in the adventure of Minnesota.

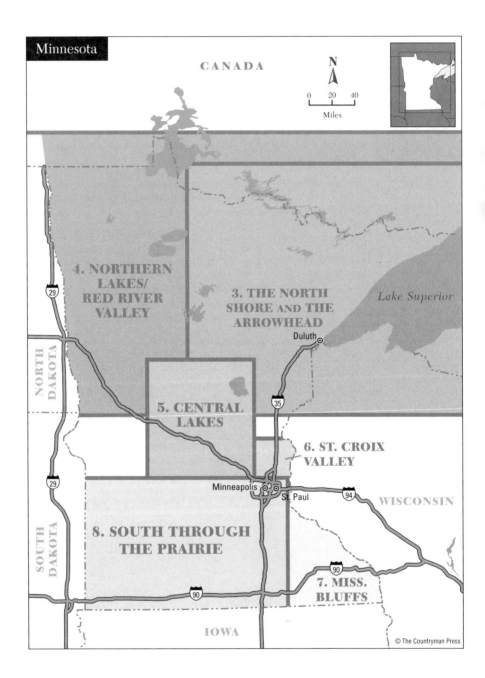

CONTENTS

ACKNOWLEDGMENTS

The people who helped, deliberately or inadvertently, is too long to list in full, but I'll give a shout-out to Antay Bilgutay, Lisa Dickinson, Mike Frickstad, Brian Malloy, Heidi Raatz, Deb Secrest, Don Sommers, and Terri Wentzka, who all provided information and interest in this book.

And for their unflagging patience, diligence, and encouragement, the editorial and PR team of Kim Grant, Jennifer Thompson, and Laura Jorstad deserve more thanks and gratitude than I can say.

INTRODUCTION

Minnesota is frequently misunderstood. For those who get their knowledge from popular media, Minnesota appears to be a land frequented by those wacky gals from *The Mary Tyler Moore Show*—except for the one corner populated by rock stars as glamorized by Prince in *Purple Rain.* The rest of the state? Garrison Keillor's *Prairie Home Companion* and the Coen brothers' classic *Fargo* tell the story: funny accents, hats with earflaps, church suppers, fish soaked in lye and served at Christmas dinner, a whole lot of snow, and backyard wood chippers.

As usual, the stereotyped images are somewhat true . . . but not the whole picture. Are there still people in small towns in Minnesota who talk like those people in *Fargo*? Sure. And while Mary Tyler Moore no longer throws her hat on Nicollet Mall, there is a sculpture immortalizing that very action. Prince? Still a Minnesota music icon, but far from the only one.

Personally, I love the above images. They represent certain facets of Minnesota. Perhaps what they best represent is the diversity inherent in the state,

ST. PAUL'S FOREPAUGH'S RESTAURANT IS HOUSED IN A HISTORIC MANSION.

where a lively metro area provides excellent access to the arts, pop culture, major-league sports, dining, and shopping. For those who want more of an outdoor experience, the state has not 10,000 lakes, but in fact more than 15,000, with opportunities for swimming, fishing (year-round: Ice fishing is nearly as popular as summer boat fishing), boating, and watersports. Campgrounds abound, as do resorts of all types and prices, from small, rustic "mom-and-pops" to the height of luxury.

In a region where the seasons are clearly different, Minnesotans have turned all four into reasons for celebration, with each offering its own activities and festivals. If ice fishing isn't your cuppa, perhaps a visit to St. Paul's Winter Carnival would be more enjoyable. Or a getaway to one of Minnesota's thousands of cabin resorts. Once there, it's your choice: Enjoy the hearty winter outdoor activities—snowshoeing, anyone?—or curl up with a good book in front of the fireplace or woodstove and listen to the peace and quiet of a snowy day.

As a Minnesotan born and raised, I've lived in both environments, the urban metro and the rural far north. One of the joys of this state is its ability to offer something for everyone to enjoy. There are visitors to Minnesota who are primarily interested in the Mall of America and base their multiple trips on that. Some come into the Twin Cities from smaller towns, happy to experience the metro life for a few days, while city dwellers set out to find a small town or rural area for a change of scenery. Others use the Twin Cities as a jumping-off point for all kinds of ventures: historical sightseeing throughout the state (ranging from Laura Ingalls Wilder sites; to literary landmarks memorializing F. Scott Fitzgerald and Sinclair Lewis; to a comprehensive, fun interactive history of the Iron Range at Ironworld), bike tours around the lakes of Minneapolis or along the Mississippi River to the headwaters in northern Minnesota, foliage hunting in fall, rest and relaxation far from the madding crowd.

In national livability surveys, Minnesota tends to rank very high, and the fac-

THE TWIN CITIES ENJOY A GROWING ETHNIC PRESENCE.

BLACKDUCK, MINNESOTA

tors that contribute to those rankings—superb quality of life, diverse leisure activities, a wide variety of cultures and habitats—make the state a leading choice for people of all ages, activity levels, and interests. Throughout the following chapters I'll lead you through a variety of places to visit, a highly diverse group from art museums to giant balls of twine, the deepest recesses of nature, and the Spam Museum. It's all here, and it's yours to pick and choose. This guide will help you learn what your options are in attractions, lodging, and dining. There will be choices of all types: deluxe hotels and resorts, small family-owned cabins, bed & breakfasts; five-star dining, small-town cafés, and quirky little restaurants with just about every cuisine imaginable. Minnesota may be known for its Scandinavian heritage, but current residents come from all over the world, with growing Somali, Asian, and Hispanic populations that have served to greatly improve the state's dining experiences. Shopping? The possibilities are nearly endless, from the massive Mall of America to the chic Galleria, the antiques stores in Stillwater, and artists' galleries in Grand Marais. It could take months to see and experience everything Minnesota has to offer, but with this guide you can plan for the time you have available, maximizing whatever experience you want to have—active or relaxed, urban or natural.

As I mentioned, I grew up and have lived in this state most of my life. But traveling its highways and byways while researching this book was like discovering it for the first time; I visited places I hadn't been in years. It sounds corny, but I came away from writing this book with a sense that Minnesota is, indeed, a highly worthwhile place to see, and one of the best things about it is how many different interests can be accommodated in one way or another. Besides that, the pride many Minnesotans take in their hometowns can be infectious; stop in any of the small regional historic museums listed in this guidebook, and you're likely to meet people who are enthusiastic and well versed in their area's history—and they might have some interesting and little-known stories to share with you. Friendliness and helpfulness are in full supply; it's hard to beat the graciousness offered by lakeside resort owners and bed & breakfast proprietors.

In conjunction with the publication of this book is the launch of my Web site, www.flyover-land.com. For those not familiar with the term *flyover land*, it's a derogatory term implying that only destinations on the East or West Coast are worth visiting. I hope this book will convince you otherwise, and please feel free to stop by the Web site to take a closer look at the *real* flyover land. I'll update the site with practical information about new accommodations, restaurants, activities, and events, as well as offering some potentially wry commentary along the way.

WHAT'S WHERE IN MINNESOTA

AREA CODE

There are seven area codes in Minnesota. In the Twin Cities area, 612 denotes Minneapolis and immediate surroundings; 651 is St. Paul and suburbs, including much of the St. Croix Valley; 763 is the northern Minneapolis suburbs; and 952 is the southern and southwestern Minneapolis suburbs. Northern Minnesota is 218; central Minnesota (outside the Twin Cities metro and suburban area) is 320; and southern Minnesota, 507.

AIRPORTS AND AIRLINES

Minneapolis/St. Paul International Airport (612-726-5555; www.mspairport.com) is the state's largest airport and is served primarily by Northwest Airlines (800-225-2525; www.nwa.com), but several other carriers serve the area as well. Flights depart to and arrive from all over the United States, as well as various international destinations, including Canada, Europe, the Caribbean, Mexico, and Asia. The following airlines serve the **Lindbergh Terminal**: Air Canada (888-247-2262; www.aircanada.com), America West (800-235-9292; www.americawest.com), American Airlines (800-433-7300; www.aa.com), Conti-

nental Airlines (800-525-0280; www.continental.com), Delta Air Lines (800-221-1212; www.delta.com), Frontier Airlines (800-432-1359; www.frontierairlines.com), KLM Royal Dutch Airlines (800-374-7747; www.klm.com), United Airlines (800-241-6522; www.ual.com), and US Airways (800-428-4322; www.usair.com). At the **Humphrey Terminal**, Air Tran Airways (800-247-8726; www.airtran.com), Champion Air (800-922-2606; www.championair.com), Icelandair (800-223-5500; www.icelandair.com), Miami Air International (305-876-3600; www.miamiair.com), Midwest Airlines (800-452-2022; www.midwestairlines.com), Sun Country Airlines (800-359-6786; www.suncountry.com), and Xtra Airways (800-258-8800) offer a mixture of commercial and charter services.

    Bemidji Regional Airport (218-444-2438; www.bemidjiairport.org), **Brainerd Lakes Regional Airport** (218-825-2166), **Chisholm/Hibbing Airport** (218-262-3451; www.hibbingairport.com), **International Falls International Airport** (218-283-8740; www.internationalfallsairport.com), **St. Cloud Regional Airport** (320-255-7292; www.stcloudairport

.com), and **Thief River Falls Regional Airport** (218-681-5585) are all served by Mesaba, linked with Northwest Airlines (800-225-2525; www.nwa.com). **Duluth International Airport** (218-727-2968; www.duluthairport.com) is also served by Mesaba/Northwest as well as Midwest Airlines (800-452-2022; www.midwest airlines.com) and Allegiant Air (702-555-8888; www.allegiantair.com). **Rochester International Airport** (507-282-2328; www.rochesterintlair port.com) is served by Mesaba/Northwest (800-225-2525; www.nwa.com), American Eagle Airlines (800-433-7300; www.aa.com), and Allegiant Air (702-555-8888; www.allegiantair.com).

AMTRAK

There is limited service in Minnesota by rail. **Amtrak** (800-USA-RAIL; www.amtrak.com) runs a train from the northwest quadrant, near North Dakota, through Minneapolis/St. Paul and on to Wisconsin and Chicago, once daily in each direction. The train is used more to transport people either east to Chicago or west to the Pacific coast than to travel within Minnesota.

AMUSEMENT PARKS

Valleyfair (800-FUN-RIDE; www.valleyfair.com) in Shakopee is Minnesota's biggest amusement park, with rides for little kids and big ones, too, along with a water park, mini golf, bumper boats, go-carts, an IMAX theater, and live music. **The Park at MOA** (952-883-8600; www.thepark atmoa.com), Bloomington, is an indoor theme park at the Mall of America with a more limited selection of rides, but at least it's open year-round.

ANTIQUARIAN BOOKS

The Twin Cities offer several good options, including **Magers & Quinn** (612-822-4611; www.magersandquinn .com), **Rulon-Miller Books** (651-290-0700; www.rulon.com), and **James & Mary Laurie Booksellers** (612-338-1114; www.lauriebooks.com), while Stillwater has **Loome Booksellers** (651-430-9805; www.loomebooks .com), which includes a theological division, and **St. Croix Antiquarian Booksellers** (651-430-0732).

ANTIQUES

Antiques shops abound in Minnesota, especially in the Twin Cities and many of the historic towns along the St. Croix, Mississippi, and Minnesota rivers. For detailed listings throughout the state, check with the **Minnesota Antiques Dealers Association** (651-426-4993; www .mnantiquesdealers.com).

AQUARIUMS

The **Underwater Adventures** (952-883-0202; www.sharky.tv) exhibit at the Mall of America in Bloomington has more than 4,500 sharks and other exotic aquatic creatures. In Duluth the **Great Lakes Aquarium** (218-740-3474; www.glaquarium.org) has extensive tanks of fish, but because most of them are freshwater species and native to the region, they may not be as interesting as the tropical sea life.

ARTISTS AND ART GALLERIES

The Twin Cities has a large, healthy arts community, and the visual arts are no exception. Galleries abound in the Warehouse District and Northeast

Minneapolis, and in downtown St. Paul. Farther north, the artist community in Grand Marais keeps several galleries busy, and the scenic drives through the southeast portion of the state (Stillwater, Lanesboro) will also yield several art galleries to visit. And don't forget about the outdoor sculpture garden in Franconia.

ART MUSEUMS

The Twin Cities are the primary sources for art museums in the state. The **Minneapolis Institute of the Arts** (MIA; www.artsmia.org) is the grande dame of art museums, with contemporary and centuries-old works of art. The **Walker** (www.walkerart.org) is the MIA's contemporary counterpoint, a museum where the building itself is a piece of art, as is the adjacent Sculpture Garden. The nearby **Weisman Art Museum** (www.weisman.umn.edu) is a newer member of the arts community, housed in a Frank Gehry building at the University of Minnesota. South Minneapolis's **Museum of Russian Art** (www.tmora.org) in a former church has a surprisingly in-depth permanent collection and visiting exhibitions. In St. Paul the **Minnesota Museum of American Art** (www.mmaa.org) is exactly what its name says. Duluth has the **Tweed Museum** (www.d.umn.edu/tma) at the University of Minnesota's Duluth campus, while down south in Winona is the **Minnesota Marine Art Museum** (www.minnesotamarineartmuseum.org), devoted to nautical artwork.

BALLOONING

Hot-air ballooning is particularly popular in Stillwater, where the scenic St.

Croix makes for a perfect bird's-eye trip. In the Twin Cities contact **Minneapolis Hot Air Balloons** (800-791-5867), **Minnesota Valley Balloons** (952-403-1064), **Balloon Adventures** (952-474-1662), or **Carousel Hot Air Balloons** (952-926-3101).

BEACHES

In the land of 10,000 (and more) lakes, it's a given that there's a beach around just about every corner. In many cases the beaches are attached to resorts that reserve those beaches for paying guests. However, most lake communities have at least one good-sized public beach, and some have several. The Central Lake District, including Brainerd, Willmar, and Mille Lacs, has hundreds of lakes with beaches public and private. Farther north the lake areas around Bemidji and up to the Canadian border, along Voyageurs National Park, have beaches, too, although the swimming season may be shorter. In the Twin Cities, Lakes Harriet, Nokomis, and Calhoun all have public swimming beaches. Many of the surrounding suburbs have city and county parks with public beaches.

BED & BREAKFASTS

Especially down the eastern side of Minnesota, B&Bs have become tremendously popular as a lodging option, particularly given the number of historic homes in those areas. Many are housed in grand 19th-century residences, some of which had prominent local citizens as the original owners. Today's owners take great pride in their properties, lovingly maintaining the historic feel, in many cases with period antiques or original furnishings and decor. The proprietors of these homes are generally well connected into their local communities as well, with valuable insights into the history and the best places to go for entertainment and food, and they're more than happy to help. Rates run anywhere from $60 to 250 per night, depending on location and amenities.

BICYCLING

All types of biking terrain are present in the state. If you like a relatively flat ride with both lakes and urban vistas, it's hard to beat the **Grand Rounds** in the Twin Cities, with 50 miles of trails winding through and around some of Minneapolis's popular lakes, along the Mississippi River, and near Minnehaha Falls. Outstate, there are literally thousands of miles of trails—paved or not, hilly or flat railway grade, wooded or riverside—located in the extensive systems of county and state parks, especially in the Brainerd lakes area and the river bluffs along

the Mississippi, Minnesota, and St. Croix rivers. The **Minnesota Department of Transportation** (651-296-2216) has detailed bike maps available on request, broken down by geographic region. **Explore Minnesota** (651-296-5029; 888-868-7476), the state tourism board, also produces bike trail brochures and maps, and many of the larger regional tourist boards have materials related to their areas.

BIRD-WATCHING

Given the number of wildlife preserves and state parks here, it's no surprise that Minnesota has numerous areas with excellent birding opportunities. The Minnesota chapter of the **Audubon Society** (http://mn.audubon.org) has detailed lists and maps showing some of the best places to observe birds, among them the **North Shore** in the northeast, **Big Bog** and **Lake of the Woods** in the north, **Itasca State Park** and **Lac Qui Parle-Big Stone** in the central and central-northwest parts of the state, the **St. Croix** and **Mississippi rivers** along the eastern border, and the **Minnesota River Valley** in southwest Minnesota.

BOOKS

It's intimidating to try to list even a fraction of the literature based in Minnesota, written by Minnesotans, or both. The literary arts community in Minnesota is thriving, and has been for decades; Minneapolis's **Open Book** (www.openbookmn.org) is a central stopping place for writing classes and author appearances, and there's a strong network of independent bookstores throughout the state,

as well as the ubiquitous **Barnes & Noble**. But if you'd like to get a sense of the literary landscape, consider reading some of the following.

F. Scott Fitzgerald, of course, produced the classic *The Great Gatsby* and *Tender Is the Night*, among other works, and lived in St. Paul with Zelda. Sinclair Lewis, author of *Babbitt* and *Elmer Gantry*, lived in Sauk Center in his youth, and despite his skewering the town in the fictional *Main Street*, the community still honors his memory. Charles Schultz of *Peanuts* fame is from Minnesota. Ole Rolvaag, author of the classic pioneer tale *Giants in the Earth*, emigrated to the United States from Norway in 1896 and lived the last half of his life in Minnesota. J. F. Powers, National Book Award winner, was a longtime professor and writer in residence at St. John's University and the College of St. Benedict. His books include *Morte d'Urban* and *Wheat That Springeth Green*. Naturalist Sigurd Olson memorably chronicled the beauty of Minnesota wilderness in books like *Reflections from the North Country* and *The Singing Wilderness*. Much-beloved children's books also have roots in Minnesota, from Laura Ingalls Wilder's *Little House* series to Maud Hart Lovelace's *Betsy-Tacy* series and Wanda Gag's *Millions of Cats*.

Contemporary writers who are from or write about Minnesota include Garrison Keillor—who, besides hosting *Prairie Home Companion*, has penned several books, including *Lake Wobegon Days* and *Happy to Be Here*. Tim O'Brien, who won the National Book Award for *Going After Cacciato* and was a Pulitzer finalist for *The Things They Carried*, was born in Austin and grew up in Worthington. *Time* named his

novel *In the Lake of the Woods* best book of the year. Robert Treuer had a wide-ranging career path, from teacher to Native American tribal organizer, before settling down as a tree farmer in northern Minnesota. His books *Voyageur Country: A Park in the Wilderness* and *The Tree Farm* are lyrical nonfiction explorations of life and issues in the northern reaches. David Mura, author of *Turning Japanese* and *Song for Uncle Tom, Tonto, & Mr. Moto: Poetry & Identity*, is a Minnesota resident, as is memoirist Patricia Hampl, who gracefully writes about growing up in St. Paul in books such as *The Florist's Daughter*. Brian Malloy's novels have detailed life for young gays in the Twin Cities, including *The Year of Ice* and *Brendan Wolf*. Anne Ursu's fictional Minnesota small town facing an emotional crisis in *Spilling Clarence* is for adults, while her trilogy of books known as the Cronus Chronicles (starting with *The Shadow Thieves*) get their start at the Mall of America. Shannon Olson gives us a Minnesotan Bridget Jones with *Welcome to My Planet: Where English Is Sometimes Spoken*. Lorna Landvik congenially covers all manner of small-town foibles and romantic mishaps in her books *The View from Mount Joy*, *The Tall Pine Polka*, and *Patty Jane's House of Curl*.

BOUNDARY WATERS CANOE AREA WILDERNESS

More than a million acres of pristine wilderness area, including 1,000 lakes, some of which are restricted to non-motorized boats, make the Boundary Waters Canoe Area Wilderness (BWCAW) one of the state's top draws. The concept of an untouched, undeveloped, protected wilderness was conceived back in 1919, when the USDA Forest Service began developing management plans for what would eventually become the BWCAW.

Beginning in 1926, roads and development were prohibited in the area, and by the late 1940s the federal government was buying out homeowners and resort owners who still had property in the protected zone. The only exception was Dorothy Molter, a long-time resident known as the Root Beer Lady, who moved into the wilderness in 1934. After locals protested her removal and the Forest Service recognized both the value of her nursing skills and her almost legendary status among the population, she was granted permission to remain in the BWCAW until her death in 1986.

The creation of this quiet, natural preserve was not without controversy. Recreationists who wanted access to the area via fly-ins, snowmobiles, and motorboats fought hard in court to preserve the right to bring engines into the area. When the BWCA Wilderness Act was finally passed in 1978, it allowed motorboats on about a quarter of the area's lakes. This remains controversial, as those who want motorboat access continue to push for more, saying the small amount of water available to them is not enough, while those who have fought for restricting access to motorboats continue their battle, wishing to reclaim that last quarter. It isn't likely that the contentious stances will soften anytime soon; when visiting the BWCAW, be sure to respect each side's territory.

One thing both sides agree on is the impressive bounty of the area. Lakes, tributaries, and forests combine to give visitors an unforgettable wilderness experience. There's something for every level of traveler—easy day trips for beginners, long portages deep into the wilderness for more experienced canoers and campers. Several outfitting companies, particularly in Grand Marais and Ely, can set up permits and equipment rentals, and can also custom-design guided trips.

During the most popular season (May 1 through September 30), permits are required for day visitors and campers. Also note that although camping reservations are not required, they are definitely recommended, because the area operates under a quota system during that season, and you could find yourself with no place to stay. For permits and reservations, contact the **USDA Forest Service** (877-550-6777; www.bwcaw.org).

One final recommendation: Seriously consider purchasing the **Superior National Forest Visitor Map**. Published by the USDA in conjunction with Superior National Forest, this is an incredibly detailed map of the BWCAW. It wouldn't hurt to buy a magnifying glass with which to read it. The BWCAW is full of back roads, often barely more than gravel strips, which don't appear on most state maps and that can get you lost unless you're very familiar with the area. The map is available in a sturdy, waterproof plastic version for about $10. Many local gas stations and convenience stores sell it, or contact the **Superior National Forest** headquarters in Duluth (218-626-4300) for information on ordering one.

BUS SERVICE

Greyhound Bus Lines (800-231-2222; www.greyhound.com) is the primary source of public transit, serving more than 70 communities around the state, including several university locations.

CAMPING

It almost seems as if the entire state is one giant campground. From the farthest northern corners of the state right down to the southern borders, state and county parks provide countless opportunities for camping, some with fairly modern campsites with electricity and facilities, others barebones in nature. Some require reservations and/or permits; others don't. Many of the major parks and forests, including Voyageurs National Park and the Boundary Waters Canoe Area Wilderness, are covered in this book. Minnesota's **Department of Natural Resources** (www.dnr.state.mn.us) has extensive information about campsites and policies in the state parks and state forests, as well as some online reservation capabilities. The **National Park Service** (www.nps.gov/voya) has camping and reservation information for Voyageurs National Park. The **USDA Forest Service** (www.bwcaw .org) provides requirements for permits and camping in the Boundary Waters Canoe Area Wilderness, but note that if you're working through an outfitter, it's likely to handle those arrangements for you; be sure to ask.

Wherever you choose to camp, always check with local authorities ahead of time as to fire restrictions. Summer droughts have become increasingly common, and the risk of wildfire is very real; you may find that campfires are prohibited.

CANOEING AND KAYAKING

Lake Superior, **Lake of the Woods**, the **Boundary Waters**,

Lake Kabetogama, the **Mississippi**, **Minnesota**, and **St. Croix rivers**, the **Chain of Lakes** in Minneapolis—these are just a few of the options for those who like to explore by water. Rentals and outfitters abound; where there is water, there is a way to get onto it. Arrangements can be as elaborate as guided canoeing or kayaking and camping tours, or they can be as simple as an afternoon's rental. Canoeing in the Boundary Waters, where there are entire waterways restricted to nonmotorized boats, needs at least a daily entry permit (or a more formal permit for multiple days and camping).

✎ CHILDREN, ESPECIALLY FOR

Minnesota is generally a child-friendly state, and throughout this guide numerous activities, museums, festivals, and restaurants have been marked with the crayon symbol ✎.

CRAFTS

Conventional wisdom would say it's the result of long winters, but love of crafts is alive and well in the North

Star State. In the Twin Cities metro area alone, dozens of craft stores, many independently owned and operated, sell fabric, yarn, beads, woodworking supplies, and scrapbooking supplies. The diversity of crafts being produced is burgeoning as well, and indie craft shows such as **No Coast Craft-o-Rama** (www.nocoastcraft .com) and **Craftstravaganza** (http:// craftstravaganza.com) showcase unusual and funky projects that definitely turn the notion of crafts as fuddy-duddy right on its head.

Which isn't to say traditional craftwork isn't valued. Most notably, the **North House Folk School** (218-387-9762; 888-387-9762; www .northhouse.org) in Grand Marais offers year-round classes in everything from knitting to bread making, canoe building, and how to construct your own yurt or outdoor brick oven.

DINING

Foodies are sitting up and taking notice at what's happening in Minnesota. No longer a culinary backwater, this state boasts many chefs who are generating interest and intrigue for their innovative menus, as well as their increased commitment to using locally grown products for seasonal menus whenever possible. In the Twin Cities most restaurants are open nightly or, at most, closed Mon. Outstate you may find eateries with more limited weekly or seasonal hours. Restaurants with strong reputations with the fine-dining crowd, such as **La Belle Vie** or **Cue**, don't require reservations, but they're strongly recommended. Another avenue that's seen an explosion in popularity is ethnic foods; the numbers of small restaurants opened and run by immigrants—thus introducing authentic Asian, African, and Hispanic foods to the state—have grown by leaps and bounds. For diners who prefer their food not to be too Americanized, there are numerous worthwhile options to choose from.

DRESS CODE

Out-of-towners often comment on the dress code, or lack thereof, at restau-

rants and events that would be considered at least semiformal outside Minnesota. It's not uncommon to see casual khakis and sweaters alongside suits and dresses at fine-dining venues and the theater. Whether this is a good thing is up for debate.

EMERGENCIES

Call **911** from anywhere in the state. In each chapter, regional hospitals are listed.

FACTORY OUTLETS

This topic is discussed in more detail in the Minneapolis chapter. Albertville, which is a community north of Minneapolis, has the **Albertville Outlet Mall** (www.premium outlets.com) with 100 stores; it's by far the largest outlet center in the state.

FALL FOLIAGE

Sept. and Oct. can be variable in terms of weather, but when the days are crisp and clear, Minnesota fall colors can be spectacular. Starting up north across the eastern half of the state (along Voyageurs National Park and the Canadian border), through the Boundary Waters, the Iron Range, and the North Shore, and down south through the Twin Cities and the St. Croix, Mississippi, and Minnesota rivers, the large areas of forest set on rolling land along water make for prime foliage viewing. Most restaurants, hotels, and bed & breakfasts are open at least weekends during fall for visitors seeking the turning of the leaves.

FARM STANDS AND FARMER'S MARKETS

Whether they're popular as a result of a long agricultural history or because today's foodies are increasingly interested in local, sustainable foods, farmer's markets and farm stands can be found in pretty much every corner of Minnesota. It may be something as simple as a teenager selling corn off the back of a pickup, or as elaborate as the revered farmer's markets in Minneapolis and St. Paul, but there's something for everyone. For complete listings, check with the **Minnesota Farmers Market Association** (www.mfma.org) or the **Minnesota Department of Agriculture** (www.mda.state.mn.us/food/minnesota grown/farmersmarkets.htm).

FESTIVALS

Minnesota is a state full of festivals. Some are cultural explorations, such as Kolacky Days and Scandinavian Midsommar Tag. Others celebrate local history or agriculture, including Irish Fest and Barnesville's Potato Days (mashed potato wrestling, anyone?). Some sound just plain goofy (Eelpout Festival, St. Urho Day), but are beloved local traditions. Some of the "best of" are listed in each chapter. Additional information and listings can be found by visiting the tourist boards listed under *Guidance* at the beginning of each chapter; or see the **Minnesota Tourism Board's** Web site, www .exploreminnesota.com.

FIRE

Wildfires are always a concern in wilderness areas, and Minnesota is no exception, especially since recent years have seen significant droughts in parts of the state. When planning a camping trip, be sure to find out if there are campfire restrictions. Because this can change from one day to the next, it's best to check upon arrival to make sure you're not violating any new restrictions.

FISHING

Fishing is a summer and winter sport in Minnesota, with options ranging from fishing out of boats on open water to dropping your line in a hole cut in the ice, usually in an ice house. Many of the lake resorts have become year-round destinations thanks to the popularity of ice fishing, and it's possible in some areas to rent a sleep-ready ice house, complete with electricity and bathroom facilities. Fishing is a licensed activity, and licenses are generally easy to obtain, usually from local DNR offices and convenience stores. For information on costs and restrictions, see www.dnr.state.mn.us.

GAMBLING

There are 18 casinos in Minnesota, scattered across 11 Indian reservations. All casinos offer slot machines and table games like blackjack and poker; most offer bingo. Live entertainment is frequently scheduled, with the larger casinos, like **Mystic Lake Casino** (www.mysticlake.com) in Prior Lake and **Grand Casino Hinckley** (www.grandcasinomn.com) in Hinckley, getting some well-known current entertainers. In addition, **Canterbury Park** (www.canterbury park.com) in Shakopee offers card games 24/7, live horse racing during summer, and simulcast horse racing from other tracks year-round.

GOLF

Minnesotans are passionate about golf, a fact demonstrated by the extreme weather golfers are willing to cope with in order to get out on the course. The state has nearly 600 courses, public and private, and the terrain varies from lush and meticulously maintained fairways to the northernmost golf course in the United States, the Northwest Angle Country Club. The **Minnesota Tourism Board** (www.explore minnesota.com) can provide complimentary golf brochures on request; or check online at www.minnesotagolf.com for a detailed directory.

HANDICAPPED ACCESS

Throughout this book, the wheelchair symbol & indicates attractions, lodgings, and restaurants that are handicapped accessible.

HIKING

Miles and miles of trails, paved and unpaved, flat and rolling, forest and prairie, await visitors statewide. The multitude of state parks offer just about every sort of terrain, wildlife viewing, and flora and fauna imaginable for the region. The **Minnesota Department of Natural Resources** (www.dnr.state.mn.us) has detailed information on each park on its Web site, and the department also offers two hiking clubs. The Hiking Club gives hikers graduated levels of awards for hiking preset mileage levels, with the ultimate awards coming in the form of free nights of camping.

The Passport Club rewards travelers for visiting state parks. The regional tourism offices listed in each chapter can provide information and maps on that region's hiking opportunities, while the **Minnesota Tourism Board** (www.exploreminnesota.com) can provide complimentary hiking brochures on request.

HISTORY

Minnesota's history runs the full gamut from pioneers and fur traders; to Native Americans and barons of industry; to famous politicians; to contentious or beloved authors, actors, and musicians; to devastating natural tragedies and scandalous murders. **Jesse James**'s epic arrival in Northfield, **Hubert Humphrey**'s presidential campaign, **John Dillinger**'s reign in St. Paul, former pro wrestler **Jesse Ventura**'s reign as governor, the quintessential pioneer **Laura Ingalls Wilder**'s travels through southern Minnesota, **Bob Dylan**'s roots on the Iron Range, **Bronko Nagurski**'s legendary football career getting its start in International Falls, musical icon **Prince**, and *A Prairie Home Companion*'s **Garrison Keillor** are just some of the legends past and present who are associated with Minnesota. And in one way or another, these people (and many more) and events throughout the state's history are commemorated in various displays, exhibits, and festivals.

HUNTING

Hunting is a licensed activity in Minnesota. Among the game that's legal to hunt (with the proper license and in-season) are bears, deer, pheasants, wild turkeys, grouse, and waterfowl.

Licenses are generally easy to obtain, usually from local DNR offices (including some by phone or on the Web site) and convenience stores. For information on cost and restrictions, see www.dnr.state.mn.us.

INFORMATION ON MINNESOTA, OFFICIAL

Explore Minnesota (651-296-5029; 888-868-7476; www.exploreminnesota) is the central state tourism organization. Visitors are welcome to the headquarters at 121 7th Place E. in St. Paul, or at one of the Travel Information Centers located in Albert Lea, Beaver Creek, Dresbach, Bloomington (Mall of America), Fishers Landing, Grand Portage Bay, Moorhead, St. Cloud, St. Croix, Duluth, and Worthington. Explore Minnesota also partners with various local tourist boards, chambers of commerce, and convention and visitor bureaus all over the state. A thorough listing of local and regional tourism groups is available on the Explore Minnesota Web site, listed above.

INTERNET

Throughout this book, Internet URLs for attractions, recreational sites, lodging, and restaurants have been given whenever they are available. The Internet has been embraced as a wonderful informational tool by smaller businesses, to the advantage of the traveling public, and it's likely that even more companies will have gone online by the time this book goes to press.

Access to high-speed Internet and WiFi, often free, is becoming more prevalent as well. Many hotels, restaurants, coffee shops, libraries, and university campuses can provide online access to visitors.

LAKES

Land of 10,000 Lakes is a slight underestimate. There are actually more than 15,000 lakes across Minnesota, nearly 12,000 of which are at least 10 acres in size. The DNR says that the state's lakes and rivers have more shoreline than California, Florida, and Hawaii combined. To the delight of visitors, those shorelines provide ample opportunities for enjoyment year-round: boating, fishing (including ice fishing in winter), swimming, waterskiing, sightseeing. Several state parks have multiple lakes, as does the one national park (**Voyageurs National Park**, www .nps.gov/voya). The **North Shore**, riding along the coast of Lake Superior, provides an almost oceanic viewing experience, while the **Brainerd Lakes District**'s bodies of water are among some of the best known in the

state for vacationers. Accommodations varying from rustic campsites to deluxe resorts with every possible amenity can be found; the demand is particularly high in summer, so booking in advance is strongly recommended.

LANGUAGE CAMPS

The northern region of Minnesota is home to **Concordia Language Villages** (218-299-4544; 800-222-4750; http://clvweb.cord.edu/prweb). The program's headquarters are in Moorhead, but most of the year-round villages are just outside Bemidji. The villages are self-contained cultural units, with different camps for Spanish, French, German, Russian, Norwegian, and Finnish. Each village is designed to look like a classic community from that country. Additional summer-only villages are offered elsewhere in the state, including camps for Chinese, Italian, Arabic, Korean, and Swedish. There are programs for

adults and children, most of them on an immersion basis, but it's not just language that's offered; students will also learn about customs, culture, and foods of their chosen regions.

Even if you aren't interested in registering for a camp, a visit to the villages is worth the side trip—the attention to detail is impressive, and the villages are nestled in stately forests, creating an otherworldly feel.

LEFSE AND LUTEFISK

Minnesota has a strong Scandinavian heritage, and—especially around the holidays or at ethnic festivals—it's inevitable that the classic Scandinavian foods lefse and lutefisk will make an appearance. Of the two, lefse is more widely enjoyed; it's a potato pastry, rolled out thin and briefly grilled. Some choose to add butter, sugar, cinnamon, or all three. Lutefisk is a horse of a different color, falling right into the "love it or hate it" category, and it's the subject of many jokes. Essentially, lutefisk is fish soaked in lye. Although not everyone's first choice, lutefisk is still very popular for holiday church dinners, at festivals, and at Christmastime.

LITTER

Littering in Minnesota is punishable on the first offense by a misdemeanor charge that goes on your driving record; subsequent offenses leave you liable for fines of several hundred dollars.

LODGING

Minnesota offers a highly diverse group of lodging choices: bed & breakfasts, resorts, cabins, motels, private homes, upscale hotels, even yurts. The rates quoted in this book reflect a per-night rate for one person, and keep in mind that rates are fluid; please don't hold us or the accommodations to the rates quoted, but instead view them as a guideline, not an absolute. In general, most bed & breakfasts don't accept children under 12 (but it's noted if they do), and many cabins or lake resorts have minimum-stay requirements (anywhere from three to seven nights) during peak periods. Pets are not accepted unless the pet symbol 🐾 is shown, and even then it's a good idea to confirm when reserving, because sizes and types of pets may be restricted, and additional fees may apply. Nearly all accept credit cards; hotels will accept a credit card as a

guarantee for arrival, while bed & breakfasts or lake resorts may require a prepaid deposit. Cancellation policies vary, so confirm the policy before committing any money.

MAPS

The **Minnesota Department of Transportation** produces a new Official State Highway Map every other year, and a free copy can be obtained by contacting **Explore Minnesota** (651-296-5029; 888-868-7476); by collecting one in person at one of the state's many Travel Information Centers (see *Information*, above); or by visiting the **DOT**'s Web site (www .dot.state.mn.us), where portions of the maps can be downloaded and printed.

For maps detailed with a significant amount of tourist information, **Professor Pathfinder's Supermaps**, published by Hedberg Maps (www .hedbergmaps.com), come in a full-state version as well as regional maps (Twin Cities, northern Minnesota, southern Minnesota, Brainerd lakes). All are clearly marked and easily read.

As noted above under *Boundary Waters*, a trip to the BWCAW wouldn't be complete without acquiring the **Superior National Forest Visitor Map** (along with a magnifying glass with which to read it). Published by the USDA in conjunction with Superior National Forest, this is an incredibly detailed map of the BWCAW and is available in a sturdy, waterproof plastic version for about $10. Many local gas stations and convenience stores sell it; or you can contact the **Superior National Forest** headquarters in Duluth (218-626-4300) for information on ordering one.

MALL OF AMERICA

The **Mall of America** (www.mallof america.com) is a shopper's paradise. Its 4-million-plus square feet include not only more than 500 stores but also 30 fast-food restaurants, 20 sitdown restaurants, an underground aquarium, a convenience store, photo studios, a 14-screen movie theater complex, a wedding chapel, and an indoor theme park. The retail anchors are Nordstrom, Macy's, Bloomingdale's, and Sears, and the surrounding stores include everything from clothing to electronics, jewelry, books, Christmas decorations, crafts, cosmetics, Irish gifts, and items made in Minnesota. Across the street you'll find home furnishings superstore IKEA and a Radisson Hotel with the Waterpark of America, so there's something for everyone to do.

MINNESOTA GROWN

Among the Minnesota-produced items available for purchase are maple syrup, cheese, meats, honey, candles, jams, and, in-season, all kinds of fresh vegetables and fruits (some of the latter available from pick-your-own farms). The **Minnesota Department of Agriculture** (651-201-6000; 800-967-2474; www.mda.state.mn.us) has online and print directories for finding locally made items.

MINNESOTA PUBLIC BROADCASTING

Minnesota has both public radio (**Minnesota Public Radio**, www .mpr.org) and public television (**Twin Cities Public Television**, www.tpt .org). Both are headquartered in the Twin Cities, but satellite stations throughout the state carry the public programming. Visit each company's Web sites for specific locations and channels. Also note that MPR has three radio options: MPR itself is a classical radio station, while KNOW is talk and news radio and The Current plays a widely diverse, eclectic selection of indie, local, and outside-the-mainstream music.

MOVIES

Popular movies are easily tracked down in most communities. For those looking for smaller, independent, foreign, or art-house movies, good bets in the Twin Cities include the **Uptown** and **Lagoon theatres** in Minneapolis and the **Edina Theatre** in Edina (www.landmarktheatres .com), as well as the venerable **Oak Street Cinema** (www.mnfilmarts.org/ oakstreet) at the University of Minnesota. The annual **Minneapolis–St. Paul International Film Fest** (www .mnfilmarts.org) is a big event each year, with nearly 70 films.

Minnesota must be given credit for its support of museums big and small. From the world-class **Minneapolis Institute of the Arts** (www.artsmia .org) and **Walker Art Center** (www .walkerart.org), which together offer significant collections of classic and contemporary art, to smaller museums like **The Museum of Russian Art** (www.tmora.org) and **Minnesota Museum of American Art** (www .mmaa.org), patrons of the arts have much to choose from. You'll also find options for families, such as the **Minnesota Children's Museum** (www .mcm.org), the **Science Museum of Minnesota** (www.smm.org), and **The Bakken Museum** (www.thebakken .org), as well as historical options including **Mill City Museum** (www .millcitymuseum.org), the **Minnesota History Center Museum** (www .mnhs.org), the **Hinckley Fire Museum** (www.seans.com/sunsetweb/ hinckley), the **Bronko Nagurski Museum** (www.bronkonagurski

.com/museum.htm), and the nearly countless city and county historical societies that provide invaluable insights into all aspects of Minnesota history. Clearly there is plenty for any museum aficionado to do here.

MUSIC

Minnesotans are passionate about their music, whether it's classical, country, rock, alternative/indie, jazz, bluegrass, or anything in between. Live venues of every size are open in the Twin Cities, from **Target Center** (www.targetcenter.com) and **Xcel Energy Center** (www.xcelenergy center.com); to **Orchestra Hall** (www.minnesotaorchestra.org) and **The Ordway** (www.ordway.org); to the **Fine Line** (www.finelinemusic .com), the **Dakota** (www.dakota cooks.com), and **First Avenue** (www .first-avenue.com). Those are just the best-known options, but literally dozens, if not hundreds, of other clubs, stages, and bars feature live music.

Besides concerts, music festivals are wildly popular in Minnesota, particularly in summer when they can be held outdoors. Among the big shows are the annual **WE Fest** (www.wefest .com), **Moondance Jam** (www.moon dancejam.com), **Sonshine Festival** (www.sonshinefestival.com), the **Minnesota Bluegrass & Old-Time Music Festival** (www.minnesotablue grass.org), and the **Boundary Waters Blues Festival** (www.elyblues.com). More are listed in each chapter.

NATURE PRESERVES

Minnesota has thousands of acres maintained as nature preserves (also called Scientific & Natural Areas, or SNAs), and as such, they provide numerous opportunities for hiking and wildlife viewing, with the heaviest concentration of such preserves in the western and southwestern parts of the state. The **Minnesota Department of Natural Resources** (www.dnr .state.mn.us) and **The Nature Conservancy** (www.nature.org) both have comprehensive listings of locations and what you can expect to find.

Areas like the **Black Dog Nature Preserve**, **Burntside Islands SNA**, **Frenchman's Bluff SNA**, **Glacial Ridge National Wildlife Refuge**, and **Bluestem Prairie SNA** are just a few of the more than 140 preserves across the state that give glimpses of now hard-to-find prairies and untouched forests, not to mention deer, prairie chickens, eagles, wolves, falcons, whooping cranes, pheasants, owls, and herons.

NEWSPAPERS AND PERIODICALS

In the Twin Cities, there are two major daily papers: Minneapolis's *Star Tribune* (www.startribune.com) and St. Paul's *Pioneer Press* (www.twin cities.com). There are also a number of independent papers that publish weekly or monthly, including *City Pages* (www.citypages.com)—an excellent resource for local events of every kind and in-depth restaurant reviews—and *The Rake* (www .rakemag.com), which covers local issues and events.

Minneapolis–St. Paul Magazine (www.mspmag.com) is a monthly publication, available at most bookstores, newsstands, and grocery stores, that has information on Twin Cities events and an extensive restaurant guide. *Minnesota Monthly* (www.minnesota monthly.com), although largely focused on the Twin Cities, does provide good resources for restaurants, lodging, and events outside the metro area. Both magazines publish several "Best Of" issues each year, often by theme or blanketing several topics (dining, shopping, et cetera).

Nearly every city of any size has at least a weekly newspaper, and several (Duluth, Bemidji, Brainerd, Rochester,

Faribault, and International Falls, to name a few) have newspapers published five to seven days a week and available for sale at local stores.

PARKS AND FORESTS, NATIONAL

Voyageurs National Park (281-283-9821; www.nps.gov/voya) is the only national park in Minnesota. It borders Canada along the state's northern edge, nudging up to **Superior National Forest** (218-626-4300; www.fs.fed.us/r9/forests/superior), which in turn surrounds the Boundary Waters Canoe Area Wilderness on the U.S. side. Voyageurs National Park and Superior National Forest comprise some of the most beautiful and remote wilderness areas in the state. Together they account for nearly 700,000 acres of forests, lakes, and streams that connect the region to Canada and provide countless opportunities for camping, hiking, canoeing, kayaking, houseboating, fishing, and hunting.

The other national area is **Chippewa National Forest**—a 1.6-million-acre preserve south and west of Voyageurs National Park and Superior National Forest. Together with the

latter two, Chippewa National Forest provides year-round recreational opportunities. Minnesota's third and fourth largest lakes, Leech Lake and Lake Winnibigoshish, are located in this forest, along with 1,300 more. Wildlife is abundant in the three national areas; wolves, bald eagles, deer, moose, bobcats, owls, and cougars are not uncommon.

PARKS AND FORESTS, STATE

The **Minnesota Department of Natural Resources** (www.dnr.state .mn.us) is the go-to organization for information about Minnesota's state parks, which rival the national parks and forests for recreation and amenities. There are more than 70 parks spread out across the state, including popular visitor sites such as **Gooseberry Falls** and **Split Rock Lighthouse** on the North Shore and **Itasca** in northern Minnesota (home to the Mississippi River headwaters); the more remote but equally beautiful **Zippel Bay** in the far north on Lake of the Woods; and **Mystery Cave** in southern Minnesota.

In addition, Minnesota has 58 state forests, also managed by the Minnesota State DNR. All but one are located in central and northern regions, while the **Richard J. Doner Memorial Hardwood Forest** is in the far southeast. Like the national parks and forests, state parks and forests offer year-round recreational opportunities, with access to a vast number of lakes and rivers.

PETS

Accommodations that accept pets are noted with the 🐾 symbol in each chapter. But be sure to call ahead;

most lodgings that take pets have restrictions regarding types and sizes, and there may be reservation and fee requirements.

POPULATION

5,167,101.

RAIL TRAVEL

Amtrak (800-872-7245; www.amtrak .com) offers basically one route across Minnesota each way, running from the Wisconsin border in the southeast through St. Paul and directly northwest until it crosses into North Dakota.

SAILING

Even though winter puts a damper on the fun, the sheer number of Minnesota lakes makes sailing a popular warm-weather pastime. In the Twin Cities sailboats can be seen on nearly all the lakes, especially **Lakes Calhoun**, **Harriet**, and **Minnetonka**. But you can expect sailboats on just about any body of water or river here, and rentals can be arranged in every resort area.

SKIING, CROSS-COUNTRY

State and national parks and forests, combined with county and city parks, provide thousands of miles of groomed and rough trails for cross-country enthusiasts. This is an activity that takes place in virtually every part of Minnesota, whether it's on flat prairie land with long-range views; through forests and challenging hills; or across lakes and along riverbanks. Rental equipment is available in most resort towns.

SKIING, DOWNHILL

Mountains isn't the first thought that comes to mind about Minnesota, but the winter season and some larger-than-average hills do keep winter visitors busy. Among the biggest and most advanced ski resorts is **Lutsen** (218-663-7281; www.lutsen.com) on the North Shore, which comes complete with slope-side accommodations and all degree of runs (there's more information in the *North Shore* chapter). Book ahead—winter weekends tend to be very popular. **Afton Alps** (651-436-5245; 800-328-1328; www .aftonalps.com), just outside Hastings, is the biggest ski resort within easy range of the Twin Cities. There are no slope-side accommodations here, but you will find several options in nearby Hastings.

Other downhill ski resorts around the state include **Buck Hill** (952-435-7174; www.buckhill.com) in Burnsville; **Spirit Mountain** (218-628-2891; 800-642-6377; www.spiritmt.com) in Duluth; **Welch Village** (651-258-4567; www.welchvillage.com) in Welch; **Buena Vista** (218-243-2231; www.bvskiarea.com) in Bemidji; **Wild Mountain** (651-465-6365; 800-447-4958; www.wildmountain.com) in Taylors Falls; and **Mount Kato** (507-625-3363; 800-668-5286; www.mountkato.com) in Mankato. Ski and snowboard lessons and rentals are available on site, and several resorts have ski lodges and tubing hills as well.

SNOWMOBILING

Snowmobiles are popular in Minnesota, used for both recreation and as a practical mode of transport, particularly in the western half of the state.

However, that doesn't mean snowmobiles can go anywhere; parts of the Boundary Waters Canoe Area Wilderness are off limits to motorized vehicles, including snowmobiles. Many state parks and forests have trails for snowmobilers, but be sure to stay on those trails; wandering off them can interfere with the work being done in nature preserves throughout the park systems. The Twin Cities metro area has varying restrictions on snowmobiles, with some cities allowing them and others banning them. To get specific information on annual regulations and requirements, check with the **Minnesota Department of Natural Resources** (www.dnr.state.mn .us/snowmobiling/index.html).

THEATER

Minnesota's commitment to the arts continues into the world of theater. Minneapolis has several world-renowned theatrical companies, including the **Guthrie Theater** (612-377-2224; 877-447-8243; www.guthrie theater.org), the **Children's Theatre Company** (612-874-0400; www .childrens theatre.org), and **Jeune Lune** (612-333-6200; www.jeunelune .org). But theaters of all shapes, sizes, and theatrical genres thrive in communities large and small across the state. The Twin Cities is also home to the **Jungle Theater** (612-822-7063; www.jungletheater.com) and the **Chanhassen Dinner Theatres** (952-934-1525; 800-362-3515; www .chanhassentheatres.com). Outstate, the **Paul Bunyan Playhouse** (218-751-7270; www.paulbunyanplayhouse .com) in Bemidji is one of the state's longest-running summer-stock theaters. On the North Shore, the **Grand Marais Playhouse** (218-387-

1284; www.arrowheadcenterforthearts
.org) offers productions year-round.
Commonweal (507-467-2525; 800-
657-7025; www.commonwealtheatre
.org) in Lanesboro offers several productions each year, and one of them is
always by Norwegian playwright Henrik Ibsen; it also sponsors the annual
Ibsen Festival. The **Great River
Shakespeare Festival** (507-474-
7900; www.grsf.org) in Winona takes
place annually in summer with highly
professional Shakespearean productions. Other theaters are noted
throughout the book.

TRAFFIC

Generally speaking, Minnesota roads
are reasonably well maintained and
well marked. That said, there are
always some trouble spots to plan
around. The webs of intertwining
freeways around and through the
Twin Cities metro area suffer routine
rush-hour slowdowns each weekday,
especially during rainy or snowy
weather. Fri. and Sun. afternoons in
spring and summer find another kind
of gridlock—the "going to the cabin"
slowdown. Highways leading north
from the Twin Cities, particularly I-
94, I-494, and I-694, can crawl along
at an agonizingly slow pace each
weekend, and even worse if it's a holiday weekend. Whenever possible, try
to plan driving at other times; you'll
get there faster with less aggravation.

Beyond the lakes traffic, be aware
that many of the communities around
the lakes and rivers have grown in
popularity with vacationers faster than
their road systems have been expanded. Driving through Brainerd or
Stillwater or along MN 61 the North
Shore on a summer's day is almost
guaranteed to be slow, with far more

vehicles crowding the roads than
usual, and bottlenecks occurring every
block thanks to stoplights or left-
turning cars. Adding to the frustration
is the increase in road construction
and repair projects that take place in
summer. A good map can give you
ideas of side roads to take, but I don't
recommend doing so on a whim; a
5-mile paved road detour might turn
into a 35-mile gravel road detour if
your choice of side road is also under-
going construction. When planning
driving routes, always check with the
**Minnesota Department of Trans-
portation** (651-296-3000; 800-657-
3774; www.dot.state.mn.us), which
publishes frequent or real-time
updates on road conditions and traffic
problems all over the state.

WEATHER

Minnesota definitely has a winter season, although it's more pronounced
the farther north you go, and not as
wicked as legends would have it. That
said, if you're traveling in winter, be
absolutely sure to keep an eye on
local weather forecasts (local radio

and TV stations carry forecasts from the **National Weather Service;** the Web site www.weather.com provides up-to-the-minute information), especially if you're headed north. Snow is one concern, but for those heading to the western part of the state, wind and cold can be an even bigger concern; the long, flat plains and prairies have nothing to break the wind, which can push snow into conditions of whiteout, and following a road can be close to impossible. When there is a travel advisory listed for a specific region, pay heed, and consider staying put.

WEB SITES

Wherever available, Web site addresses have been included for accommodations, restaurants, attractions, tourist boards and chamber of commerce, and hospitals. When one isn't listed, none was offered at time of publication. In addition, feel free to visit www.flyover-land.com—my own Web site, with additional and updated information on all things Minnesota.

WINERIES

Several hearty and entrepreneurial souls have attacked the notion that wine cannot be produced in a wintry seasonal climate. Wineries have begun to appear in all regions of Minnesota, some using specially cultivated grapes that are better able to withstand winter, and others using fruits besides grapes (blueberries, rhubarb) to create unusual and fun wines. **Alexis Bailly Vineyard** (651-437-1413; www.abwines.com) in Hastings was one of the first to work with grapes in Minnesota, producing its first vintage in 1978. Today there's even a **Wine Trail** (www.threerivers winetrail.com)—a group of six wineries in the St. Croix Valley in southeast Minnesota, all producing wines that are increasingly enjoying acclaim and success. At this point most of the state's wineries are still in its southern half, where the climate is a bit more temperate, but not far from Bemidji is **Forestedge Winery** (www.forest edgewinery.com), which works with local fruits (chokecherries, raspberries, Honeycrisp apples) to create some flavorful vintages.

Minneapolis 1

MINNEAPOLIS AND
NEIGHBORING COMMUNITIES

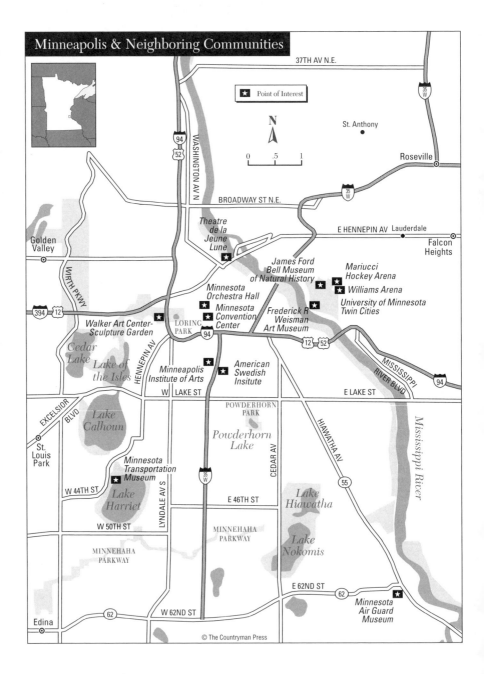

Minneapolis & Neighboring Communities

★ Point of Interest

N

0 .5 1

37TH AV N.E.

St. Anthony

Roseville

BROADWAY ST N.E.

E HENNEPIN AV Lauderdale

Golden Valley

Falcon Heights

WASHINGTON AV N

WIRTH PKWY

Theatre de la Jeune Lune ★

James Ford Bell Museum of Natural History ★

Mariucci Hockey Arena ★
★ Williams Arena

Minnesota Orchestra Hall ★

Minnesota Convention Center ★

Frederick R Weisman Art Museum ★

University of Minnesota Twin Cities

Walker Art Center-Sculpture Garden ★

LORING PARK

Cedar Lake

Lake of the Isles

HENNEPIN AV

Minneapolis Institute of Arts ★

American Swedish Insitute ★

MISSISSIPPI RIVER BLVD

Mississippi River

W LAKE ST

POWDERHORN PARK

E LAKE ST

St. Louis Park

EXCELSIOR BLVD

Lake Calhoun

Powderhorn Lake

CEDAR AV

HIAWATHA AV

Minnesota Transportation Museum ★

LYNDALE AV S

W 44TH ST

Lake Harriet

E 46TH ST

Lake Hiawatha

W 50TH ST

MINNEHAHA PARKWAY

Lake Nokomis

MINNEHAHA PARKWAY

E 62ND ST

Minnesota Air Guard Museum ★

Edina

W 62ND ST

© The Countryman Press

MINNEAPOLIS AND
NEIGHBORING COMMUNITIES

It's called the City of Lakes, and for a reason: Minneapolis is home to seven lakes, five of them—Harriet, Lake of the Isles, Calhoun, Cedar, and Brownie—connected by trails through the Grand Rounds National Scenic Byway. The lakes serve as a present-day memento from glacier movement centuries ago, and today they are a center of social and recreational activity. But it's not so much the lakes that brought Minneapolis into prominence as its location on the Mississippi River. The Mississippi was a crucial thoroughfare for the development of the logging and milling industries that set Minneapolis on the path from sleepy river town to thriving economic and cultural force.

The land surrounding Minneapolis was originally settled by Dakota Indians, who turned over that parcel to the US government in 1805. It's thought that the first white man to explore the area was Father Louis Hennepin, a French missionary. Whether or not that's true, he is remembered today for giving his name to both the county and one of the major avenues through the city. Originally the area had two towns, St. Anthony (named for the St. Anthony Falls on the Mississippi) and Minneapolis, but in 1872 the two merged. What followed was an economic boom as Minneapolis became the leading lumber and flour milling center in the United States.

Those glory days were gone by 1930, as northern woods became deforested and logging mills shut down. Flour milling began to take hold in other parts of the country, reducing Minneapolis's lock on the market. Today flour milling is still an important industry—General Mills is headquartered here. Other agricultural and industrial companies related to the food industry began here and remain powerful, including Cargill and SuperValu. Still more industry giants that either were or remain headquartered in the City of Lakes include Honeywell, Medtronic, Best Buy, and Target. The University of Minnesota's Minneapolis campus grew exponentially during this time—and particularly the medical and research departments, which have been leading innovators in medical procedures, including the first open-heart surgery.

With major companies bringing in people and money, Minneapolis began to see growth of cultural institutions. The Guthrie Theater, now a world-renowned company, opened in 1960; the Minneapolis Institute of the Arts began receiving visitors in 1915, and the Walker Art Center began focusing on contemporary art in 1940s. Sports fans were given something to cheer about when the major-league Minnesota Twins debuted in 1960 and went on to win the World Series in 1987 and 1991. The Minnesota Vikings brought NFL football to the state and have played in the Super Bowl four times. More recently, professional basketball teams (the men's Timberwolves and women's Lynx) have brought crowds to Target Center.

A dynamic combination of history, industry, arts, and popular culture has made Minneapolis a vibrant city to visit. Oh, and the lakes are fun, too.

GUIDANCE

All offices are open year-round unless noted otherwise.

Minneapolis Regional Chamber of Commerce (612-370-9100; www.minneapolischamber.org), 81 S. 9th St., Suite 200. Open weekdays 8–5. The chamber's Web site includes a thorough overview of the cultural, entertainment, sports, and outdoor activities available in the city, as well as links and order forms for informational brochures and maps.

Greater Minneapolis Convention and Visitors Association (612-767-8000; www.minneapolis.org), 250 Marquette Ave. S., Suite 1300. Open weekdays 8:30–5. An extensive listing of tourist info, including online booking for air and hotel reservations.

Northeast Minneapolis Chamber of Commerce (612-378-0050; www.nemplschamber.org), 2535 Central Ave. NE. Less a tourist site than a residents' compendium of local information, the NE Chamber provides a comprehensive listing of local events that may be of interest to visitors.

THE MINNEAPOLIS SKYLINE FROM LAKE OF THE ISLES

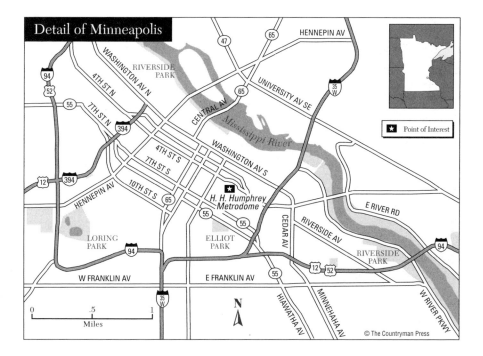

Detail of Minneapolis

HENNEPIN AV

RIVERSIDE PARK

Mississippi River

H. H. Humphrey Metrodome

LORING PARK

ELLIOT PARK

RIVERSIDE PARK

E RIVER RD

W FRANKLIN AV

E FRANKLIN AV

Point of Interest

© The Countryman Press

N

0   .5   1
Miles

GETTING THERE

By car: Interstates 94, 394, and 35W all lead into downtown Minneapolis.

By bus: **Greyhound** has a terminal downtown (612-371-3325; www.greyhound .com).

By rail: **Amtrak** (800-872-7245; www.amtrak.com) has a rail station off University Avenue between Minneapolis and St. Paul (730 Transfer Rd.).

By air: The primary airport is the Lindbergh Terminal at the **Minneapolis–St. Paul International Airport** (612-726-5555; www.mspairport.com); next door is the **Hubert Humphrey Terminal** (612-726-5800), a smaller secondary airport serving mostly no-frills and charter airlines. Both airports are in Bloomington, a western suburb. Taxis, limos, rental cars, and light-rail service are available from the airports into the city.

GETTING AROUND

For travel within the city, **Metro Transit** (612-373-3333; www.metrotransit.org) provides extensive service designed primarily to transport students and employees from outlying homes to work and school within the city. Currently the only light-rail service runs from downtown Minneapolis to the Metrodome stadium, Historic Fort Snelling, the Mall of America, and the airport; more service has been proposed, but hasn't been built. For maximum flexibility, a car is recommended, unless you're staying in the downtown area and can walk or take a brief taxi ride to other downtown destinations.

MINNESOTA'S "FIFTH SEASON"

Like any northern clime, Minnesota struggles to get as much road construction and repair done during the warm months as possible. Consequently, the old phrase *you can't get there from here* seems to be an unfortunate truth at various points during the summer construction season. Spring, summer, and fall can hold other inconveniences, such as rare but not unheard-of flooding that closes roads. The bottom line: When planning your travel, particularly if you're traveling by car, check out current road conditions by visiting the Minnesota Department of Transportation's road and traffic conditions Web site (www.511mn.org). You can also call 511 (or 800-657-3774) for updated information.

WHEN TO COME

The warmer months of spring, summer, and fall are always popular in the Twin Cities, but even the colder months can be an attractive time to visit. Those visitors staying in downtown hotels may have access to the city's extensive system of skyways, which allow foot travel across the heart of the city without stepping outdoors. And while the temperatures may be cold, the city's theater season, nightclub scene, and basketball/football seasons are going strong. But for those who like winter, outdoor events and sports are in full bloom Jan. through Mar., including cross-country and downhill skiing, ice skating, snowshoeing, and ice fishing.

MEDICAL EMERGENCY

Call **911**.

In the downtown area, the closest hospital is **Hennepin County Medical Center** (612-873-3000; www.hcmc.org), 701 Park Ave. Elsewhere in Minneapolis are the following hospitals: **University of Minnesota–Fairview Medical Center**, located at the University of Minnesota (612-273-3000; www.fairview-univeristy .fairview.org), at either 2450 Riverside Ave. or 500 Harvard St.; **Abbott Northwestern** (612-863-4000; www.abbottnorthwestern.com), 800 E. 28th St.; and **Children's Hospital**, located next to Abbott Northwestern (612-813-6000; www .childrensmn.org), 2525 Chicago Ave. S.

✳ To See

All attractions are open year-round unless noted otherwise.

MUSEUMS

✐ ♿ **Minneapolis Institute of the Arts** (612-870-3100; 800-642-2787; www .artsmia.org), 244 3rd Ave. S. Open Tues.–Sat. 10–5, Thurs. until 9; Sun. 11–5. General admission is free, but special traveling exhibits may require paid tickets, varying in price. The Art Institute, Minneapolis's so-called traditional museum, has seen significant growth over the past decade, with funding and donations reaching record levels and culminating with the 2006 grand opening of a new addition to the venerable neoclassical building. Exhibits are varied and lively, including an impressionist gallery, an extensive collection of American photography, a gallery showcasing local artists, a display of Frank Lloyd Wright architectural pieces, and a wide array of ancient Asian and African artifacts. The institute has proven itself willing to take risks with its visiting exhibitions, which in recent years have included such diverse offerings as an Egyptian exhibit; a Villa America exhibit featuring such contemporary American artists as Georgia O'Keeffe, Grant Wood, and Arthur Dove; an exhibit featuring completed and in-progress works from the St. John's Bible Project; and an exhibit of artifacts from the *Star Wars* franchise, including works tying the movies to their mythological foundation. The institute offers a variety of programs, including Family Sundays, docent-led tours, lecture series, and the annual Art in Bloom fund-raiser. The premises include a **D'Amico & Sons Café** for lunch and a gift shop with a wide variety of art-related gifts. Parking is free in the attached parking ramp, but only if you get there early—there are few spots, and competition is fierce from the Children's Theatre and the Minneapolis College of Art and Design, which are all part of the institute complex. Street parking is available with meters. Bring quarters.

♿ Y **Walker Art Center** (612-375-7600; www.walkerart.org), 1750 Hennepin Ave. Open Tues.–Sun. 11–5, Thurs.–Fri. until 9. $8 adults, $6 seniors 65 and older, $5 students/teens with student IDs. Free for Walker Center members, for children under 12, for visitors with a same-day event ticket, and on Thurs. night after 5 and the first Sat. of each month. The Art Institute is known as the traditional museum, while the Walker focuses solely on contemporary pieces. The artwork here is done in a wider variety of media: painting, sculpture, video, performance art, and Internet art. The Walker offers special events tailored for

MINNEAPOLIS INSTITUTE OF THE ARTS

families, gays, singles, and film buffs; traveling exhibitions include the famed Diane Arbus retrospective, an examination of Picasso and his influences, and a rare Frida Kahlo exhibit. Diners have a choice between two restaurants by Wolfgang Puck—**Café 8**, a casual eatery, and the more formal **20.21**. The Minneapolis Sculpture Garden (see *Green Space*) is free. Parking is available in a ramp beneath the museum or a pay lot across the street. Some street parking is available, but it can be difficult to get.

♿ **Frederick R. Weisman Art Museum** (612-625-9494; www.weisman.umn .edu), 333 E. River Rd. Open Tues.–Fri. 10–5, Thurs. until 9, Sat.–Sun. 11–5. Admission is free. Looming over Washington Avenue on the University of Minnesota's East Bank is a large modern structure designed by Frank Gehry. A building both loved and hated, the Weisman Art Museum is visually hard to miss, and inside is a collection of 20th- and 21st-century art masters, including Georgia O'Keeffe and Alfred Maurer, as well as a large collection of Korean furniture and international ceramics. While the Weisman doesn't have a restaurant on site, there are several small but good restaurants in the nearby Stadium Village (walking distance). The museum offers a parking ramp for a fee; free parking is pretty much nonexistent at this end of the university.

♿ **The Museum of Russian Art** (612-821-9045; www.tmora.org), 5500 Stevens Ave. S. Open Mon.–Fri. 10–5, Thurs. until 8, Sat. 10–4. $5 adults, with voluntary donations asked of adults over 60. Located in a small South Minneapolis building whose architecture is reminiscent of Spain, the Museum of Russian Art is the only permanent museum of Russian art and artifacts in North America. The building itself is worth a visit; originally a church, it eventually was used as a funeral home before providing its current occupant with an unexpectedly perfect venue for Russian art. Galleries range in size from small, low rooms in the basement to a two-story chapel-esque gallery on the main floor. Be sure to visit the gift shop on the second floor, behind the main gallery; it's full of Russian treasures, including a fine collection of hand-painted lacquered boxes.

✎ ♿ **The American Swedish Institute** (612-871-4907; www.americanswedish inst.org), 2600 Park Ave. S. Open Tues.–Sat. noon–4, Wed. until 8, Sun. 1–5; Nov.–Dec., open Sat. 10–5. $6 adults, $5 ages 62 and over, $4 ages 6–18; under 6 free. Free admission is offered the first Wed. of every month. Housed in the opulent Turnblad mansion (which is on the National Register of Historic Places), the institute houses an extensive collection of artwork and craft pieces from Sweden, as well as a permanent exhibition examining the relationship between Sweden and Swedish immigrants to Minnesota. This may sound subdued, but make no mistake, the institute is entirely child-friendly. The first Saturday of every month, a special story hour is held in the story attic, a third-floor space where new and classic Swedish tales are told. Folk-song fests, Midsummer Celebrations, a packed holiday season, and quarterly Swedish smorgasbords are just a few of the events on the museum's busy calendar.

✎ ♿ **The Bell Museum of Natural History** (612-624-7083; www.bellmuseum .org), 10 Church St. SE (on the East Bank of the University of Minnesota). Open Tues.–Fri. 9–5, Sat. 10–5, Sun. noon–5. Admission is free for museum members, University of Minnesota staff, faculty, and students; otherwise, $5

AMERICAN SWEDISH INSTITUTE

adults, $3 seniors 62 and over, non–University of Minnesota students, and ages 3–16. Children under 3 are free. The Bell Museum is located at the University of Minnesota–Minneapolis campus—an apt location, because it's both a working scientific facility and a center of nature in the heart of the city. The diorama halls introduce the natural world of Minnesota, while other galleries delve into nature and wildlife from around the world. The Touch & See room is ideal for kids, or anyone just curious as to what a live snake or the skull of a long-dead mammal looks and feels like.

✇ ♿ **The Mill City Museum** (612-341-7555; www.millcitymuseum.org), 704 S. 2nd St. Open Tues.–Sat. 10–5, Thurs. 10–9, Sun. noon–5. Holiday hours may apply. Admission is free for Minnesota Historical Society members and children 5 and under; $8 adults, $6 seniors and college students, $4 ages 6–17. Mill City, built along the Mississippi River in downtown Minneapolis, gives visitors a vivid glimpse of Minneapolis's role in the history of grain production and milling. The museum has several interactive exhibits; groups that book ahead can participate in a baking session in the kitchen. A partially demolished remnant of the original mill exists and can be explored, or enjoyed as the venue for occasional outdoor concerts sponsored by the museum.

✇ ♿ **The Bakken Museum** (612-926-3878; www.thebakken.org), 3537 Zenith Ave. S. Open Tues.–Sat. 10–5, Thurs. 10–8. $7 adults, $5 seniors and students; free ages 3 and under. The Bakken is a family-friendly museum that offers kids a chance to do some hands-on experiments involving electricity and magnetism. Not as dry as it sounds, the Bakken keeps things lively, yet its science research is

MILL CITY MUSEUM

scholarly and impressive. The surroundings are worth a visit, too: The museum is located in a Tudor mansion near Lake Calhoun.

The Carl W. Kroening Interpretive Center (763-694-7693), 4900 Mississippi Ct. Open Mon.–Sat. 9–5, Sun. noon–5. Admission is free. This center is a small but informative resource on anything you ever wanted to know about the heritage of the proud Mississippi. Call ahead to find out which organized programs are being offered; events vary seasonally.

✳ To Do

BICYCLING

Minneapolis isn't called the City of Lakes for nothing, and one of the highlights of the city's chain of water is the 50-mile bike trail that connects the **Four Lakes Loop** (**Lake Harriet**, **Lake Calhoun**, **Lake of the Isles**, and **Lake Nokomis**). Well maintained and clearly marked, the trails offer vistas of the best the city has to offer: blue waters, wildlife, houses of the rich and famous, and excellent people-watching. Trails are available in other parts of the city as well, including along the Mississippi River, a route that takes riders into Minnehaha Park. **Calhoun Cycle**, located near the lake of the same name, rents bikes and in-line skates.

BOATING

Those who would rather be on the lake than biking past it can bring their own or stop by Lake Calhoun's boat rental station to rent canoes, kayaks, or paddle boats. Motorboats are not allowed. Depending on the weather, rentals are available seasonally, daily 11–7. Sailboats and sailboards are also allowed on the chain of lakes, and the **Lake Calhoun Sailing School** offers classes for adults and children (612-927-8552; www.lakecalhoun.org/lcss).

✳ Green Space

Minneapolis might be known as the City of Lakes, but it could also be known as the City of Green Space. Nearly every community and neighborhood has some kind of park, with facilities varying from playground equipment to basketball courts, tennis courts, and swimming pools. For full details about the range of park offerings, check with the **Minneapolis Park & Recreation Board** (www .minneapolisparks.org). What follows is a selected list of outdoor spaces to enjoy.

✧ ♿ **Minneapolis Sculpture Garden** (612-370-4929; http://garden.walkerart .org), 726 Vineland Pl. The garden is open daily 6 AM–midnight; the Cowles Conservatory, Tues.–Sat. 10–8, Sun. 10–5. The Sculpture Garden is a joint exhibit created and managed by the Minneapolis Park & Recreation Board and the Walker Art Center. There are 11 beautifully manicured acres, with both indoor and outdoor floral gardens and more than 40 sculptures, including the iconic *Spoonbridge and Cherry Fountain*. Although most of the exhibits are permanent, some temporary sculptures have also appeared, including a mini golf course one summer in which each hole was designed by a different contemporary artist. Admission is free. Parking is easiest in an adjoining pay lot. Some free or metered street parking is available, but it goes quickly.

♿ **Loring Park** (612-370-4929; www.minneapolisparks.org), 1382 Willow St. Across Hennepin Avenue from the Sculpture Garden, Loring Park is an oasis in the city. The small but charming park offers a community pool, a basketball court, and a boat dock for the small lake at its heart. Bike and walking trails through the park are connected to trails leading to other parts of the city. Annual

TRAILS RING LAKE OF THE ISLES

AT THE MINNEAPOLIS SCULPTURE GARDEN

festivals, such as the Pride Festival and the Loring Park Art Festival, are held here each year. And if you're hungry after enjoying nature, **Café Lurcat** (see *Where to Eat*) and **Joe's Garage** are right across the street.

🐾 ♿ **Minnehaha Park** (612-230-6400; www.minneapolisparks.org), 4801 Minnehaha Ave. S. Perhaps one of the most beautiful spaces in Minneapolis, Minnehaha (which means "laughing waters") is a 193-acre park that encompasses Minnehaha Falls, limestone bluffs, and views of the river. A small rail museum pays homage to the park's history as a railway station, and Longfellow Gardens and Pergola Garden showcase both formal gardens and wildflower displays. Hiking trails wind through the park, including near the waterfall. Picnic tables and a bandstand combine for relaxed weekend outings. **Wheel Fun Rentals** (www.wheelfunrentals.com) rents bicycles, and **Sea Salt Eatery** (www.seasalteatery.com; see *Where to Eat*), open Apr.–Oct., serves fresh seafood, wine, and beer for your dining pleasure.

🐾 ♿ **Lake Harriet** (612-230-6475; www.minneapolisparks.org), 43rd St. W. and E. Lake Harriet Pkwy. Located near the charming Linden Hills neighborhood, Lake Harriet has a public beach, a boat launch (it's a popular sailboating lake), a beautiful rose garden, and a band shell that features live music in summer. Walking and biking trails give you the chance to enjoy the view, both of the lake and of the historic mansions that surround it.

🐾 ♿ **Lake Calhoun** (3000 Calhoun Pkwy.) and **Lake of the Isles** (2500 Lake Isles Pkwy.; www.minneapolisparks.org), 612-230-6400. These neighboring lakes give you the best of both lake worlds: Calhoun is another favorite of boaters, not to mention sunbathers and people-watchers. **Tin Fish** (see *Where to Eat*) gives you a quick and tasty meal before you strap on your blades and go for a ride. When you cross over to Lake of the Isles, you'll find a quieter, more scenic lake, with elegant historic homes lining the way.

✳ Lodging

Unless noted otherwise, all lodging is open year-round.

HOTELS

Downtown Minneapolis
 ✿ ♈ **The Nicollet Island Inn** (612-331-1800; www.nicolletislandinn.com), 95 Merriam St. Visitors looking for historic charm and ambience will be most successful at this small (24 rooms) but upscale hotel on Nicollet Island. Built in 1893, this limestone building with its timber-and-beam interior originally housed a door-manufacturing company, then a men's shelter run by the Salvation Army, before the Minneapolis Park & Recreation Board bought it and turned it into an inn. All rooms have views of the Mississippi River and the Minneapolis skyline. Rooms include plasma-screen TV, plush robes, and 400-thread-count Egyptian cotton bedding. The inn has its own highly regarded dining room, but many other Minneapolis dining and entertainment spots are within walking distance or a few minutes' drive. Rates run $200–265, with the higher fees charged for corner rooms, which are larger and have more views; the Deluxe Corner Room has a four-poster bed. Packages and specials available.

✿ ♈ **The Grand Hotel** (612-288-8888; www.grandhotelminneapolis.com), 615 2nd Ave. S. Housed in the former Minneapolis Athletic Club, this hotel matches its predecessor in quiet elegance. A boutique hotel represented by Preferred Hotels, it features 140 rooms, many of which offer four-poster bed and marble soaking tub. Ideally located for visitors staying downtown, the Grand Hotel also offers a 58,000-square-foot athletic area (a well-preserved remnant from its days as an upscale athletic club) and one of the city's trendiest restaurants, **Martini Blu** (see *Where to Eat*). Rates run $369–489, with some specials and packages offered.

✿ ♈ **Graves 601** (612-677-1100; www.graves601hotel.com), 601 1st Ave. N. One of the city's newest hotels is this high-fashion, high-tech establishment with tasteful, comfortable rooms and suites. It is by far the best thing to come to the Block E entertainment complex, with its stylish and spacious rooms and public spaces, and a well-regarded restaurant. Room rates start at $250, with special packages available.

🐾 ✿ ♈ **Chambers Hotel** (612-767-6900; www.chambersminneapolis.com), 901 Hennepin Ave. This newcomer to the local hotel scene offers its own brand of trendy charm. Billing itself as a "fine art hotel," Chambers is housed in a restored building near the Orpheum and State theaters. The hotel offers only 60 rooms and suites, but they are designed for luxury and comfort. An extensive collection of art pieces runs through the hotel, including the guest rooms; paintings, sculptures, and even video art are available for viewing 24 hours a day. Chambers is also the home of the **Chambers Kitchen** (see *Where to Eat*), run by star chef Jean-Georges Vongerichten.

Rates start at $345, going up to $1,100 for the Chambers Suite. Packages are available.

🐾 ♿ ♈ **The Radisson Plaza** (612-339-4900; www.radisson.com), 35 S. 7th St. The Radisson is attached to Macy's in the heart of downtown and across the street from the Marriott. Small but comfortable rooms, each furnished with a Sleep Number bed, and the well-regarded restaurant **FireLake Grill** (see *Where to Eat*) make this a good choice both for business travelers and tourists in for a weekend of major-league sports or theater and shopping. Rates start at $319, with weekend discounts and packages available.

🐾 ♿ ♈ **Marriott Minneapolis City Center** (612-349-4000; www.marriott.com), 30 S. 7th St. The Marriott was recently renovated and has, besides its standard hotel rooms, bi-level suites and a private concierge level. The hotel also has the **Northern Shores Grille**, which serves standard American fare, but for guests with more adventurous tastes a trip into City Center itself to dine at **Fogo de Chao** (see *Where to Eat*) is recommended. Rates start at $259, with packages and weekend discounts offered.

🐾 ✎ ♿ ♈ **The Westin Hotel** (612-333-4006; www.starwoodhotels.com), 88 S. 6th St. The Westin should be a case study in how to renovate a historic building. The company took Farmers and Mechanics Bank building and created a luxury hotel with a highly touted bar and restaurant (appropriately named **B.A.N.K.**; see *Where to Eat*). It kept the bank's vintage accoutrements while providing guest rooms with ergonomic work chairs and iPods. Rates start at $299,

with packages and weekend discounts offered.

♿ ♈ **The Hyatt** (612-370-1234; www.hyatt.com), 1300 Nicollet Mall. On Nicollet Avenue, where downtown Minneapolis begins to segue into neighborhoods, resides this active conference hotel. The Hyatt is close enough to walk to several downtown attractions. But with two of the city's most popular restaurants (**Manny's** for steak and **Oceanaire** for seafood; see *Where to Eat*) on site, you may not need to go far. Rates start at $299, with packages and weekend discounts offered.

♿ ♈ **The Millennium Hotel** (612-332-6000; www.millenniumhotels.com), 1313 Nicollet Mall. Across the street from the Hyatt, the Millennium is a comfortable hotel that caters to the business crowd and is connected by skyway to the Convention Center. Rates start at $235, with packages and weekend discounts offered.

🐾 ♿ ♈ **The Hilton Minneapolis** (612-376-1000; www.hilton.com), 1001 Marquette Ave. The Hilton is in a prime location for convention visitors, as it's connected by skyway to the Convention Center. It offers standard hotel rooms and suites, along with a recently refurbished set of Executive Rooms featuring upscale furnishings and amenities. The hotel restaurant **Skywater** is open three meals a day, but for variety's sake, many options are within blocks of the hotel. Rates start at $279, with packages and weekend discounts offered.

✎ ♿ ♈ **The Holiday Inn Metrodome** (612-333-4646; www.metrodome.com), 1500 Washington Ave. S. It's not the most luxurious of choices in the city, but the Holiday Inn was recently refurbished and offers convenient access to major sporting events at the Metrodome. Rates start at $120, with packages and weekend discounts offered.

The Depot Minneapolis

There are three lodging options at the the Depot Minneapolis (612-375-1700; www.thedepotminneapolis .com), 225 S. 3rd Ave.—an old Milwaukee Road railway depot that's been converted into an entertainment complex, complete with a 15,000-square-foot indoor water park and a seasonal ice rink.

♂ �& ᵞ The **Renaissance Hotel**, while still historic in nature, is geared more toward business travelers with smaller rooms and extensive technological amenities. However, the deluxe **Historic Suites** section of the Renaissance lives up to its name with generous suites decorated in early-20th-century style; large windows overlook the city. Rates begin at $269, with packages and weekend discounts offered.

🐾 ♂ �& ᵞ The **Residence Inn** is an extended-stay format, with each unit containing a full kitchen. Rates begin at $229, with packages and weekend discounts offered.

University of Minnesota— East Bank

�& ᵞ **The Radisson University** (612-379-8888; www.radisson.com), 615 Washington Ave. SE. This hotel is an attractive option close to restaurants and within easy walking distance of Northrop Auditorium and the Weisman Museum. Rates start at $129.

🐾 �& **The Days Inn University of Minnesota** (612-623-3999; www .daysinn.com), 2407 University Ave. SE. A bit farther down the road, the Days Inn is on the edge of the East

Bank, but still within walking distance of many university locations. Rates start at $69, with packages and weekend discounts offered.

✳ Where to Eat

The Minneapolis restaurant scene continues to expand, both in quality and in types of foods offered. Visitors who think of Minnesota as the land of white food—Swedish meatballs, mashed potatoes, lutefisk, and lefse—will be in for a tasty surprise. Some of the upper-end restaurants have gained national attention (D'Amico Cucina, for instance, and Vincent: A Restaurant), while numerous small ethnic cafés have begun to change the city's culinary landscape to reflect its growing ethnic diversity. A caveat: The restaurant industry is always a volatile one, and Minneapolis is not immune to the rapid turnover that can occur. Use the contact info here to check a restaurant's current status before arrival.

All restaurants are open year-round unless otherwise noted.

DINING OUT

Downtown

Minneapolis is now a foodie destination—but many visitors to the area are surprised by the generally casual approach to dining out. For better or worse, Minnesota diners tend to err on the informal side when it comes to dressing for dinner. That's not to say that you won't see suits and ties, but it's not uncommon to see people in business casual—or even jeans and T-shirts—at some of the leading restaurants.

�& ᵞ **D'Amico Cucina** (612-338-2401; www.damico.com), 100 N. 6th

St. Open Mon.–Sat. for dinner at 5:30. Closed Sun. The D'Amico brothers have built a restaurant empire that started with this thoughtful, upscale Italian restaurant, which is a longtime leader in the local restaurant scene. Open only for dinner, D'Amico Cucina is located on the edge of the Warehouse District, within steps of the Hennepin Theatre District and the Target Center, making it perfectly suited for an evening out. The restaurant's theme continues into its wine list, which is exclusively Italian. Entrées are $35 and up.

🚻 ⍟ **Café Lurcat** (612-486-5500; www.cafelurcat.com), 1624 Harmon Pl. Open daily for dinner at 5. Another D'Amico establishment, Café Lurcat overlooks Loring Park and delights patrons with an inventive and tasty à la carte menu. The adjoining **Bar Lurcat** offers live music as well as an extensive wine list, including 40 wines served by the glass. Entrées start at $20.

🚻 ⍟ **Masa** (612-338-6272; www.masa -restaurant.com), 1070 Nicollet Mall. Open Mon.–Fri. 11:30–2:30 for lunch, Mon.–Sat. at 5 for dinner. Also a D'Amico venture, Masa provides authentic Mexican food. While the Hispanic food scene is thankfully growing in the Twin Cities, providing numerous small outlets for great food, Masa is one of the few upscale, "night-out" Mexican restaurants. Lunch entrées start at $11, dinner entrées at $17.

🚻 ⍟ **Fogo de Chao** (612-338-1344; www.fogodechao.com), 645 Hennepin Ave. Open Mon.–Fri. 11–2 for lunch; Mon.–Fri. at 5 for dinner, Sat. at 4:30, Sun. at 4. This is a carnivore's fantasy swathed in Brazilian traditions. Rather than ordering from a menu,

diners are served by gauchos who sidle through the restaurant, cutting meat to order off sizzling skewers. Sides are served family-style, all at a fixed price. The sumptuously decorated interior, lined with murals of Brazilian ranch life, dark woods, and endless bottles of wine, inspires a true feeling of decadence. Lunch is $22, dinner $39.

🚻 ⍟ **B.A.N.K.** (612-656-3255; www .bankmpls.com), 88 S. 6th St. Open daily for all three meals. Located at the Westin Minneapolis Hotel in the old Farmers and Mechanics Bank, B.A.N.K.'s developers wisely took the banking theme and ran with it, creating an unusual but lovely tribute to the olden days of finance. The food plays up the opulent setting. Breakfast entrées start at $7, lunch at $9, and dinner at $14.

🚻 ⍟ **Cosmos** (612-312-1168; www .cosmosrestaurant.com), 601 1st Ave. S. Open daily for all three meals. Another hotel restaurant that rises above standard hotel food. Quite possibly one of the most beautiful restaurants in the Twin Cities, Cosmos offers world-class cuisine, a stellar wine list, and desserts by the master, pastry chef Khan Tranh. Breakfast and lunch entrées start at $9, dinner at $18.

🚻 ⍟ **Chambers Kitchen** (612-767-6999; www.chambersminneapolis .com), 901 Hennepin Ave. Open daily for all three meals. This buzz-worthy restaurant run by chef Jean-Georges Vongerichten is easily one of the best in the Twin Cities, located in one of the area's best hotels. Breakfast and lunch entrées start at $8, dinner at $20.

🚻 ⍟ **FireLake Grill** (612-216-3473; www.firelakerestaurant.com), 31 S. 6th St., in the Radisson Plaza

Hotel. Open daily for all three meals. The restaurant has won considerable acclaim for its attention to local produce, cheese, and meat producers and artisan-quality fare. A seasonal menu allows the chef to tailor dishes to what's in-season, such as locally fished walleye during summer, prepared over a real fire and seasoned to perfection. Breakfast and lunch entrées start at $7, dinner at $15.

&. ⅄ **Martini Blu** (612-752-9595; www.martiniblu.com), 615 2nd Ave. S. Open daily for all three meals. A coolly contemporary bar and restaurant tucked away on the second floor of the Grand Hotel, Martini Blu's trendy decor stands in contrast with the aristocratic grandeur of the hotel's entrance, but the change in ambience works, as does the haute cuisine menu and outstanding sushi bar. At press time Martini Blu offered all-you-can-eat sushi on Sunday; call ahead for reservations, because it's a very popular event. But no doggie bags allowed. Breakfast entrées start at $8, lunch $14, dinner $18.

&. ⅄ **Oceanaire** (612-333-2277; www.theoceanaire.com), 1300 Nicollet Mall (in the Hyatt Hotel). Open daily at 5 for dinner. This eatery fast became a local favorite both for its vintage interior harking back to the 1940s and for its extensive fresh seafood menu. Entrées start at $25.

✍ &. ⅄ **Palomino** (612-339-3800; www.palomino.com), 825 Hennepin Ave. Open Mon.–Sat. for lunch, daily for dinner. Located across the street from the Orpheum and down the street from the State Theatre, Palomino accommodates theatergoers with early dining specials and brunches on Sunday matinee days. Its casual American fare is well executed, if not

especially innovative, but it's a good choice for those looking for convenient pretheater arrangements. Lunch entrées start at $12, dinner at $20.

&. ⅄ **Vincent: A Restaurant** (612-630-1189; www.vincentrestaurant .com), 1100 Nicollet Mall. Open Mon.–Fri. for lunch, Mon.–Sat. for dinner; closed Sun. The eponymous restaurant of Vincent Francoual, this establishment was a success from the moment it opened. Vincent has earned national acclaim for its southern French food, served at lower-than-expected prices, as well as its casually elegant interior. Stop by for the happy hour. Lunch entrées start at $12, dinner at $17.

✍ &. ⅄ **La Belle Vie** (612-874-6440; www.labellevie.us), 510 Groveland Ave. Open daily at 5 for dinner. Originally located in Stillwater, La Belle Vie moved into the former 510 Groveland space (near Loring Park and the Walker Art Center) to great acclaim in 2005. Chef and proprietor Tim McKee is widely considered one of the best chefs in the state, and his commitment to high quality and using local ingredients has made him a local darling. In 2007 La Belle Vie launched a **Junior Gourmet Club**, with occasional events designed to teach younger eaters about the joys of fine food. Outings include a multi-course dinner designed and explained by McKee as well as a field trip to the Mill City Farmer's Market, introducing kids to the concept of farming and buying local. Entrées start at $22.

Warehouse District
A number of small restaurants and bistros in the Warehouse District have built niches as destination dining for aficionados.

STEAK HOUSES

Minnesotans love their fish and seafood, but few will turn their back on a prime piece of beef. Downtown Minneapolis is home to several outstanding steak houses, which all seem to coexist peacefully; apparently there are plenty of steak lovers to keep them busy.

&. Y **Murray's** (612-339-0909; www.murraysrestaurant.com), 24 S. 6th St. Open Mon.–Fri. for lunch, daily for dinner. The original Minneapolis steak house, famous for its "silver butter knife" tender meat. Its reputation as a hometown favorite, as well as its tremendous steaks, keep it a serious contender. Lunch entrées start at $10, dinner at $17.

&. Y **Ruth's Chris** (612-672-9000; www.ruthschris.com), 920 2nd Ave. S. Open daily for dinner. One of the more economical offerings in the often expensive steak house category, but the restaurant doesn't spare quality for price. Entrées start at $20.

&. Y **Morton's** (612-673-9700; www.mortons.com), 555 Nicollet Mall. Open daily for lunch and dinner. Morton's rises above its chain image to serve impeccable steaks in portions generous enough to feed a crowd. Lunch entrées start at $11, dinner at $25.

&. Y **Rossi's** (612-312-2880; www.rossissteakhouse.com), 90 S. 9th St. Open Mon.–Fri. for lunch, daily for dinner. Rossi's takes the steak house back to its retro supper-club roots. Lunch entrées start at $8, dinner entrées at $14.

&. Y **Manny's** (612-339-9900; www.mannyssteakhouse.com), 1300 Nicollet Mall (in the Hyatt Hotel). Open daily for dinner. Serves a loyal local and tourist clientele. Entrées start at $20.

&. Y **The Capital Grille** (612-692-9000; www.thecapitalgrille.com), 801 Hennepin Ave. Open Mon.–Fri. for lunch, daily for dinner. This is where local people of prominence go for steaks, as well as to store their personal wine selections in the cellar. Lunch entrées start at $10, dinner at $25.

&. Y **Origami** (612-333-8430; www.origamirestaurant.com), 30 N. 1st St.; also in Minnetonka. Open Mon.–Fri. for lunch, daily for dinner. Origami's location in a historic, narrow stone building in the Warehouse District gives it a perpetual cool factor, but it's the extraordinary sushi and other Japanese entrées, as well as a well-stocked bar, that keep people coming back. All the sushi is made to order, which means it's tremendously fresh, but it also means service can be slow when the restaurant is busy. It's worth the wait, as long as you're prepared. Lunch entrées start at $8, dinner at $18.

&. Y **Babalu** (612-746-3158; www.babalu.us), 800 Washington Ave. N. Open Mon.–Sat. for dinner. This popular spot has a lively Cuban atmosphere and menu in a white-tablecloth environment. Call ahead to find out when live music will be available to get the full tropical experience. Entrées start at $14.

♿ ⚊ **Sapor** (612-375-1971; www .saporcafe.com), 428 Washington Ave. N. Open Mon.–Fri. for lunch, Mon.–Sat. for dinner. Sapor has a quiet, comfortably upscale feel, and the chefs provide some truly inspired melding of cuisines. Lunch entrées start at $10, dinner at $20.

♿ ⚊ **Café Havana** (612-338-8484), 119 Washington Ave. N. Open Tues.–Sat. for dinner. The Old World interior, combined with far-better-than-average Cuban food and drinks, makes this a worthy destination. Word of warning: Café Havana is located on a transitional block and counts Sex-World and Sinners as its close neighbors. That hasn't stopped people from flocking in for Cuban food. Entrées start at $11.

♿ ⚊ **Cue at the Guthrie** (612-225-6499; www.cueatguthrie.com), 818 S. 2nd St. Open Tues.–Sun. for lunch and dinner. *The* place for dining at the Guthrie, not just because it's located in the same building, but also because both its culinary offerings and its dramatic interior satisfy all senses. The restaurant complements the theater's building beautifully, and at night the lighting is spectacular. Lunch entrées start at $11, dinner at $18.

South Minneapolis

♿ ⚊ **Chino Latino** (612-824-7878; www.chinolatino.com), 2916 S. Hennepin Ave. Open daily for dinner. Chino Latino pulls off a melding of Asian and Hispanic cuisine while maintaining its cutting-edge social reputation. Expect crowds and a noisy

atmosphere, but also expect to have an exciting culinary experience. Entrées start at $17.

♿ ⚊ **Figlio's** (612-822-1688; www .figlio.com), 3001 Hennepin Ave. Open daily for lunch and dinner. One of the few constants in the Calhoun Square development in Uptown. For nearly 30 years the restaurant has attracted hip locals who are looking to meet others, or just to have a decent meal and a drink. Lunch entrées start at $10, dinner at $12.

♿ ⚊ **Lucia's** (612-825-1572; www .lucias.com), 1432 W. 31st St. Open Mon.–Sat. for lunch and dinner. A small, intimate bistro quietly tucked away from the bustle of the Lake–Hennepin intersection, Lucia's is a romantic eatery directed by the inestimable Lucia Watson, a local culinary legend. Menu changes daily; local foods are used whenever possible. Lunch entrées start at $10, dinner at $16.

⚉ ♿ ⚊ **Fuji-Ya** (612-871-4055; www .fujiyasushi.com), 600 W. Lake St. (also in St. Paul). Open Tues.–Sun. for dinner only. Fuji-Ya made a welcome transition from its previous smaller quarters on Lyndale Avenue to larger facilities on West Lake Street. Part of the expansion was adding Japanese tearooms (reservations are a must) in which diners can enjoy their meal quietly in a small, enclosed room, sitting on the floor in the traditional Japanese way. But tearoom or no tearoom, Fuji-Ya serves some of the best Japanese food in the state. Its sushi is top quality, freshly made to order, and beautifully presented. Beyond sushi, Fuji-Ya also shines, with a wide variety of Japanese salads, noodle bowls, bulgogi, and meat and seafood entrées. Possibly because so much care is

OUTDOOR EATING

Whether it's because Minnesota is a state rich in nature, or because the winter months make everyone long to be outdoors, Minnesotans are very fond of eating alfresco. The good news is that many restaurants have options for doing just that; the bad news is, often the outdoor venues are as dismal as seating on a sidewalk adjacent to a busy road with heavy bus traffic or overlooking vast asphalt parking lots. Here's a quick list of places where excellent food—and excellent outdoor views—come together perfectly.

&. ♈ **Solera** (612-338-0062; www.solera-restaurant.com), 900 Hennepin Ave. Open daily for dinner. Solera serves a huge variety of tapas, and in summer

taken with preparation, service is slow; be prepared to relax and enjoy. Entrées start at $14.

EATING OUT

There are almost countless options for more casual, less expensive quality dining throughout Minneapolis. What follows should be viewed as great suggestions rather than a fully comprehensive list.

♪ &. **Hell's Kitchen** (612-332-4700; www.hellskitcheninc.com), 89 S. 10th St. (also in Duluth). Open daily for breakfast and lunch. Hell's Kitchen is a Gothic haunt in downtown Minneapolis, open only for breakfast and lunch weekdays, brunch on weekends. The signature "damn good" breakfast foods can't be beat, and weekend servers might show up for work in their PJs. Entrées start at $9.

its rooftop patio is the perfect place to enjoy tasty morsels while taking in views of the city. Tapas start at $4.

🍴 ♿ 🍸 **Brit's Pub** (612-332-3908; www.britspub.com), 1110 Nicollet Mall. Open daily for lunch and dinner. A casual British pub with exemplary British dishes (fish-and-chips, ploughman's lunch), Brit's also has a rooftop bowling green surrounded by tables and umbrellas. The bowling green isn't just for looks—there are leagues that play through summer. It's a bit of British refinement above the city. Entrées start at $12.

🍴 ♿ 🍸 **It's Greek to Me** (612-825-9922), 626 W. Lake St. Open Tues.–Sun. for lunch and dinner. A long-term fixture at the corner of Lake and Lyndale, It's Greek to Me has food that's tasty and reasonably priced, and a lovely, secluded private patio. Lunch entrées start at $8, dinner at $11.

🍴 ♿ 🍸 **The Black Forest** (612-872-0812; www.blackforestinnmpls.com), 1 E. 26th St. Open daily for all three meals. This neighborhood standby has an unexpectedly charming garden hidden behind the main restaurant for German food lovers. Breakfast entrées start at $4, lunch at $5, dinner at $11.

🍴 ♿ 🍸 **Psycho Suzi's Motor Lounge and Tiki Garden** (612-788-9069; www.psychosuzis.com), 2519 Marshall St. NE. Open daily for lunch and dinner. Psycho Suzi's made great use of an old drive-in restaurant by building a delightful patio where bikers, gays, families, and businesspeople all gather to enjoy the soul-satisfying bar grub. Entrées start at $7.

🍴 ♿ **The Tin Fish** (612-823-5840; www.thetinfish.net), 3000 Calhoun Pkwy. E. Open daily for lunch and dinner, May–mid-Oct., weather permitting. It's hard to beat the scenery of Tin Fish, located right on the shores of one of the city's most popular lakes, Lake Calhoun. Entrées start at $10.

🍴 ♿ 🍸 **Sea Salt Eatery** (612-721-8990; www.seasalteatery.com), 4801 Minnehaha Ave. S. Open daily for lunch and dinner, summer months only. This one gives Tin Fish a run for its scenic money, placed as it is in the lovely Minnehaha Park overlooking Minnehaha Falls. Entrées start at $5.

🍴 **Annie's Parlour** (612-379-0744) 313 14th Ave. SE. Open daily for lunch and dinner. This friendly café has been a Dinkytown/University of Minnesota fixture for decades, and for good reason: The burgers and fries are close to perfect. But save room for the hot fudge sundaes—the hot fudge is so delicious you won't need the ice cream. Entrées start at $6.

🍴 ♿ 🍸 **The Sample Room** (612-789-0333; www.the-sample-room.com), 2124 NE Marshall St. Open daily for lunch and dinner. A casual noshing spot located in a historic building in the northeast area. An eclectic menu includes one of the best meat loaf dinners ever. Entrées start at $14.

🍴 ♿ 🍸 **Pizza Luce** (612-333-7359, 119 N. 4th St.; 612-827-5978, 3200

Lyndale Ave. S.; 612-332-2525, 2200 Franklin Ave. E.; also in St. Paul and Duluth; www.pizzaluce.com). Open daily for lunch and dinner. From lunch to late night, Pizza Luce serves some of the best pizza the Twin Cities offers. Whether you prefer traditional pizzas or feel adventurous, Pizza Luce has something for you. This is also a good spot for vegans, with several non-animal-product offerings. Entrées start at $6.

& **Betty Jean's Chicken 'n' Waffles** (612-339-1968; http://bjschicken nwaffles.com), 319 1st Ave. N. Open Tues.–Sun. for lunch and dinner. Closed Mon. A casual restaurant in the Warehouse District that offers—you guessed it—chicken and waffles, sometimes together. Betty Jean's serves home cooking at its best, and on weekend nights it's open until 2 AM (also open later on event nights; call before stopping by). Entrées start at $8.

& **Holy Land Deli** (612-781-2627, www.holylandbrand.com), 2513 Central Ave. NE (also an outlet at the Midtown Global Market). Open daily for all three meals. Open later in summer. Half restaurant, half grocery store, and wholly worth the drive, Holy Land Deli doesn't look like much from the outside, but drop by for the hearty and flavorful lunch and dinner buffets (or order à la carte), then pop into the grocery side for Middle Eastern staples not found elsewhere. Entrées start at $7.

& ¥ **Broder's Pasta Bar and Deli** (612-925-9202; www.broders.com), 5000 Penn Ave. S. Open daily for dinner. Broder's is a reasonably priced neighborhood pasta bistro with far-above-average offerings. Open only for dinner, but across the street is Broder's Deli, available for lunch and takeout and also open daily. Stop by for some lunch to take to Lake Harriet for a perfect afternoon picnic. Entrées start at $8.

& **Café Zumbro** (612-920-3606), 2803 W. 43rd St. Open Tues.–Sun. for breakfast and lunch. Closed Mon. This small café in the Linden Hills neighborhood is something of a local tradition. The specialty is breakfast (the huevos and eggs Benedict are both popular), and a limited breakfast

---

& ¥ **Midtown Global Market** (www.midtownglobalmarket.org), Lake St. and Chicago Ave. Open daily for all three meals (restaurants' opening hours vary). The Midtown Global Market represents a major effort on the part of the city to not only revitalize a faltering neighborhood and restore a long-vacant Sears tower, but also pay tribute to the ever-growing ethnic and culinary diversity in the area. Most of the food outlets here are quick service, but of surprisingly good quality and reasonable prices. This is an excellent place to wander on a weekend afternoon, trying different cuisines while taking in the live music or dancing in the central plaza. Try the foods of **Holy Land Deli**, **A La Salsa**, **Jakeeno's Trattoria**, **Everest Café**, and **Manny's Tortas**, all of which have restaurants in other parts of the Twin Cities; also worthy of a stop are **La Loma Tamales**, **Safari Express**, **Taqueria Los Ocampo**, and **Andy's Garage**.

menu is available over the lunch hour as well, but you'd miss out on the gourmet sandwiches, soups, and salads. Entrées start at $6.

 ⛿ Ⓨ **Café Twenty Eight** (612-926-2800; www.cafetwentyeight.com), 2724 W. 43rd St. Open Tues.–Sun. for lunch and dinner. Also located in the small Linden Hills neighborhood. The menu is limited, but a deft hand with local seasonal ingredients and a relaxed atmosphere make this a great place to stop after a walk around Lake Harriet or a shopping spree. Entrées start at $9.

⛿ **Rice Paper** (612-926-8650; www.ricepaperrestaurant.com), 2726 W. 43rd St. Open Mon.–Sat. for lunch and dinner. Rice Paper serves Asian fusion food in hearty portions and inventive combinations. The shrimp spring rolls are in demand, as is the homemade peanut sauce. Entrées start at $9.

✍ ⛿ Ⓨ **El Meson** (612-822-8062; www.elmesonbistro.com), 3450 Lyndale Ave. S. Open Mon.–Sat. for lunch and dinner, Sun. for dinner only. El Meson bills itself as a Spanish-Caribbean bistro, and this longtime neighborhood favorite knows what it's doing. Allow extra time for the paella; it's worth the wait. If you're in a hurry for lunch, check out the buffet, full of vegetable- and meat-based Caribbean dishes of varying spiciness. Entrées start at $12.

✍ ⛿ **The Egg and I** (612-872-7282), 2828 Lyndale Ave. S. (also in St. Paul). Open daily for breakfast and lunch. The Egg and I knows a thing or two about breakfasts. Pancakes are huge and fluffy; egg dishes, perfectly cooked in generous portions. Lunch is served, but breakfast is what you'll want. Entrées start at $5.

✍ ⛿ **Al's Breakfast** (612-331-9991), 413 14th Ave. SE. Open daily for breakfast. A minuscule venue with just 14 seats. There's nearly always a wait, but waiting is worth it when it comes to Al's breakfast fare—though service can be less than friendly. Don't miss the pancakes. Entrées start at $4.

✍ ⛿ Ⓨ **Loring Pasta Bar** (612-378-4849; www.loringpastabar.com), 327 14th Ave. S. Open daily for lunch and dinner. Tucked into the Dinkytown/University of Minnesota area, the Loring serves global food in a sumptuous interior. Sun. nights feature a live tango band. Lunch entrées start at $8, dinner at $11.

✳ Entertainment

LIVE PERFORMANCES

Minneapolis is a theater and music lover's town. From large, internationally renowned companies like the Guthrie Theater and the Children's Theatre Company; to arena rock at the Target Center; the theaters that host Broadway tours; and smaller inventive and experimental groups like Theatre de la Jeune Lune, the Jungle Theater, and the intimate jazz space of the Dakota Jazz Club—there's something for every taste.

✍ ⛿ Ⓨ **The Guthrie Theater** (612-377-2224; www.guthrietheater.org), 818 S. 2nd St. This internationally renowned theater company completed an ambitious move in 2006 when it left its original location adjacent to the Walker Art Center for the growing arts and restaurant area near the Mississippi River. Besides three separate stage areas, the Guthrie also includes what is considered some of the city's top-end dining with Cue at

EAT STREET

For the most part, none of the restaurants clustered together over several blocks on Nicollet Avenue just outside downtown is formal. But they do make up a broad ethnic swath, mostly at reasonable prices and of excellent quality. You could spend days exploring the world in just a few blocks.

✏ ♿ **Bad Waitress** (612-872-7575), 2 E. 26th St. Open daily for all three meals. The name might seem like a warning, but actually it's a tease: Diners fill out their own order sheets at their tables and turn them in to the cashier to get their choice of delectable pancakes and sandwiches. Entrées start at $6.

♿ ♟ **Azia** (612-813-1200; www.aziarestaurant.com), 2550 Nicollet Ave. S. Open Mon.–Sat. for lunch and dinner, Sun. for dinner only. Across the street from Bad Waitress, Azia has built a solid reputation as a trendy Asian fusion restaurant, and the Caterpillar Lounge in the back has become a busy hot spot, offering an extensive sake menu. Entrées start at $18, with lunch versions offered for slightly less as specials.

✏ ♿ **Peninsula Malaysian Cuisine** (612-871-8282; www.peninsulamalaysian cuisine.com), 2608 Nicollet Ave. Open daily for lunch and dinner. Offers a broad and fascinating overview of Malaysian food. Prices are surprisingly low, given the range of food options. Entrées start at $9.

✏ ♿ ♟ **Christos** (612-871-2111; www.christos.com), 2632 Nicollet Ave. S. (also in St. Paul and Minnetonka). Open daily for lunch and dinner. Serves a solid Greek menu, from the traditional gyros and hummus to lamb, chicken, and pork dishes as well as a lengthy vegetarian menu. Lunch entrées start at $6, dinner at $12.

✏ ♿ **Quang** (612-870-4739), 2719 Nicollet Ave. S. Open Wed.–Mon. for lunch and dinner; closed Tues. Provides jumbo Vietnamese noodle bowls, delicious and inexpensive, although the service is not always friendly. Entrées start at $6.

✏ ♿ ♟ **Taco Morelos** (612-870-0053), 14 W. 26th St. Open daily for all three meals. One of the best sources around for authentic Mexican food. Besides, you can get real Mexican Coca-Cola here. Entrées start at $7.

✏ ♿ ♟ **Rainbow Chinese** (612-870-7084; www.rainbowrestaurant.com), 2739

the Guthrie (see *Where to Eat*). The Wurtele Thrust Stage hosts large-scale productions, such as classics and musicals, while the McGuire Proscenium Stage hosts more contemporary works, as well as productions from touring companies. The Dowling Studio acts as a training ground for University of Minnesota and Guthrie Theater acting students. Even if you don't want to see a particular play, a visit to the building itself is worth the

Nicollet Ave. Open daily for lunch and dinner. Does for Chinese what Taco Morelos does for Mexican, and the prices are quite reasonable for top-notch food. Entrées start at $8.

✐ ♿ **Pho 79** (612-871-4602), 2529 Nicollet Ave. (also in St. Paul). Open daily for lunch and dinner. Serves heaping bowls of Vietnamese pho, perfectly seasoned. Wear easy-wash clothing, as slurping your soup can get messy, but it's worth it. Entrées start at $7.

✐ ♿ ⏧ **Salsa a la Salsa** (612-813-1970; www.salsaalasalsa.com), 1420 Nicollet Ave. Open daily for lunch and dinner. Farther down Nicollet, Salsa a la Salsa has a menu encompassing both authentic and Americanized Mexican food. While some restaurants interpret *spicy* as slightly more than mild, Salsa a la Salsa takes the word seriously, especially in the Chicken Chiltepin. Be sure to have one of the homemade margaritas. Entrées start at $10.

PENINSULA MALAYSIAN CUISINE

time; the dramatic Endless Bridge, a cantilevered lobby with spectacular views of the Mississippi River falls, is a perfect place to start, followed by a stop at one of the building's restaurants or bars. Most of the public spaces are open to the public every day except Monday, even when no play is in production.

✐ ♿ **The Children's Theatre Company** (612-874-0400; www.childrens theatre.org), 2400 3rd Ave. S. The

THE GUTHRIE THEATER'S ENDLESS BRIDGE

CTC has an international reputation for its outstanding and innovative productions. The theater itself is adjacent to the **Minneapolis Institute of the Arts** (see *Museums*). Appropriately family-friendly, the stage area has comfortable stadium seating with extra spacing between rows—helpful when transporting young children to the bathrooms during productions with minimal discomfort to other theatergoers. Snacks and coffee are sold in the lobby during intermission and after the show. Each season includes a variety of productions geared toward different age groups. Some of the classics that appear periodically include *The 500 Hats of Bartholomew Cubbins* (which leaves both kids and adults wondering, "How did they do that?"), *How the Grinch Stole Christmas*, and *A Year with Frog and Toad*. Free parking is available in a ramp next to the theater, but arrive early: The spaces are limited, and on busy museum days the competition for those spots is heavy. Street parking (metered on weekdays) is also available.

♂ ♿ ⚇ **The Hennepin Theatre District** (612-673-0404; www.hennepin theatredistrict.org). The district is made up of a series of renovated theaters in downtown Minneapolis: the **State**, the **Orpheum**, **Hennepin Stages**, and the **Pantages**, all located between 7th and 10th streets on Hennepin Avenue. The Orpheum and the State are Minneapolis's home base for Broadway touring productions as well as headlining music, magic, and comedy acts. Hennepin Stages presents smaller-scale musical productions and concerts. Pantages is home to an intimate concert venue for touring musicians.

THE CHILDREN'S THEATRE

🖋 ♿ **The Music Box Theatre**, 1407 Nicollet Ave. The Music Box sells tickets to its long-running comedy production, *Triple Espresso* (www.tripleespresso.com) through the Hennepin Theatre District office, although the theater itself is just off the main Theatre District corridor.

🖋 ♿ **Theatre de la Jeune Lune** (612-333-6200; www.jeunelune.org), 105 N. 1st St. Jeune Lune uses a large warehouse as its staging area to produce a unique merging of theatrical conventions: plays, circuses, operas, all combined into one production. Don't be fooled by the bare-bones look of the theater—this company produces some highly thought-provoking performances, as well as some distinct eye candy.

♿ **The Jungle Theater** (612-822-7063; www.jungletheater.com), 2951 Lyndale Ave. S. A small (150 seats) theater focused on intimate productions, mainly of a contemporary nature.

🖋 ♿ 🍸 **Northrop Auditorium** (612-624-2345; www1.umn.edu/umato), 84 Church St. SE. Situated at the top of Northrop Mall on the University of Minnesota's East Bank, Northrop's stately architecture gives access to a wide variety of performances: musicians of nearly every genre, comedians, and the annual Northrop Dance Series, which features a diverse selection of touring and local dance troupes.

🖋 ♿ 🍸 **Target Center** (612-673-0900; www.targetcenter.com), 600 1st Ave. N. Home to the **Minnesota Timberwolves** (see *Sporting Events*) as well as many touring musical acts. There are two large parking ramps connected by skyway, and Target Center also offers a "parents' room" for adults who bring offspring to concerts that the parents don't necessarily want to attend. Some of the music industry's most popular performers stop here, but it's not because of the great acoustics; St. Paul's Xcel Energy Center is a much better musical setting. When that certain band comes to town, though, Target Center may be where it ends up playing anyway.

♿ 🍸 **Brave New Workshop** (612-332-6620; www.bravenewworkshop.com), 2605 Hennepin Ave. S. The long-standing home of improvisational and sketch comedy on Hennepin Avenue near Uptown. The company develops and produces original shows made up of several short pieces built around one theme, usually societal or political. Weekend shows often have improv after the official performances. Beer, wine, and snacks are available.

♿ 🍸 **Fine Line Music Café** (612-338-8100; www.finelinemusic.com), 318 1st Ave. N. Located in the Consortium Building, a historic site in the warehouse district, the Fine Line quickly established itself as a first-rate music club, showcasing both local and national performers. This is not so much a dance club as an actual music club; the Cowboy Junkies, Aimee Mann, and the Neville Bros. have all performed here. Acoustics are great, and the crowd ambience is calmer than at nearby First Avenue or Quest.

♿ 🍸 **Dakota Jazz Club & Restaurant** (612-332-1010; www.dakotacooks.com), 1010 Nicollet Ave. Located right in the heart of downtown Minneapolis. Truly a jazz and blues lover's haven, the Dakota has a packed schedule of musicians in its intimate performance space, and it offers excellent food as well.

&. ⚲ **First Avenue** (612-332-1775; www.first-avenue.com), 701 1st Ave. N. The granddaddy of rock venues. Still operating at its original location, the nationally acclaimed First Avenue continues to serve the rock and alternative scene with both major players and up-and-coming musicians, including a wide range of local groups. This bar is truly about the music—the environment itself does not lend itself well to comfort, and the smell of stale beer permeates the air (replacing the cigarette odors that dominated until the city banned smoking in all indoor public places). If ambience is what you want, this isn't the place. But for a true rock music experience, it can't be beat.

&. **The Varsity Theater** (612-604-0222; www.varsitytheater.org), 1308 4th St. SE. Located in the University of Minnesota's Dinkytown neighborhood, the Varsity is rapidly becoming another popular destination for local and smaller touring bands. Although heavily frequented by students, the Varsity is by no means college-only; the theater has been lauded for its sound and light systems and for its comfortable interior, as well as its willingness to book a wide variety of acts.

&. ⚲ **The Nomad World Pub** (612-338-6424; www.nomadpub.com), 501 Cedar Ave. If you'd like to experience the Twin Cities jazz scene at its finest—and most diverse—check out the Nomad, which features established jazz performers early in the evening, up-and-comers later at night.

OTHER ENTERTAINMENT

♿ &. ⚲ **Block E** (Hennepin Ave. between 6th and 7th sts.). This was supposed to be the centerpiece of urban renewal, but most locals were disappointed when a series of chains came in. Nonetheless, if you've got a hankering to engage in some heavy-duty arcade action, **Gameworks** has over 200 electronic games, virtual bowling, and real bowling, along with a bar and grill. Upstairs, **Hard Rock Café** does its hard-rock thing with its bar menu and pulsing music. **Crown Theatres** offers 15 screens of stadium-seating movie goodness.

♿ &. ⚲ **Elsie's** (612-378-9701; www.elsies.com), 729 Marshall St. NE. If bowling is what you want, venture northeast to this neighborhood favorite for a bite to eat and some rounds of glow-in-the-dark bowling.

&. ⚲ **Bryant Lake Bowl** (612-825-3737; www.bryantlakebowl.com), 810 W. Lake St. As its name implies, Bryant Lake Bowl offers bowling, but it doubles as a live theater venue as well.

&. ⚲ **The Cedar Cultural Center** (612-338-2674; www.thecedar.org), 416 Cedar Ave. S. The Cedar has had a lasting impact on the Twin Cities' live-music scene, presenting musicians from all over the world.

&. ⚲ **El Nuevo Rodeo** (612-728-0101; www.elnuevorodeo.com), 3003 27th Ave. S. An example of the growing Hispanic influence on the Twin Cities. Both restaurant and nightclub, El Nuevo Rodeo provides live music and a lively Mexican menu.

SPORTING EVENTS

♿ &. ⚲ **Target Center** (612-673-1600; www.targetcenter.com), 600 1st Ave. N. Home to the Minnesota Timberwolves men's basketball team and the Minnesota Lynx women's basketball team. The Wolves and Lynx both have loyal fan bases; call ahead for tickets. Target Center also hosts touring sports exhibitions, such as figure skating and the timeless Harlem Globetrotters.

🖌 ♿ ☂ **The Metrodome** (612-332-0386; www.msfc.com), 900 S. 5th St. The Metrodome is—for now—the home of the Minnesota Twins baseball team and the Minnesota Vikings football team. The Twins plan to build a new stadium outside Minneapolis, and the Vikings are considering doing the same. But for the time being, their regular seasons are played at the Metrodome.

🖌 ♿ **The Minnesota Gophers** (www.gophersports.com) The official sports teams of the University of Minnesota are spread out across several athletic facilities, including the Metrodome and the university-sited Mariucci Arena and Williams Arena.

✳ Selective Shopping

Linden Hills
This small neighborhood in South Minneapolis, near Lake Harriet, offers several fun shops. Some have additional locations—mentioned in the description—but Linden Hills has them all in one place. All are open year-round and daily unless noted otherwise.

Bibelot (612-925-3175, 4315 Upton Ave.; 300 E. Hennepin Ave., 612-379-9300; also in St. Paul; www.bibelotshops.com). Gifts and novelties. But this is not another tacky souvenir shop; the Bibelot stores carry all kinds of guilty pleasures, from locally made jewelry to unique women's clothing to off-the-wall kitchen and bath items. Their greeting card selection is good for more than a few giggles, and there

is a well-chosen line of toys for kids.

Great Harvest Bread Co. (612-929-2899; www.greatharvest.com), 4314 Upton Ave., also in St. Paul, Minnetonka, Burnsville, and Woodbury. Where healthy and delicious are combined to the best effects of both (be sure to try the whole wheat chocolate chip cookies).

🖌 **Creative Kidstuff** (612-929-0653; www.creativekidstuff.com), 4313 Upton Ave., also in St. Paul, Edina, Minnetonka, Woodbury, and Maple Grove. This is a mecca for young children. The store, housed in three sections of an old office building, is chock-full of toys, educational and otherwise, and—perhaps even better—is well staffed by knowledgeable, helpful clerks who aren't against the idea of kids trying out toys before buying them.

The Garden Sampler (612-925-4859; www.thegardensampler.com), 4301 Upton Ave. A gift shop themed around gardening, with a wide variety of prices for the gardening guru.

Coffee & Tea Ltd. (612-920-6344; www.coffeeandtealtd.com), 2730 W. 43rd St., also at the Mall of America in Bloomington. Don't be deceived by its hole-in-the-wall size and ambience; this little shop has an excellent variety of coffee and tea products, and staff are passionate on the topic.

🖌 **Wild Rumpus** (612-920-5005; www.wildrumpusbooks.com), 2720 W. 43rd St. One of the best children's bookstores ever. The store comes complete with its own pets, including a tailless cat and a chicken; the front door has a small-fry door as well. Whatever you need to know, just ask; staff seem to know everything worth knowing about children's literature.

Linden Hills Yarns (612-929-1255; www.lindenhillsyarn.com), 2720 W. 43rd St. Closed Sun. Down the street from Wild Rumpus (just past Café Twenty-Eight and Rice Paper) is this haven for yarn enthusiasts. The upscale hand-painted yarns are every knitter and crocheter's dream; but be aware—service can vary depending on the mood of the proprietor.

BOOKSTORES

Barnes & Noble and Borders both have several locations throughout the Twin Cities metro area, but there is a group of sturdy independent stores that are holding steady in the competitive retail book field. All shops are open year-round and daily unless noted otherwise.

✍ **Birchbark Books** (612-374-4023; www.birchbarkbooks.com), 2115 W. 21st St. A small, cozy, family-friendly bookstore owned by novelist Louise Erdrich. The store specializes in Native American items, but also carries a good selection of fiction and has a children's area with a "treehouse."

Uncle Edgar's Mystery (612-824-9984) and **Uncle Hugo's Science Fiction** (612-824-6347) bookstores (2864 Chicago Ave. S.; www.uncle hugo.com). Next door to each other down the road from Abbott Northwestern Hospital, Uncle Edgar's and Uncle Hugo's have developed strong followings with their extensive selections of mysteries and sci-fi books.

Amazon Books (612-821-9630; www .amazonfembks.com), 4766 Chicago Ave. S. Amazon (not the online retailer) specializes in women's and lesbian studies and sponsors frequent book events.

Dreamhaven Books (612-823-6161; www.dreamhavenbooks.com), 912 W. Lake St. A sci-fi/fantasy/comic-book shop near the Uptown area. The shop has a busy schedule of readings and author visits from prominent writers, and also publishes a line of books.

Magers & Quinn (612-822-4611; www.magersandquinn.com), 3038 Hennepin Ave. S. One of the premier independents in the Twin Cities. Located in the Uptown area, Magers & Quinn sells new and used books, including collectible items.

Big Brain Comics (612-338-4390; www.bigbraincomics.com), 1027 Washington Ave. S. As its name implies, Big Brain specializes in comics of all sizes and genres for all ages.

YARN

Possibly because of the climate in winter, or just because arts and creativity are prized in this community, the Twin Cities metro area has an unusually large selection of yarn shops. A section in the St. Paul chapter details yarn shops on that side of the river. Shops listed below are in Minneapolis unless otherwise noted.

Depth of Field (612-340-0529; www .depthoffieldyarn.com), 405 Cedar Ave. Open daily. Located on the West Bank of the University of Minnesota, Depth of Field has an impressive array of yarn and supplies, including a second-story discount area.

Linden Hills Yarn. See *Linden Hills*, above.

Needlework Unlimited (612-925-2454; www.needleworkunlimited .com), 4420 Drew Ave. S. Open daily. Supplies for knitters, crocheters, and needlework enthusiasts.

Crafty Planet (612-788-1180; www
.craftyplanet.com), 2318 Lowry Ave.
NE. Open daily. Not just for knitters,
but for sewers and needleworkers as
well, Crafty Planet carries what could
be considered "alternative" projects,
including "subversive" cross-stitch
kits.

Coldwater Collaborative. See
Excelsior in "Neighboring
Communities."

Amazing Threads (763-391-7700;
www.amazing-threads.com), 11262
86th Ave. N., Maple Grove. Open
daily. It may take some patience to
wind through the suburban sprawl to
find this shop, but it's worth the
effort.

✳ Special Events

✍ ♿ **Minneapolis Farmer's Markets** (612-333-1718; www.mpls
farmersmarket.com), 312 E. Lyndale
Ave. N. Open 6–1 daily from mid-Apr.
to mid-Nov. While there are several
offshoots (once-weekly offerings on
Nicollet Mall and at the Mill City
Museum), this is the granddaddy of
the Minneapolis Farmer's Market
scene. It can take some patience to
get there—the fact that the signature
red shed roofs are visible from the
freeway don't necessarily mean it's
easy to find. But a huge selection of
local produce and crafts that vary
throughout the season make it a
worthwhile visit, if only for the chance
to munch on samples of bread, nuts,
cheese, and syrup, as well as seasonal
fruits and vegetables.

♿ **Minneapolis/St. Paul International Film Festival** (612-331-7563;
www.mspfilmfest.org), various locations. More than 75 films, from local
filmmakers and worldwide documen-

tarians, are presented across several
venues in late Apr. Several events and
galas are also scheduled, and discussions with film directors are offered.

♿ ♈ **Art-a-Whirl** (612-788-1679;
http://art-a-whirl.org). This annual
event, which takes place the third
weekend of May, serves to highlight
the growing and active Northeast
Minneapolis arts community. Local
and national artists exhibit their work;
visitors get to see a rich variety of art
while enjoying the artistic ambience
of this corner of Northeast.

♿ ♈ **Pride Festival and Parade**
(612-305-6900; www.tcpride.org).
This is one of the nation's largest
GLBT Pride events, occurring every
year in June. The raucous parade is a
centerpiece of the festival, which also
includes an art show, boat cruise, pic-
nics, and Grand Marshal's Ball. An
outdoor component of the festival is
held at Loring Park; booths and tents
are set up with informational, retail,
and food vendors.

♿ ♈ **Basilica Block Party** (612-317-
3511; www.basilicablockparty.org),
Hennepin Ave. and 17th St. Who says
Minnesotans can't be tolerant? This
annual event, a two-day rock concert
sponsored in part by local radio station Cities 97, takes place on the
grounds of the Basilica of St. Mary.
Besides nationally prominent acts, the
Block Party also has a fiercely competitive Battle of the Bands for local
acts. Taking place each year in early
July, the weather is often ideal and
the music is good. You're also on the
edge of downtown, where you can
wander to other venues if the outdoors become too much.

✍ ♿ ♈ **Aquatennial** (612-338-0634;
www.aquatennial.com). Billed as the
"Best 10 days of summer," the mid-

summer Aquatennial is spread across various venues in Minneapolis. Events include sailing regattas, tennis tournaments, classic car shows, triathlons, sand-castle competitions, milk-carton boat races (yes—full-sized boats built out of milk cartons), historic exhibits, a block party, and a torchlight parade. With a history stretching more than 65 years, the Aquatennial is a well-organized and fun batch of events.

𝒮 & ♀ **The Metris Uptown Art Fair** (612-823-4581; www.uptown minneapolis.com/art-fair). The Twin Cities are home to several annual art fairs, but this is the biggest, busiest, and perhaps best located—within easy walking distance of Lake Calhoun. Taking place each year in Aug., the three-day juried art event allows 450 artists to take their highly coveted spot near the Uptown area. Besides art of all sorts, food and beverage vendors also set up shop. This event attracts upward of 350,000 visitors each year, so parking can be a problem; either plan to arrive early and park locally, or consult bus maps for routes from downtown. In a nice twist, recent years have seen the Uptown Art Fair join forces with two other local art fairs, the Powderhorn Park Art Fair and the Loring Park Art Festival, and complimentary city bus service is available to transport visitors among the three.

& ♀ **Minnesota Fringe Festival** (612-872-1212; www.fringefestival .org). Admission to any event requires a $3 Fringe Festival button; individual shows are $12 in advance, $14.50 at the door for adults, $10 for students, seniors, and Minnesota Public Radio members, with valid ID; $5 ages 12 and under. A five-show punch card is available for $45. A growing and popular event, the Fringe Festival takes place over roughly 11 days in early Aug. During that time more than 20 venues present over 160 shows, some live, some recorded, nearly all an hour or less in length. Quality and themes vary wildly, but enthusiasm is universal.

🐾 𝒮 & ♀ **Minnesota Renaissance Festival** (952-445-7361; 800-966-8215; www.renaissancefest.com), US 169 S., Shakopee. Open weekends and Labor Day mid-Aug.–Sept., 9–7. $18.95 adults, $16.95 seniors, $9.95 ages 6–12; under 6 free. Discount tickets are available on the Web site. Dogs (on leashes) and cats welcome at $10 per pet, per day, through the Pet Gate (proof of immunizations required). A rowdy, sometimes bawdy re-creation of the Renaissance era. Live music, jugglers, comedians, craft demonstrations and sales, and endless amounts of food (the turkey legs and sweet corn are not to be missed). Most weekends have a theme, such as Irish Heritage or Highland Fling. *Note:* A good time to go is the weekend before or the weekend of Labor Day, when crowds are sparser than normal thanks to the Minnesota State Fair.

𝒮 & **Medtronic Twin Cities Marathon** (763-287-3888; www .mtcmarathon.org). Taking place the first weekend in Oct., the Twin Cities Marathon begins near the Metrodome in Minneapolis and finishes 26.2 miles later at the State Capitol in St. Paul. For those not willing to go the distance, the event also offers a 10-mile and a 5K run/walk, and family events including a Diaper Dash and a Toddler Trot. *Note:* All events require pre-registration; see the Web site for details. Some of the events end up in a lottery, so register early.

⚲ ♿ **Holidazzle** (www.holidazzle .com). A cherished holiday event, the Holidazzle Parade takes place several nights a week from Thanksgiving to Christmas Eve. Fairy-tale characters come to life, dressed in extravagantly lit (with real lights) costumes. Plan ahead if you'd like to eat downtown— Holidazzle brings in hundreds of viewers who want dinner ahead or after the parade.

NEIGHBORING COMMUNITIES

There are several tiers of communities surrounding Minneapolis. The dreaded S-word—*suburb*—technically defines them, but many started out as small towns in their own right before the sprawl of the city reached out and made them part of the metro area. Nevertheless, many of these communities have developed attractions, dining, and shopping venues that make them worth stepping outside the Minneapolis city limits.

✳ Edina

SHOPPING

Southdale (952-925-7874; www.southdale.com), 66th St. and France Ave. Edina is the city that gave the United States enclosed shopping malls. Southdale, which opened in 1956, was the first to offer the indoor shopping-mall experience, and as the decades have passed the mall has renovated and remodeled to keep up with changing tastes and clientele. It's still a bustling, busy mall, anchored by primary tenants Macy's and JCPenney department stores and AMC Theatres. A robust mix of smaller stores includes the Apple Store, the Gap, Ann Taylor, Abercrombie & Fitch, Sonnie's, Easy Spirit, and Dell Direct. Food options include a few fast-food outlets in the food court, or sit-down dining at P. F. Chang's, Maggiano's Little Italy, and the Cheesecake Factory. While parking is ample on all sides of the mall, this is a very popular shopping destination—plan ahead and arrive early to avoid parking in the outfield.

The Galleria (952-925-4321; www.galleriaedina.com), 69th St. and France Ave. Right across the street from Southdale is this smaller, more upscale shopping center. The Galleria offers more boutiques than large-scale stores. While the center is anchored by Barnes & Noble and Gabberts Design Studio and Fine Furnishings, shops include brand boutiques Cole Haan, Coach, Bang & Olufsen, Brighton Collectibles, and L'Occitane. Other establishments include local kids' toy store Creative Kidstuff; clothiers Blue Willi's, Epitome, Len Druskin, and Fawbush's; and home accessories stores ATAZ, Pottery Barn, and Ampersand. There is no food court, but there are four restaurants to visit, all popular and busy at main mealtimes: the Good Earth, serving healthy, hearty meals; Big Bowl, a fast-paced Asian restaurant with a "pick your own" stir-fry bar; Kozy's, a steak house; and Crave, a New American cuisine restaurant with a sushi bar.

50th and France (952-922-1524; www.50thandfrance.com), 50th St. and France Ave. A small neighborhood collection of upscale shops and restaurants, this isn't an enclosed shopping mall, but it's in a small enough area to make it easy to walk.

Women's clothing stores include Acorn, Hot Mama, Monique Lhuillier, and Bluebird Boutique; gourmet kitchen items can be found at Cooks of Crocus Hill and Sur La Table. Hand-painted tiles and plates can be found at Gather, while Jeri Kaplan Jewelry specializes in custom-designed pieces.

BLOOMINGTON

Bloomington may reside near Edina and its chic shopping areas, but it has a claim to fame that no other suburb can match: the nation's largest shopping mall.

The Mall of America (952-883-8800; www.mallofamerica.com), 60 E. Broadway. This behemoth of retail and entertainment opened in 1992 and encompasses over 4 million square feet that house not only stores but also 30 fast-food restaurants, 20 sit-down restaurants, an underground aquarium, a 14-screen movie theater complex, a wedding chapel, and an indoor theme park. During its planning, locals wondered why the area needed so much retail; in general, the Twin Cities are not short of malls and other retail venues. But since its opening, the Mall of America has proven a major draw for both locals and visitors from outside the Cities (and even outside the country).

So what can you do at the mall? For starters, you can walk; there are over 4,000 registered participants in the mall-walking club (walking around one level is slightly over 0.5 mile). You can visit the retail anchors: Nordstrom, Macy's, Bloomingdale's, and Sears. You can browse through any of the more than 500 stores in just about every conceivable category: There are clothing stores for men, women, and kids; video games, electronics, and computer stores; jewelry, art, book, gift, athletic wear, Christmas decoration, bathing suit, and craft stores; cosmetics and body product shops: toys, Irish gifts, made-in-Minnesota items, photo studios, and even a convenience store. Across the street is home furnishings superstore IKEA.

🎣 ♿ **The Water Park of America** (952-854-8700; www.waterparkof america.com), I-494 and Cedar Ave. For the members of your traveling party who are not as inclined to spend hours at the mall, book a stay at the Water Park of America's Radisson Hotel. The hotel has over 400 rooms, and the park comes complete with slides, a mile-long family raft ride, a wave pool, and a Flow Rider. Not interested in water activities? There's also a huge arcade and a spa. The Water Park is available without a hotel stay for a fee, but plan ahead—hotel guests get first priority, and public admission closes when the park fills up.

In the midst of the retail is the **Landmark Edina Theatre**, which has four screens showing a mix of popular and art-house movies.

The area is not short of places to eat. **Tejas** serves New Mexican foods that are innovative and fresh (be sure to try the guacamole, prepared tableside). **Salut Bar Americaine** offers a friendly and occasionally cheeky casual French ambience ("Le Basic Burger," anyone?). **Beaujo's** is a wine bar with a limited but thoughtful menu of salads, small plates, and entrées. **Pearson's** is a visit to another era, a 1950s dining-out type of restaurant with Swedish meatballs and breakfast specials. The **Edina Grill** bills itself as an urban diner, and that's exactly what you'll get, but with a larger selection (beer-battered green beans, eggplant Parmesan) and better quality than you might expect. The casual Italian restaurant **Arezzo Ristorante** can seem pricey, but the food redeems the cost. If you're looking for a quick-but-quality option, check out **D'Amico & Sons**, which is the casual quick-food outlet of the D'Amico group. Finally, don't pass up the chance to enjoy some locally made ice cream at the **Edina Creamery**.

Complimentary parking ramps are available on each side of 50th, but watch the signs—some parking areas are reserved for local grocer Lunds Foods. Also pay attention to the maximum parking times allowed on the lower levels—the parking police do closely monitor these ramps, and tickets will be issued if you overstay the time allotted.

✳ Shakopee

This small town, southwest of Minneapolis along the Minnesota River, is home to four popular attractions, all very different.

♪ ♿ **Valleyfair** (800-FUN-RIDE; www.valleyfair.com), 1 Valleyfair Dr. Open daily Memorial Day–Labor Day; weekends only in early May and late Sept. Visitors 48 inches and taller pay $35.95; kids 3 years old and under 48 inches tall, as well as senior citizens, pay $11.95. Kids under 2 are free. There is no discount admission for nonriding chaperones. Parking is $10, or $12 if you're using an oversized vehicle such as an RV that requires more than one space. A permanent outdoor amusement park, Valleyfair has something for almost everyone. You'll find a wide variety of gentle rides, including a miniature roller coaster, for younger park adventurers; there are also more intense rides and coasters for thrill seekers, including the 2007 addition of a new wooden roller coaster, the Renegade, bringing the park's total to eight coasters. The Whitewater Country Waterpark, included in admission, offers respite from hot summer days (swimsuits are available for sale, and a changing area is provided). The six-story IMAX theater runs giant-sized movies, and live performances around the park occur throughout the season. Challenge Park, which requires both park admission and additional fees, offers a mountainous mini golf course, bumper boats, go-carts, and RipCord, a bungee-jumping assimilation.

♪ ♿ **Murphy's Landing** (763-694-7784; www.threeriversparkdistrict.org), 2187 E. MN 101. Open daily Memorial Day–Labor Day. Year-round special events and private tours available. Weekday admission is $5; weekend and special-event admission is $8.50 adults, $7 ages 3–17 and seniors. Right down the road from

Valleyfair is this historic site, a pioneer village comprising 40 buildings set up to demonstrate life for Minnesota pioneers in the late 1800s. Visitors on summer weekends will find the addition of a "living history" component, with guides dressed in clothing specific to that period, explaining how life was lived in those days. The Pioneer Kids Play House is exactly what it says—a house set up to be hands-on for kids, who can try on pioneer costumes, do laundry in a washtub, use printing blocks to make a newspaper, and simulate cooking.

& Ÿ **Canterbury Park** (952-445-7223; www.canterburypark.com), 1100 Canterbury Rd. Live horse racing is offered early May–Labor Day; simulcast racing is available year-round. The Card Club allows you to indulge your whims for blackjack and poker.

✐ **Sever's Corn Maze** (952-974-5000; www.severscornmaze.com), next to Canterbury Park. Open Sat.–Sun. 11–6; also open the Thurs. and Fri. of MEA (Minnesota Education Association) weekend, usually the third weekend in Oct. Admission is $10 for ages 3 and up; under 3 is free. Local farm stand company Sever's opens this cornfield every year late Sept. through late Oct. The field is given a different look each year (past mazes have included the *Titanic*, the United States, and an Egyptian sphinx), and participants are given a map with clues to find their way through. A smaller hay-bale maze is set up for younger kids, along with a petting zoo and camel rides. The Corn Pit acts like a ball pit, only with kernels of corn (an oddly soothing place to play, even for adults), and if you need to get some aggression out, try the Pumpkin Slinger. Concessions available. Be sure to wear sturdy shoes or boots, and be sure you don't mind if they get dirty—if there's been rain, the field will be muddy.

✳ Prior Lake

& Ÿ **Mystic Lake Casino** (952-445-4000; www.mysticlake.com), 2400 Mystic Lake Blvd. Open 24 hours. Casinos are a popular attraction throughout Minnesota, but the sheer size of Mystic Lake is astonishing. Slots are big business here, with over 4,000 machines, and sprawling displays of table games as well. Bingo is available. The mass of Mystic Lake can look intimidating, but inside the casino is kept in sparkling condition, with ample nonsmoking areas. Food is available at one of several cafés and restaurants nearly 24/7. An attached theater is a fine venue for the many live performances that the complex books, which in the past have included such well-known entertainers as Tony Bennett and Carrie Underwood. The Mystic Lake Casino Hotel and Spa has 600 rooms and suites, but if you're staying elsewhere, it also offers complimentary bus service around the Twin Cities.

✳ Chanhassen

North of Bloomington is the small town of Chanhassen. It's a busy and rapidly growing community, and for visitors there is a notable place to visit.

✐ & Ÿ **The Chanhassen Dinner Theatres** (800-362-3515; 952-934-1525; www.chanhassentheatres.com), 501 W. 78th St. This long-standing Chanhassen venue serves full dinner and drinks with each production in its three theaters.

Primarily musical in nature, the Chanhassen Dinner Theatres companies are definitely of professional stature, and while the food may not be on par with many of the Twin Cities' top restaurants, it's reasonably good and completes the experience.

✳ Chaska

Bordering Chanhassen, Chaska offers one of the loveliest green spaces in the suburbs.

✔ ♿ **Minnesota Landscape Arboretum** (952-443-1400; www.arboretum .umn.edu), 3675 Arboretum Dr. Open daily except Thanksgiving and Christmas, 8–8 (or sunset, whichever comes first). $7 adults, free for arboretum members and ages 15 and under. The University of Minnesota is the proprietor of this 1,000-plus-acre stretch of gardens, landscaping, woodlands, wetlands, and trails. Open year-round, the arboretum has a 3-mile paved road used by motorists and people on foot. Several off-road trails—including cross-country ski and snowshoe paths—wind throughout the grounds. The Oswald Visitor Center has a large gift shop and cafeteria; picnic lunches are available with preorder. Seasonal programs and events include annual and perennial exhibits, demonstrations about making maple syrup, an annual holiday decoration sale and Christmas tea, and fall foliage walks.

✳ Excelsior

Just down the road from Chanhassen, this small town on the southern shores of Lake Minnetonka is a visitor's dream, especially in summer. Small shops, intimate restaurants, and parks and trails make for an inviting place to relax and unwind—once you've found a place to park.

✔ ♿ **The Excelsior Streetcar** (www.trolleyride.org). The Minnesota Streetcar Museum offers a ride through Excelsior's past with a summer service of vintage streetcar riding. Available early May–early Sept., the streetcar is $2 per person; children under 3 are free. Reservations are not necessary; just arrive early at the Water Street Station, at the intersection of Water and George streets.

✔ ♿ **The Steamship *Minnehaha*** (952-474-2115; www.steamboatminnehaha .org). If you'd like your history on water, take a ride on the little yellow steamboat with the colorful history. Part of a fleet of steamboats that were workhorses in the early 1900s, the *Minnehaha* was scuttled and sank to the bottom of Lake Minnetonka, where she remained until rediscovered 50 years later. Brought up to the surface and refurbished, the *Minnehaha* now provides scenic tours of the lake.

WHERE TO EAT

St. Alban's Boathouse (952-474-6260; www.stalbansboathouse.com), 21960 Minnetonka Blvd. A casual supper club on the shores of Lake Minnetonka, St. Alban's offers a hearty meat-and-seafood menu for lunch and dinner. During the summer season, a made-to-order pasta bar is also available.

Adele's (952-470-0035), 800 Excelsior Blvd. Open Feb.–Christmas Eve. A tiny café near MN 7 coming into Excelsior, Adele's doesn't look like much on the outside—just a run-down little house with a deck. But inside, along with a limited sandwich menu, is homemade frozen custard, available in cones, sundaes, and malts. Flavors vary daily. Forget about counting calories and indulge.

Antiquity Rose (952-474-2661), 429 2nd St. A small lunch-only restaurant within an antiques shop, Antiquity Rose brings back the best of yesteryear entrées: salmon loaf with creamed peas and new potatoes, tortilla casserole. Be sure to try the bran muffins (the sugar content must outweigh any nutritional benefit) and pick up a copy of the café's cookbook on the way out.

Bielle Ristorante (952-474-8881), 227 Water St. Open for dinner only, this sumptuous restaurant provides top-notch cuisine with an admirable wine list.

318 Café (952-401-7902; www.three-eighteen.com), 318 Water St. Located in the historic Excelsior Mill, 318 is a small, cozy establishment with a fireplace, rough-hewn wood floors, an outdoor patio, and delectable soups, salads, sandwiches, and baked goods. Wine bar by night, 318 also offers live music on a regular basis.

SHOPPING

The Excelsior Mill (www.excelsiormill.com), 310–340 Water St. This former lumber mill is now a miniature shopping mall with a handful of specialty shops, all worth a visit.

DB & Company (952-474-7428). A store filled with whimsical home accessories, with special emphasis on quality tea and the items with which to serve it. The Christmas season finds the store full of ornaments, decorations, and vintage candies.

Ta-Dah! (952-474-5997). A women's clothing and accessory store. Check out the handbags.

Provisions (952-474-6953). A kitchen and home gift store.

Lily Accent Furnishings (952-474-3581). Upholstery store, offering goods for sale or for special order.

Coldwater Collaborative (952-401-7501; www.coldwateryarn.com), 347 Water St. A cozy yarn shop across from the Excelsior Mill with a wide variety of materials and tools for fiber enthusiasts.

Bay Tree (952-470-8975; www.baytreeonline.com), 261 Water St. Home accessories and gift baskets, as well as Minnesota-themed clothing.

Capers (952-474-1715), 207 Water St. A gift shop with a solid line of humor-filled gifts, as well as inexpensive jewelry and kids' items.

Heritage II (952-474-1231; www.heritageii.com), 50 Water St. Also in White Bear Lake. The source for Scandinavian and British Isles merchandise, including clothing, tableware and accessories, and gifts.

✳ Wayzata

Like Excelsior, Wayzata (pronounced *why-ZET-ta*) has the good fortune to be situated on Lake Minnetonka, and it counts as its residents and visitors many well-heeled lake lovers. The city is busy during the summer months, but don't discount a visit in winter, when the shops and restaurants aren't quite as busy.

TO DO

⚓ ♿ **Minnetonka Center for the Arts** (952-473-7361; www.minnetonkaarts .org), 2240 North Shore Dr. Just outside town, the Minnetonka Center for the Arts has become a thriving school and gallery for local artists, budding and professional. The center is open year-round and offers a variety of events (check the Web site or call for specifics).

WHERE TO EAT

Blue Point Restaurant (952-475-3636; www.bluepointrestaurantandbar.com), 739 E. Lake St. Open daily at 4 for dinner. Blue Point is a sleek seafood restaurant right across the street from Lake Minnetonka. The seafood choices range well beyond what's found in Minnesota lakes, with mussels, shrimp, and salmon among the many options. Entrées start at $15.

Sunsets (952-473-5253; www.sunsetsrestaurant.com), 700 E. Lake St. (also in Woodbury). Open daily for lunch and dinner. Sunsets is a very popular casual restaurant, due in no small part to its location right on the lake. During summer months patio dining is available, but be prepared to wait. The menu includes a broad assortment of pastas, sandwiches, and various grilled specialties. Lunch entrées start at $10, dinner at $14.

⚓ **Gianni's Steakhouse** (952-404-1100; www.giannis-steakhouse.com), 635 E. Lake St. Open for dinner only, Gianni's is a congenial steak house with a traditional menu full of steaks, ribs, and fish. Bring the kids on Thurs. and Fri., when a magician can be summoned for a tableside show. Entrées start at $20.

Patrick's Bakery and Bistro (952-345-6100; www.patricksbakerycafe.com), 331 Broadway Ave. S. Open daily for all three meals. French baker and chef Patrick Bernet serves up French fare that looks almost as good as it tastes. Saving room for dessert is a must, and you might consider taking some home. Entrées start at $19.

NorthCoast (952-475-4960; www.northcoastwayzata.com), 294 E. Grove Ln. Open daily for lunch and dinner. The primarily American menu here includes all the standbys (steak, chicken, fish), but serves them attractively and with a few twists. Lunch entrées start at $9, dinner at $17.

SELECTIVE SHOPPING

The Bookcase (952-473-8341; www.bookcaseofwayzata.com), 607 E. Lake St. An independent and busy bookstore that opens at 6:30 AM for those who are up and ready for reading. The store hosts many author events each year; check the Web site for current information.

Blanc de Blanc (952-473-8275; www.blancdeblancltd.com), 691 Lake St. True to its name, Blanc de Blanc is themed in white, and the store carries a wide variety of upscale products: home and kitchen, bed and bath, holiday, even pet items.

Old World Antiques (952-929-1638; www.owantiques.com), 305 Minnetonka Ave. S. The proprietors of this shop acquire their antiques themselves with frequent buying trips to Europe. They carry artwork, rugs, accessories, and furniture.

Polly Berg (952-920-0183; www.pollyberg.com), 712 E. Lake St. Polly Berg specializes in luxurious bed linens and lingerie.

✴ Maple Grove

From small town to one of the most rapidly expanding suburbs, Maple Grove saw intense growth during the 1990s. Where there were once empty fields, you'll now find acres of retail and restaurants. Maple Grove implemented the idea of a "walkable downtown," something other communities are looking at and considering emulating. But be warned—the main shopping area can be slow going for motorists. There are countless stoplights, and lines can form.

The Shoppes at Arbor Lakes (763-424-0504; www.shoppesatarborlakes.com), I-94/I-694 and Hemlock Ln. Despite the rather prissy name, Arbor Lakes has made progress in reducing the ambience of "soulless suburb" by providing a mix of retail and dining in actual city blocks with sidewalks to give it all a small-town-center feel. While many of the usual chain-store suspects are present (Gymboree, Abercrombie & Fitch, Smith & Hawken, J. Crew and J. Jill, Pottery Barn), the strolling-friendly layout over four city blocks makes the shopping experience feel less *suburban mall* and more *charming village*. Dining options are pretty much casual, with a mix of fast food (Qdoba Mexican, Potbelly Sandwiches) and sit-down dining (Biaggi's Ristorante Italiano, Granite City Food & Brewery). Pittsburgh Blue, an independent steak house, opened in late 2007.

✴ Albertville

On the far northern end of the Minneapolis area is the town of Albertville, which is home to a massive outlet mall.

Albertville Premium Outlets (763-497-1911; www.premiumoutlets.com), 6415 Labeaux Ave. NE. A sprawling collection of 100 outlet stores, including Polo Ralph Lauren, Tommy Hilfiger, Banana Republic, Nike, Coach, Claire's Accessories, Le Creuset, Mikasa, Harry & David, and Bath & Body Works. The outlet center offers occasional live concerts outdoors during summer months, and the Web site lists events and promotions offered by individual retailers.

St. Paul 2

ST. PAUL AND NEIGHBORING COMMUNITIES

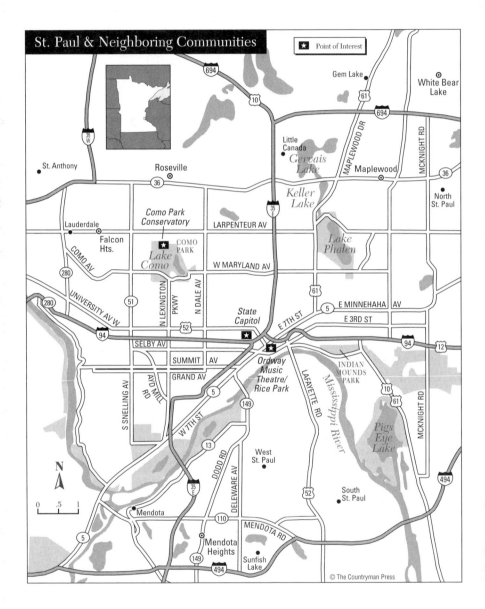
St. Paul & Neighboring Communities

★ Point of Interest

ST. PAUL AND NEIGHBORING COMMUNITIES

S t. Paul serves as the capital for the state; it also suffers at times from being neglected in favor of its twin across the river. Take in a concert at the Xcel Energy Center and see what happens if the performer onstage makes the mistake of thanking the Minneapolis audience; it's a frequent and unfortunate occurrence.

While not as cutting edge as Minneapolis in terms of dining and shopping, St. Paul holds its own for sheer beauty in its neighborhoods and downtown area. The ornate buildings downtown and grand mansions along many of the city's prominent streets (Summit Avenue being the most noticeable) reflect the city's historical roots. Named by a French priest who felt that the city's original name, Pig's Eye Landing, was not grand enough, St. Paul became the state capital in 1849, an event that caused a population explosion of sorts—the city doubled in size in just three weeks. But the expansion didn't come without criticism; in the late 1800s, a New York newspaper cast aspersions on the local climate, saying it wasn't fit for human habitation. Officials disagreed, and thus was born one of the city's most cherished annual events, the St. Paul Winter Carnival.

The 20th century brought highs and lows to the city on the river. The 1920s saw increased crime and the presence of gangsters, due to the tolerance of the local police department. But when the US government determined that the favored hiding spot of John Dillinger needed attention, police began to crack down on crime and make St. Paul a safer place to be.

Regardless of safety, St. Paul lagged behind Minneapolis in terms of cultural growth, at least until the 1990s. As St. Paul became more aggressive in drawing visitors, development funds were given to projects like the Ordway Center for the Performing Arts—a popular and beautiful live-performance venue—and RiverCentre, a convention center that's also home to the Xcel Energy Center, the acoustically superior counterpart to Minneapolis's Target Center. The Science Museum benefited from a move down the street to a larger home and has become one of the premier science museums in the country.

Today St. Paul continues to grow, adding new entertainment and dining options. One note for visitors: Former governor and pro wrestler Jesse Ventura once commented, to the consternation of loyal St. Paulites, that the city's streets had apparently been designed by a "drunken Irishman." Whoever conceived

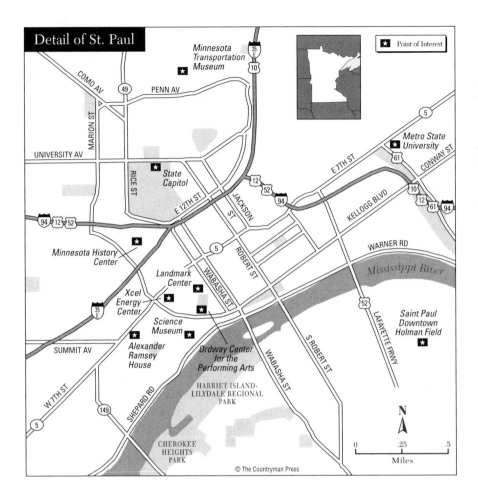

© The Countryman Press

them, Ventura had a point: The winding one-ways and dead ends can be confusing, especially during rush hour. A good downtown city map is crucial for finding your way, and don't hesitate to ask for help.

GUIDANCE

St. Paul Convention and Visitors Bureau (651-265-4900; 800-627-6101; www.stpaulcvb.org), 175 W. Kellogg Blvd., Suite 502. Offers extensive lodging and activity information for St. Paul.

GETTING THERE

By car: I-94, I-35E, US 12, US 61, and US 10 all lead into downtown St. Paul.

By bus: **Greyhound** has a terminal a few blocks from the Capitol (612-371-3325; www.greyhound.com).

By rail: **Amtrak** (800-872-7245; www.amtrak.com) has a rail station off University Ave. between Minneapolis and St. Paul (730 Transfer Rd.).

By air: The primary airport is the Lindbergh Terminal at the **Minneapolis–St. Paul International Airport** (612-726-5555; www.mspairport.com); next door is the **Hubert Humphrey Terminal** (612-726-5800), a smaller secondary airport serving mostly no-frills and charter airlines. Both airports are in Bloomington, a western suburb. Taxis, limos, rental cars, and light-rail service are available from the airports into the city.

GETTING AROUND

For travel within St. Paul, **Metro Transit** (612-373-3333; www.metrotransit.org) provides extensive service designed primarily to transport students and employees from outlying homes to work and school within the city. For maximum flexibility, a car is recommended, unless you're staying in the downtown area and can walk or take a brief taxi ride to other downtown destinations.

Having a vehicle is a necessity when traveling around the northern lakes region.

WHEN TO COME

The warmer months of spring, summer, and fall are always popular in the Twin Cities, but even the colder months can be an attractive time to visit. Those visitors staying in downtown hotels may have access to the city's extensive system of skyways, which allow foot travel across the heart of the city without stepping outdoors. And while the temperatures may be cold, the city's theater season, night-

IN ST. PAUL'S CATHEDRAL HILL NEIGHBORHOOD

club scene, and basketball/football seasons are going strong. But for those who like winter, outdoor events and sports are in full bloom Jan.–Mar., including cross-country and downhill skiing, ice skating, snowshoeing, and ice fishing.

MEDICAL EMERGENCY

Call **911**.

Regions Hospital (651-254-3456; www.regionshospital.com), 640 Jackson St.

Children's Hospital St. Paul (651-220-6000; www.childrensmn.org), 345 N. Smith Ave.

United Hospital (651-241-8000; www.unitedhospital.com), 333 N. Smith Ave.

St. Joseph's Hospital (651-232-3000; www.stjosephs-stpaul.org), 69 W. Exchange St.

✳ To See

Attractions are open year-round unless otherwise noted.

MUSEUMS

✑ ₺ **Minnesota History Center** (651-259-3000; www.mnhs.org), 345 Kellogg Blvd. W. Open daily Memorial Day–Labor Day, Tues.–Sun. the rest of the year. The center is sometimes open Mon. holidays; call for information. $8 adults, $6 seniors, $4 ages 6–17; free for those under 6 and for Minnesota Historical Society members. Despite its rather dull name, the History Center takes a lively, hands-on approach to history that makes it interesting and fun, even (and especially) for kids. Serious history buffs can find specialized research help; kids can crawl through a grain silo and explore the world of Minnesota music in a recording booth. An A-to-Z display gives a great overview of history, culture, and society. The gift shop is fun, and even the cafeteria is far above average.

✑ ₺ **State Capitol** (651-296-2881; www.mnhs.org/statecapitol), University Ave. between Dr. Rev. Martin Luther King Jr. Boulevard and Cedar Street. Open daily. General tours are free; special events may have varying admission fees. Groups of 10 or more should reserve tours two weeks in advance. Just down the street from the History Center is another piece of Minnesota's past and present. Guided and self-guided tours are available through the venerable white marble building. Weather permitting, group tours explore the rooftop to visit the golden horses sculpture.

✑ ₺ **Minnesota Museum of American Art** (651-292-4355; www.mmaa-org), 50 Kellogg Blvd W. Open Tues.–Sun. Admission is free. This museum may not have the size and status of Minneapolis's Institute of Arts or Walker Art Center, but with its focus only on American art, it deserves a wider audience.

✑ ₺ **The James J. Hill House** (651-297-2555; www.mnhs.org/places/sites/jjhh), 240 Summit Ave. Open Wed.–Sun. $8 adults, $6 seniors, $4 ages 6–17; free for those under 6 and for Minnesota Historical Society members. This was the residence of railroad impresario James J. Hill, and his prominence shows in the rich mansion open to the public. Inside, besides a piece of history, is a two-story art

MINNESOTA STATE CAPITOL

gallery with several pieces from Hill's own collection, focused primarily on French landscapes.

*The Wabasha Street Caves** (651-292-1220; www.wabashastreetcaves.com), 215 S. Wabasha St. The caves have a legendary history involving moonshiners and mobsters—and besides, they're caves. Tours are offered year-round, both with the caves as the primary attraction and as part of other tours (Ghosts, Graves, and Caves in October).

The Science Museum of Minnesota (651-221-9444; www.smm.org), 120 Kellogg Blvd. W. Open Tues.–Sun. Admission for Science Museum exhibits only is $10 adults, $7.50 children and seniors; free for museum members. Admission to the 3D Cinema, the Omnitheater, and special exhibitions costs extra. The Science Museum has utilized its executive and marketing staffs to become one of the premier science museums in the United States. A large permanent collection covers all aspect of science, mostly from a hands-on perspective; visiting exhibits tend to be major events, with past visits including the Body Worlds exhibit. The OmniTheater includes a giant surrounding movie screen, with specially made movies (many by the Science Museum's staff) on view. When the weather's nice, stop by the mini golf course behind the museum to learn some geology lessons while having fun with a golf club.

Minnesota Children's Museum (651-225-6000; www.mcm.org), 10 W. 7th St. Open Tues.–Sun. Admission is $8; children under the age of 1 and museum members are free. A large, rollicking space for kids and adventurous parents. Displays are highly active and interactive; education is important here, but fun always rules.

Historic Fort Snelling (612-726-1171; www.mnhs.org/places/sites/hfs),

SCIENCE MUSEUM OF MINNESOTA

MN 5 and MN 55, near the Minneapolis–St. Paul Airport. Open daily Memorial Day–Labor Day; open Sat.–Sun. in May, Sept., Oct. $8 adults, $6 seniors, $4 ages 6–17; free for those under 6 and for Minnesota Historical Society members. This fort, an army outpost at the junction of the Minnesota and Mississippi rivers, was built in the early 1800s to establish control of river traffic, but it quickly became a regional center for trade and social activities as well. The fort was still used through World War II, when it was a processing and training camp, but it closed after the war's end. Today it's a living history museum with costumed guides and hands-on activities in summer and home to several events each year, often focused on some aspect of fort life, whether it's cooking, the blacksmith's shop, or WWII military intelligence.

✳ Green Space

Rice Park, 109 W. 4th St. It's tiny, only one city block, but it has the Ordway Center on one side, the St. Paul Hotel across the way, and the St. Paul Public Library alongside, all of which are beautiful and, with the exception of the Ordway, decades-old buildings. The park itself has a walking path and a fountain; it's a prominent gathering place for visitors to the Ordway, and many of the city's festivals utilize the space for events and displays.

✎ **Como Park, Zoo, and Conservatory** (651-487-8201; www.comozoocon servatory.org), 1225 Estabrook Dr. Open daily. Admission is free, but a donation of $2 per adult and $1 per child is requested for the park's maintenance. It's like a city within a city; Como Park and Zoo comprise several acres with a lake, pool, mini golf, and golf course (the last three open summer only), walking trails, even a mini amusement park. **The Marjorie McNeely Conservatory** has an exten-

HARRIET ISLAND

An island on the Mississippi across from downtown St. Paul, Harriet Island has gained prominence in recent years as not only a public park but also a venue for concerts and festivals. Amenities include a band shell, stage, public boat launch, playground, Riverwalk, and jumping-on points for a number of trails. The wide, flat space at the river's edge is ideal for setting up large-scale events, and the view of the St. Paul skyline makes a perfect backdrop.

But that's not all. Harriet Island is also home to the Minnesota Centennial Showboat (see *Entertainment*), the Covington Inn Bed and Breakfast (see *Lodging*), the St. Paul Yacht Club, and the Padelford Packet Boat Company, which offers public river cruises.

Harriet Island has also become a central location for many of St. Paul's festivals, at least those that can be held outdoors. Besides being easier logistically and in terms of security for the city, many of the festivals offer patrons the option of parking in downtown St. Paul, then catching a free shuttle bus for the quick ride across the bridge. There is some parking near the island, but it's limited. See *Special Events* for such listings as the St. Paul Winter Carnival, Taste of Minnesota, and the Irish Fair—just a few of the regular events scheduled for Harriet Island.

sive, lush indoor garden, a favorite for weddings and parties. For a slightly different kind of experience, sign up for the **Como Pedicab Tour** (651-646-3648), which will take you on a rickshaw ride through the park.

Indian Mounds Park (651-632-5111; www.stpaul.gov/depts/parks/userguide/), Earl Street at Mounds Boulevard. Open daily. Across the river from downtown St. Paul is Indian Mounds, which serves both as a public park and a historic site with six Native American burial mounds. It offers beautiful views of downtown St. Paul as well.

Crosby Regional Park (651-632-5111; http://www.stpaul.gov/depts/parks/user guide), Shepard Road at Homer Street. Open daily. A nature area with several miles of paved trails for hiking and biking, lakes for fishing, and a boat launch.

✳ Lodging

Accommodations are open year-round unless otherwise noted.

Downtown
& ⵏ **The St. Paul Hotel** (651-292-9292; 800-292-9292; www.saintpaul hotel.com), 350 Market St. This elegant Old World hotel is situated on Rice Park, right across from the Ordway Center and just steps from Xcel Energy Center, the Science Museum, and several excellent restaurants (as well as hosting two top-notch restaurants itself; see *Where to Eat*). Its 250-plus sumptuously appointed rooms are among the loveliest in the city, and if you're feeling posh, the Penthouse Suite has a dining room that seats 12, a fireplace, surround sound in the living room, a full kitchen, and two bedrooms and baths. Rates start at $209; packages are available.

THE ST. PAUL HOTEL

COVINGTON INN BED & BREAKFAST

Covington Inn Bed and Breakfast
(651-292-1411; www.covingtoninn
.com), 100 Harriet Island Rd. Four
suites are available aboard perma-
nently moored towboat the *Covington*,
which spent its first 30 years as a river
towboat, moving cargo ships into
place. Now it's a luxury guest house;
all rooms have a private bath, fireplace, and air-conditioning. The decor
reflects the glorious days past of river
travel, and there are several salvaged
fixtures and antiques. Rates start at
$140; packages are available.

♦ ₺ ⴹ **Crowne Plaza St. Paul
Riverfront** (651-292-1900; 800-593-
5708; www.ichotelsgroup.com), 11 E.
Kellogg Blvd. This popular conference hotel overlooks the river and is
just blocks away from the Ordway
Center and Xcel Energy Center.
There's an indoor pool and whirlpool,
and the Carousel restaurant offers
wonderful (revolving!) river views (see
Where to Eat). Rates start at $169.

♦ ₺ ⴹ **Embassy Suites** (651-224-
5400; 800-362-2779; www.embassy
suites1.hilton.com), 175 E. 10th St.
This all-suite hotel is within easy
walking distance or very short drives
to downtown St. Paul attractions, dining, and entertainment options.
There's an indoor pool, and a daily
cooked-to-order breakfast is included
in the rates. Two restaurants, the
casual **Cork's Pub** and the more formal **Woolleys**, are both open daily for
lunch and dinner. Rates start at $160;
weekend discounts and packages are
available.

🐾 ♦ ₺ ⴹ **Best Western Kelly Inn**
(651-227-8711; www.bestwesternst
paul.com), 161 St. Anthony Ave.
Located near the State Capitol, this
Best Western offers less expensive
accommodations for visitors to the
area. The hotel has an indoor pool
and restaurant. Rates start at $99;
packages are available.

✳ Where to Eat

Restaurants are open year-round unless otherwise noted.

DINING OUT

Downtown

Y **Forepaugh's** (651-224-5606; www.forepaughs.com), 276 S. Exchange St. Open Mon.–Fri. for lunch, daily for dinner; Sun. brunch. A fine restaurant in an old historic mansion on the edge of downtown St. Paul. The layout of the mansion results in several small, intimate dining rooms; the Victorian decor fits the house, and the food—classics such as beef Wellington—is served on china from the period. The food is excellent, as is the wine list, and if you're going to the Minnesota Opera (or selected special events) at the Ordway afterward, make arrangements for the shuttle bus—you can park for free at Forepaugh's if you eat there before going to the Ordway. Entrées start at $17.

✿ ち Y **St. Paul Grill** (651-224-7455; www.stpaulgrill.com), 350 Market St. Open daily for lunch and dinner. Located in the St. Paul Hotel (see *Lodging*), the St. Paul Grill is right across Rice Park from the Ordway Theater. It's definitely a special-occasion restaurant, with an upscale American menu including steaks, lobster, and lamb chops. The bar is a great stop for a before-dinner or after-theater visit, with extensive wine and scotch lists. Entrées start at $18.

ち Y **Pazzaluna** (651-223-7000; www.pazzaluna.com), 360 St. Peter St. Open daily for dinner. Chef's table available; reserve in advance. This informal but upscale Italian restaurant offers a menu that changes seasonally but is always tasteful. Service can vary in terms of friendliness, but fortunately the food is consistent in quality. Entrées start at $14.

ち Y **Kincaid's Fish, Chop, and Steak House** (651-602-9000; www.kincaids.com; also in Bloomington), 380 St. Peter St. Open Mon.–Fri. for lunch, daily for dinner. Kincaid's offers all the usual steak house suspects, beautifully prepared, and with the occasional fun twist; try the

FOREPAUGH'S

bacon-wrapped Kobe meat loaf with horseradish mashed potatoes. Entrées start at $17.

✑ ₺ ℽ **Fuji-Ya** (651-310-0111; www .fujiyasushi.com), 465 Wabasha St. (also in Minneapolis). Open Mon.– Fri. for lunch, Sat. for dinner only. Fuji-Ya serves some of the best Japanese food in the state. The sushi is top quality, freshly made to order, and beautifully presented. But beyond sushi, Fuji-Ya also shines, with a wide variety of Japanese salads, noodle bowls, bulgogi, and meat and seafood entrées. Possibly because so much care is taken with preparation, service is slow; be prepared to relax and enjoy. Entrées start at $14.

✑ ₺ ℽ **Mancini's Char House & Lounge** (651-224-7345; www.man cinis.com), 531 W. 7th St. Open daily for dinner. This venerable family-run steak house has been serving charbroiled steaks and lobster, along with generous martinis, for over 40 years. Live music is offered in the lounge several times a month. Entrées start at $16.

✑ ₺ ℽ **Sakura Restaurant and Sushi Bar** (651-224-0185; www .sakurastpaul.com), 350 St. Peter St. Open daily for lunch and dinner. Sakura has come a long way from its humble beginnings as a tiny Japanese restaurant. Now the two-story restaurant has a sushi bar and private tearooms. Best of all is the sushi, splendidly fresh and beautifully prepared. Entrées start at $11.

✑ ₺ ℽ **Carousel Restaurant** (651-292-0408), 11 E. Kellogg Blvd, 22nd floor of the Crowne Plaza hotel (see *Lodging*). This restaurant provides expansive views of the river, especially since the restaurant itself slowly revolves. The view is probably the

most notable aspect; the food is expensive and varying in quality, but if vistas are what you want, this is the place to go. Entrées start at $18.

Cathedral Hill

₺ ℽ **W. A. Frost** (651-224-5715; www.wafrost.com), 374 Selby Ave. Open daily for dinner and lunch. One of the most romantic restaurants in the area. The interior, dark but not gloomy with high copper ceilings, speaks of intimacy, while the outdoor patio garden is a gem for nature lovers. Entrées start at $16.

₺ ℽ **Moscow on the Hill** (651-291-1236; www.moscowonthehill.com), 371 Selby Ave. Open Tues.–Sat. for lunch, daily for dinner. Russian food served Russian-style—don't plan on eating in a hurry, but not in a bad way. This upscale bistro provides hearty Russian food and, of course, an excellent array of vodka (available in tasting flights). Entrées start at $15.

  ♿ ♉ **Zander Café** (651-222-5224), 525 Selby Ave. Open Mon.–Fri. for lunch, daily for dinner. Chef Alexander Dixon has guided this neighborhood mainstay through good times and bad, and the reward is a simple but delicious seasonal menu, focused on fish and vegan options. Live jazz is offered on weekends. Entrées start at $17, but appetizers are huge and can act as an entrée for around $8.

  ♪ ♿ ♉ **The Happy Gnome** (651-287-2018; www.thehappygnome.com), 498 Selby Ave. Open daily for lunch and dinner. A neighborhood bar and grill with a more sophisticated menu. Try the lamb scaloppine or the venison burger. Entrées start at $8.

  ♪ ♿ ♉ **The Muddy Pig** (651-254-1030; www.muddypig.com), 162 Dale St. Open daily for lunch and dinner. A more traditional bar-and-grill menu, including burgers and sandwiches, but also heartier fare like chicken cordon bleu. Entrées start at $9.

  ♿ ♉ **Vintage Restaurant and Wine Bar** (651-222-7000), 579 Selby Ave. Open daily for dinner. Housed in a historic home, Vintage is a cozy, romantic spot to enjoy casual dining. The extensive wine list is worthy, and other alcoholic beverages are available. Entrées start at $12.

Other Areas

  ♿ ♉ **Heartland** (651-699-3536; www .heartlandrestaurant.com), 1806 St. Clair Ave. Open Tues.–Sun. for dinner. Wine bar open daily. Heartland prides itself—and justifiably so—on its creative use of local and regional culinary specialties and produce. The adjacent wine bar is considered a worthy destination on its own. Entrées start at $24, and fixed price menus are offered.

MULTICULTURAL UNIVERSITY AVENUE

Minneapolis has Eat Street and the Midtown Global Market; St. Paul has its own ethnic neighborhoods filled with immigrants and authentic and delicious home cooking. University Avenue is home to dozens of small, casual Asian restaurants that don't always rely on Americanization to sell their foods.

  ♪ ♿ ♉ **Café Bonxai** (651-644-1444), 1613 University Ave. Open Mon.–Sat. for lunch and dinner. The somewhat garish interior is quickly eclipsed by the food, which brings in swarms of locals each night. The food is an intriguing mix of Thai, Italian, and French, and it works. Entrées start at $10.

  ♪ ♿ **Hoa Bien** (651-647-1011), 1105 University Ave. Open daily for lunch and dinner. Excellent Vietnamese food, especially the seafood dishes.

  ♪ ♿ **Que Nha Vietnamese** (651-290-8552), 849 University Ave. Open daily for lunch and dinner. Authentic, flavorful Vietnamese cuisine, including several noodle bowls and variations on pho. Entrées start at $6.

  ♪ ♿ ♉ **Ngon Vietnamese Bistro** (651-222-3301), 799 University Ave. Open daily for lunch and dinner. An unexpectedly elegant entry into the city's

& ♈ **Ristorante Luci** (651-699-8258; www.ristoranteluci.com), 470 Cleveland Ave. Open for dinner Tues.–Sat. A tiny, very romantic bistro serving lovingly made Italian food, including not just pasta but sharp takes on meat dishes as well. Entrées start at $10; Tuesday is "2 for 40" night, when a four-course taster's dinner is offered at $20 per person for at least two people.

✍ & ♈ **Muffuletta** (651-644-9116; www.muffuletta.com), 2260 Como Ave. Open daily for lunch and dinner. This cozy restaurant with its changing-daily menu is tucked into a little neighborhood just blocks from the St. Paul campus of the University of Minnesota. Using local and seasonal foods when possible, Muffuletta provides inventive and delicious food, such as Argentine pot roast with sweet potatoes and black beans. Entrées start at $12.

Downtown

✍ & ♈ **M Street Café** (651-228-3855; www.mstreetcafe.com), 350 Market St. Open daily for breakfast and lunch. Located in the lower level of the St. Paul Hotel, the M Street Café offers breakfast classics and soups, salads, and sandwiches. Entrées start at $9.

✍ & **Cossetta's** (651-222-3476), 211 W. 7th St. Open daily for lunch and dinner. Cossetta's has been in its West 7th location for almost a century, and there's a reason for that. The casual Italian restaurant cooks up seriously delicious pastas and pizzas, and the adjacent Italian market has fresh ingredients to take home. Entrées start at $6.

✍ **Mickey's Diner** (651-222-5633), 36 W. 7th St. Open 24 hours daily.

Asian restaurant scene, Ngon has extensive wine and beer lists and fusion food—and some of the best pho around. Entrées start at $10.

✍ & **Saigon Restaurant and Bakery** (651-225-8751), 601 University Ave. The extensive Asian menu here is backed up by excellent cooking and low prices. Entrées start at $5.

✍ & **Cheng Heng** (651-222-5577), 448 University Ave. Open daily for lunch and dinner. Cambodian food, varied and tasty. Try the Asian crêpes. Entrées start at $10.

✍ & **Krua Thailand** (651-224-4053), 432 University Ave. Open Mon.–Sat. for lunch and dinner. Thai food for serious Thai food foodies. The chefs don't buy into the "Minnesotans can't handle spice" urban legend; when they say something is spicy, beware. The interior could use some refurbishing, but that shouldn't stop you from trying this spot. Entrées start at $10.

✍ & ♈ **Little Szechuan** (651-222-1333; www.littleszechuan.com), 422 University Ave. Open daily for lunch and dinner. With a casual but attractive interior and a menu listing more than 200 items, this Asian cookery focuses on its specific cuisine with educated and inspired results. Entrées start at $9.

INSIDE MICKEY'S DINER

This is truly a St. Paul institution, listed on the National Register of Historic Places. A rehabbed dining car with a tasty breakfast-and-burger grill menu, Mickey's is the classic quick-and-cheap eating spot. The waitresses are trained to deliver food, not make friends—and make sure you follow the posted rules regarding minimum dollars spent and maximum time allowed. Entrées start at $4.

✂ ᕦ **Keys Café** (651-731-5397; www.keyscafe.com), 767 Raymond Ave. Open daily for breakfast and lunch. Breakfast is served all day at this location, and you really don't need to look at the lunch menu (although it's good, too). Enormous cinnamon rolls and giant omelets (including a "Loon" omelet with wild rice and mushroom sauce) will take care of your appetite. Entrées start at $5.

✂ ᕦ ᖗ **The Liffey** (651-556-1420; www.theliffey.com), 175 W. 7th St. Open daily for all three meals. An Irish pub with an American and Irish menu, so you can have corned beef and cabbage or a burger. Entrées start at $10.

Grand Avenue

Parking on or near Grand Avenue can be difficult. There is a ramp at Grand and Victoria, but given that the retail and dining area stretches more than 30 blocks, it may still be quite a hike from your destination—and restaurants often don't have their own parking lots. When looking for side-street parking, pay close attention to road signs; many side streets are for residents with permits only, and violating that can lead to tickets and towing.

✂ ᕦ ᖗ **Saji-Ya** (651-292-0444; www.sajiya.com), 695 Grand Ave. Open Mon.–Sat. for lunch and dinner, Sun. for dinner only. Japanese cuisine, including extensive sushi options and teppanyaki tables. Entrées start at $17.

✂ ᖗ **Barbary Fig** (651-290-2085), 720 Grand Ave. Open Mon.–Sat. for lunch and dinner, Sun. for dinner only. Moroccan and North African cuisine in this rehabbed two-story house. Try the garlic sausage. Entrées start at $8.

✂ ᕦ **Grand Ole Creamery** (651-293-1655), 750 Grand Ave. Open daily at 10 AM. Homemade ice cream. Need I say more? Treats start at $2.

✂ ᕦ ᖗ **Wild Onion** (651-291-2525; www.wild-onion.net), 788 Grand Ave. Open daily for lunch and dinner. A neighborhood bar and grill with a menu heavy on sandwiches, burgers, and pizza. Prime rib is offered on Fri. and Sat. Entrées start at $7.

✂ ᕦ **Café Latte** (651-224-5687; www.cafelatte.com), 850 Grand Ave. Open daily for lunch and dinner. It

THE DISTRICT DEL SOL

Across the Mississippi from St. Paul, the District del Sol (www.districtdel
sol.com) is a large Hispanic settlement with tempting food options. If you're
in town for Cinco de Mayo, stop by for the festivities (see *Special Events*).

El Burrito Mercado (651-227-2192; www.elburritomercado.com), 175 Cesar
Chavez. Open daily. This longtime Mexican grocery has served the district
for more than 25 years, offering Hispanic foods at low prices. Summer often
finds a corn feed of sorts on the sidewalk outside, with ears of corn served
with chile powder and sour cream.

El Café Restaurant is a restaurant in the back of the Mercado that has both
cafeteria and table service, but—more importantly—excellent food at low
prices. You can go for the "Americanized" versions, or stick to the more
authentic foods, such as steamed mussels or carnitas platters. Mexican
beer and wine are offered.

El Amanecer Restaurant (651-291-0758), 194 Cesar Chavez. A small restaurant also focused on tasty, authentic Mexican food.

Don Panchos Bakery (651-225-8744), 140 Cesar Chavez. A block away, in an
unassuming white house, is this little bakery. It may not look like much outside or in, but the aroma of fresh bakery goods wafting out the door will
make you forget about the ambience. Look for the guava-cheese turnovers.

Blue Cat Coffee & Tea (651-291-7676), 153 Cesar Chavez. Across from the
Mercado is this neighborhood caffeine provider, a cozy bistro.

Boca Chica (651-222-8499; www.bocachicarestaurant.com), 11 Cesar
Chavez. Mexican foods made from scratch on site. Minnesota's favorite fish,
the walleye, is given an exemplary Mexican take. Live mariachi music
offered monthly; call for schedule.

IN THE DISTRICT DEL SOL

may be a cafeteria, but forget tasteless casseroles and limp iceberg salads. Latte serves up fresh, lively food, often taking advantage of seasonal produce for a changing-daily menu of soups and salads. Whatever you choose, leave room for dessert—Café Latte has one of the most decadent bakeries in the Twin Cities. Entrées start at $7.

♪ 占 **Uptowner Café** (651-224-0406), 1100 Grand Ave. Open daily for breakfast and lunch, Fri. and Sat. for late-night munching. This small but delicious café prepares impeccable breakfast foods, served late on weekends for the postbar crowds. Entrées start at $7.

♪ 占 ▼ **Everest on Grand** (651-696-1666; www.hotmomo.com; also at the Midtown Global Market, see "Minneapolis"), 1278 Grand Ave. Open daily for lunch and dinner. Nepali food served in a friendly atmosphere. The kothe (deep-fried meat) is delicious, as are the many curries. Vegetarians have lots of choices. Entrées start at $8.

Other Areas
♪ 占 **Nina's Coffee Cafe** (651-292-9816), 165 Western Ave. N. Open daily for all three meals. A coffee shop with a limited but quality menu of pastries, sandwiches, and soups, Nina's is a neighborhood hangout enhanced by its location upstairs from Common Good Books. Free WiFi is available to patrons, and November finds Nina's acting as the unofficial gathering spot for the locally active NaNoWriMo group (**National Novel Writing Month,** www.nanowrimo .org). Entrées start at $4.

♪ 占 ▼ **Luci Ancora** (651-698-6889; www.ristoranteluci.com), 2060 Randolph Ave. Open Tues.–Fri. for lunch, daily for dinner. The sister restaurant to **Ristorante Luci** (see *Dining Out*) is more casual and relaxed than the dinner-only bistro. It's also slightly larger, but reservations are still recommended. Entrées start at $8.

♪ 占 ▼ **Kum Gang San** (651-645-2000), 694 N. Snelling Ave. Open daily for lunch and dinner. A Korean restaurant with servers in traditional Korean dress, appropriate for the authentic menu. Specialties are the Korean grilled meats, served (as all entrées are) with panchan, six or seven small side dishes. The Korean sushi is quite good, too. Entrées start at $8.

✳ Entertainment

LIVE PERFORMANCES

The Fitzgerald Theater (651-290-1200; www.fitzgeraldtheater.public radio.org), 10 E. Exchange St. This downtown St. Paul venue is the home of Garrison Keillor's radio program, *A Prairie Home Companion.* Call ahead for tickets, as this is a local favorite when in production. When it's not hosting Keillor's troupes, the Fitzgerald also offers other performances, often in conjunction with **Minnesota Public Radio** (www.mpr.org) across the street.

Ordway Center for the Performing Arts (651-224-4222; www .ordway.org), 345 Washington St. The Ordway is a spectacular theater at the edge of downtown St. Paul on Rice Park, within easy walking distance of several prime St. Paul restaurants (**Pazzaluna, Sakura, St. Paul Grill;** see *Where to Eat*). Home of the renowned Minnesota Opera, the Ordway also hosts touring musicians,

ORDWAY CENTER FOR THE PERFORMING ARTS

dancers, and Broadway musicals as well as presenting several locally developed theatrical shows each year. Dress up for the theater night out, and place your bar order ahead of time to have it ready and waiting during the intermission.

Landmark Center (651-292-3233; www.landmarkcenter.org), 75 W. 5th St. Across the street from the Ordway is this impressive building, originally built in 1902 to serve as a federal courthouse and post office. Today it's a cultural center, with a variety of events—music, dance, theater—taking place throughout the year. The building also houses several art galleries.

Minnesota Opera (612-333-2700; www.mnopera.org), Ordway Center (see previous entry). The Minnesota Opera formed in the 1970s, and in the mid-1980s it became one of the original tenants of the new Ordway Center. Today the company produces four or five full operas each year, using both local and international opera performers in innovative stagings. The primary focus is bel canto, and each season includes at least one bel canto masterpiece.

Penumbra Theatre (651-224-3180; www.penumbratheatre.org), 270 N. Kent St. Penumbra is one of only three African American theaters in the country to produce a full season each year. Creative director Lou Bellamy has led the company to national prominence with quality productions and high-profile theatrical premieres, including several August Wilson works. The company's *Black Nativity* is one of the Twin Cities' most popular holiday events each year.

St. Paul Chamber Orchestra (651-291-1144; www.spco.org), 408 St. Peter St., 4th floor. The SPCO is a full-time professional chamber orchestra, and it's a busy group; besides performing in its own music hall on St. Peter Street, it headlines the Ordway Center and offers concerts at suburban venues such as Wayzata and Eden Prairie. The company gives more than 150 performances each year, including a set of children's concerts and occasional international tours.

Minnesota Centennial Showboat (651-227-1100; www.showboat.umn.edu), Harriet Island. A theater on a boat, docked at Harriet Island across the river from downtown St. Paul. The theater showcases acting talent from the University of Minnesota's Theater Department, with emphasis on comedies and mysteries.

Xcel Energy Center (651-265-4800; www.xcelenergycenter.com), 175 W. Kellogg Blvd. Part of the larger River-Centre entertainment and convention complex, the Xcel Energy Center is home to the Minnesota Wild HNL team (see *Sporting Events*) and plays host to a wide variety of touring performers. Like its counterpart across

the river, the Target Center, Xcel brings in top-level entertainers and bands; unlike Target Center, Xcel was built with concert acoustics in mind. Locals rejoice when their favorites play here, because the sound is much better.

History Theatre (651-292-4323; www.historytheatre.com), 30 E. 10th St. A theater company devoted to original plays focused on the American experience, primarily Minnesotan, both historical and current.

Artists' Quarter (651-292-1359; www.artistsquarter.com), 408 St. Peter St. Open daily. Live jazz every evening, from local gems to national acts. The Quarter does not accept reservations, so plan on arriving early, especially for weekend performances. No food is served, but two nearby restaurants can deliver.

✎ **Circus Juventas** (651-699-8229; www.circusjuventas.org), 1270 Montreal Ave. Circus Juventas is a performing arts circus school for people ages 3–21. Besides offering workshops and camps, the Juventas troupes put

THE MINNESOTA CENTENNIAL SHOWBOAT

on two shows annually. Call or check the Web site for a schedule.

SPORTING EVENTS

St. Paul Saints (651-644-6659; www .saintsbaseball.com), 1771 Energy Park Dr. The Saints are the Twin Cities' minor-league baseball team, owned in part by actor Bill Murray. Until the Twins' new stadium is complete, the Saints are the only professional baseball team offering outdoor play; Midway Stadium is wide open to beautiful sunsets and views of the lights from the State Fair at the end of August. They may not have the name power of the Minnesota Twins, but the Saints do have goofy activities and displays between innings, including a live pig as mascot.

Minnesota Wild (651-602-6000; www.wild.nhl.com), 175 W. Kellogg Blvd. Minnesota's hockey team plays its home games at the Xcel Energy Center.

Minnesota Thunder and **Minnesota Lightning** (651-817-8326; www .mnthunder.com), 275 Lexington Pkwy. N. Professional men's and women's soccer teams. While professional soccer hasn't quite achieved the popularity of baseball, football, and hockey in the Twin Cities, interest is growing.

✳ Selective Shopping

Stores are open year-round unless otherwise noted.

BOOKS

Common Good Books (651-225-8989; www.commongoodbooks.com), 165 Western Ave. N. Open daily. Garrison Keillor's contribution to the world of independent bookstores. Small, but with a diverse selection of

books, Common Good resides in the same building as Nina's Café and across the street from **W. A. Frost** and **Moscow on the Hill** (see *Where to Eat*).

Micawbers (651-646-5506; www .micawbers.com), 2238 Carter Ave. Open daily. This small but well-stocked bookstore is a local favorite, with frequent book events and a knowledgeable, friendly staff. Located around the corner from **Muffuletta** (see *Where to Eat*).

⚓ **Red Balloon Bookshop** (651-224-8320; www.redballoonbookshop.com), 891 Grand Ave. This bookstore in a refurbished house focuses solely on children's books, and its expertise is considerable. The shop carries a wide range of books and hosts several events every month. Staff are knowledgeable and friendly.

Sixth Chamber Used Books (651-690-9463; www.sixthchamber.com), 1332 Grand Ave. Open daily. Books bought and sold daily, and the inventory is attractively displayed in a comfy, cheerful shop.

YARN

Possibly because of the climate in winter, or just because arts and

COMMON GOOD BOOKS

GRAND AVENUE

Just outside downtown St. Paul is Grand Avenue, which runs parallel to Summit Avenue, home to many sumptuous St. Paul mansions (including the governor's home). Grand Avenue itself is a walker's paradise of restaurants and shops, many in rehabbed homes. The heart of the area is Victoria Crossings, the intersection of Grand Avenue and Victoria, where a public parking ramp and several restaurants are situated. An annual festival showcases the neighborhood (see *Special Events*). Following is an overview of some of the shops to visit; see www.grandave.com for details.

Bibelot (651-222-0321, 1082 Grand Ave.; 2276 Como Ave., 651-646-5651; also in Minneapolis; www.bibelotshops.com). Bibelot stores carry all kinds of guilty pleasures, from locally made jewelry to unique women's clothing to off-the-wall kitchen and bath items, greeting cards, and toys for kids.

✐ **Creative Kidstuff** (651-222-2472; www.creativekidstuff.com), 1074 Grand Ave.; also in Woodbury. Open daily. This store is chock-full of toys, educational and otherwise, and—perhaps even better—is well staffed by knowledgeable, helpful clerks who aren't against the idea of kids trying out toys before buying them.

Cooks of Crocus Hill (651-228-1333; www.cooksofcrocushill.com), 877 Grand Ave.; also in Edina. Open daily. All the fine cooking supplies you ever thought, or never knew, you needed.

Garden of Eden (651-293-1300; www.gardenofedenstores.com), 867 Grand Ave. Open daily. A luxurious assortment of bath and body goods, many of which are natural products. Customers can create their own fragrances.

Northern Brewer (651-223-6114; www.northernbrewer.com), 1150 Grand Ave. Open daily. Supplies for home-brewing and wine-making beginners and aficionados.

Treadle Yard Goods (651-698-9690), 1338 Grand Ave. Open daily. Fabric and supplies for those interested in sewing, including some unusual and high-end items.

My Sister's Closet (651-222-2819), 1136 Grand Ave. Open Mon.–Sat. Vintage and upscale women's consignment shop.

The Yarnery (651-222-5793; www.yarnery.com), 840 Grand Ave. Open daily. A compact and packed shop full of choice yarns and knitting/crocheting accessories.

Quince (651-225-9900; www.quincegifts.com), 850 Grand Ave. Open daily.

Tucked behind Café Latte is this gift and women's clothing shop, carrying fun and funky items.

Susan Metzger for C'est Fou (651-602-9133), 1128 Grand Avenue. Open Tues.–Sat. This local designer's shop carries her own one-of-a-kind outfits for women. Accessories are usually made by local artists.

Golden Fig (651-602-0144; www.goldenfig.com), 790 Grand Ave. Open Tues.–Sun. It may not look like much from the outside, but this is a small gem offering gourmet foods, treats, spices, local artisan cheeses, and heavenly chocolates. The proprietors care enough about their local products (including award-winning chocolatiers B. T. McElrath and Sweet Goddess Chocolates) that during the warm summer months, they personally pick up the products directly from the makers to make sure chocolates aren't allowed to languish in a hot delivery truck.

Red Balloon Bookshop and **Sixth Chamber Used Books**. See *Books* earlier in this section.

ALONG GRAND AVENUE

creativity are prized in this community, the Twin Cities metro area has an unusually large selection of yarn shops. A section in the Minneapolis chapter details yarn shops on that side of the river. Shops listed below are in St. Paul unless otherwise noted.

Borealis Yarns (651-646-2488; www.borealisyarn.com), 1340 Thomas Ave. Open daily. A large, rambling yarn store with a wide selection of yarns and supplies, plus a room at the back with sale items.

The Yarnery. See the *Grand Avenue* sidebar.

Three Kittens Needle Arts (651-457-4969; www.threekittensyarnshoppe.com), 805 Sibley Memorial Hwy. (MN 13). Open daily. Looks small from the outside, but it's made up of several small rooms, leading to a big selection of yarn.

Sheepy Yarn Shoppe (651-426-5463; www.sheepyyarnmn.com), 2185 3rd St., White Bear Lake. Open Mon.–Sat. A cozy shop, complete with fireplace, for yarn lovers to relax, shop, or pursue their favorite yarn activity.

Knit'n from the Heart (651-702-0880; www.heartknits.com), 1785 Radio Dr., Woodbury. Open daily. Carries a wide and changing variety of yarns, including new and unusual brands.

Yarn Garage (651-423-2590; www.yarngarage.com), 2980 W. 145th St., Rosemount. Open daily. Run by the self-proclaimed Glitter Knitter Steven, the Yarn Garage is housed in an old retail building on a vintage small-town street, but inside you'll find pretty much anything a yarn enthusiast needs. The store is floor-to-ceiling yarns and supplies, as well as vintage buttons and handles, numerous samples, cheeky gift ideas, and plentiful help.

✳ Special Events

✇ ♿ **Minnesota Historical Society** (http://events.mnhs.org/calendar). The historical society, which maintains sites all over the state, has numerous events, some annual, some one-time-only. Check its Web site for information on upcoming festivities at the St. Paul headquarters, as well as around St. Paul and the state, including Historic Fort Snelling. Special events around various holidays, including haunted State Capitol tours for Halloween and multitudes of historical Christmas celebrations, are of special interest.

✇ ♿ **Winter Carnival** (651-223-4700; www.winter-carnival.com), various sites. Legend has it that this festival began in response to a New York reporter, who commented that St. Paul winters were "unfit for human habitation." This carnival sets out to prove that not only is winter *not* uninhabitable, it can in fact be quite hospitable and even fun. For 10 days starting in late January, St. Paul hosts a wide variety of events, including a coronation of winter royalty, a torchlight parade, snow-sculpting and ice-carving contests, a medallion treasure hunt, numerous kids' activities, and a "Frozen" 5K and half-marathon. Check the Web site for details of each year's events; some years have included the building of an ice palace.

✇ ♿ **Festival of Nations** (651-647-0191; www.festivalofnations.com), River-Centre, 175 W. Kellogg Blvd. Held annually in early May, this festival celebrates the melting-pot diversity of America and, increasingly, Minnesota. Nearly 100 different ethnic groups are represented with shops, cafés, musical and dance performances, craft demonstrations, and displays of cultural traditions.

♂ ⅋ **Cinco de Mayo** (651-222-6347; www.districtdelsol.com), District Del Sol. St. Paul's vibrant West Side, already home to many Hispanic restaurants and shops (see *Where to Eat*), hosts this annual event. Two days of food, fun, live entertainment, a low-rider car show, parade, 5K and 1-mile races, salsa-tasting contests, and children's activities are all part of the celebration. Proceeds are reinvested into the neighborhood.

🐾 ♂ ⅋ ⅋ **Grand Old Day** (651-699-0029; http://grandave.com/grandoldday), Grand Ave. Held the first Sunday in June. It's only one day, but what a day. Grand Old Day kicks off with races of varying lengths (8K, 5K, 0.5 mile, 0.25 mile), followed by food, parades, an art fair, kids' activities, live music, and a teen battle of the bands.

♂ ⅋ ⅋ **Taste of Minnesota** (651-772-9980; www.tasteofmn.org), Harriet Island. This six-day food and fun festival celebrating the Fourth of July used to be held near the State Capitol, but has been centralized at Harriet Island. It may have lost something from its days of celebrating near the heart of the state's government and near the cathedral, but logistically it's easier to manage on the island. Food vendors, kids' activities, live music, and spectacular evening fireworks each night.

St. Paul Bike Classic Bike Tour (952-882-3180; www.bikeclassic.org), University of St. Thomas. Not a race, but an actual tour; there are two routes, 15 and 30 miles, for bikers to choose from, both meandering along the Mississippi River

---

♂ ⅋ ⅋ **Minnesota State Fair** (651-288-4400; www.mnstatefair.org), 1265 N. Snelling Ave. Open for 10 days through Labor Day. Regular admission is $11 adults, $9 seniors, $8 ages 5–12; free for those under 5. Various discounts are offered; check the Web site for details. Billed as the "Great Minnesota Get-Together," the fair is the classic rite of passage from summer to fall. Attended by well over a million people each year, the State Fair is held on permanent fairgrounds in St. Paul. Parking can be tricky and expensive; most public transit companies around the Twin Cities offer State Fair buses that bypass the parking issue. The fair has something for everyone: animals (farm and pets), farm machinery, rides small and large, live entertainment all day (some included in the admission, some incurring extra costs—especially the grandstand shows, which tend to feature name performers), exhibits with crafts and fine arts, games, a Miracle of Birth Center where animals are on display during their birth process, parades, haunted house, hands-on exhibits from vendors, and food. The fair is well known for its food, much of which lacks a healthy component but makes up for it in taste. Most of it's on a stick: pizza on a stick, pickle on a stick, you-name-it on a stick. And where else could you get SPAM curds? Go early, go often.

and then continuing to either Summit Avenue or Indian Mounds Park and around Lake Phalen. Routes can change; check the Web site for details. The Bike Tour is an early-Sept. fund-raiser for the **Neighborhood Energy Connection** (www.firstgiving.com/nec).

St. Paul Art Crawl (651-292-4373; www.stpaulartcrawl.org), downtown. The St. Paul Art Crawl is held twice each year, in spring and fall, and allows more than 200 local artists and galleries to open their studios to visitors and potential buyers.

♂ ♿ **Hmong New Year** (651-265-4800; www.rivercentre.org), RiverCentre, 175 W. Kellogg Blvd. This annual Nov. holiday celebrates and educates visitors about the Hmong New Year with traditional foods, clothing, music, dance, and shopping. The Hmong population in the Twin Cities is one of the largest in the United States, and this celebration has taken place for more than 30 years.

NEIGHBORING COMMUNITIES

✳ Apple Valley

♂ ♿ **Minnesota Zoo** (952-431-9200; 800-366-7811; www.minnesotazoo.org), 13000 Zoo Blvd. Open daily. $12 adults, $8.25 seniors, $7 ages 3–12; free for those under 3 and zoo members. Parking is additional, as is admission to the IMAX theater. This is the *other* major zoo in the Twin Cities area. Como Zoo is the one in the heart of St. Paul; the Minnesota Zoo is out in the country, and the two are different enough to justify visiting both. The emphasis at the Minnesota Zoo is on natural habitat, so instead of regular cages, many of the larger animals have large parcels of land to call their own. While you won't see some traditional zoo animals, such as elephants and giraffes, here (unless they're in a visiting exhibition), there's plenty to take in, including a wide variety of monkeys and large cats. A new dolphin area has regular shows. The adjacent IMAX theater offers a variety of nature programs interspersed with popular movies on the giant screen. The zoo offers numerous special events each year, including an indoor sandbox and beach day in February. Check the Web site for details.

✳ Mendota

Sibley House Historic Site (651-452-1596; www.mnhs.org/places/site/shs), 1357 Sibley Memorial Hwy. (MN 13). Open May and Sept., Sat.–Sun.; Memorial Day–Labor Day, Fri.–Mon. $5 adults, $4 seniors, $3 ages 6–17; free for those under 6 and members of the Minnesota Historical Society. Some of the state's oldest remaining buildings are at this site, the former home of Henry Hastings Sibley, who worked at the trade center for the American Fur Company in the mid-1800s and eventually became governor. Guides are available to lead visitors through three buildings, including the residence and the fur company cold store.

✳ Maplewood

Ÿ **Myth Nightclub** (651-779-6984; www.mythnightclub.net), 3090 Southlawn Dr. Open Fri.–Sat. at 9 PM. They said it couldn't be done, but apparently they

were wrong. When gigantic nightclub Myth opened in this far-flung St. Paul suburb, many people wondered how it would stay in business. It seems that presenting a wide variety of performers (metal to hip-hop to country) in an acoustically
top-notch club does indeed draw the crowds. Myth has a strong reputation as a
great live venue; for nights when there isn't a live concert scheduled, DJs pick
up the slack.

✳ White Bear Lake

This small town on a lake has risen above its suburban roots to become a destination for the dining and shopping crowds.

WHERE TO EAT

& ♈ **Ursula's Wine Bar and Café** (651-429-9600; www.ursulaswb.com), 2125
4th St. Open daily for dinner. This cozy bistro has a limited but tasteful menu of
appetizers, pasta, and meat to go with the more extensive wine list. Entrées start
at $22.

⌀ & ♈ **Ingredients Café** (651-426-6611; www.ingredientscafe.com), 4725 US
61 N. Open daily for lunch and dinner. A menu that changes monthly—focusing
on fresh, locally available foods—and good wine and martini lists make this place
worth a visit. Entrées start at $14.

⌀ & ♈ **Rudy's Redeye Grill** (651-653-6718; www.rudysredeye.com), 4940 US 61
N. Open daily for lunch and dinner.
An upscale steak house with a wide
variety of steaks, seafood, and pasta,
plus a full bar. Entrées start at $14.

DOWNTOWN WHITE BEAR LAKE

⌀ & ♈ **Washington Square Bar &
Grill** (651-407-7162), 4736 Washington Square. Open daily for lunch and
dinner. This neighborhood bar and
grill features outstanding burgers. The
outdoor patio is used three seasons
and is a lovely spot. Entrées start at $8.

⌀ & **Ban Thai Restaurant** (651-
407-8424), 2186 3rd St. Open daily
for lunch and dinner. This little
restaurant is often said to be one of
the best Thai restaurants—if not *the*
best—in the Twin Cities. Entrées
start at $7.

WHERE TO SHOP

Truly (651-426-8414; www.trulyon
line.com), 2175 4th St. Open Tues.–
Sat. Specializing in handmade gifts by
independent artists and artisans.

Backdoor Candy Store (651-762-8200; www.backdoorcandystore.com), 4746 Washington Sq. Open Mon.–Sat. Treats for the young and the young-at-heart, including a wide selection of nostalgia candy.

Mélange (651-426-0388; www.melange.com), 4764 Banning Ave. Open daily. A gift shop carrying items for the home, bath, and body, along with jewelry and other accessories.

Heritage II (651-429-4541; www.heritageii.com), 2183 3rd St. Also in Excelsior. Open daily. The source for Scandinavian and British Isles merchandise, including clothing, tableware and accessories, and gifts.

The Farmer's Daughter (651-653-6768; www.mnhandmade4u.com), 4905 Long Ave. Open daily. Featuring handmade gift items from local artists and artisans.

❋ Woodbury

Woodbury Lakes (651-251-9500; www.woodburylakes.com), 9000 Hudson Rd. Open daily. Opened by the same company that handled the Shoppes at Arbor Lake, Woodbury Lakes is designed to feel more like a small-town shopping center than a giant mall by providing a mix of retail and dining in actual city blocks with sidewalks to give it a small-town-center feel. While many of the usual chain-store suspects are present (Gap, Banana Republic, Victoria's Secret, and J. Jill), the strolling-friendly layout over four city blocks makes the shopping experience feel less *suburban mall* and more *charming village*. Dining options are much more limited than in Maple Grove, with only two sit-down restaurants, an ice cream shop, and a Starbucks.

North Shore and the Arrowhead 3

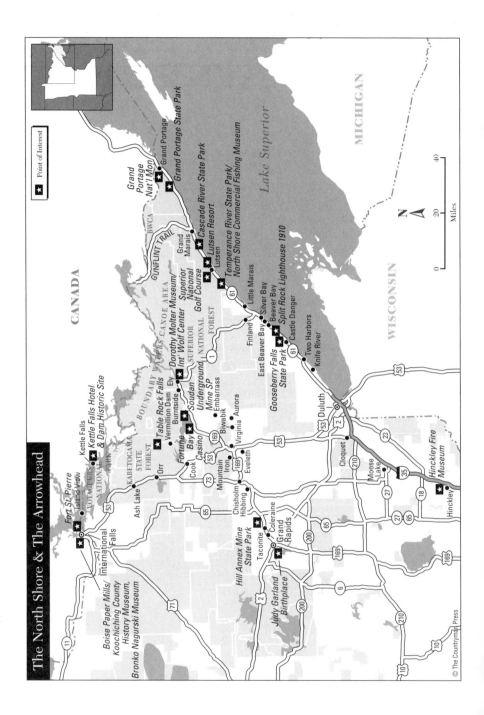

The North Shore & The Arrowhead

Point of Interest ★

CANADA

Lake Superior

MICHIGAN

WISCONSIN

Fort St. Pierre
Island View
Kettle Falls
Kettle Falls Hotel
& Dam Historic Site
VOYAGEURS NATIONAL PARK
International Falls

Boise Paper Mills/
Koochiching County
History Museum,
Bronko Nagurski Museum

Ash Lake
Orr

KABETOGAMA STATE FOREST

BOUNDARY WATERS CANOE AREA

Table Rock Falls
Vermillion Dam Ely
Burntside
Soudan Underground Mine SP
Fortune Bay Casino
Cook

Dorothy Molter Museum/
Int'l Wolf Center
Superior National Golf Course

GUNFLINT TRAIL

BWCA

Grand Portage Nat'l Mon
Grand Portage
Grand Portage State Park

Grand Marais
Lutsen Resort
Lutsen
Cascade River State Park

SUPERIOR NATIONAL FOREST

1

Embarrass
Biwabik
Aurora
Virginia
Mountain Iron
Eveleth

169
53
73
65

Chisholm
Hibbing

Coleraine
Grand Rapids
Taconite

Hill Annex Mine State Park

Judy Garland Birthplace

Temperance River State Park/
North Shore Commercial Fishing Museum

Little Marais

Finland
East Beaver Bay
Silver Bay
Beaver Bay
Castle Danger
Split Rock Lighthouse 1910

Gooseberry Falls State Park

Two Harbors
Knife River

Duluth

Cloquet
Moose Lake
Hinckley
Hinckley Fire Museum

210
35
23
27
65
18
53
2
200
6
169
210
10
11
71

N

0   20   40
Miles

© The Countryman Press

NORTH SHORE AND THE ARROWHEAD

In a state that encompasses stately forests, lakes small and large, prairies, and rolling countryside, it's hard to pick one area as the most scenic. But the North Shore and the Arrowhead region (named for its shape) have arguably some of the loveliest vistas in Minnesota, and the region is one of the most popular among visitors.

The eastern edge of the Arrowhead runs along the shores of Lake Superior, while the northern border runs along Canada, both swaths rich in geological and historical interest. Much of the Lake Superior area was inhabited by the Ojibwe before the arrival of the Europeans, who came searching for trade routes and posts. The French were prominent explorers and settlers here, looking for furs and other goods for trade, and their influence is seen in community names like *Grand Marais* and *Grand Portage*. Fur trading was a central activity until about 1840, when most of the traders and trappers moved elsewhere, including the Mississippi headwaters area. However, the arrival of railroads in 1869, combined with increased ship traffic on Lake Superior, led to a population boom. Soon the commercial fishing and iron ore industries were booming; the subsequent evolution of infrastructure and shipping led not only to established communities but to the beginning of the tourism industry as well. The area's heyday lasted until the Depression years, which saw increased competition from other parts of the country.

Today the North Shore and Arrowhead region still enjoys considerable commercial fishing and mining activity. But tourism has come to play an ever-increasing role in the local economy. The establishment of the million-plus-acre Boundary Waters Canoe Area (BWCA), which has preserved this wilderness nearly as it was in the days of the voyageurs, brings thousands of visitors each summer for camping, hiking, and boating. But whereas visitors used to come only in the summer for fishing and hiking, now they come year-round, taking advantage of the area's winter landscape for activities like skiing, snowmobiling, snowshoeing, and even dogsledding.

All offices are open year-round unless noted otherwise.

Hinckley (800-952-4282; www.hinckleymn.com). Contact the tourism association via phone or Web to order a visitor's guide to the area.

Duluth Convention and Visitors Bureau (218-722-4011; 800-438-5884; www.visitduluth.com), 21 W. Superior St., Suite 100. The Duluth CVB has extensive information about the city on the lake, but be aware that the Web site is very "busy" in terms of graphics and ads; it may take some persistence to find the information you want.

Lutsen-Tofte Tourism Association (218-663-7804; 888-616-6784; www.americasnorthcoast.org), 392 MN 61. Provides information for visitors to this popular ski resort.

Grand Marais Area Tourism (218-387-2524, ext. 1; 888-922-5000; www.grandmarais.com), 13 N. Broadway Ave. Open year-round: July–Oct., daily; Nov.–May, Mon., Tues., and Thurs.–Sat.; June, Mon.–Sat. Local resource for all things Grand Marais.

Gunflint Trail (612-767-8000; 800-338-6932; www.gunflint-trail.com). An online and phone service providing information for tourists to the Gunflint Trail area.

Boundary Waters Canoe Area Wilderness Permit Reservation Center (877-550-6777; www.bwcaw.org). The center for the required permits for visitors to the is very "busy" in terms of graphics and ads; it may take some persistence to find the information you want.

Ely Chamber of Commerce (218-365-6123; 800-777-7281; www.ely.org), 1600 E. Sheridan St. The Ely Chamber can provide help and information not just on Ely itself, but on the Boundary Waters as well.

IN THE BOUNDARY WATERS

Iron Range Tourism Bureau (218-749-8161; 800-777-8497; www.ironrange .org), 403 N. 1st St., Virginia. The Iron Range Tourism Bureau offers a free print guide to the Iron Range as well as online information.

International Falls and Rainy Lake Convention and Visitors Bureau (800-325-5766; www.rainylake.org), 301 2nd Ave., International Falls. A well-organized CVB devoted to tourism along the Canadian border and into the Voyageurs National Park area.

Voyageurs National Park Association (612-333-5424; www.voyageurs.org), 126 N. 3rd St., Suite 400, Minneapolis. Provides information and resources for visitors to the state's only national park.

Kabetogama Lake Tourism Bureau (800-524-9085; www.kabetogama.com), 9903 Gamma Rd., Lake Kabetogama. Tourist information for the Lake Kabetogama region.

GETTING THERE

By car: From the Twin Cities, I-35W North will take you up to Duluth and scenic MN 61, which leads all the way up to the Canadian border. If you're heading to the eastern half of the Boundary Waters or the Gunflint Trail, this is the best route to take. If you're looking for the western parts of the Boundary Waters, you can take I-35W toward Duluth, and then follow MN 61 north of Silver Bay to MN 1; this leads you directly to Ely and parts west.

If you're driving toward Voyageurs National Park, you can take US 169 north out of the Twin Cities through the Iron Range to Chisholm; here you can pick up MN 73, which merges farther north with US 53, which in turn continues to International Falls. An alternate route is I-94 West to St. Cloud, crossing over to US 10 to MN 371 through Brainerd and merging with US 71 south of Bemidji. US 71 then continues north to International Falls.

By air: The primary commercial airport in the region is the Duluth airport, served by Northwest with flights to Minneapolis–St. Paul and Detroit; Midwest Airlines with flights to Milwaukee; and Allegiant Air with flights to Las Vegas. International Falls also has an airport served by Mesaba Airlines (a subsidiary of Northwest) with a feeder route from Minneapolis–St. Paul. Taxis, limos, rental cars, and light-rail service are available from the airports into Duluth and surrounding areas.

GETTING AROUND

Duluth has a public bus system that covers the metro area, with reduced service on weekends and holidays. The service is designed primarily to transport students and employees from outlying homes to work and school within the city. Contact the **Duluth Transit Authority** for more information: 218-722-7283; www.duluthtransit.com. For maximum flexibility, a car is your best bet—and it's a necessity for those traveling outside Duluth. If you're staying in the downtown Duluth area and can walk or take a brief taxi ride to other downtown destinations, you could survive without a car.

The remaining regions of northeastern Minnesota require a vehicle.

THE GLENSHEEN CARRIAGE HOUSE AND GARDENS IN DULUTH

WHEN TO COME

The summer months are a particularly popular time in the Duluth, Greater North Shore, and Voyageurs National Park areas, where the cooler temperatures generated by Lake Superior keep the heat from rising to intolerable levels. The scenery is beautiful, and countless events and festivals up and down the shore take advantage of that. Autumn months draw foliage visitors to all parts of the North Shore and Arrowhead region, while winter draws sports enthusiasts, particularly skiers to Lutsen and snowmobilers, snowshoers, and ice fishers to the more remote areas. Be aware that the winter months can produce some bitterly cold temperatures, particularly in the far-northern reaches, but local stores are well prepared to provide the necessary outerwear. And if you're not fond of cold weather, bundle up in one of the many bed & breakfasts or lodges with cozy fireplaces and enjoy the snowy scenery from the warmth of indoors.

MEDICAL EMERGENCY

Call **911**.

St. Luke's Hospital (218-249-5555; 800-321-3790; www.slhduluth.com), 915 E. 1st St., Duluth.

Lake View Memorial Hospital (218-834-7300; www.lvmhospital.com), 325 11th Ave., Two Harbors.

Cook County North Shore Hospital (218-387-3040), Grand Marais.

Fairview University Medical Center-Mesabi (218-262-4881; www.range.fairview.org), 750 E. 34th St., Hibbing.

Ely Bloomenson Community Hospital (218-365-3271; www.ebch.org), 328 W. Conant St., Ely.

Grand Itasca Clinic & Hospital (218-326-3401; www.granditasca.org), 1601 Golf Course Rd., Grand Rapids.

Falls Memorial Hospital (218-283-4481; www.fmh-mn.com), 1400 US 71, International Falls.

HINCKLEY

About halfway between the Twin Cities and Duluth on I-35W is the small community of Hinckley.

✳ To See and Do

All attractions are open year-round unless otherwise noted.

✍ ♿ **Hinckley Fire Museum**, 1060 Old Hwy. 61 S. Open May–mid-Oct., Tues.–Sun. On September 1, 1894, a historic event occurred in the quiet logging town of Hinckley, just south of Duluth: A fire started. And while any fire that burns out of control in the wilderness can be considered a wildfire and therefore devastating, the fire that consumed Hinckley was worse. Its technical name is *firestorm*; flames shot up 4 miles into the air, and 20 square miles of land was destroyed in less than four hours. The firestorm evolved much like a natural disaster, with cyclones of fire advancing and wreaking havoc. The only comparable events in the 20th century were related to the launching of atomic bombs in Hiroshima.

The Hinckley Fire Museum is housed in the town's former railroad depot (it was built to replace the one destroyed by the firestorm). Though small, it has a

HINCKLEY FIRE MUSEUM

sizable collection of fire artifacts, a brief documentary movie, and Native American items. The friendly staff know the history of the firestorm well and are happy to answer questions or provide information on the individual artifacts.

  ሐ ፕ **Grand Casino Hinckley** (800-472-6321; www.grandcasinomn.com), 777 Lady Luck Dr. Grand Casino offers extensive opportunities for slots, blackjack, and bingo. Five restaurants are available for dining, and the on-site Kids Quest provides care for kids too young to be on the casino floor.

✳ Where to Stay

✐ ሐ ፕ **Grand Casino Hinckley Hotel** (800-468-3517; www.grand casinomn.com), 777 Lady Luck Dr. This is the larger of the Grand Casino Hinckley hotels, with 281 rooms and suites. Rates start at $65.

✐ ሐ ፕ **Grand Hinckley Inn** (800-468-3517; www.grandcasinomn.com), 111 Lady Luck Dr. The inn has 154 rooms and suites as well as an indoor pool. Rates start at $44.

✐ ሐ **Dakota Lodge** (320-384-6052; www.dakotalodge.com), 40497 MN 48. The Dakota offers a wide variety of accommodations: four bed & breakfast lodge rooms, all with private bath and fireplace; cabins; and a two-

bedroom guest house. The B&B rooms come with a full breakfast daily. The property is a naturalist's haven, with easy access to nearby St. Croix State Park. Rates start at $119.

Woodland Trails Bed & Breakfast (320-655-3901; www.woodlandtrails .net), 40361 Grace Lake Rd. Built in 2003, this country charmer is situated on 500 acres of woodland. The property includes 4 miles of trails for hiking as well as access to Grace Lake for bird-watching, paddle boating, or catch-and-release fishing. The five guest rooms all have private bath and electric fireplace; full breakfast is included. Rates start at $145.

DULUTH

✳ To See

All attractions are open year-round unless otherwise noted.

✐ ሐ **The Tweed Museum of Art** (218-726-8222; www.d.umn.edu/tma), 1201 Ordean Ct., University of Minnesota–Duluth. Open Tues. 9–8, Wed.–Fri. 9–4:30, Sat.–Sun. 1–5. Closed Mon. Admission free, with a requested donation of $2 for individuals, $5 for families, $1 for seniors and students. UMD students with ID and children under 6 are free. Named for art collectors George and Alice Tweed, the Tweed Museum focuses both on early-20th-century American and European artwork as well as on bringing in exhibits from regional artists past and present.

✐ ሐ **The Lake Superior Railroad Museum** (218-733-7594; www.lsrm.org), 506 W. Michigan St. Open daily. $10 ages 14 and over, $5.50 ages 3–13; free for

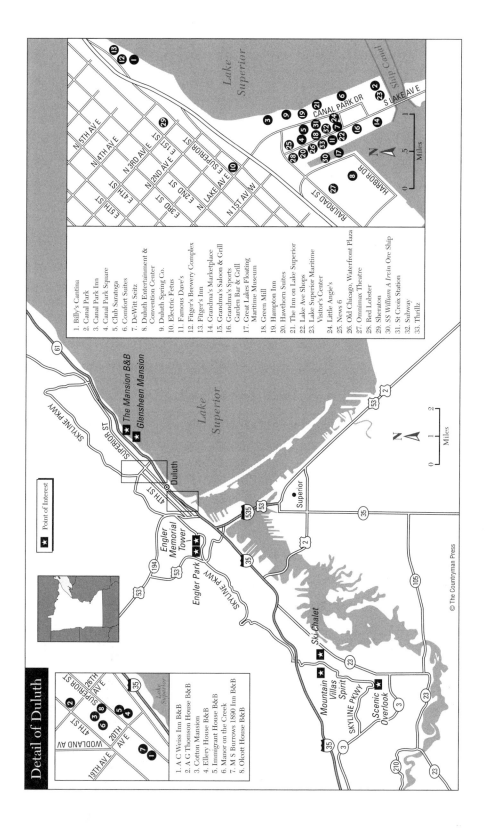

Detail of Duluth

★ Point of Interest

1. A C Weiss Inn B&B
2. A G Thomson House B&B
3. Cotton Mansion
4. Ellery House B&B
5. Immigrant House B&B
6. Manor on the Creek
7. M S Burrows 1890 Inn B&B
8. Olcott House B&B

1. Billy's Cantina
2. Canal Park
3. Canal Park Inn
4. Canal Park Square
5. Club Saratoga
6. Comfort Suites
7. DeWitt Seitz
8. Duluth Entertainment & Convention Center
9. Duluth Spring Co.
10. Electric Fetus
11. Famous Dave's
12. Fitger's Brewery Complex
13. Fitger's Inn
14. Grandma's Marketplace
15. Grandma's Saloon & Grill
16. Grandma's Sports Garden Bar & Grill
17. Great Lakes Floating Maritime Museum
18. Green Mill
19. Hampton Inn
20. Hawthorn Suites
21. The Inn on Lake Superior
22. Lake Ave Shops
23. Lake Superior Maritime Visitor's Center
24. Little Angie's
25. News 6
26. Old Chicago, Waterfront Plaza
27. Omnimax Theatre
28. Red Lobster
29. Sheraton
30. SS William A Irvin Ore Ship
31. St Croix Station
32. Subway
33. Thrillz

The Mansion B&B ★
Glensheen Mansion ★

Engler Memorial Tower ★

Ski Chalet ★

Mountain Villas Spirit ★

Scenic Overlook ★

© The Countryman Press

children under 3 and museum members. Admission includes entrance to Depot Square (see below). This small museum devoted to Duluth's locomotive history features vintage wood-burning steam engines (including the largest one ever built), railroad snowplows, and an operating model train exhibit. Between Memorial Day and Labor Day, visitors can ride a vintage electric trolley around the museum, or sign up to take a ride on the North Shore Scenic Railroad, which has a number of options. Visitors who purchase a ride on the North Shore Scenic Railroad are eligible for discounts on museum admission.

✔ ⚐ **Depot Square** (218-733-7594; www.lsrm.org), 506 W. Michigan St. Open daily. $10 ages 14 and over, $5.50 ages 3–13; free for children under 3 and museum members. Admission includes entrance to the Lake Superior Railroad Museum (see above). This historic complex is a re-creation of two Duluth streets set in 1910. Also on site are the **Duluth Children's Museum** (218-733-7543) and **Duluth Art Institute** (218-733-7560).

✔ ⚐ **Glensheen** (218-724-8863; www.d.umn.edu/glen), 3300 London Rd. Open daily from Memorial Day–mid-Oct., weekends only mid-Oct.–late May. Tours $5–24. Just north of downtown Duluth, on a stretch of Lake Superior shoreline, is the 39-room mansion Glensheen. Built in the early 1900s by the prosperous Congdon family, Glensheen is now open as a historic site (maintained by the University of Minnesota). There are three levels of tours available: the home's exterior and grounds; its exterior, grounds, and first and second floors; or all of these plus the third floor, attic, and basement. The last tour takes the longest (and can be toasty in warmer weather—central air was not an available amenity when the mansion was built), but it's worth the extra time. The docents are well trained and full of interesting tidbits about the history and construction of the 36-room mansion, filled with mostly original furniture, decorating, and artwork. Ahead of their time, the Congdons incorporated electricity throughout (but maintained gaslights, too, as Chester Congdon was not convinced that electricity wasn't just a fad), as well an early version of a central vacuum system. The

GLENSHEEN

grounds, set on a wide expanse of shoreline, include a rocky beach, boathouse, carriage house, and gardener's home, as well as extensive, lavish gardens.

One thing that isn't mentioned on the tour, but which you can now ask about at the end of the tour (in earlier years, docents were not allowed to talk about it), is the murder of Elisabeth Congdon and her nurse at Glensheen in 1977. For some, this is reason enough to visit Glensheen, but even if you have no interest in the real-life murder and subsequent trials, visiting the mansion provides an unusually detailed and carefully preserved view into a lost way of life.

ATTRACTIONS

🐾 ⟨♿⟩ **Duluth OMNIMAX** (218-727-0022; 888-666-4629; www.duluthomnimax .com), 301 Harbor Dr. (Duluth Entertainment Convention Center). Open daily Memorial Day–Labor Day, Fri.–Sun. Tickets start at $5.50. The 99-foot dome screen draws viewers into the movie experience by surrounding them with sight and sound. Located near Canal Park.

🐾 **SS William A. Irvin** (218-727-0022, ext. 234; www.williamairvin.com), 301 Harbor Dr. (Duluth Entertainment Convention Center). Open daily Memorial Day–mid-Oct. $9 adults, $6 children. Run by the Great Lakes Floating Maritime Museum, the SS *William A. Irvin* spent more than 40 years delivering coal and iron ore as well as transporting dignitaries around the Great Lakes region. Daily tours are available in-season; in October, special "Ship of Ghouls" tours are offered.

🐾 ⟨♿⟩ **Great Lakes Aquarium** (218-740-FISH; www.glaquarium.org), 353 Harbor Dr. Open daily. $12.95 adults, $9.95 seniors, $6.95 ages 3–11; free for those under 3. Located along the shore near Canal Park, the Great Lakes Aquarium specializes in freshwater fish and aquatic life. Given that most regional fish are fairly monochromatic, the exhibits may be of more interest to people with a strong interest in marine biology than for families with kids who want to see colorful tropical fish. Recent exhibitions have included more fanciful creatures, such as seahorses, in an effort to broaden the appeal.

🐾 ⟨♿⟩ ⟨Y⟩ **Vista Fleet Sightseeing and Dining Cruises** (218-722-6218; 877-883-4002; www.vistafleet.com), 323 Harbor Dr. Rates vary. Vista offers several daily cruises during the season, some of which board in Duluth and some across the Lake in Superior. Sightseeing, natural history, brunch, lunch, and dinner cruises are offered.

✳ Green Space

Skyline Parkway. A narrow road that winds through residential and rural areas, Skyline Parkway can be maddening to follow (it's not terribly well marked, especially on the northern end), but it's worth the effort if you want to catch some spectacular views of Lake Superior, the city of Duluth, and western Wisconsin. Take a detailed Duluth map with you, and be aware that parts of the road are closed during winter months. Don't forget your camera.

Enger Park. Located along Skyline Parkway, Enger Park is a small but lush picnic area complete with its own stone tower. During summer months the floral

A HARBOR VIEW FROM THE SKYLINE PARKWAY

display is breathtaking, and shaded picnic tables are spread generously through-out the grounds. Climb the tower for a wide-open view of Duluth and Lake Superior.

Leif Ericson Park. A large park set along Lake Superior, Leif Ericson has a wide variety of amenities: an open-air amphitheater that hosts live performances in sum-mer, strolls along the lakeside, and a lovely and (in-season) fragrant rose garden.

Spirit Mountain (218-628-2891; 800-642-6377; www.spiritmt.com), 9500 Spirit Mountain Place. While the word *mountain* might be overstating things a bit, the Spirit Mountain area is a popular stop for winter visitors to Duluth. Skiing is available daily, and though there aren't nearly as many runs or levels of difficulty as northern neighbor Lutsen-Tofte offers, for those who want to get a little skiing in without venturing farther north, Spirit Mountain works fine. During summer, campsites are available for rent with panoramic views of Lake Superior and the city. Book lodging at the Mountain Villas Resort, a collection of 14 octag-onal tree houses that make up the only lodging on the mountain.

ENGER PARK

Superior Whitewater Rafting (218-384-4637; www.minnesotawhitewater .com), 950 Chestnut Ave., Carlton. Open daily May–Sept. Must be 12 or older. Fifteen miles south of Duluth, Superior Whitewater Rafting offers rafting and sea kayaking on the St. Louis River. Kayaking can be done as a guided tour or as a rental only. Reserve early for Saturday excursions.

✻ Where to Stay

Unless otherwise noted, all lodgings are open year-round.

Canal Park

There are several hotels in the compact Canal Park area, all offering convenient access to shops, dining, and strolling along the Lake Walk. Given the popularity of visiting Duluth in summer, plan ahead—many of these hotels fill to capacity in advance, especially on weekends.

♦ ♿ **Canal Park Lodge** (218-279-6000; 800-777-8560; www.canalpark lodge.com), 250 Canal Park Dr. One of the newer properties in Canal Park, the lodge has 116 rooms with pool, hot tub, and high-speed and WiFi access. Full breakfast included with accommodations. Rates start at $110, with weekend discounts and packages available.

♦ ♿ **Comfort Suites Canal Park** (218-727-1378; 800-424-6423; www .stayinduluth.com), 408 Canal Park Dr. One of the smaller Canal Park properties, this all-suite hotel has a pool and whirlpool as well as some in-room whirlpools, high-speed Internet, and WiFi access. All rooms come with refrigerator, microwave, and coffeemaker. Continental breakfast is included with accommodations. Rates start at $99, with weekend discounts and packages available.

♦ ♿ **Hampton Inn-Duluth** (218-720-3000; 800-426-7866; www.hamptoninn .com/hi/duluth), 310 Canal Park Dr. This Canal Park lodging has mostly

THE LEIF ERICSON PARK ROSE GARDEN

hotel rooms with a handful of Jacuzzi suites and offers high-speed and WiFi access. The property also includes a pool, whirlpool, and daily continental breakfast with accommodations. Rates start at $89, with weekend discounts and packages available.

🐾 🌿 ♿ **The Inn on Lake Superior** (218-726-1111; 888-668-4352; www .theinnonlakesuperior.com), 350 Canal Park Dr. The inn is one of the larger properties in Canal Park, offering both hotel rooms and suites. All rooms have refrigerator, microwave, and coffeemaker. Some rooms have fireplace and whirlpool. The property has two pools, one indoor and one outdoor, and in an unusual twist for this climate, the outdoor pool is open year-round; it's situated on the roof with a sheltering wall, and the water

DULUTH'S RADISSON HOTEL

is kept luxuriously warm. Also year-round is the evening s'mores tradition, where kids of all ages can come out by the shoreline and toast marshmallows. Rates start at $137, with weekend discounts and packages available.

🌿 ♿ **The Suites Hotel** (218-727-4663; 877-766-2665; www.thesuites duluth.com), 325 Lake Ave. S. This all-suite hotel also has an indoor pool, a full kitchen in each suite, continental breakfast daily, and charging privileges at several local restaurants, including Bellisio's, Grandma's, and Little Angie's Cantina. Rates start at $179, with weekend discounts and packages available.

City of Duluth
🌿 ♿ 🍸 **Fitger's Inn** (218-722-8826; 888-348-4377; www.fitgers.com), 600 East Superior Street. Located lakeside within walking distance of Canal Park, Fitger's Inn is part of the Fitger's Brewery complex (see Where to Eat and Selective Shopping). The hotel has 62 rooms and suites, several with excellent views of Lake Superior, as well as complimentary high-speed and WiFi access, Aveda personal products, a specialty pillow menu, complimentary continental breakfast, and access to the Arrowhead Tennis & Athletic Center. The rooms have been decorated to complement the building's historic and charming character. Rates start at $129, with packages available.

🐾 🌿 ♿ 🍸 **Radisson** (218-727-8981; 800-333-3333; www.radisson.com/ duluthmn), 505 W. Superior St. The Radisson is the distinctly circular building in downtown Duluth, with views of Lake Superior from many of its rooms. It's a local landmark both because of its shape and because it was one of the first upscale hotels in the area. The property has a pool, sauna, hot tub, whirlpool, and high-speed and WiFi access. The hotel's signature restaurant, Top of the Harbor (see *Where to Eat*), is open daily for breakfast, lunch, and dinner, in a revolving space at the top of the hotel. Rates start at $89, with weekend discounts and packages available.

✑ ᕒ ᛏ **Sheraton Duluth** (218-733-5660; 800-325-3535; www.starwood hotels.com), 301 E. Superior St. Opened in 2007, the Sheraton is just a few blocks from the Canal Park area in downtown Duluth. The hotel has an indoor pool and rooms with flat-screen TV and high-speed Internet access; the Sheraton Club level offers larger rooms with sitting area, as well as daily breakfast and afternoon appetizers. Rates start at $109, with weekend discounts and packages available.

✳ Where to Eat

All restaurants are open year-round unless otherwise noted.

DINING OUT

✑ ᕒ ᛏ **At Sara's Table** (218-723-8569; www.astccc.net), 1902 E. 8th St. Open Mon.–Sat. for all three meals; Sun. for breakfast and lunch. Located near the University of Minnesota campus, At Sara's Table goes by two other names as well: Chester Creek Café and Taran's Market Place. Don't let the abundance of names intimidate you; this restaurant, casual and friendly, serves delicious meals, often using local food sources in-season. Breakfasts are hearty and plentiful; lunch and dinner can be simple or elaborate, depending on your mood. A library in the back is available for lounging, or even purchasing the books. Free WiFi

is offered to customers. Entrées start at $5.

✑ ᕒ **New London Café** (218-525-0777), 4721 E. Superior St. Open daily. This is where the locals gather for breakfast and lunch. A tiny café on Duluth's busy London Road, it's not fancy, but it does prove that simple food prepared well can be outstanding. Be sure to try the New London potatoes. Entrées start at $4.

✑ ᕒ ᛏ **Hell's Kitchen** (218-727-1620; www.hellskitcheninc.com), 310 Lake Ave. S. Open daily for all three meals. This is the Duluth branch of the Minneapolis restaurant, and currently Duluth proves itself the winner in that this restaurant serves not only breakfast and lunch, but also dinner (not available in Minneapolis). The devilishly black-and-red interior, combined with the proclamation that they serve "damn good food," is tongue-in-cheek, but the quality of the food is no joke. Entrées start at $8.

✑ ᕒ ᛏ **Fitger's Brewhouse and Grill** (218-279-2739; www.brew house.net), 600 E. Superior St. Open

AT SARA'S TABLE

BED & BREAKFASTS

Just north of the center of Duluth is a stretch of historic homes (including the Congdon mansion, Glensheen, open for tours; see *To See*). Within this area, not on Lake Superior itself but a short drive or doable walk, is a cluster of bed & breakfasts.

A. Charles Weiss Inn (218-724-7016; 800-525-5243; www.acweissinn.com), 1615 E. Superior St. A mansion built by A. Charles Weiss, a former editor and publisher of the *Duluth Herald*. This inn, built in 1895, has five rooms with private bath. Massage is available by appointment. Rates start at $110.

The Mathew S. Burrows 1890 Inn (218-724-4991; 800-789-1890; www.1890inn .com), 1632 E. 1st St. This late-19th-century home has seen many changes since its days as a "bachelor pad," complete with third-floor ballroom, but it now offers five rooms, all with private bath. Rates start at $95.

The Olcott House (218-728-1339; 800-715-1339; www.olcotthouse.com), 2316 E. 1st St. This 1904 mansion includes luxurious accommodations in five suites in the home with private bath, as well as a separate carriage house suite. Several of the suites have fireplace and whirlpool tub; all have air-conditioning, LCD TV, and either four-poster or canopy bed. Rates start at $150; some packages are available.

The Ellery House (218-724-7639; 800-355-3794; www.elleryhouse.com), 28 S. 21st Ave. Ellery House's four elegant suites all have private bath, robes, and

daily for lunch and dinner. Located in the historic Fitger's complex, the Brewhouse is a cheerful take on the "burger and beer" concept. Hearty sandwiches, burgers, and quesadillas all available with your choice of brew. Entrées start at $8.

✍ & ♈ **Baja Billy's Cantina & Grill** (218-740-2300; www.bajabillys.com), 600 E. Superior St. Open daily for lunch and dinner. The menu may not be unique, but the skillfully Americanized Mexican entrées are prepared in hearty portions and are especially tasty when combined with the house margarita. Entrées start at $9.

✍ & ♈ **Grandma's Saloon & Grill** (218-727-4192; www.grandmas restaurants.com), 522 Lake Ave. S. Open daily for lunch and dinner. This hometown favorite is open for lunch and dinner daily, with a cheerfully American menu packed with steaks, sandwiches, and pasta. Summer is especially popular at Grandma's, which offers deck seating overlooking the Aerial Lift Bridge. Entrées start at $10.

✍ & ♈ **Bellisio's** (218-727-4921; www .grandmasrestaurants.com), 405 Lake Ave. S. Open daily for lunch and dinner. This upscale offshoot from the Grandma's Restaurant group offers excellent Italian cuisine and a sizable wine list. Entrées start at $14.

✍ & ♈ **Little Angie's Cantina** (218-727-6117; www.grandmasrestaurants

featherbed; one suite has a private sunporch, while another has a separate sitting area. WiFi is available throughout the property. Breakfast can be served in the rooms if requested. Rates start at $109; some packages are available.

A. G. Thomson House (218-724-3464; 877-807-8077; www.thomsonhouse.biz), 2617 E. 3rd St. Built in 1909 by architect Edwin H. Hewitt, the A. G. Thomson House has four rooms with private bath in the main house as well as three rooms with private bath in the adjacent carriage house. Full breakfast is available in the dining room, or a continental breakfast can be served to your room. Rates start at $119; some packages are available.

Cotton Mansion (218-724-6405; 800-228-1997; www.cottonmansion.com), 2309 E. 1st St. This 16,000-square-foot 1908 Italianate mansion offers seven rooms and suites, all sumptuously appointed. A full breakfast is served each morning by candlelight, and an afternoon wine-and-cheese service is provided daily. Rates start at $135; some packages are available.

Solglimt (218-727-0596; 877-727-0596; www.solglimt.com), 828 S. Lake Ave. This inn is not grouped with the others on or near Superior Street, but is located across the Aerial Lift Bridge from Canal Park. Rather than a mansion, Solglimt is more of a seaside cottage; three suites have private bath. Amenities include full breakfast daily, robes, beach towels, and binoculars. Rates start at $135; some packages are available.

.com), 11 E. Buchanan St. Open daily for lunch and dinner. Southwest and American foods, served in jumbo portions with an agreeable assortment of margaritas and cocktails. Try the black bean tacos. In summer, enjoy Little Angie's outdoor deck while having a drink and people-watching the crowds on Canal Park. Entrées start at $10.

♿ 🍸 **Top of the Harbor** (218-727-8981), 505 W. Superior St. (in the Radisson Hotel). Top of the Harbor's major claim to fame is its status as a revolving restaurant providing generous views of Duluth and Lake Superior. The food is basic American cuisine. Open daily for breakfast, lunch, and dinner. Breakfast entrées start at $6, dinner entrées at $14.

✷ Entertainment

LIVE PERFORMANCES

Duluth Entertainment Convention Center (218-722-5573; www.decc.org), 350 Harbor Dr. The DECC is home to touring concerts and productions that come through Duluth, as well as host to the Duluth-Superior Symphony Orchestra and the Minnesota Ballet. Besides the theater and convention center, the DECC is also home to the Duluth OMNIMAX and the SS *William Irvin* (see *To See*).

✳ Selective Shopping

The Canal Park area, geared as it is for tourists, has several enticing shops.

The Dewitt-Seitz Marketplace (218-722-0047; www.dewitt-seitz .com), 394 Lake Ave. S. Located in the heart of Canal Park, the marketplace is housed in a century-old manufacturing and warehouse site that's now on the National Register of Historic Places. Tourist shops worth a stop include **Inland Coast Traders**, purveyor of sportswear; **Minnesota Gifts**, full of northwoods-themed apparel and souvenirs; and **Cruisin' by Sandra Dee**, a small, casual shop for the T-shirt and sweatshirt shopper. **J. Skylark** is an engaging toy and game shop for kids, while **Blue Heron Trading** has cooking items

SHOPPING IN CANAL PARK

and gifts. **The Art Dock** sells regional art and crafts. **Hepzibah's Sweet Shoppe** can easily take care of that chocolate craving. For a quick bite to eat, stop by either the **Amazing Grace Bakery & Café**, which offers heavenly baked goods, or **Lake Avenue Café**, a small but surprisingly creative deli.

Fitger's Brewery (218-722-8826; www.fitgers.com), 600 E. Superior St. Besides a hotel (see *Lodging*) and restaurants (see *Where to Eat*), Fitger's also has a variety of retail establishments to explore through its ambling hallways. Not immune to a downturned economy, some of Fitger's is sadly empty, but there are still enough retailers to while away some shopping time while waiting for your dinner reservation. **Benetton** has a store here with its trademark "world of Benetton" colors. **Fitger's Wine Cellars** is a small but carefully stocked wine and spirits shop. **Jake's Lake Place** is full of the "Life is Good" clothes and products. **Wintergreen Clothing** is a retail outlet for the Ely, Minnesota, outdoor clothing manufacturer. **Frost River** continues the outdoor theme with its line of rugged canoe packs. **The Bookstore at Fitger's** is a charming store with a mix of popular and literary books and gift items.

The Electric Fetus (218-722-9970; www.electricfetus.com), 12 E. Superior St. Just steps away from the waterfront, the Electric Fetus has one of the largest music inventories in the state (along with its sister locations in the Twin Cities and St. Cloud), as well as gifts and jewelry.

Blue Iris Gallery (218-720-3300; www.blueirisgalleryduluthmn.com), 723 Lake Ave. S. Carries a range of regional artists, particularly in photography, prints, jewelry, and fine crafts.

Blue Lake Gallery (218-725-0034; www.bluelakegallery.com), 395 Lake Ave. S. Regional artists are represented with their pottery, jewelry, and sculpture (some of which is located in an outdoor sculpture garden).

Northern Lights Books and Gifts (218-722-5267; 800-868-8904; www.norlights.com), 307 Canal Park Dr. Sells a fine variety of books, with emphasis on local and regional authors and topics.

✷ Special Events

✺ **Winterfest** (www.visitduluth.com/promo_events/winterfest), various locations. The months of Jan.–Mar. may be the coldest, but Duluth keeps everyone warm and happy with a brisk schedule of special events ranging from ski races to snowshoe championships to the Polar Plunge (are you ready for a dip in Lake Superior in midwinter?). Check the organization's Web site for specific events and dates.

John Beargrease Sled Dog Marathon (218-722-7631; www.beargrease.com). One of the most beloved events in this region, the late-Jan. Beargrease (as it's known) celebrates its 25th year in 2008 and is the longest sled dog event in the lower 48 states. The event draws dogsled teams and visitors from across the country.

✺ **Grandma's Marathon** (218-727-0947; www.grandmasmarathon.com),

Duluth. Taking place over the third weekend of June, Grandma's Marathon is one of the premier marathon events in Minnesota. You'll find a variety of activities besides the marathon itself—a health and wellness expo, kids' races and a 5K run, live evening entertainment, and a spaghetti dinner. Plus, of course, the actual marathon.

✺ ♿ **Duluth Festival of Cultures** (www.duluthfestivalofcultures.com), Bayfront Festival Park. The Festival of Cultures is held in early Aug. and includes performers representing a variety of cultures, as well as a global market.

✺ ♿ **Bayfront Blues Festival** (www.bayfrontblues.com), Bayfront Festival Park. This annual three-day celebration of the blues in early Aug. is a popular and long-running event; ordering tickets early and making hotel or camping reservations well in advance is recommended.

Glensheen's Festival of Fine Art and Craft (218-726-8910; 888-454-4536; www.d.umn.edu/glen/visit/calendar.html), Glensheen Mansion, 3300 London Rd. Glensheen is itself worthy of a visit (see *To See*), and in mid-Aug. it hosts a fine art festival on its grounds that attracts thousands of people annually. It's hard to imagine a better setting than this opulent 19th-century mansion and its sumptuous gardens.

GUIDANCE

Once you leave Duluth, you will want a car, if for no other reason than to be able to stop on a whim and visit scenic overlooks, trails, shops, and cafés. Make sure you take Scenic Highway 61 out of Duluth; you'll miss the lake views if you take Superior Street instead.

✷ To See

All attractions are open year-round unless otherwise noted.

🐾 🐾 ♿ **Gooseberry Falls** (218-834-3855; www.dnr.state.mn.us), 3206 MN 61 E., Two Harbors. Open daily 9–5. Admission is free. This waterfall area is by no means the largest in the United States, but it's visitor-friendly, with a sizable visitor center and extensive trails and walkways. Pets are allowed, and there are "doggie bags" strategically placed to encourage dog owners to clean up after their pets. The park twists and turns around the base of the falls, allowing access to both sides. Be sure to wear sturdy shoes; crossing wet rocks is a tricky proposition in the best of footgear, and flip-flops could be downright dangerous.

🐾 ♿ **Split Rock Lighthouse** (218-226-6372; 888-727-8386; www.mnhs.org), 3713 Split Rock Lighthouse Rd., Two Harbors. Open daily May 15–Oct. 15, 10–6. Call for winter hours. $8 adults, $6 seniors and college students with ID, $4 ages 6–17. North of Duluth on MN 61 is Split Rock Lighthouse. This safety beacon for passing ships is not large in stature, but given its location on a dramatic, steep cliff, it proved its worth for decades. Now it's open for tourists to visit, along with a large visitor center with gift shop and video presentation. If you're feeling fit, take the trail that leads down the side of the cliff to the beach below (171 steps each way) for amazing views of the lighthouse and surrounding shorelines. The lighthouse grounds are connected to the Gitchi-Gami State Trail, which can be used by bikers or in-line skaters.

🐾 ♿ **North Shore Commercial Fishing Museum** (218-663-7804; www.commercialfishingmuseum.org), 7136 MN 61, Tofte. Open Apr. 1–Dec. 1, daily 9–5. $3 adults, $1 ages 6–16; under 6 free. This museum is dedicated to preserving and giving insight into the long history of commercial fishing on Lake Superior.

GOOSEBERRY FALLS

☀ To Do

The North Shore is all about the outdoors, whether it's summer or winter.

Superior Hiking Trail (218-834-2700; www.shta.org). Run by the Superior Hiking Trail Association (SHTA), this collection of hiking byways and trails covers over 200 miles along the Lake Superior shoreline from Jay Cooke State Park south of Duluth to the Canadian border west of Grand Portage. It's a work in progress; one of its special features is that it has been constructed mostly by volunteers over the past 20 years, with a tentative completion date of 2010. Frequent campsites and parking lots allow visitors to choose between backpacking and taking short day hikes. Contact the SHTA for information on the Lodge-to-Lodge Hiking Programs.

SPLIT ROCK LIGHTHOUSE

Gitchi-Gami State Trail (www.ggta.org). Long-term plans show an ambitious 86 miles of nonmotorized trails extending from Two Harbors to Grand Marais. At presstime about 28 miles have been completed and are open for visitors. A large section is open beginning at Gooseberry Falls through to Tofte.

Lutsen Mountains (218-663-7281; www.lutsen.com), Ski Hill Rd. (C5), Lutsen. Lutsen is Minnesota's largest ski area, with 90 runs of varying difficulty across four mountains. Downhill skiers, snowboarders, and cross-country skiers have 1,000 acres of land at their disposal, along with an Alpine Slide and a mountain tram for prime sightseeing. Horse-drawn sleigh rides are available in winter. Lutsen isn't just popular in winter, although that's its prime season; hiking, horseback riding, mountain biking, rock climbing, kayaking, and canoeing are all offered in summer, when the lush greenery attracts skiers and nonskiers alike.

North Shore Charters and Tours (218-663-7384; www.northshorevisitor .com/charterfishing), 6921 W. MN 61, Tofte. North Shore Charters offers Lake Superior sightseeing tours as well as sportfishing packages, available in half- or full-day segments.

Stoney Creek Kennels (218-663-0143; www.stoneycreeksleddogs.com), 142 Sawbill Trail, Tofte. Experience firsthand the thrill of riding behind a team of well-trained sled dogs. Excursions can run anywhere from 15 minutes to a full day.

Temperance River State Park (218-663-7476; www.dnr.state.mn.us/state _parks/temperance_river/index.html), MN 61, Schroeder. A heavily wooded state park with waterfalls, rivers, and trails for hiking, camping, snowmobiling, cross-country skiing, and rock climbing.

There is a seemingly endless supply of lodging along the North Shore from Duluth to Lutsen, from small mom-and-pop motels to bed & breakfasts to large, deluxe resorts. But despite the number of accommodations you see, they do book up during prime seasons (winter for the Lutsen area, summer along the North Shore in general), so plan ahead. Accommodations are open year-round unless otherwise noted.

🐾 ✎ ♿ ♉ **Superior Shores Resort & Conference Center** (218-834-5671; 800-242-1988; www.superior shores.com), 1521 Superior Shores Dr., Two Harbors. This large resort complex has all the bells and whistles: a pebbled beach on Lake Superior, lodge rooms or lake homes, indoor and outdoor pools, and easy access to hiking, cross-country skiing, and snowmobile trails; it's located near an 18-hole golf course. Rates start at $49; weekend discounts and packages are available.

✎ **Northern Rail Traincar Bed and Breakfast** (218-834-0955; 877-834-0955; www.northernrail.net), 1730 CR 3, Two Harbors. It's not false advertising—this is a bed & breakfast built out of actual traincars. The cars have been developed into surprisingly tasteful and comfortable suites. Guests check in at the "depot" before arriving at one of the 18 suites (all are themed, including northwoods, Victorian, and safari themes). The property provides guests with private bath, continental breakfast, trail access, snowshoe rental, and summer bonfires, all tucked into a quiet wooded area. Rates start at $69; packages are available.

Lighthouse Bed & Breakfast (218-834-4898; 888-832-5606; www.light housebb.org), 1 Lighthouse Point, Two Harbors. Open May–Oct. Built in 1892, this B&B is on the National Register of Historic Places; proceeds from guests contribute to the lighthouse's ongoing restoration. There are four rooms with shared bath, all with views of Lake Superior. A full Scandinavian breakfast is served daily by candlelight.

Baptism River Inn (218-353-0707; 877-353-0707; www.baptismriverinn .com), 6125 MN 1, Silver Bay. *Cozy* doesn't do justice to this charming three-bedroom bed & breakfast. Each room has a private bath; all have the rustic qualities of a log cabin. Situated on the Baptism River, with easy access to hiking and skiing. Rates start at $100.

🐾 ✎ ♿ ♉ **Cascade Lodge** (218-387-1112; 800-322-9543; www.cascade lodgemn.com), 3719 W. MN 61, Lutsen. Open Apr.–mid-Dec. The best of both worlds, Cascade Lodge is nestled into Cascade River State Park with access to several trails, and stellar views of Lake Superior. Accommodations vary from motel rooms, lodge rooms, and cabins to two private homes. Stop at the restaurant for dinner (see *Where to Eat*). Rates start at $53; packages are available.

🐾 ✎ **Solbakken Resort** (218-663-7566; 800-435-3950; www.solbakken resort.com), 4874 W. MN 61, Lutsen. Another combination resort, with motel rooms, lodge rooms, and lakeshore cabins and homes. Solbakken offers direct access to cross-country ski trails. Rates start at $50.

❄ ✎ ♿ ♉ **Bluefin Bay on Lake Superior** (800-258-3346; www.blue finbay.com), 7192 W. MN 61, Tofte. Studios and condominium units are available for rent at this resort right on Lake Superior. The property boasts year-round indoor and outdoor pools as well as dining at the Bluefin Grille (see *Where to Eat*) and massage therapy by appointment. Rates start at $48; packages are available.

❄ ✎ ♉ **Caribou Highlands Lodge** (218-663-7241; 800-642-6036; www .caribouhighlands.com), 371 Ski Hill Rd., Lutsen. A year-round resort nestled into Sawtooth Mountain in Lutsen, Caribou Highlands offers lodge rooms, town homes and condos, and Poplar Ridge homes—log cabins with multiple bedrooms and fireplaces. During winter the property offers ski-in, ski-out access to Lutsen Mountain. There is a restaurant and coffee shop at the lodge, as well as indoor and outdoor pools, saunas, tennis courts, evening bonfires, and massage and WiFi. In summer the Mountain Kids Camp offers half- or full-day themed camp programs for kids ages 4–10. Rates start at $69, with packages available.

✎ **Temperance Landing** (877-723-6426; www.temperancelanding.com), Temperance Trail, Schroeder. Composed of 3,000-square-feet log cabins, Temperance Landing is a Lake Superior luxury option. Each cabin has at least three bedrooms and baths; all come with fireplace (some gas, some wood-burning), fully equipped kitchens, access to hiking trails and canoe/kayak launch areas, and a fully restored classic Finnish sauna. Rates start at $195.

✳ Where to Eat

All restaurants are open year-round unless otherwise noted.

✎ ♿ **Betty's Pies** (218-834-3367; 877-269-7494; www.bettyspies.com), 1633 MN 61, Two Harbors. Open daily for all three meals. Local legend Betty's Pies has everything, from attitude ("Pies just like Mom used to make, before she took up bingo, cigarettes & beer") to truly delectable pies. A limited short-order menu includes broasted chicken, burgers, sandwiches, salads, and "pie shakes." But it's the pies that will bring you back again and again. Entrées start at $5.

✎ ♿ **Rustic Inn Café** (218-834-2488; www.rusticinncafe.com), 2773 MN 61, Two Harbors. Open daily for all three meals. Breakfast is served all day, but there are separate lunch and dinner menus that include burgers, sandwiches, and slow-roasted pork and beef. Entrées start at $6.

✎ ♿ ♉ **Bluefin Grille** (218-663-6200; www.bluefinbay.com), 7192 West MN 61, Tofte. Open daily for all three meals. Located at the Bluefin Bay resort (See *Lodging*), Bluefin Grille serves American food with an emphasis on local, particularly Lake Superior seafood when available. Entrées start at $7.

✎ ♿ **Cascade Lodge** (218-387-1112; 800-322-9543; www.cascadelodge mn.com), 3719 W. MN 61, Lutsen. Open daily for all three meals. The restaurant at Cascade Lodge provides hearty American fare in a casual, North Shore–themed setting. Entrées start at $7.

✳ Selective Shopping

MN 61 has about as many small shops along the way as it does small restaurants and cafés. Because winter sports have increased the traffic farther north, many of these shops stay open year-round.

Playing with Yarn (877-693-2221; www.playingwithyarn.com), 276 MN 61, Knife River. Open Wed.–Sun. This small but packed yarn shop, located right on the shores of Lake Superior, offers everything needed for the fiber enthusiast. Even better if you're a dog lover—the owner's dogs reside in the house next door and can be introduced upon request.

Russ Kendall's Smoke House (218-834-5995), MN 61, Knife River. Open Mon.–Sat. As the name suggests, this is a great spot for smoked items, especially the fish—lake trout, herring, salmon. Gifts are also available.

Northwoods Pioneer Gallery & Gifts (218-834-4175; www.pioneer crafts.com), 2821 MN 61, Two Harbors. Open daily Memorial Day–mid-Oct.; Fri.–Sun. mid-Oct.–Dec.; Sat.–Sun. Jan.–mid-May. Art and craft items made by local artisans.

✳ Special Events

St. Urho's Day (218-353-7337; www .finlandmnus.com), 7344 MN 1, Finland. Possibly one of the oddest historical festivals in Minnesota. In Finland, a tiny town just north of Silver Bay, St. Urho is celebrated each year with a four-day festival in mid-Mar. What's odd is that there is no St. Urho; the people of Finland (the town, not the country) created him to have something to celebrate. Ostensibly he drove the grasshoppers out of Finland (the country) in an act similar to St. Patrick driving the snakes out of Ireland. Regardless of veracity, the festival goes on; even in the country of Finland, St. Urho has a pub named for him.

Two Harbors Kayak Festival (www.kayakfestival.org). This annual event, usually the first weekend in Aug., is about all things kayak: kayak races, beginning and advanced lessons, equipment demonstrations, and a gear swap.

North Shore Inline Marathon/Half-Marathon (218-723-1503; www.northshoreinline .com). Held on a Sat. in mid-Sept., the Inline Marathon begins in Two Harbors and flies 26.2 miles along Scenic Highway 61, ending at the Duluth Entertainment Convention Center. The half-marathon begins at the 13.1-mile point, ending at the same destination. Participants must be 13 and older; there is a kids' sprint on Fri. night.

Master's Bluegrass Festival (218-387-1284, ext. 4; www.boreal.org/ music), Lutsen Resort. This annual festival takes place the first weekend in Nov., a perfect time to cozy up to the fireplace and listen to the masters of bluegrass.

Annual *Edmund Fitzgerald* Memorial Beacon Lighting (651-259-3000; 800-657-3773; www.mnhs.org/ places/site/srl/ed.html), Split Rock Lighthouse, 3713 Split Rock Lighthouse Rd., Two Harbors. On November 10, 1975, the freighter *Edmund Fitzgerald* sank in raging gales in Lake Superior; all 29 men aboard were lost. The somber anniversary, commemorated in the Gordon Lightfoot song "The Wreck of the *Edmund Fitzgerald*," is marked each year with a ceremony at Split Rock Lighthouse. If you plan to visit, please dress appropriately, as the weather can be cold and windy; the Minnesota Historical Society recommends bringing a flashlight.

GRAND MARAIS/GRAND PORTAGE/GUNFLINT TRAIL

The farthest-northeast corner of the state, running along the Canadian border through the Boundary Waters, is a nature lover's paradise. The opportunities for kayaking, canoeing, fishing, hunting, bird-watching, hiking, biking, and observing wildlife are countless. Which is not to say there aren't other things to do in the area—but they act as accompaniments to the natural centerpiece.

GETTING AROUND

A car is pretty much a necessity here, and if you're planning on venturing into the Boundary Waters, I strongly recommend that you purchase the Superior National Forest Visitor Map. Published by the USDA in conjunction with Superior National Forest, this is an incredibly detailed map of the BWCAW. It wouldn't hurt to buy a magnifying glass with which to read it. The BWCAW is full of back roads, often barely more than gravel strips, which don't appear on most state maps and which can get you lost unless you're very familiar with the area. The map is available in a sturdy, waterproof plastic version for about $10. Many local gas stations and convenience stores sell it, or contact the **Superior National Forest** headquarters in Duluth (218-626-4300) for information on ordering one. Also be sure to check out *To Do* for some suggested outfitters.

✳ To See

Attractions are open year-round unless otherwise noted.

North House Folk School (218-387-9762; 888-387-9762; www.northhouse.org), MN 61, Grand Marais. North House is a nonprofit organization committed to rekindling interest in and developing abilities of old-style crafts and survival techniques. Over 200 courses are offered each year, some as short as a day, some taking several days. Courses include not only how to cook and bake in an outdoor brick oven, but how to build the oven; constructing kayaks and canoes; building yurts and a facsimile of Thoreau's cabin; knitting, papermaking, jewelry, and ancient Native American techniques for basket weaving.

Grand Marais Art Colony (218-387-2737; 800-385-9585; www.grandmaraisart colony.org), Grand Marais. The city itself is known as an art colony, a quiet seaside-like community with diverse seasons that attracts resident and visiting artists. It's no wonder, then, that the official Grand Marais Art Colony is a popular and active organization. The colony sponsors year-round art classes, art events and competitions, and an annual arts festival (see *Special Events*).

Grand Portage Casino (800-543-1384; www.grandportage.com), Grand Portage. This casino takes the northwoods theme and runs with it, including a northern lights display in the carefully designed ceiling. Open 24/7, the casino has a hotel (see *Lodging*) and offers a shuttle to Thunder Bay, Ontario (US citizens will need passports to cross the border).

Grand Portage National Monument (218-387-2788; www.nps.gov/grpo), 211 Mile Creek Rd., Grand Portage. The stockade is open late May–mid-Oct., daily 9–5. The Grand Portage and Mount Rose Trail are open year-round dawn–dusk. $3 adults, $6 families; children 15 and under are free, as are holders of the Annual, Senior, and Access passes. This monument is really a don't-miss for visitors to the area. An extensive re-creation of the life of traders and Native Americans before there was a United States or Canada, the monument includes a traditional Ojibwe village, a reconstruction of the Northwest Company's stockade (including a great hall and kitchen), a fur trader's canoe under construction, and historic gardens that represent what the original trading villages grew. Kids' programs are offered in summer, and costumed historical guides are available to answer questions. Trails outside the stockade take visitors deep into the northern wilderness, and there are snowshoe trails available during winter. The monument also serves as the departure point for the ferry to Isle Royale, the largest island in Lake Superior (technically part of Michigan).

✳ To Do

From Grand Marais north you'll find an abundance of state parks and wildlife areas. Be sure to check local conditions before visiting—nearly annual droughts have brought severe fire restrictions in parks and campsites in recent years, and some park access is limited during wildfires. Check with individual parks for up-to-the-minute information.

Judge C. R. Magney State Park (218-387-3039; www.dnr.state.mn.us/state _parks/judge_cr_magney/index.html), 4051 E. MN 61, Grand Marais. Open daily Apr. 1–Oct. 31. This park, located between Grand Marais and Grand Portage, is home to the Brule River. The Brule leads to Devil's Kettle, a unique

50-foot waterfall that is rumored to have a bottomless cauldron. Nine miles of hiking trails, including an ascent to Devil's Kettle, are open in-season, as are several fishing sites. Campsites are available; reservations are recommended.

Grand Portage State Park (218-475-2360; www.dnr.state.mn.us/state_parks/ grand_portage/index.html), 9393 E. MN 61, Grand Portage. Open daily. This is the only Minnesota state park operated managed jointly with an Indian tribe. During summer months, naturalists who are also tribe members are on hand to speak about local Ojibwe history. The park boasts Minnesota's highest waterfall, the 120-foot High Falls. Camping is not available, but the falls are easily accessible for day visitors via a 0.5-mile trail and boardwalk.

Gunflint Trail (218-387-3191; 800-338-6932; www.gunflint-trail.com). A 57-mile paved road leading from Grand Marais to Saganaga Lake near the Canadian border, the Gunflint Trail is hands-down one of the most beautiful drives in the region. Acres of forest uninterrupted by more than the occasional café or shop, the Trail also has an extensive collection of lodging options nestled within the trees. Watch your speed as you drive; it's not unusual for a deer, wolf, or even moose to appear on the road, and all of these animals can do as much harm to you and your vehicle as you can do to them. The area has seen a boom in year-round tourism thanks to the increased popularity of winter sports, which join the ranks of favored pastimes such as birding, mountain biking, fall foliage viewing, canoeing and kayaking, camping, fishing, and even mushroom and berry picking.

BWCAW OUTFITTING

Be aware that visitors to the Boundary Waters, except for day-only visitors, need to reserve a permit ahead of time. Your outfitter can do this for you, or you can contact the **Boundary Waters Canoe Area Wilderness Permit Reservation Center** (877-550-6777; www.bwcaw.org).

Boundary Country Trekking (218-388-4487; 800-322-8327; www.boundary country.com), 11 Poplar Creek Dr., Gunflint Trail. Ted and Barbara Young, proprietors of the Poplar Creek Guesthouse (see *Lodging*), offer a variety of adventure arrangements in the Gunflint Trail/Boundary Waters area. They can organize lodge-to-lodge hiking and biking trips, canoe/biking trips, mountain biking, and canoeing trips.

Clearwater Canoe Outfitters & Lodge (218-388-2254; 80-527-0554; www .canoebwca.com), 774 Clearwater Rd., Gunflint Trail. Residing along Clearwater Lake in the Boundary Waters area, Clearwater offers both a lodge (see *Lodging*) and an outfitting company. The proprietors can assist you with canoeing, hiking, fishing, birding, even wildlife photography trips.

Sawbill Canoe Outfitters (218-663-7150; www.sawbill.com), 4620 Sawbill Trail, Tofte. The folks at Sawbill have been arranging BWCAW trips for over 50 years, and they've got keen insight into navigating the wilderness. Sawbill offers full and partial outfitting, canoe touring, even food-only arrangements.

✳ Lodging

Grand Marais

Accommodations are open year-round unless otherwise noted.

❦ ✐ ♿ **Best Western Superior Inn & Suites** (218-387-2240; 800-842-8439; www.bestwestern.com/superior inn), MN 61. A solid choice for mid-price travelers, the Best Western offers high-speed Internet, microwaves, and refrigerators; upgraded rooms have fireplace. There are winter vehicle plug-ins, plus parking for trailers and snowmobiles. Rates start at $79.

❦ ✐ ♿ **East Bay Suites** (218-387-2800; 800-414-2807; www.eastbay suites.com), 21 Wisconsin St. Located right on Lake Superior, close to restaurants and shops, East Bay Suites all have deck or patio overlooking the lake as well as full kitchen, fireplace, washer and dryer, and WiFi. Accommodations vary in size from studio to three-bedroom, with some suites offering bunk beds. Rates start at $149.

✐ ♿ **Cobblestone Cove Villas** (218-387-2633; 800-247-6020; www.cobble stonecovevillas.com), 17 S. Broadway. Located on the harbor in the city of Grand Marais, Cobblestone Cove Villas is a newer townhouse property whose upscale accommodations are within easy walking distance to the shops and restaurants of Grand Marais. Rates start at $149.

✐ **Opel's Lakeside Cabins** (800-950-4361; www.opelslakesidecabins .com), Croftville Rd. Open mid-May–mid-Oct. Opel's has five cabins, all directly on the Lake Superior shoreline. The cabins are rustic but charming, and the views and location are hard to beat. Rates start at $85.

Superior Overlook Bed and Breakfast (218-387-9339; 877-387-9339; www.superioroverlookbb.com), 1620 E. MN 61. Two well-appointed rooms, each with private bath, overlook Lake Superior. A sauna is available for guests. Rates start at $105.

Skara Brae (218-387-2861; 866-467-5272; www.skarabraebb.com), 1708 E. MN 61. This small but charming Scottish-themed bed & breakfast offers, for adults and children ages 12 and up, lovely accommodations in two rooms and a cottage, all with private bath. Breakfast and afternoon tea are available daily, and discounts for North House Folk School students are offered. Rates start at $75.

Gunflint Trail

✐ **Poplar Creek Guesthouse** (800-322-8327; www.littleollielodging.com), 11 Poplar Creek Dr. Tucked into a peaceful wooded area off the Gunflint Trail, the Poplar Creek Guesthouse offers two guest rooms, each with private bath, and a suite. The rooms are graciously appointed, and they share a common room with kitchenette, fireplace, and private deck. The suite has a private kitchen area as well as deck. Hosts Barbara and Ted have run a bed & breakfast in the northwoods for many years, and they know exactly how to do it, especially when it comes to the full breakfast served in the cheerful, welcoming breakfast room. Poplar Creek can arrange a variety of lodge-to-lodge tours (see *To Do*). Also available are two cabins and a year-round yurt (see "Boundary Waters/Ely"). Rates start at $85; packages are available.

❦ ✐ **Moosehorn Lodge** (888-238-5975; www.moosehorn.com), 196 N. Gunflint Lake Rd. Open May–Oct. and Dec.–Mar. Moosehorn is situated on Gunflint Lake. The property offers two lovely bed & breakfast rooms, each with private bath, and four cabins near or on the lake with fireplace, complete kitchen, and deck with barbecue. Rates start at $110.

Pincushion Bed & Breakfast (218-387-1276; 800-542-1226; www.pincushionbb.com), 968 Gunflint Trail. Pincushion is on 43 acres just 3 miles from Grand Marais and, sitting on the Sawtooth Mountain ridgeline, has impressive views and on-site access to hiking trails. This peaceful inn offers four rooms, all with private bath, and a common living area with fireplace. Full breakfast served daily. Rates start at $98.

🐾 **Bearskin Lodge** (218-388-2292; 800-338-4170; www.bearskin.com), 124 E. Bearskin Rd. Located almost 30 miles from Grand Marais on the Gunflint Trail, Bearskin Lodge is a model of peace and retreat. The resort has 11 cabins and two lodges with townhouse accommodations. There's a hot tub and sauna on site, and massage can be arranged. In summer boats, canoes, and pontoons are available, as well as bikes; children's naturalist programs can be arranged. Rates start at $136.

🐾 🛶 **Clearwater Canoe Outfitters & Lodge** (218-388-2254; 800-527-0554; www.canoebwca.com), 774 Clearwater Rd. This lodge has seven cabins, plus a suite and two bed & breakfast rooms in the lodge (breakfast is served daily for lodge guests only). The resort also offers full outfitting and tour services (see *To Do*). Rates start at $80.

🐾 🛶 🍸 **Gunflint Lodge** (218-388-2294; 800-328-3325; www.gunflint.com), 143 S. Gunflint Lake. Gunflint Lodge has 23 cabins of varying ameni-

COMMON AREA AT THE POPLAR CREEK GUESTHOUSE

ties, from the more rustic Canoers Cabins (bunk beds, shared bath in a nearby building) to the Romantic Cottages (lakeview cabins with fireplace, hot tub, and full kitchen) to the Gunflint Lake Home (with two to four bedrooms, fireplace, hot tub, and sauna). A restaurant on site offers an alternative to self-cooking in the cabin, and an extensive list of year-round activities includes winter and summer sports as well as massage. Rates start at $99.

Grand Portage

🛶 ♿ **Naniboujou Lodge** (218-387-2688; www.naniboujou.com), 20 Naniboujou Trail. Open daily mid-May–late Oct.; specific weekends Christmas–Mar. Call for dates. Naniboujou is listed on the National Register of Historic Places, and its colorful history matches its bright interior. Built in the 1920s as a private club for founding members that included Babe Ruth and Jack Dempsey, the club never reached its potential as the country hit the Depression years. Eventually reborn as a hotel and lodge, Naniboujou has a beautifully decorated Great Hall, painted in designs reflective of the Cree Indians. The rooms are tastefully and comfortably set up, and there are no TVs or telephones in order to preserve the sense of getting away from it all. Rates start at $70.

♪ ⟨ ⟩ Υ **Grand Portage Lodge & Casino** (800-543-1384; www.grand portage.com), Located just south of the Canadian border, the Grand Portage Lodge has spacious rooms and friendly staff ready to help with anything you need. The hotel offers an indoor pool and sauna, a full-service restaurant overlooking Lake Superior, and a seasonal (mid-May–mid-Oct.) RV park. Rates start at $85.

✳ Where to Eat

Grand Marais

As befitting a small town with a reputation as an arts colony and an almost seaside ambience, Grand Marais has a good selection of restaurants. All are open year-round unless otherwise noted.

The Pie Place (218-387-1513), 2017 W. MN 61. Open daily for all three meals. This pie shop gives Betty's Pies in Two Harbors serious competition. Flaky crusts with traditional and innovative fillings will leave you wanting more. Entrées start at $5.

My Sister's Place (218-387-1915), MN 61. Open daily in summer, Mon.–Sat. off-season, for lunch and dinner. Not much to look at on the outside, but My Sister's Place has friendly service and solid soups and sandwiches that will satisfy any taste and hunger (including some vegetarian options, such as "The Fungi" mushroom sandwich). Entrées start at $6.

South of the Border (218-387-1505), MN 61. Open daily for breakfast and lunch. Don't be confused by the name—the "border" referred to is the Canadian border, not the US–Mexico border. Instead of Mexican food, you'll find hearty home cooking for breakfast and lunch. Entrées start at $5.

Dockside Fish Market & Deli (218-387-2906; www.docksidefish market.com), 418 W. MN 61. Open Apr.–Dec. daily for lunch and dinner. This retail market also has a deli with a limited but delicious menu, including several varieties of fish caught locally. Entrées start at $7.

The Wild Onion Café (218-387-1191; www.bytheharbor.com/rest .html), in the Harbor Inn. Open daily for all three meals. Hearty breakfasts, salads, soups, sandwiches, and entrées include variations on old favorites, such as the Salmon BLT and the Sol Burger, made with venison and deep-fried pickles. Breakfast entrées start at $6, dinner at $15.

The Crooked Spoon (218-387-2779), 17 W. Wisconsin St. Open daily for lunch and dinner. Contemporary American cuisine, presented as dress-up food in a casual atmosphere. Entrées start at $7.

World's Best Donuts (218-387-1345), 10 E. Wisconsin St. Open mid-May–mid-Oct. daily at 7 AM (the walk-up window opens at 4:30 AM). No matter that the name doesn't seem modest; the doughnuts are truly wonderful. Prices start under $1.

Sven and Ole's (218-387-1713; www
.svenandoles.com), 9 W. Wisconsin
St. Open daily for lunch and dinner.
You can't have a northern Minnesota
experience without the quintessential
Sven and Ole's. Contrary to the
name, this is no bland Scandinavian
fare, but a local pizza haunt with
hearty, flavorful pizzas. The menu
does include an option for a lutefisk
pizza, but unless you have the requi-
site $1 million in cash, better to order
one of the other offerings. Entrées
start at $5.

Angry Trout Café (218-387-1265;
www.angrytroutcafe.com), 416 W.
MN 61. Open May–mid-Oct., daily
for lunch and dinner. The Angry
Trout has indoor and outdoor dining,
with a strong focus on local ingredients and sustainability. Be sure to
check out the artsy bathrooms.
Entrées start at $9.

Chez Jude (218-387-9113; www.chez
jude.com), 411 W. MN 61. Open
May–Oct., Tues.–Sun.; Nov.–Dec.,
Thurs.–Sat. (groups can reserve a special catered event other nights during
Nov. and Dec.); serving lunch, dinner,
and afternoon tea. Chez Jude is small
in size, but big in flavor. Proprietor
Judi Barsness brings an international
flair to her locally inspired menu.
Afternoon tea provides the option of a
traditional British tea, or a North
Shore tea complete with smoked trout
and lingonberry jam. A well-chosen
wine list and good selection of micro-
brews completes the experience.
Entrées start at $12.

Gunflint Trail
Trail's End Café (218-388-2212;
800-346-6625; www.wayofthe
wilderness.com/cafe.htm), 12582
Gunflint Trail. Open mid-May–mid-

Oct. daily for breakfast, lunch, and
dinner. The knotty-pine interior fits
well with the wooded wonderland
outside, and the Trail's End serves
basic but hearty meals, including
burgers, sandwiches, and pizzas.
Entrées start at $5.

Old Northwoods Lodge (218-388-
9464; 800-682-8264; www.oldnorth
woods.com), 7969 Old Northwoods
Loop. Open daily for all three meals.
If you're looking for something
beyond a café, check out the Old
Northwoods Lodge. Seating is at large
wooden tables, under massive wooden
beams and beside a large stone fireplace. Three meals a day are served,
and the options vary from pancakes
and bacon to Mango Walleye and rib-
eye steaks. A wine list is offered.
Entrées start at $12.

❋ **Entertainment**
Grand Marais Playhouse (218-387-
1284; www.arrowheadcenterfort
hearts.org), 51 W. 5th St., Grand
Marais. The playhouse runs local theatrical productions periodically during
the year, primarily the summer and
pre-Christmas seasons.

❋ **Selective Shopping**
Stores are open year-round unless
otherwise noted.
Drury Lane Books (218-387-3370;
888-887-3370; www.drurylanebooks
.com), 12 E. Wisconsin St., Grand
Marais. Open daily. A small shop, but
an excellent book selection for all
your North Shore needs, whether
escapist fiction or local information.
Authors frequently make appearances, and writing workshops are
occasionally offered.

Northern Light Jewelry and Gifts (218-387-2969; www.northernlight -jewelry.com), 8 W. 1st Ave., Grand Marais. Open daily. Northern Light carries jewelry made from local stones and can also custom-design pieces. Gifts and artwork from local artists are available for sale.

Beth's Fudge & Gifts (218-387-2081), 11 S. Broadway, Grand Marais. Open Mon.–Sat. If the doughnuts and pie in Grand Marais haven't satisfied your sweets craving, Beth's Fudge will. Creamy, smooth, and very much a treat.

Lake Superior Trading Post (218-387-2020; www.lstp.com), Grand Marais. Open daily. Part souvenir shop, part outfitter for rural experiences, the Trading Post is staffed with friendly people who know their stock. The log cabin construction gives it a northwoods feel, and Lake Superior is right outside the door.

Gunflint Mercantile (218-387-9228; www.gunflintmercantile.com), 12 1st Ave. W. Open daily. A food store for backpackers and general visitors alike. Come in for the free fudge sample, view the extensive supply of lightweight foods for the trail, and stay for the coffee and soup.

Wilderness Waters (218-387-2525; www.wilderness-waters.com), MN 61, Grand Marais. Open daily. Wilderness Waters is one-stop shopping for outdoor survival gear, from books and maps to clothing and gear. It also provides canoe outfitting services.

❈ Special Events

❦ **Winter Tracks** (218-387-3191; 800-338-6932; www.wintertracks .com), Gunflint Trail. This annual event, taking place in early Mar., is the result of a collaboration by resort and inn owners on the Gunflint Trail. For

DRURY LANE BOOKS

three days there are various activities including scavenger hunts, snow sculpture, sled dog rides, skiing, snowshoeing, sledding, and geocaching.

Grand Marais Arts Festival (218-387-2737; 800-385-9585; www.grand maraisartcolony.com), Grand Marais. An annual juried art show held annually in mid-July.

Crossing Borders Studio Tour (800-388-8698; www.crossingborders studiotour.com). An autumn tour of artist studios along Lake Superior's northern end, including stops in Lutsen, Grand Marais, Grand Portage, and Thunder Bay, Ontario. *Note:* The Western Hemisphere Travel Initiative could require passport identification for land border crossings between the United States and Canada as early as January 2008. Be sure to check the status of the initiative before making travel plans that include crossing the border.

🎣 **Moose Madness** (218-387-2524; 888-922-5000; www.grandmarais .com), Grand Marais. The third weekend in Oct. is the annual statewide teacher's convention, which means kids are out of school, and moose are being sighted in Grand Marais and along the Gunflint Trail. This festival has contests, moose tours, a treasure hunt, and moose essay- and poetry-writing contests.

Doe Camp (888-616-6678; www .americasnorthcoast.org), various locations. Usually the first weekend in Nov., this gives "hunting widows" the option of enjoying a relaxing weekend in the northwoods that's not spent in a hunting stand. The tourism associations for Lutsen-Tofte, Grand Marais, and the Gunflint Trail join forces to present several events that are decidedly nonhunting in nature.

BOUNDARY WATERS

South of Grand Marais, MN 61 connects with MN 1, a brief stretch of highway that moves inland from Lake Superior to Ely, a gateway city into the Boundary Waters. Ely is a tourist town, and one well prepared for the outdoor enthusiasts who flock through the area each year.

GETTING AROUND

A car is pretty much a necessity here, and if you're planning on venturing into the Boundary Waters, I strongly recommended that you purchase the Superior National Forest Visitor Map. Published by the USDA in conjunction with Superior National Forest, this is an incredibly detailed map of the Boundary Waters Canoe Area Wilderness. It wouldn't hurt to buy a magnifying glass with which to read it. The BWCAW is full of back roads, often barely more than gravel strips, which don't appear on most state maps and which can get you lost unless you're very familiar with the area. The map is available in a sturdy, waterproof plastic version for about $10. Many local gas stations and convenience stores sell it, or contact the **Superior National Forest headquarters** in Duluth (218-626-4300) for information on ordering one.

IN THE BOUNDARY WATERS

❊ To See and Do

BOUNDARY WATERS

The Boundary Waters is an amazing natural preserve, encompassing over a million acres of woods and at least 2,500 of Minnesota's famed lakes, teeming with wildlife. It is largely meant to be explored as explorers of old traveled: by canoe, with backpack and tent. While a few areas have opened up to motorized vehicles, the beauty of this area is the peacefulness resulting from the lack of motors, allowing visitors to hear the myriad bird calls, wolf howls, and the sounds of water and wind.

It is possible to day-trip in the Boundary Waters, or least along the edges, by starting from Ely or the Gunflint Trail (see "Grand Marais/Grand Portage/Gunflint Trail"). More ambitious travelers may want to portage in with canoes and set up camp. Experienced canoers and campers can plot their routes, but if you're fairly new to this type of adventure, you might consider working with an outfitter. There are several in the Ely area, listed in *To Do*.

Be aware that visitors to the Boundary Waters, except for day-only visitors, need to reserve a permit ahead of time. Your outfitter can do this for you, or you can contact the **Boundary Waters Canoe Area Wilderness Permit Reservation Center** (877-550-6777; www.bwcaw.org). Camping permits are required to limit the number of entrances each day into the BWCAW—an effort made to keep the wilderness, well, wild.

ELY

❊ To See

Attractions are open year-round unless otherwise noted.

⚓ **Dorothy Molter Museum** (218-365-4451; www.rootbeerlady.com), MN 169, Ely. Memorial Day–Labor Day, open Mon.–Sat. 10–5:30, Sun. noon–5:30. May and Sept., open Sat. 10–5:30, Sun. noon–5:30. Tours are $5 adults, $3 ages 6–12; free for children under 6. This is a loving tribute to the last living person in the Boundary Waters. Dorothy Molter lived a great deal of her adult life in a cabin in the BWCAW, and even when the US government evicted other tenants when declaring the area a wilderness, she was granted lifetime tenancy. During her many years in her rustic cabin, she brewed homemade root beer for boaters and fishers coming through her area, earning the nickname "the root beer lady." After her death, her log cabin was painstakingly disassembled, reassembled on

DOROTHY MOLTER MUSEUM

the eastern edge of Ely, and turned into a museum. The cabin is crammed full of Dorothy's things, and the adjacent gift shop sells books about her as well as cases of root beer (worth the purchase). The only downside is the noise of traffic from nearby MN 169, which can make visitors (this one, at least) wonder why they couldn't have sited the museum just a bit farther down the road to recapture something more similar to the peace of nature Molter enjoyed.

✔ ✦ **The International Wolf Center** (218-365-4695; www.wolf.org), 1396 MN 169, Ely. Open May 15–June 14, daily 10–4; June 15–Labor Day, daily 10–6; Labor Day–Oct. 14, Wed.–Sun. 10–4; Oct. 15–May 14, Sat.–Sun. 10–4. Open additional hours for the Minnesota Education Association school break in Oct. and the Ely Winter Festival in Feb.; check the Web site for specific dates. $7.50 adults, $6.50 seniors, $4 ages 3–12; children under 3 are free. The International Wolf Center is an internationally renowned center for wolf education and infor- mation. It tries to address public fears and concerns about wolf behaviors through press relations and through public visits. The center has hands-on exhibits and Wolf Cams, allowing visitors to watch wolves from a great distance; it also coordinates Learning Vacations, which bring visitors into the wilderness to meet "ambassador" wolves.

✔ ✦ **North American Bear Center** (218-365-7879; www.bear.org), 1926 MN 169. Open May–Labor Day, daily 9–6, Sat. until 8. $8.50 adults and teens, $7 seniors, $4.50 ages 3–12; children under 3 and members free. One mile west of Ely is this center, similar in intent to the International Wolf Center. Visitors can learn more about bears through videos and exhibits, then watch the bears in their 2-acre habitat from a viewing deck.

✒ **Soudan Underground Mine** (218-753-2245; www.dnr.state.mn.us/state _parks/soudan_underground_mine/index-html), MN 169, Soudan. Open May–Sept., daily 9:30–5:30; Oct., Sat.–Sun. 9:30–5:30. Tour admission $10 adults, $6 ages 5–12; children under 5 free. The Soudan Mine gives visitors insight into the daily life of miners in this once operational mine. Adventurous tourists can take the tour, which carries them 27 stories beneath the ground. (*Note:* Extensive walking is required, some of it through confined areas.) Those who don't wish to go below can wander the grounds for free. The scenery from the hillside mine is breathtaking, particularly during fall foliage season.

✒ **Wintergreen Dogsled Lodge** (218-365-6022; 800-584-9425; www.dogsled ding.com), 1101 Ring Rock Rd., Ely. With nearly 30 years of dogsled adventures under their belt, the proprietors of the Wintergreen Dogsled Lodge know a thing or two about taking visitors on a dogsled trip, whether it's first-timers or seasoned sledders. Trips can be arranged with stays at the lodge itself, just east of Ely, as lodge-to-lodge treks, or as camping excursions. Multiple-night or one-day-only trips are available. Special opportunities include parent–daughter trips and photography workshops.

✳ To Do

The following Ely-based outfitting companies offer full-service arrangements, including canoe and kayak rental and sales, permits, camping reservations, and guided tours.

✒ **River Point Outfitting Company** (800-456-5580; www.elyoutfitters .com), 12007 River Point Rd.

SOUDAN UNDERGROUND MINE

✒ **Piragis Northwoods Company** (218-365-6745; 800-223-6565; www .piragis.com), 105 N. Central Ave.

✒ **Wilderness Outfitters** (218-365-3211; 800-777-8572; www.wilderness outfitters.com), 1 E. Camp St.

✒ **Echo Trail Outfitters** (218-365-3156; 888-811-3156; www.echotrail outfitters.com), 3811 Fenske Lake Rd.

✒ **Moose Track Adventures** (218-365-4106; 800-777-7091; www.moose trackadventures.com), 593 Kawishiwi Trail.

✒ **Boundary Waters Canoe Adventures** (218-365-2129; 800-510-2947; www.boundarywaterscanoetrips.com), 3060 Echo Trail.

✒ **North Country Canoe Outfitters** (218-365-5581; 800-552-5581; www .boundarywaters.com), 474 Kawishiwi Trail.

⏴ **Spirit of the Wilderness Outfitters** (218-365-3149; 800-950-2709; www.ely canoetrips.com), 2030 E. Sheridan St.

✳ Lodging

Not surprisingly, the Boundary Waters area is surrounded by countless places to stay, everything from rustic mom-and-pop resorts to more elaborate, deluxe accommodations. What follows is a sample of recommended places, which also represents the diverse offerings available. Accommodations are open year-round unless noted otherwise.

🐾 ⏴ ⚐ ❦ **Grand Ely Lodge** (218-365-6565; 800-365-5070; www.grand elylodge.com), 400 N. Pioneer Rd., Ely. Just outside the city of Ely is this resort—the largest in Ely with 61 rooms and suites. The resort is very family-friendly, with kids under 10 staying and eating free with paid adult. There's an indoor pool and sauna, and lake activities are provided at the marina on Shagawa Lake. The Evergreen Restaurant is open all day; there's also a lounge. Mountain bikes are available to guests who want to use the Trezona Trail across the street, which connects to the International Wolf Center. Rates start at $90.

🐾 ⏴ **Adventure Inn** (218-365-3140; www.adventureinn-ely.com), 1145 E. Sheridan St., Ely. Right in the heart of downtown Ely, this small but charming motel has economy and standard/deluxe rooms that are clean and comfortable; several boast hand-made quilts. Rates start at $49.

🐾 ⏴ **Timber Trail Lodge** (218-365-4879; 800-777-7348; www.timber trail.com), 629 Kawishiwi Trail, Ely. Timber Trail has 15 cabins ranging from one to six bedrooms as well as four motel units with kitchenette. The resort can arrange boat rentals and guides; massage is offered on site, and once-weekly floatplane rides are offered to guests. Rates start at $69.

🐾 **Blue Heron Bed & Breakfast** (218-365-4720; www.blueheronbnb .com), 827 Kawishiwi Trail, Ely. Five beautifully decorated rooms, some with exposed log walls, make up this charming bed & breakfast. Rooms come with private bath, lake views, full breakfast, use of canoes or snowshoes, and use of the sauna. Rates start at $129.

🐾 ⏴ **Tall Pines Yurt** (800-322-8327; www.littleollielodging.com), 11 Poplar Creek Dr., Boundary Waters. For a true wilderness experience, the Tall Pines Yurt is open year-round for summer or winter adventures. Four guests can sleep on bunk beds or a futon, although additional bedding can be provided for more. A fully equipped kitchen is included; an outhouse is steps away, as is a traditional Finnish sauna. Rates start at $69.

⏴ **Log Cabin Hideaways** (218-365-6045; www.logcabinhideaways.com), 1321 N. CR 21, Ely. For those truly wanting the wilderness experience, Log Cabin Hideaways provides hand-hewn log cabins on the edge of the BWCAW. Each cabin comes with a canoe, but no electricity or indoor plumbing. Propane is provided for cooking; most units have a Finnish sauna. Some of the cabins are accessible by water only. But none of the cabins has "neighbors"; each is on its own secluded site. Rates start at $90.

Burntside Lodge (218-365-3894; www.burntside.com), 2755 Burntside Lodge Rd., Ely. Open mid-May–late Sept. West of Ely on Burntside Lake, Burntside Lodge has been offering gracious hospitality to guests for nearly a century, and it's arguably one of Minnesota's most famous accommodations. The resort offers several cabins in varying sizes, all tucked into the woods or near the lake; the peaceful ambience is assisted by the lack of TVs or telephones. The lodge itself is on the National Register of Historic Places, and its dining room (open daily for dinner during the season, weekends only for breakfast) serves delicious food in a large, open room. The adjoining gift shop has several items of local interest. Rates start at $135.

FRONT PORCH OF THE BURNTSIDE LODGE

Fortune Bay Resort Casino (800-555-1714; www.fortunebay.com), 1430 Bois Forte Rd., Tower. Seemingly in the middle of nowhere, this newer resort and casino is on Lake Vermilion and offers attractive rooms and suites, an indoor pool, a dining room, a 24-hour casino, and a golf course. An on-site marina has fishing boats, pontoons, canoes, and paddle boats available for rent, or you can bring your own boat and dock it at the marina. Rates start at $79; packages are available.

Where to Eat

Ely

Restaurants are open year-round unless otherwise noted.

Sir G's (218-365-3688), 520 E. Sheridan St. Open daily for lunch and dinner. Italian food, including pasta made on-site. Entrées start at $7.

The Chocolate Moose (218-365-6343), 101 N. Central Ave. Open summer only, daily for all three meals. A popular cabinlike restaurant serving casual lunch and dinner daily during the summer. Entrées start at $7.

Journey's End Café and Smokehouse (218-365-3398; www.elysmokehouse.com), 528 E. Sheridan St. Open daily for lunch and dinner. Be prepared for a wait, but it's worth it at this small café offering meat smoked on-site. Entrées start at $10.

Front Porch Coffee and Tea (218-365-2326; www.frontporchcoffeeandtea.com), 343 E. Sheridan St. Open daily for breakfast and lunch. A cozy, inviting coffeehouse with a limited but tasty menu of soups and pastries. Free WiFi with purchase. Food starts at $2.

THE CHOCOLATE MOOSE

Ely Steak House (218-365-7412), 216 E. Sheridan St. Open daily for dinner. Steak house and bar with fresh fish specials, prime rib on weekends, and steak whenever you like. Entrées start at $14.

✳ Selective Shopping

Ely has several blocks of shops, with a good variety of merchandise, from regular tourist things like shirts and mugs to specialty items, including art and model train supplies. Shops are open year-round unless otherwise noted.

Brandenburg Gallery (877-493-8017; www.jimbrandenburg.com), 11 E. Sheridan St. Open daily. The gallery showcases the award-winning nature photography of Jim Brandenburg, who has traveled the world for *National Geographic* and has a special love for the Boundary Waters area (he makes it his home part of the year).

Wintergreen Designs (218-365-6602; www.wintergreennorthern wear.com), 205 E. Sheridan S. Open daily. Specializing in high-quality and attractive outdoor apparel, Wintergreen produces its work in Ely and sells it at this local retail store (another store is open in Duluth).

Piragis Northwoods Company (218-365-6745; 800-223-6565; www.piragis .com), 105 N. Central Ave. Open daily. This large outfitting shop sells and/or rents all manner of outdoor gear, including canoes and camping gear. Piragis offers guided canoeing and camping trips in the BWCAW.

Lisa's Second-Floor Bookstore (218-365-6745), 105 N. Central Ave. Open daily. On the second floor of Piragis is this bookstore, accessibly only by going through Piragis. A small but congenial gathering space for book lovers, the shop has a solid selection of both fiction and local resource books.

SANTA'S NORTH POLE, ELY

Chapman Street Market (218-365-6466; www.chapmanstreetmarket .com), 141 E. Chapman St. Open Mon.–Sat. An upscale gourmet food shop providing artisan breads, imported cheeses, specialty meats, and a variety of deli items.

Steger Mukluks & Moccasins (800-685-5857; www.mukluks.com), 100 Miners Dr. Open daily. Inspired by Native American designs, these mukluks and moccasins are made in Ely from moosehide and are highly regarded for their comfort and winter protection.

Upper Lands (218-365-2156; www .greatnorthcoast.com), 22 W. Sheridan St. Open Tues.–Sat. A gift shop

including cards, jewelry, candles, and home and garden items.

Santa's North Pole (218-365-2063), 134 E. Sheridan St. Open Mon.–Sat. This whimsical shop is less about Christmas—unless you're a model train enthusiast—and more about finding the perfect additions to your model train collection.

✳ Special Events

🛶 **Ely Winter Festival** (www.ely winterfestival.com), Ely. It's never too cold for a festival, as this annual mid-winter event shows. Snow-sculpting lessons and contests, Nordic ski racing, the Mukluk Ball, snowshoe tours, snowmobile races, and musical concerts are all part of the fun during the 10-day event.

Blueberry Art Festival (218-365-6123; 800-777-7281), Ely. Annual three-day arts fair held in late July.

🛶 ♿ **Harvest Moon Festival** (218-365-6123; 800-777-7281), Ely. This annual Sept. festival includes three days of art and craft exhibits, children's activities, live musical performances, and food.

INTERNATIONAL FALLS/ VOYAGEURS NATIONAL PARK

✳ To See

Attractions are open year-round unless otherwise noted.

🛶 ♿ **Koochiching County Historical Museum/Bronko Nagurski Museum** (218-283-4316; http://bronkonagurski.com/museum.htm), 214 6th Ave., International Falls. Open Mon.–Fri. 9–5. Admission of $2 adults, $1 students gains entrance to both museums. Two museums share one building, each focused on history specific to the region. Bronko Nagurski is a local legend, a farm boy who became one of the best professional football players in the sport's history. His side of the museum details not only his life and sports career, but also the impact of the times (Depression, World War II) on his life and those of others. The County Historical Museum features a well-rounded collection of artifacts reflecting the area's history with Native Americans and French voyageurs, as well as its relationship to Canada. Museum volunteers and staff are well versed in the collections and can answer questions and offer insightful tales.

Boise Cascade Paper Mill (218-285-5011), 2nd St. June–Aug., Mon.–Fri. No admission fee. Children under 10 not allowed; cameras prohibited. Boise Cascade, one of the world's largest papermaking companies, offers both mill and woodland tours. Call ahead for reservations—these tours are very popular.

✳ To Do

Not surprisingly, this area is full of activities in the great outdoors, some more rustic than others.

Waters of the Dancing Sky (www.watersofthedancingsky.org), MN 11. Named for the northern lights, this stretch of highway travels over 190 miles from the North Dakota border into Voyageurs National Park. It covers a full range of northern Minnesota scenery: rivers, lakes, prairies, farmland, and a host of small towns. *Note:* The western edge of the byway is completed when MN 11 connects with US 59, then MN 175.

Falls Country Club (218-283-4491; www.fallscc.com), 4402 CR 152. Designed by Joel Goldstrand, the Falls Country Club golf course is a challenging and beautiful course, and it's open to the public.

Rainy Lake/Rainy River (www.rainylake.org). Rainy Lake, which stretches north into Canada, has some of the best fishing in the state, particularly for walleye, and there are many resorts and houseboats offering accommodations and fishing guides (see *Lodging*). Rainy River connects Rainy Lake with Lake of the Woods to the west; its 80 miles of river provide not only excellent fishing opportunities (walleye, smallmouth bass) but great canoeing and kayaking trips as well.

✳ Lodging

Accommodations open year-round unless otherwise noted.

International Falls

Within International Falls itself are several small motels or budget hotels, such as the Days Inn and Super 8 on US 53. Most accommodations that provide more of the "northern" experience are on the outskirts, or along MN 11 east to Voyageurs National Park.

✺ ⅄ **Holiday Inn** (218-283-8000; 800-331-4443; www.hiifalls.com), 1500 US 71. A well-appointed hotel within International Falls, the Holiday Inn also has an indoor pool, restaurant, and even a garden walk down to the river, where guests can fish. Rates start at $89.

✺ **Camp Idlewood** (218-286-5551; www.campidlewood.com), 3033 CR 20, International Falls. Camp Idlewood has nine cabins with knotty-pine interior and full kitchen; the resort itself has a beach, canoe, and paddle boat, with inner tubes and towropes available at no fee. Boats and motors

Voyageurs National Park (218-283-6600; www.nps.gov/voya), 3131 US 53, International Falls. Centuries ago, French traders paddled these waters on their way to Canada, looking to trade animal pelts and goods with the Natives. Today Voyageurs National Park is a haven for those who love to be on the water, whether by canoe, kayak, or houseboat. Hikers, snowshoers, and cross-country skiers travel the grounds year-round. A series of connected lakes and bays, as well as miles of untouched forest, provide an intimate northwoods experience. Wildlife is abundant.

There are three visitor centers. The **Rainy Lake Visitor Center** (218-286-5258) is the primary source and the only one open year-round. Located 10 miles east of International Falls, the Rainy Lake Center is open late May–Sept., daily 9–5; Oct.–Memorial Day, Wed.–Sun. 10–4. The **Kabetogama Lake Visitor Center** (218-875-2111) and the **Ash River Visitor Center** (218-374-3221) are both open late May–Sept. only.

There are campgrounds available on a first-come, first-served basis (groups can reserve ahead of time with one of the visitor centers), but note that the campgrounds within the park are accessible only by boat. A free permit is required for camping, which can be obtained at the visitor centers or at self-permit stations within the park. If you're interested in camping, but would rather be able to drive up to your campsite, look into reserving a site at the **Woodenfrog State Campground** (218-365-7229), CR 122, Ray. Located in Kabetogama State Forest, part of Voyageurs National Park, Woodenfrog has campsites available mid-May–mid-Sept. that don't require boat access.

LAKE KABETOGOMA

can be rented, or you can bring your own; each cabin has one dock space included, and additional spaces can be rented. Weekly rates start at $665.

⚓ **Bear Ridge Guest House** (218-286-5710; www.bearridgeguesthouse.com), 210 4th Ave., International Falls. Offering just two accommodation choices, the Bear Ridge Guest House is nevertheless a great choice for visitors to Rainy Lake. Located on a hill overlooking the lake, with a private deck to enjoy the view, Bear Ridge has a guest house suite with separate bedroom, full kitchen, and fireplace; a separate guest room has its own bath and living area. Rates start at $110.

🐾 ⚓ ℠ **Island View Lodge and Cabins** (218-286-3511; 800-777-7856; www.rainy-lake.com), 1817 MN 11 E., International Falls. Actually located 12 miles east of International Falls, Island View sits on the edge of Rainy Lake with gorgeous views and direct lake access. There are 15 cabins available, as well as several lodge rooms. An adjacent spa has a hot tub and sauna, and the lodge has a dining room and lounge. Rates start at $90.

⚓ ℠ **Woody's Rainy Lake Resort** (218-286-5001; 866-410-5001; http://fairlyreliable.com), 3481 Main St., Ranier. Woody's offers seven cabins with full kitchen, all near or on Rainy Lake. The lodge has a pub with pizza and beer, and is the headquarters for Woody's Fairly Reliable Guide Service. The tongue-in-cheek name reflects the jovial nature of Woody's resort, but is an understatement in terms of service; Woody's staff know Rainy Lake, and they can help with summer and winter fishing needs. Weekly rates start at $795.

⚓ ℠ **Rainy Lake Inn & Suites at**

Tara's Wharf (218-286-5699; 877-724-6955; www.taraswharf.com), 2065 Spruce St. Landing, Ranier. Near Woody's, the Rainy Lake Inn offers four suite accommodations in a charming "seaside" setting. The ice cream shop will keep everyone happy. Rates start at $95.

Voyageurs National Park

⚓ ℠ **Kettle Falls Hotel** (218-240-1724; www.kettlefallshotel.com), 10502 Gamma Rd. Open early May–early Oct. While I have not visited this hotel personally, it's enough of a legend that it can't be ignored. Located on an odd geographic twist that allows you to stand in Minnesota and look south to Canada, this hotel is the only lodging within Voyageurs National Park, and it's accessible solely by plane or boat. Nearly a century old, Kettle Falls Hotel has a rich history that includes bootleggers selling whiskey during Prohibition. Today the hotel has 12 rooms with shared baths, a full-service restaurant, and a saloon that still bears the marks of wilder early years. Rates start at $50.

Lake Kabetogama

🐾 ⚓ **Voyageur Park Lodge** (218-875-2131; 800-331-5694; www.voyageurparklodge.com), 10436 Waltz Rd., Kabetogama. Ten cottages along Lake Kabetogama, along with a lodge suite, offer guests peaceful privacy. Full kitchen, barbecue grill, and campfire site are included with each cabin (campfires only when conditions allow). Use of canoes, kayaks, and paddle boats is free; fishing boats, pontoons, and motors can be rented on-site. Rates start at $145.

🐾 ⚓ **Herseth's Tomahawk Resort** (218-875-2352; 888-834-7899; www.geocities.com/~lherseth), 10078

HOUSEBOATS

An alternative to hotels and resorts is the houseboat experience. Rainy Lake has two companies that offer several houseboats for rental.

Northernaire Houseboats (800-854-7958; www.northernairehouseboats .com), 2690 CR 94, International Falls. Open May–Sept. Northernaire offers 10 houseboats of varying sizes and levels of amenities, including some with an open deck and some with a screened-in. Rentals include a tow-behind boat, free delivery on the lake twice weekly (for groceries and the like), and a guide service for the first 4 miles to orient you to the maps and buoy systems. Order ahead and your boat's kitchen will be stocked with the foods and beverages of your choice. Rates start at $235.

Rainy Lake Houseboats (218-286-5391; 800-554-9188; www.rainylake houseboats.com), 2031 Town Road 488, International Falls. Open mid-May– mid-Oct. Rainy Lake has several fully equipped houseboats with kitchen, a tow-behind boat, swim platforms and waterslides, and deck table and chairs. Guide service is available with prearrangement, and groceries can be ordered ahead as well. Rates start at $235.

Gappa Rd., Ray. Herseth's offers eight cabins and one mobile home. The resort has a large sand beach with free canoes and paddle boats. Motorized boats are available for rent. The proprietor is a certified scuba diver and is happy to arrange diving excursions into Lake Kabetogama. Rates start at $123.

Moosehorn Resort (218-875-3491; 800-777-7968; www.moose hornresort.com), 10434 Waltz Rd., Kabetogama. Moosehorn has nine cabins stretched along Lake Kabetogama with a sandy beach. This is an especially family-friendly resort, located in a quiet bay that keeps the lake waters calmer than in other spots. Canoes, kid-sized kayaks, and a playground area are included for guests. Boats are available for rent. Weekly rates start at $665.

Kec's Kove Resort (218-875-2841; 800-777-8405; www.fishand game.com/kecs), 10428 Gamma Rd., Kabetogama. Kec's has eight cabins and a lodge with whirlpool and sauna. A massage therapist is available for guests, and motorized boats can be rented. If you go fishing and need some help afterward, Kec's can provide fish cleaning and freezing services. Paddle boats, canoes, and kayaks are complimentary. Weekly rates start at $675.

Northern Lights Resort, Outfitting, and Youth Quest (612-805-9646; 800-318-7023; www.nlro.com), 12723 Northern Lights Rd., Kabetogama. With 10 cabins along Lake Kabetogama, Northern Lights has a number of planned activities for all interest levels: Guides can be arranged for fishing or other expeditions; a Ladies' Pontoon Cruise is offered weekly, with coffee and muffins; an adults social cruise is also offered weekly in the evening; and the Youth Quest program is offered for kids ages 5–17, with planned events including kayaking, canoeing, tomahawk-throwing training, and island cookouts. Younger kids are separated from the older kids, and activities are age-appropriate. Weekly rates start at $475.

✳ Where to Eat

Restaurants are open year-round unless otherwise noted.

✎ **Giovanni's** (218-283-2600; www.giosifalls.com), 301 3rd Ave., International Falls. Open daily for lunch and dinner. A cheerful, family-friendly American Italian restaurant with pizza, pasta, pierogi, and burgers. A buffet is available, as is an arcade area for kids. Entrées start at $6.

Coffee Landing (218-283-8316; www.coffeelanding.com), 444 3rd St., International Falls. Open daily. This full-service coffee, espresso, and tea shop also offers a limited but tasty food menu including breakfast items, pastries, and quiche. Entrées start at $4.

19th Hole Restaurant and Lounge (218-286-3364), Crystal Beach, International Falls. Open daily for dinner. 19th Hole revisits the supper-club concept with a large watering-hole decor and hearty entrées starting at $14.

Rose Garden Restaurant (218-283-4551), 311 4th Ave., International Falls. Open daily for lunch and dinner. Classic Chinese American food, large portions at reasonable prices. Entrées start at $6.

Chocolate Moose Restaurant Company (218-283-8888), US 53 S., International Falls. Open daily for all three meals. The Chocolate Moose serves up platter-sized portions of pancakes, burgers, pasta, and dinner entrées including steak and shrimp. Entrées start at $7.

Woody's Pub (218-286-5001; 855-410-5001; http://fairlyreliable.com), 3481 Main St., Ranier. Pizza, wine, and beer on the shores of Rainy Lake. Nice days are meant for enjoying the outdoor patio. Entrées start at $6.

Grandma's Pantry (218-286-5584), 2079 Spruce St., Ranier. Open for breakfast, lunch, and early dinner Mon.–Fri., breakfast-only on Sat. Breakfast is the specialty, and it's served all day in gigantic portions, but the homemade sandwiches, soups, and dinners are tasty, too. Entrées start at $5.

✳ Selective Shopping

Shops are open year-round unless otherwise noted.

Border Bob's (218-283-4414), 200 2nd Ave., International Falls. Open daily Memorial Day–Labor Day. The quintessential souvenir shop, with local goods such as maple syrup,

WOODY'S PUB

commemorative Minnesota/Canada items, T-shirts, and other tourist goods. Also a great place to stop for ice cream.

Pine Ridge Gift Shop (218-875-3313; www.pineridgegiftshop.com), 9903 Gamma Rd., Lake Kabetogama. Open daily May–Sept. Pine Ridge is housed in a log cabin on Gamma Road, near CR 122. Located near a cluster of resorts on Lake Kabetogama, the shop is easy to find, and its merchandise runs the gamut from touristy to collectible. Local arts, crafts, quilts, cabin amenities, Christmas decorations, candles, locally produced foods (including their own roasted coffee), and clothing make up the bulk of this shop, staffed by cheerful locals who know the area well.

✷ Special Events

✎ **Blast on the Border** (218-283-9400; 800-325-5766; www.intlfalls .org), International Falls. Formerly known as Ice Box Days, this annual festival includes such winter fun as frozen turkey bowling, smoosh races (four people on two skis), a human sled dog race, snowshoe races, a talent contest, and the Freeze Yer Gizzard Blizzard Run. Occurs in late Feb.

Birders Spring Rendezvous (218-286-5258; www.nps.gov/voya), Voyageurs National Park. Held the first weekend in June, the Birders Spring Rendezvous is a series of events and activities designed to help beginning and expert birders discover what can be seen in Voyageurs National Park. Theme walks, canoeing, a cruise along Kettle Falls, expert speakers, and of course plenty of birdwatching are offered.

Paddle Fest (218-283-6670; www .nps.gov/voya), Voyageurs National Park. An end-of-summer celebration in late Aug., Paddle Fest offers a variety of canoe and pontoon boat adventures through the lakes of Voyageurs National Park. Many events are free, but reservations are required and often fill up in advance.

BORDER BOB'S IN INTERNATIONAL FALLS

✳ To See

Attractions are open year-round unless otherwise noted.

🖉 ♿ **Ironworld** (218-254-7959; 800-372-6437; www.ironworld.com), 801 SW US 169, Chisholm. Open Tues.–Sun. 10–5, until 9 on Thurs. $8 adults, $7 seniors, $6 ages 7–17; free for children 6 and under, and free for everyone on Thurs. after 5 PM. Despite its rather grim name, Ironworld is a wonderful stop for visitors to the Iron Range. The grounds themselves are beautiful (and frequently used for weddings and receptions). An indoor museum details the Iron Range's extensive history and hosts traveling exhibits, while a trolley takes visitors to the Glen Location—a former mining town where people can explore the historic buildings. Heritage Park includes a series of re-created pioneer homes. In summer visitors can opt to add a guided bus tour to Hibbing Taconite, a working open-pit mine, for an additional $5 per person (Wed.–Thurs. only).

🖉 ♿ **Greyhound Bus Museum** (218-263-5814; www.greyhoundbus museum.org), 1201 Greyhound Blvd., Hibbing. Open mid-May–Sept., Mon.–Sat. 9–5, Sun. 1–5; by request for groups in the off-season. $5 adults, $4 seniors, $2 students, $1 ages 6–12; free for under those 6; $10 for families, and $3 per person for tour groups. Documents the development of the US bus industry from its days as a single vehicle in Hibbing to the current national route.

🖉 ♿ **US Hockey Hall of Fame** (800-443-7825; www.ushockeyhall .com), 801 Hat Trick Ave., Eveleth. Open Memorial Day–Labor Day, Mon.–Sat. 9–5, Sun. 10–3; Labor Day–Memorial Day, Sat.–Sun. 9–5. $8 adults, $7 seniors and students ages 13–17, $6 ages 6–12; under 6 free. A must-see for hockey fans, the Hall of Fame includes memorabilia not just from local hockey teams— and the Iron Range tends to have a lot of local hockey fans—but from national events, including the 1980 "Miracle on Ice" Olympic team and the 1998 women's gold-medal Olympic team.

🖉 **Finnish Heritage Homestead Tours** (218-984-2084), MN 135 and CR 21, Embarrass. A three-hour

IRONWORLD

guided tour to the small town of Embarrass illustrates the Finnish part of Minnesota's history. Handcrafted log structures, antique farm and weaving machinery, and a gift shop are all part of the tour.

✇ **Bob Dylan's Childhood Home,** 2425 Dylan Dr., Hibbing. While it's not open for tours, fans of Bob Dylan can drive by the childhood home on the renamed street.

✇ ♿ **Paulucci Space Theatre** (218-262-6720; www.spacetheatre.mnscu.edu), 1502 E. 23rd St., Hibbing. A 3-D IMAX screen shows films about space and planets.

✇ ♿ **Forest History Center** (218-327-4482; 888-727-8386; www.mnhs.org), 2609 CR 76, Grand Rapids. Open Memorial Day–mid-Oct., Mon.–Sat. 10–5, Sun. noon–5. Mid-Oct.–Memorial Day, weekdays (except for holidays) 8–4:30. Cross-country ski trails open daily. $5 adults, $4 seniors, $3 ages 6–15; free for children under 6. $12 maximum per household. The Forest History Center has a visitor center and a re-created turn-of-the-20th-century logging camp with costumed characters for guides. Visitors can board a floating cook shack, climb a 100-foot fire tower, and crawl through a decayed log while learning about Minnesota's logging history. A trail system takes visitors through the forest and along the Mississippi River.

✇ ♿ **The Judy Garland Museum** (800-664-5839; www.judygarlandmuseum .com), 2727 US 169 S., Grand Rapids. Open Mon.–Sat. 10–5, Sun. noon–5; closed New Year's Day, Easter Sunday, Thanksgiving, and Christmas Day. Admission is $6 for all, which includes the Children's Discovery Museum (see below). Judy Garland was born in Minnesota in 1922 and spent her first four years here. The home she lived in has been moved from its original street to a location on US 169, a busy highway across from Home Depot, which detracts slightly from its charm. The house has been lovingly restored with considerable attention to detail, and the curators have procured a wide variety of artifacts, including the carriage Dorothy rode in upon her arrival at Oz. The museum did have a pair of ruby slippers, but those were stolen in 2005, and it's clearly a theft that the community still grieves.

✇ ♿ **Children's Discovery Museum** (218-326-1900; 866-236-5437; www.cdm kids.org), 2727 US 169 S., Grand Rapids. Open Mon.–Sat. 10–5, Sun. noon–5; closed New Year's Day, Easter Sunday, Thanksgiving, and Christmas Day. Admission is $6 and includes the Judy Garland Museum (see above). This hands-on children's museum includes a kid-sized town, a river forest with talking tree (but a friendlier tree than the ones encountered by Dorothy on her way to Oz), a "Dino Dig," and an art room.

✳ To Do

✇ **Wellstone Memorial and Historic Site** (651-645-3939; www .wellstone.org), US 53 and Bodas Rd., Eveleth. A wooded 5-acre site is the memorial to Minnesota senator Paul Wellstone and the other travelers who died when their plane crashed near this site in 2002. Trails are lined with boulders naming the victims and interpretive signs explaining Wellstone's work and legacy.

ᶜ **Hill Annex Mine State Park**
(218-247-7215; www.dnr.state.mn.us/
state_parks/hill_annex_mine/index
.html), US 169, Calumet. Open daily
9–5. This area was mined for 65
years, ending in 1978, and can now be
explored during summer months by
taking one of three guided tours
offered daily Fri., Sat., Sun., and holidays: a mine tour, a boat tour, and a
fossil hunt.

ᶜ **Mineview in the Sky** (218-741-
2717), US 53, Virginia. Open
May–Sept., daily 9–6. No admission,
but donations are welcome. An overlook of the Rouchleau Group of
mines, with an observation deck originally used by site foremen to observe
the mine's operation in an open pit
almost 3 miles long and 450 feet deep.

THE HOME WHERE JUDY GARLAND WAS
BORN

✳ Lodging

Accommodations are open year-round
unless otherwise noted.

ᶜ ৬ **Americinn Lodge & Suites**
(218-741-7839; 888-741-7839;
www.americinn.com), 5480 Mountain
Iron Dr., Virginia. The Americinn
chain is a solid, reliable choice with
hotel rooms and suites (some with
fireplace), an indoor pool, and daily
continental breakfast. Rates start at
$95.

ᶜ **Chisholm Inn & Suites** (218-254-
2000; 877-255-3156; www.chisholm
inn.com), 501 Iron Dr., Chisholm.
Similar to the Americinn, the
Chisholm Inn offers hotel rooms and
suites, and breakfast is included for
guests. Larger rooms have whirlpool
bath. The hotel also has an indoor
pool and sauna. Rooms start at $89.

ᶜ ৬ ⍦ **Coates Plaza Hotel** (218-
749-1000; www.coatesplazahotel
.com), 502 Chestnut St., Virginia.

Located in downtown Virginia, the
rooms at the Coates Plaza all overlook
the indoor pool area, which includes a
whirlpool and sauna. The hotel's
restaurant, Chestnut on 5th (see
Where to Eat), serves three meals a
day in a semiformal environment, and
the Hob Nob Club provides full bar
service. Rates start at $59.

ᶜ ৬ **Hibbing Park Hotel** (800-262-
3481; www.hibbingparkhotel.com),
1402 E. Howard St., Hibbing. One of
Hibbing's nicest hotels, the Hibbing
Park has 120 rooms and suites, as well
as an indoor pool. The hotel was
recently renovated, and the rooms
have been updated. The hotel's
restaurant, Grandma's in the Park (see
Where to Eat), is similar to the
Duluth-area Grandma's. Rates start at
$89.

Mitchell-Tappan House (218-262-
3862; 888-662-3862; www.mitchell

-tappanhouse.com), 2125 4th Ave. E., Hibbing. Built in 1897 for a mine superintendent, the Mitchell-Tappan House was moved, as many Hibbing houses were, in the early 1920s when it was discovered that ore ran right underneath. Today this bed & breakfast has five rooms, four with shared bath, plus cozy common areas. Full breakfast is included. Rates start at $70.

✳ Where to Eat

Restaurants are open year-round unless otherwise noted.

✍ よ ﹗ **Grandma's in the Park** (800-262-3481; www.hibbingparkhotel .com), 1402 E. Howard St. Open daily for lunch and dinner. While not a direct branch of the Duluth Grandma's restaurants, this dining spot, in the Hibbing Park Hotel, is related and has a similar menu, complete with ribs, pasta, steak, and fish. Entrées start at $11.

よ ﹗ **Chestnut on 5th** (218-749-1314; www.coatesplazahotel.com/restaurant), 502 Chestnut St., Virginia. Open daily for all three meals. Steak, ribs, and pasta are served in generous portions. Entrées start at $14.

✍ よ **A&W Drive In** (218-229-2240), 103 Main St. S., Aurora. Open mid-May–mid-Sept., weather permitting. An honest-to-goodness drive-in restaurant, where you receive your burgers and fries in your car and eat on the spot. Be sure to order a big frosty mug of root beer. Entrées start at $4.

✍ よ **K&B Drive In** (218-744-2772; www.kandbdrivein.com), US 53 and Cedar Island Dr., Eveleth. Open daily for lunch and dinner. K&B ups the ante by having a drive-in open year-

round. Besides the typical drive-in fare of burgers and hot dogs, K&B also has gyros and pasties. Entrées start at $4.

✍ よ ﹗ **Zimmy's Bar & Restaurant** (218-262-6145; 866-305-3849; www .zimmys.com), 531 E. Howard St., Hibbing. Open daily for lunch and dinner. Located in a historic building that has seen many incarnations in Hibbing, Zimmy's other claim to fame is its extensive collection of Bob Dylan memorabilia. The lunch and dinner menus are peppered with Dylan references, while the food is hearty American-style: burgers, ribs, sandwiches, steaks, and pasta. A gift shop sells Dylan-related clothing and items. Entrées start at $11.

✍ よ ﹗ **The Old Howard Saloon & Eatery** (218-262-1031; www.theold howard.com), 413 E. Howard St., Hibbing. Open daily for lunch and dinner; open Sun. at 8 AM for brunch. The Howard is housed in a building that's had an operating restaurant for more than 80 years. The current decor, with Tiffany lamps and a brass-railed, marble-topped bar, pays homage to its Victorian beginnings. Steaks are the major entrée here, but chicken, pork, fish, and pastas are also served. Entrées start at $7.

✍ よ ﹗ **Adventures** (218-741-7151; www.adventuresrestaurants.com), 5475 Mountain Iron Dr., Virginia. Open daily for lunch and dinner; Sat.–Sun. for breakfast. Themed for northwoods exploration, Adventures breaks its menu into sections for "Tenderfoots," "Light Hiker," and "Less Adventurous." Burgers, sandwiches, salads, and pasta are typical entrées; walleye sandwiches and wild rice meat loaf are great choices. Entrées start at $9.

♫ & ▽ **Grandma's Saloon & Grill** (218-749-1960; www.grandmas restaurants.com), 1302 12th Ave. S., Virginia. Open daily for lunch and dinner. A member of the Duluth Grandma's Restaurants family, this branch, like its Duluth siblings, provides reliable grill food and a sturdy drink menu. Entrées start at $11.

✳ Special Events

♫ & **Laskianen Finnish Sliding Festival** (218-638-2551; www.iron range.org), Aurora. The first weekend of Feb. brings this annual celebration of ethnic—particularly Finnish—traditions. The three-day event includes a ball, sleigh and carriage rides, theater, special dinners, and of course sliding.

Dylan Days (218-262-6145; 866-305-3849; www.dylandays.com), Hibbing. This Iron Range city celebrates its musical hero with the annual Dylan Days, taking place each year in May, around the time of Dylan's birth date (May 24). Special events include dinners, a Dylan Days Bus Tour of historic Dylan sites, and live musical concerts (but don't expect Dylan himself).

♫ & **Land of the Loon Festival** (218-749-5555; www.landoftheloon festival.com), Virginia. Taking place annually the third weekend of June, Land of the Loon bills itself as an Ethnic Arts and Crafts Festival. The two-day festival offers a parade, over 300 vendors, live music, and a kids' area with a petting zoo and face painting. A variety of ethnic foods (German, Finnish, Mexican, Greek, and Cuban, among others) is for sale.

♫ & **Judy Garland Festival** (800-664-5839; www.judygarlandmuseum .com), Grand Rapids. The Judy Garland Museum (see *To See*) sponsors this annual festival in late June, after Garland's birth date (June 10). It's a popular event, attracting visitors from around the country, so plan ahead if you'd like to attend. The festival includes speakers on Judy Garland, informal sing-alongs, screenings of *The Wizard of Oz*, a gala dinner and fund-raiser, a collector's exchange, a seminar on the dangers of drug use, and occasional visits from the actors who portrayed some of the Munchkins.

♫ & **Chisholm Fire Days** (218-254-7930; www.chisholmchamber.com), Chisholm. Ten days of festival fun beginning after Labor Day. Events include special dinners, tournaments of the sports and games types, a parade, a Kid's Day, and a craft fair.

Northern Lakes/ Red River Valley

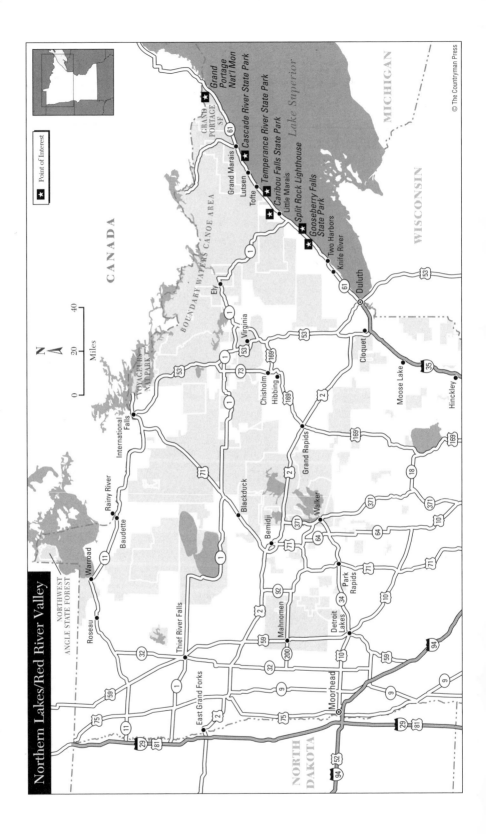

Northern Lakes/Red River Valley

★ Point of Interest

CANADA

Lake Superior

MICHIGAN

WISCONSIN

NORTH DAKOTA

N

0 20 40
Miles

NORTHWEST
ANGLE STATE FOREST

BOUNDARY WATERS CANOE AREA

VOYAGEURS NAT'L PARK

Grand Portage Nat'l Mon
GRAND PORTAGE SF
Cascade River State Park
Temperance River State Park
Grand Marais
Lutsen
Tofte
Caribou Falls State Park
Little Marais
Split Rock Lighthouse
Gooseberry Falls State Park
Two Harbors
Knife River

Ely

Virginia

Chisholm
Hibbing

Duluth

Cloquet

Moose Lake

Hinckley

Grand Rapids

Walker

Blackduck

Bemidji

International Falls

Rainy River

Baudette

Warroad

Roseau

Thief River Falls

Mahnomen

Park Rapids

Detroit Lakes

East Grand Forks

Moorhead

61

61

1

1

1

1

53

53

53

73

169

169

169

169

2

2

2

2

71

71

71

71

71

53

53

35

18

10

371

371

64

64

92

34

200

59

59

59

9

9

9

10

10

32

32

75

75

29

29

81

81

11

11

11

94

94

52

© The Countryman Press

NORTHERN LAKES/RED RIVER VALLEY

The northern lakes region and the Red River Valley provide visitors with a range of geological vistas. The lakes area is made up of rolling and heavily forested land, while the valley, contradictory to its name, is flat agricultural plains, where you can drive for miles and see nothing but sunflowers, corn, and soybean crops. This is a region shaped by former glacial lakes and settled by Chippewa Indians, followed by French traders and eventually Scandinavians, looking for fertile farmland.

The lakes that punctuate the region are known for excellent fishing and boating. The fishing season has grown in popularity thanks to better winter technology; today many northern lakes are dotted by buildings ranging from little more than shacks to larger, heated structures (with attached portable toilets) known as "sleepers," but all are considered ice houses to be used for winter fishing. Ice fishing and other winter sports such as cross-country skiing, snowmobiling, and snowshoeing have made the northern region a year-round destination rather than a summer-only spot.

Rivers, as well as lakes, play an important role here. The Mississippi River has its starting point here in Itasca State Park, where the headwaters—first accurately identified by explorer Henry Schoolcraft in 1832—can be crossed easily by foot, giving no sign of turning into the Mighty Mississippi. The Red River on the northwestern side of the state is not the most scenic of rivers, but the flatlands surrounding it are an agricultural center for the state.

The plains give way to the lake-heavy region around Detroit Lakes, bodies of water carved by the glaciers that moved through centuries ago. Now the region is a popular tourist destination for lake lovers. Tourism plays a major role in this area's economy, and the annual WE Fest has become one of the nation's largest country music festivals, attracting 50,000 people each year.

GUIDANCE

Leech Lake Chamber of Commerce (218-547-1313; 800-833-1118; www .leech-lake.com), 205 Minnesota Ave. W., Walker.

Park Rapids Chamber of Commerce (218-732-4111; 800-247-0054; www .parkrapids.com), US 71 S., Park Rapids.

Visit Bemidji (800-458-2223, ext. 105; http://visitbemidji.com). An online and phone-based tourism affiliate for the Bemidji area.

Lake of the Woods Tourism Bureau (218-634-1174; 800-382-3474; www .lakeofthewoodsmn.com), MN 11, Baudette. Open daily in summer, Mon.–Fri. the rest of the year. Tourism information for the general Lake of the Woods area that runs along the Canadian border, including Baudette, Warroad, and the Northwest Angle.

Roseau Tourism Bureau (800-815-1824; www.city.roseau.mn.us). Information on lodging and events in the Roseau area.

Riverland Tourism Association (800-827-1629; www.visitthiefriverfalls.com), 2017 US 59 SE, Thief River Falls. A tourist board for all things Thief River Falls.

Moorhead Travel Information Center (218-236-2720), eastbound I-94, 1 mile east of US 75. Provides information for visitors to the twin city of Fargo, North Dakota.

Detroit Lakes Regional Chamber of Commerce (800-542-3992; www.visit detroitlakes.com). Serves as the central tourist information center for the Greater Detroit Lakes area.

GETTING THERE

By car: Park Rapids is served by MN 34 and US 71. MN 34 ends at MN 200 in Walker; MN 200 and MN 371 are the primary routes through Walker. MN 371 ends at US 2, while MN 200 merges with US 71, both of which are the major highways through Bemidji. Follow US 71 north to MN 72 in order to head north to Baudette; from Baudette, MN 11 is the major road crossing west to Warroad and Roseau. The primary highway to East Grand Forks is US 2; to Moorhead (and Fargo, North Dakota), I-94 is the major freeway, while US 10 also serves Moorhead, as well as Detroit Lakes.

The Northwest Angle, a ridge of land bordering Canada, is the northernmost part of the contiguous United States, and it can be accessed by car through Canada (with proper U.S. identification), or by seaplane or boat. **Lake of the Woods Passenger Service** (218-556-9444; 800-862-8602) can arrange transportation across the water.

THREE ISLAND COUNTY PARK, NORTH OF BEMIDJI

By rail: Amtrak's Empire Builder route offers rail service between Minneapolis–St. Paul and Fargo-Moorhead.

By air: Regional commercial airlines, primarily Northwest and its Mesaba branch, serve the cities of Bemidji, Thief River Falls, and Fargo (across the river from Moorhead). Taxis and rental cars are available from the airports into the city.

GETTING AROUND

Having a vehicle is a necessity when traveling around the northern lakes region.

WHEN TO COME

The summer months see an influx of tourists who come to enjoy the multitude of lakes and beaches. Still, summer isn't the only popular time, especially for fishing enthusiasts who cast their lines in open water in summer and through holes in the ice in winter. Hunters and winter sports aficionados appreciate the fall and winter seasons as well.

MEDICAL EMERGENCY

Call **911**.

St. Joseph's Hospital (218-732-3311; 800-556-3311; www.sjahs.org), 600 Pleasant Ave. S., Park Rapids.

North Country Health Services (218-751-5430; www.nchs.com), 1300 Anne St. NW, Bemidji.

Roseau Area Hospital and Homes (218-463-2500; www.rahhinc.com), 715 Delmore Dr., Roseau.

Northwest Medical Center Hospital (218-681-4240; www.nwmc.org), 120 LaBree Ave., Thief River Falls.

MeritCare Hospital (701-234-2000; www.meritcare.com), 801 Broadway N., Fargo, ND.

St. Mary's Regional Health System (218-847-5611; www.smrhc.com), 1027 Washington Ave., Detroit Lakes.

PARK RAPIDS/WALKER

✳ To See

Attractions are open year-round unless otherwise noted.

& ⅋ **Northern Lights Casino and Hotel** (800-252-7529; www.northern lightscasino.com), 6800 Y Frontage Rd. NW, Walker. Open daily. Slots, poker, and blackjack are open 24/7. Two restaurants and a snack bar are in the casino, while the attached hotel has an indoor pool and sauna and extensive arcade.

⅋ **Forestedge Winery** (218-224-3535; www.forestedgewinery.com), 35295 MN 64, LaPorte. Open Mother's Day–Dec., Tues.–Sun. Northwest of Walker is this

winery, which produces wines from hardy northern crops including chokecherries, blueberries, raspberries, and plums. Forestedge's rhubarb wine has won several awards. Stop by for a sample, and enjoy the beautiful gardens. Tables are available if you'd like to enjoy a bottle right on the spot.

✿ **Northland Bison Ranch** (218-652-3582; 877-453-9499; www.northlandbison .com), 22376 Glacial Ridge Trail, Nevis. Open mid-June–Labor Day. Tour prices are $7.50 adults, $5 kids. This working bison ranch offers guided tours by appointment in summer. See the bison in their habitat and learn their history.

✳ To Do

Heartland Trail (www.dnr.state.mn.us/state_trails/heartland/index-html), Park Rapids. This 49-mile trail uses old railroad grades to create a multiuse trail system. The trail is paved and can be used by hikers, bicyclists, and bladers (but be aware that the terrain is very steep in some areas and rough in others); an adjacent grass trail can be used by horseback riders and mountain bikers. Snowmobile enthusiasts will find the trail is groomed all winter long.

Leech Lake (www.leechlake.org). North of the popular Brainerd Lakes area is Leech Lake, a favored fishing spot surrounded by forests and opportunities for year-round outdoor activities. Hundreds of resorts flank the lake (see *Lodging* for some examples), and boaters, anglers (both summer and winter), skiers, snowmobilers, and hunters have all contributed to the growth of this area as a four-season destination.

✳ Lodging

Accommodations are open year-round unless otherwise noted.

❀ ✐ ♿ **Breezy Point Resort** (218-573-3125; 800-939-2630; www.breezy point.com), 54852 MN 34, Osage. Breezy Point has nine log cabins with knotty-pine interiors, spacious and comfortable. A mobile home farther away from the lake is the 10th accommodation. The resort offers boat and motor rentals, and guided fishing trips can be arranged. There's a sandy beach with a variety of "beach toys" included in the rates: paddle boats, hydro-bikes, and kayaks. Pets accepted in the off-season. Rates start at $78.

Red Bridge Inn (218-237-7337; 888-733-7241; www.redbridgeinn.com), 118 Washington Ave. N., Park Rapids. A bed & breakfast offering seven rooms, some with private patio or deck. Located on Fish Hook Lake, the inn has a dock and offers direct water access. Rates start at $145.

Heartland Trail Bed and Breakfast (218-732-3252; www.heartland bb.com), Dorset. The Restaurant Capital of the World (see *Where to Eat*) is also home to this charming bed & breakfast, a renovated 1920s community school building. The inn has five spacious guest rooms, all with private bath and fireplace; full breakfast is served daily. Located on the Heartland Trail. Rates start at $80.

✐ ♿ **Crow Wing Crest Lodge** (218-652-3111; 800-279-2754; www.crow wing.com), 31159 CR 23, Akeley. Open mid-May–Oct. Nineteen cabins on a pristine lake. Cabins vary from rustic to upscale. The resort prides itself on its environmental stance: The proprietors recycle lake water, use no pesticides or herbicides, and use only all-natural cleaning products. They also take a holistic approach to vacations, and reflexology, aromatherapy, massage, and yoga are available. Kids' activities are offered daily in summer—that is, if they aren't entertained enough on the sandy beach with the beach toys, paddle boats, and kayaks; or on the playground; or on the fishing dock. Rates start at $76.

✐ **Brindley's Harbor Resort** (888-547-5477; www.brindleysharbor.com), 9530 Pine Point Rd. NW, Walker. A quiet resort on Leech Lake with 15 cottages, a lake home, and three luxury log cabins. A huge sandy beach has four piers for fishing as well as a boat slip and marina. Canoes, kayaks, sailboats, bikes, and hammocks are all included in rental rates; the staff will clean and freeze your catch of fish. Boats and ice houses are available for guest rental. Rates start at $100.

✳ Where to Eat

Restaurants are open year-round unless otherwise noted.

✐ ♿ ♟ **The Velvet Antler** (218-652-3623; www.velvetantler2.com), 24025 MN 34, Nevis. Open daily for lunch and dinner, Sat.–Sun. for breakfast. This northwoods-themed restaurant serves supper-club dinners in a log cabin environment. Steaks, prime rib, duck, and an extensive collection of soups are on the menu. The adjacent Whitetail Tavern has a full bar, daily drink specials, and live music on weekends. Entrées start at $9.

✐ **MinneSoda Fountain** (218-732-3240), 205 S. Main, Park Rapids. The MinneSoda falls in the category of "don't miss." This 17-stool confectionary has seen over 80 years of service in the heart of this small town. Leave the calorie counter at home. Treats start at $3.

⚓ ♿ � **Goose Crossing Food and Spirits** (218-732-2700; www.goose crossing.com), 17789 MN 34 E., Park Rapids. Open daily for dinner in summer; Thurs.–Sat. for dinner the rest of the year. This cozy restaurant provides a fireplace for winter warmth and a unique copper tree in the center of the dining room, as well as goose sculptures outside. A standard menu includes the usual supper-club items, such as steak and prime rib; an "Up North Favorites" menu has beef tips over rice, and chicken-fried pork or steak (either is highly recommended). Entrées start at $11.

♿ � **The Boulders** (218-547-1006; www.thebouldersrestaurant.com), 8363 Lake Land Trail NW, Walker. Open daily for dinner. An upscale restaurant with a casual atmosphere,

---

DORSET—RESTAURANT CAPITAL OF THE WORLD

This tiny burg has, tongue firmly in cheek, billed itself as the Restaurant Capital of the World. Certainly it's hard to believe any other town has as many restaurants per capita: With just 26 residents, Dorset has 4 restaurants, one for every 6.5 villagers. (This is also a town that elected a local five-year-old as its mayor for the 2007–08 term.) What's more surprising is that while the restaurants may not be profiled in *Food & Wine* anytime soon, they are worthy of a visit if you're in the neighborhood (east of Park Rapids on CR 18, north of MN 34). Just follow the boardwalk down the main street (or take a detour from the Heartland Trail if you're out hiking or biking), and you'll find a good meal somewhere.

⚓ ♿ ♲ **LaPasta Italian Eatery** (218-732-0275; www.dorset-lapasta.com/ lapasta.htm). Open daily June–Aug. for all three meals; May and Sept., Sat.–Sun. for all three meals. Breakfast includes the standard pancakes and omelets, along with stuffed French toast and potato pancakes; lunch offers a few pasta items plus burgers and sandwiches; dinner is a changing roster of Italian foods. Entrées start at $5.

⚓ ♿ ♲ **Dorset Café** (218-732-4072). Open year-round Mon.–Fri. for dinner, Sat.–Sun. for lunch and dinner. This dinner-only café serves steaks and seafood and has a full bar.

⚓ ♿ ♲ **Dorset House Restaurant and Soda Fountain** (218-732-5556). Open in summer, daily for lunch and dinner. Choose from the buffet or from a pizza and burger menu; homemade pies and, of course, ice cream for dessert. Entrées start at $4.

⚓ ♿ ♲ **Companeros** (218-732-7624; www.companerosofdorset.com). Open June–Aug. daily for lunch and dinner; May and Sept., open Thurs.–Sun. for dinner, Sun. for brunch. Americanized Mexican food served in cheerful abundance. Entrées start at $8.

the Boulders offers steak, salmon, lamb chops, even paella, which is beautifully prepared and served. A good special-occasion choice. Entrées start at $14.

♂ ♿ ☙ Lucky Moose Bar and Grill (218-547-3295; www.luckymoose bargrill.com), 441 Walker Bay Blvd., Walker. Open daily for lunch and dinner. A casual bar and grill housed in a log building. Entrées start at $9.

♿ ☙ Ranch House Supper Club (218-547-1540), 9420 371 NW, Walker. Open daily for dinner. An old-fashioned supper club with steaks and prime rib, plus all-you-can-eat specials each night. Entrées start at $12.

✳ Entertainment

Long Lake Theater (218-732-0099; www.longlaketheater.net), CR 6, Hubbard. Open selected Wed.–Sat., June–Sept. This summer-stock theater offers four or five productions each year, along with holiday presentations of *A Christmas Carol*.

Northern Light Opera Company (218-237-0400; www.northernlight opera.org), 11700 Island Lake Dr., Park Rapids. Productions on occasion; check the Web site for a schedule. The name of this company is a play on words; the *light* refers to "light opera" more than "northern lights." This grassroots organization has diligently been putting together productions, primarily of Gilbert and Sullivan, since 2001. Its success is demonstrated by its growth and its branching out, including performances of *Oklahoma* and *Amahl and the Night Visitors.*

♂ Jaspers Jubilee Theater (218-237-4333; www.jasperstheater.com), MN 34, Park Rapids. Open

June–Aug., Thurs. and Sat. $18 adults, $17 seniors, $9 ages 4–16; free for those under 4 if sitting on an adult's lap. A lively family-friendly live show incorporating music, magic, juggling, yodeling, dancing, and comedy skits.

♂ Woodtick Musical Theater (218-652-4200; 800-644-6892; www.wood ticktheater.com), MN 34, Akeley. Open Wed.–Sat., mid-June–mid-Sept.. $14.50 adults, $13.50 seniors, $9.50 ages 13–17, $6.50 ages 6–12; under 6 free. Billing its show as similar to those in Branson, Missouri, the Woodtick Theater offers a musical variety production each summer that's appropriate for all ages. The music encompasses country, folk, bluegrass, and gospel, and is accompanied by comedy.

✳ Special Events

Eelpout Festival (218-547-1313; www.eelpoutfestival.com), Walker. Admission is $10. Held mid-Feb. each year, the Eelpout Festival, besides having one of the odder names for a state festival, is a good-natured celebration of winter and the joys of ice fishing. Events during the three-day event include, of course, ice fishing, as well as a 5K run, an ice-house decorating contest, on-ice auto and snowmobile races, rugby on ice, and the Polar Plunge, an opportunity to raise money for the local community center by collecting pledges and agreeing to jump in the lake—in Feb.

Moondance Jam (877-666-6526; www.moondancejam.com), Walker. Ticket prices for the four-day festival start at $90 for the basic ticket and $350 for a VIP ticket. The latter includes special seating, a VIP tent with free beer, pop, and water, discounted cocktails, occasional meet and greets with some of the bands, dinner and hors d'oeuvres daily, and preferential parking. Tickets go on sale nearly a year in advance, and the closer to festival date, the more they cost. Campsites should be reserved ahead of time. The classic rock version of WE Fest (see "Detroit Lakes"), this four-day event held in early July draws thousands of people from across the country to hear live concerts by the likes of Def Leppard, Kansas, Alice Cooper, and REO Speedwagon. Children are not pro-hibited, but organizers note that this is an event intended for adults and may not be appropriate for kids. A country music version of this event was launched in 2007; information can be found at www.jammincountry.com.

Leech Lake Regatta (218-547-1819; www.shoresofleechlake.com/regatta), 6166 Moriss Point Rd., Walker. Race participation is $80; additional fees apply for boat mooring. This early-Aug. event is a multiclass sailboat race for those of all skill levels. Many sailors opt to spend several days after the race on the water.

BEMIDJI AREA

✷ To See

Attractions are open year-round unless otherwise noted.

🐾 ♿ **Bemidji Art Walk** (218-759-0164; 800-458-2223, ext. 105). Open daily. Stop at the lakefront tourist information center to begin your tour of sculptures and murals that appear lakeside and into downtown.

🐾 ♿ **Beltrami County History Center** (218-444-3376; www.beltramihistory.org), 130 Minnesota Ave. SW. Open Mon.–Sat. $5 adults, $4 seniors and children under 12; free for Historical Society members. The History Center resides in the restored 1912 Great Northern Railway Depot, which was the last depot built by railroad baron James J. Hill. The building's architecture itself is worth a visit, but the collection within is entertaining and enlightening, from Native American artifacts to a restored telegraph office. A separate research area offers historians access to archival materials.

🐾 ♿ **Headwaters Science Center** (218-444-4472; www.hscbemidji.org), 413 Beltrami Ave. Open daily. Admission is $4 for visitors 12 and older, $3 for kids under 12, $20 maximum per household; free with HSC membership. Essentially a children's science museum, the HSC offers a variety of hands-on activities as well as a collection of live animals (snakes, turtles, salamanders) for kids to learn about and handle.

🐾 ♿ **Concordia Language Villages** (218-586-8600; 800-450-2214; http://clvweb.cord.edu/prweb), 8607 Thorsonveien NE. This renowned language school, headquartered in Moorhead, holds the majority of its classes and camps at an expansive site just outside Bemidji. The languages (including French, German, Spanish, Korean, Russian, Norwegian, and Swedish) are taught in villages created to resemble a town in the country of origin. Most are centered near Turtle Lake, but a few are about 10 miles north. Each village is separate from the others; programs are offered for kids and adults. Even if you're not planning on learning a foreign language, the beautiful sightseeing and loving re-creations of international villages make this worth a stop.

EXHIBIT AT THE BELTRAMI COUNTY HISTORY CENTER

✂ & **Bemidji Community Art Center** (218-444-7570; http://bcac.word press.com), 426 Bemidji Ave. Open Tues.–Sat. Located in the historic Carnegie Library building on the lakeshore, which is listed on the National Register of Historic Places. Inside are three galleries that display national and regional artists, as well as hosting live music and poetry readings. New exhibits appear monthly from Feb.–Dec. The center also sponsors a series of First Fridays, which showcase art and live performances both in the building and around Bemidji.

✂ & **Paul Bunyan and Babe the Blue Ox**. Lakefront, near the tourist information center. Daily. A visit to Bemidji isn't quite complete without a photo opportunity near the statues of the legendary Paul Bunyan and his faithful ox. Besides, it's a good starting point for the Bemidji Art Walk.

AT THE HEADWATERS SCIENCE CENTER

THE CONCORDIA GERMAN VILLAGE

✳ To Do

Chippewa National Forest (218-335-8600; www.fs.fed.us/r9/forests/chippewa), 200 Ash Ave. NW, Cass Lake. With over 666,000 acres, Chippewa National Forest has ample opportunity for outdoor adventures. The forest has 160 miles of hiking trails and cross-country ski trails, 330 miles of snowmobiling trails, 23 developed campgrounds and 380 camping sites, and a sandy swimming beach. Three visitor centers have programs and information: Norway Beach, Cut Foot Sioux, and Edge of the Wilderness Discovery Center. For water fans, the forest holds two of Minnesota's five biggest lakes, and there are nine canoe routes across various rivers and Leech Lake. *Note:* Some of these routes are more treacherous than others; when planning a canoe trip, check with the Chippewa National Forest for recommendations based on your skill level.

Itasca State Park/Mississippi Headwaters (218-266-2100; www.dnr.state.mn.us/state_parks/Itasca/index.html), 36750 Main Park Dr., Park Rapids. Open daily. This is Minnesota's oldest state park, and it's also well known as the starting point of the Mississippi, where you easily walk across the river. But Itasca State Park has several other spots to visit, including an Indian cemetery and Wegmann's Cabin, a pioneer artifact. Pines inhabit the Wilderness Sanctuary, a 2,000-acre stand of white and red pines, some upward of 300 years old. The Bohall Wilderness Trail guides you through the pines and onto an overlook at Bohall Lake. Plan ahead if you'd like to stay at Douglas Lodge (see *Lodging*), located right within the park.

Lake Bemidji State Park (218-755-3843; www.dnr.state.mn.us/state_parks/lake_bemidji/index.html), 3401 State Park Rd. NE, Bemidji. Open daily 8–4:30.

BUENA VISTA RANCH

It may not have the Mississippi headwaters, but Lake Bemidji State Park is a worthy stop with acres of forest, access to Lake Bemidji for boating and fishing, a paved bike trail, and scores for birds for watching.

Buena Vista Ski Village (218-243-2231; 800-777-7958; www.bvskiarea.com), 19276 Lake Julia Dr. NW, Bemidji. Open for winter sports mid-Nov.–Mar., depending on the weather. The mountains may not be the highest, but Buena Vista has beautiful scenery to enjoy with its 16 runs.

Cross-country skiing, tubing, snowboarding, and horse-drawn sleigh rides are all offered while there's snow. See below for summer activities.

Buena Vista Ranch (218-243-2231; 800-777-7958; www.bvskiarea.com/ranch), 19276 Lake Julia Dr. NW, Bemidji. The winter ski resort becomes a logging village and visitor center during summer months. Activities include covered wagon tours, horsemanship training clinics, and fall foliage rides. Reservations are recommended; call for information.

Big Bog State Recreation Area (218-647-8592; www.dnr.state.mn.us/state _parks/big_bog/index-html), 55716 MN 72 NE, Waskish. Open daily. Opened in 2005, this recreation area provides a way for visitors to explore the ecology of a bog without overly disturbing it. A mile-long boardwalk allows you to go deep into the natural area without damaging the plant life. Signs posted frequently along the way explain the significance of the bog and point out different aspects of plants and wildlife that you can see from the walk.

✳ Lodging

Accommodations are open year-round unless otherwise noted.

🎣 ♿ ☗ **Hampton Inn** (218-751-3600; 800-426-7866; www.hamptoninn .com), 1019 Paul Bunyan Dr. S., Bemidji. The Hampton Inn is right on Lake Bemidji, a short walk from the tourist information center and the beginning of the Art Walk. Full breakfast is included in the rates, and all rooms have high-speed Internet access. The hotel also has a Green Mill pizza restaurant (see *Where to Eat*) for lunch and dinner. Rates start at $103.

🎣 ♿ **Americinn Motel & Suites** (218-751-3000; 800-396-5007; www .americinn.com), 1200 Paul Bunyan Dr. NW, Bemidji. Near the Paul Bunyan Mall, the Americinn offers 59 units, 26 of which are suites. The property has an indoor pool, whirlpool, and sauna, and the rates include continental breakfast. Rooms start at $75.

🎣 ♿ **Holiday Inn Express** (218-751-2487; www.ichotelsgroup.com), 2422 Ridgeway Ave. NW, Bemidji. A basic but comfortable Holiday Inn. Most

AT THE BIG BOG

rooms have two queen beds, while a few upgraded rooms have king beds and Jacuzzi bath. The Holiday Inn is near the Paul Bunyan Mall. Rates from $86.

🐾 ♿ ⅋ **Northern Inn Hotel & Suites** (218-444-9500; 800-667-8485; www.bemidjinortherninn.com), US 2 W., Bemidji. This hotel, close to the Bemidji airport, has an indoor pool with poolside and pool-view rooms. There are also four Presidential Suites with separate living area and Jacuzzi bath. Breakfast is included in the rates; a restaurant, **Gangelhoff's**, is open only for dinner June–Sept., while a lounge with comedy club is open Sept.–May. Rates start at $75.

🐾 🐾 ♿ ⅋ **Ruttger's Birchmont Lodge** (218-444-3463; 888-788-8437; www.ruttger.com), 7598 Bemidji Rd. NE, Bemidji. A family resort that's something of a tradition on Lake Bemidji, Ruttger's offers both lodge and cabin accommodations. The Cedar Lodge has the most luxurious suites, with lakefront setting and fireplace, while the Main Lodge offers the more economical rooms. Cedar Lodge is open year-round; the Main Lodge, only in summer. In addition, there are 22 cottages (mostly open only mid-May–Labor Day) and seven villas (larger than the cottages), which are open year-round. The resort has a restaurant and bar open in summer. You'll also find an indoor pool and hot tub, open all year, and boat and bike rentals during summer. A large sandy beach makes for a great summer resting spot, and in summer Ruttger's offers a supervised kids' program for ages 4–12. Rates start at $37.

Villa Calma Bed and Breakfast (218-444-5554; www.villacalma.com), 915 Lake Blvd. NE, Bemidji. This bed & breakfast, located near Lake Bemidji, offers four rooms, two with private bath and two that share. All rooms have upgraded bed coverings and bathrobes, and full breakfast is included, as is an early-evening glass of wine. A common great room serves as the breakfast point, with lovely views of the lake, and the backyard has a fire pit and double hammock for guest relaxation. Villa Calma is on the Paul Bunyan Trail, a 17-mile paved trail open to bikers and in-line skaters. Rates start at $79; packages are available.

🐾 **Douglas Lodge** (866-857-2757; www.stayatmnparks.com), Itasca State Park. This lodge was built in 1905 with timber from Itasca State Park and houses five guest rooms, a dining room, and a lounge. There is also a Club House which has rooms available, as well as several cabins. Campgrounds can be reserved, too. Rates start at $69.

❋ Where to Eat

Bemidji has been growing thanks to the university and the local health care system, but its restaurant scene has not quite kept pace. There are plenty of chains to choose from, including Applebee's, Ground Round, Perkins, Country Kitchen, Bonanza, McDonald's, Burger King, Pizza Hut, Subway, and Quiznos. But there are also some restaurants that don't carry a major chain behind them and offer good dining options. The following choices are open year-round unless otherwise noted.

🐾 ♿ ⅋ **Peppercorn's** (218-759-2794; www.peppercornrestaurant.com), 1813 Paul Bunyan Dr. Open daily for lunch and dinner. A steak house with friendly staff and generous portions.

Peppercorn's emphasis is on steak, ribs, and seafood. Mon.–Thurs. nights is a rotating all-you-can-eat selection, varying from crab legs to chicken and ribs. The food is good and the service is quick. Entrées start at $10.

✐ ⌖ **Raphael's Bakery Café** (218-759-2015; www.gr8buns.com), 319 Bemidji Ave. Open Mon.–Sat. for breakfast and lunch. The quintessential small-town bakery and café, Raphael's serves delicious breakfasts and lunches and sells baked goods to go. The menu may be limited (salads, sandwiches, soups), but the baked goods are pleasingly fresh, and the soups are homemade and worth buying extra for takeout. Entrées start at $4.

✐ ⌖ ♆ **Brigid's Cross** (218-444-0567; www.brigidsirishpub.com), 317 Beltrami Ave. Open daily for lunch and dinner. A cheerful Irish pub with the usual suspects (fish-and-chips, ploughman's platter, shepherd's pie) and the not-so-Irish variations (macaroni-and-cheese bites, mini burger basket). The food is hearty, a full bar is available, and a variety of events is offered, from open mike to trivia contests to live music. Entrées start at $7.

✐ ⌖ ♆ **Keg & Cork** (218-444-7600), 310 Beltrami Ave. NW. Open daily for lunch and dinner. A friendly neighborhood bar and grill. The locals love it, so you know it's good. Entrées start at $7.

✐ ♆ **Dave's Pizza** (218-751-3225), 422 W. 15th St. Not much to look at, but Dave's has been filling pizza lovers' needs for decades. Entrées start at $7.

✐ ⌖ ♆ **Green Mill Pizza** (218-444-1875; www.greenmill.com), 1025 Paul Bunyan Dr. S. Open daily for lunch and dinner. Yes, it's a chain, but it's also got a prime location at the Hampton Inn with great views of Lake Bemidji. Plus, the pizza is excellent. Entrées start at $6.

✻ **Entertainment**

Paul Bunyan Playhouse (218-751-7270; www.paulbunyanplayhouse .com), 314 Beltrami Ave. With over 55 years of productions, this is one of the country's longest continuously operating summer-stock theaters. The Paul Bunyan Playhouse uses both national professional actors and locals for its summer season. Veterans of the playhouse have gone on to professional theater careers in the Twin Cities.

✐ **Paul Bunyan Amusement Park**, on the lakeshore. Open daily Memorial Day–Labor Day, 10 AM–dusk, weather permitting. Rides for small children and old-fashioned miniature golf.

✻ **Selective Shopping**

Stores are open year-round unless otherwise noted.

Paul Bunyan Mall (218-751-3195; www.paulbunyanmall.com), 1401 Paul Bunyan Dr. NW, Bemidji. Open daily. The Paul Bunyan Mall is anchored by JCPenney, Herberger's, and Kmart; other stores include Foot Locker,

PAUL BUNYAN'S GRAVE IN KELLIHER

Claire's, Bath & Body Works, and General Nutrition Center.

Bemidji Woolen Mills (888-751-5166; www.bemidjiwoolenmills.com), 391 Irvine Ave. NW, Bemidji. Open daily. Closed Thanksgiving, Christmas, and Easter. Manufacturer and retailer of woolen apparel. Woolen Mills' products are high in quality; the store also carries Hudson's Bay, Woolrich, and Dale of Norway wool clothing.

✳ Special Events

The northern lakes region isn't short of festivals and events. *Note:* This list does not include an extensive, ongoing list of events that take place at Concordia Language Villages (see *To See*). Check Concordia's Web site for detailed information on its festivals and weekend events.

Bemidji Polar Daze (218-444-3451; 800-458-2223; www.bemidji.org/chamber/polardaze), Bemidji. This festival, which is often jokingly called the "Brrrrmidji Polar Daze" (*Bermidji* being a common mispronunciation of the city's name), is held the third weekend in Jan. each year. Activities include the "Taste of Northern Minnesota"—a dining event featuring several local eateries—a poker tournament, a 5K run/walk, night skiing, snowshoeing, and stock car ice racing.

✏ **Logging Days** (218-243-2231; 800-777-7958; www.bvskiarea.com),

Buena Vista Ski Area, 19276 Lake Julia Dr. NW, Bemidji. Admission is $5 for those 13 and over, $3 ages 6–12; those 5 and under are free, while the family rate (up to 6 people) is $25. This annual festival on the first Sat. in Feb. is a day packed with logging and winter activities. Stump and log pulling, chain saw sculptures, roping contests, a treasure hunt, square dancing, all-you-can-eat flapjacks, live music, and craft displays are all part of the fun.

Chippewa Triathlon (800-356-8615; www.casslake.com), Cass Lake. The traditional June triathlon elements of a run (7 miles) and bike ride (28 miles) are combined with a 14-mile canoe ride.

Art in the Park (218-444-7570; http://bcac.wordpress.com), Lake Bemidji. This annual event, which has taken place for 40 years, showcases local and national artists and offers food and live entertainment. Dates are scheduled for mid-July.

Woodcarver's Festival (218-835-4949; www.blackduckmn.com/community/woodcarvers.html), Blackduck. This annual festival has grown from its beginnings in 1983 to include woodcarvers from across the United States and Canada. Held the last Sat. in July, the outdoor festival (rain or shine) brings visitors from all over the region. Carvers exhibit their wares for purchase, and food is available for sale. Look for the Uffda Taco.

✳ To See

The northwestern border of Minnesota is all about the outdoors and year-round outdoor activities: fishing, hiking, snowmobiling, skating, cross-country skiing. There are some attractions and historic sites, but the emphasis here is outside, not inside. Attractions are open year-round unless otherwise noted.

✐ ⚅ **Willie Walleye**. Bayfront Park, Baudette. No visit to the northern lakes would be complete without a photo op at the walleye equivalent of Paul Bunyan. Forty feet long and weighing 2 tons, Willie represents Baudette's claim of being "Walleye Capital of the World."

✐ ⚅ **Lake of the Woods County Museum** (218-634-1200), 119 8th Ave. SE, Baudette. Open mid-May–Labor Day, Tues.–Sun.; off-season by appointment. No admission fee. This small but well-stocked museum has exhibits on various aspects of northern Minnesota's history and development, including a re-created homestead kitchen, school, country store, and tavern, as well as information on the geology of the area.

✐ ⚅ **The Polaris Experience** (218-463-4999; www.polarisindustries.com), 205 5th Ave. SW, Suite 2, Roseau. Open Mon.–Sat. No admission fee. One of the leading manufacturers of snowmobiles, Polaris built this visitor center adjacent to its plant to showcase the company's history. The exhibits range from the earliest snowmobile prototypes to today's sleeker machines, as well as history and trivia from the age of snowmobiles. Tours of the Polaris plant itself are scheduled daily at 2 PM; call ahead or stop by the office to sign up. Admission is free.

THE POLARIS EXPERIENCE

AT PIONEER VILLAGE

✍ ♿ **Pioneer Village** (218-463-3052; www.roseaupioneerfarm.com), MN 11, Roseau. Open May–Aug., Mon.–Fri. noon–5; other times by appointment. Admission is free. This lovingly preserved village is a testament to the pioneer agricultural days of northwestern Minnesota. Most of the 16 buildings are restored artifacts, completed primarily by volunteer labor (volunteer opportunities are available on Tuesday; call the village for more information). Visitors are welcome to explore on their own or take a guided tour through the post office, parish hall, church, barn, blacksmith shop, and log cabin. Bathroom facilities are, fittingly, of an outhouse nature, in a vintage portable toilet.

✍ **Fort St. Charles** (218-223-4611), The Point, Lake St. NE, Warroad. Open daily, weather permitting. In the early 1700s a French explorer and trader by the name of Pierre Gaultier de Varennes, Sieur de la Verendrye, established this fort as a base for trading and for launching expeditions. Lack of food and hostility from local Sioux made the fort difficult to maintain, however, and it was abandoned after 1760. The buildings were discovered and reconstructed as a historic site in the mid-1900s.

✍ ♿ **Wm. S. Marvin Training and Visitor Center** (218-386-4334; www .marvin.com), MN 11 and 313, Warroad. Open daily. Admission is free. The Marvin Visitor Center is a historic and industrial exhibition celebrating the growth and technology behind Marvin Windows and Doors. Theatrical highlights include a description of the fire that destroyed the Marvin plant in 1961 and how the Marvin company rebuilt and expanded. Tours of the plant itself are available by appointment at 218-386-4333, Mon.–Fri. only.

✍ ♿ **Christian Brothers, Inc.** (218-386-1111), 1001 State Ave. NE, Warroad. The manufacturer of the well-regarded hockey sticks offers plant tours. Call for appointments.

✳ To Do

The northwestern stretch of the state is geared primarily toward visitors who want to enjoy outdoor activities, including fishing (both summer and winter), boating, hiking, hunting, snowmobiling, snowshoeing, and cross-country skiing. Consequently, many resorts in this area are open year-round to cater to clients who favor activities in the different seasons. *Note:* Because winter can be unpredictable, don't head out to this part of the state in the middle of January without a snow emergency kit in your vehicle, as well as a charged-up cell phone. Pay close attention to the weather, because snowstorms (complete with dangerous winds and windchills) can arise quickly.

SUNFLOWER FIELDS

FISHING

Lake of the Woods is one of the nation's largest lakes (after the Great Lakes and Salt Lake), and it's become a favored place of anglers from all over the country and Canada. The region is proud of its walleye population (although its claim as "Walleye Capital of the World" is disputed), but there are many kinds of fish for the catching: Lake sturgeon, northern pike, smallmouth and largemouth bass, perch, and muskie are just some of the plentiful species. You can bring your own boat and manage your fishing yourself, or you can hire a guide through one of the many guide services (and through many of the dozens of resorts in the area) to assist you.

There are separate summer and winter fishing seasons. Winter's ice fishing has gained considerable ground as more resorts offer ice houses for rent, many of which are outfitted with propane heaters and cooktops. The popularity of "sleeper" fish houses, outfitted like rustic cabins, also continues to grow. Fish spearing is another activity seeing increasing interest.

Official seasons and regulations can be found through the **Minnesota Department of Natural Resources** (DNR) (651-296-6157; 888-646-6367; www.dnr .state.mn.us/regulations/fishing/index.html).

HUNTING

Deer hunting in Minnesota begins in late October for bow hunters and early November for firearms. Besides deer, duck, grouse, and goose hunting are all

LAKE OF THE WOODS

popular activities. Because there's so much open land near Lake of the Woods, it's easy to mistake private property for public hunting grounds. Check with the local tourist offices or with your resort owners, who can provide necessary information to help you avoid trespassing. **Minnesota DNR** has specific licensing and regulation information (651-296-6157; 888-646-6367; www.dnr.state.mn.us/regulations/hunting/index.html).

CANOEING

Lake of the Woods, north through the Northwest Angle, makes for excellent canoeing, as does the meandering Rainy River.

SNOWMOBILING

There are over 400 miles of snowmobile trails in the Lake of the Woods area, most groomed and maintained by a local snowmobiling organization, the **Lake of the Woods Drifters Snowmobile Club** (218-634-3042; www.lowdrifters .org), Baudette. The Drifters can provide maps and trail conditions during the winter season. If you're going to be using the trails extensively, it's worth considering a membership in the Drifters (the annual individual fee is $25; the family rate is $35) in order to participate in one of the many events they sponsor during the snowmobiling season.

GOLF

Golf's charm is felt this far north. There are several courses available to the public across the region:

Oak Harbor Golf Course (218-634-9939; www.oakharborgolfcourse.com), 2805 24th St. NW, Baudette. Open May 1–Oct. 15, weather permitting. Nine-hole course.

Oakcrest Golf Club (218-463-3016; www.oakcrestgolfcourse.com), 5th St. S., Roseau. Open mid-May–mid-Oct., weather permitting. An 18-hole championship course that winds along the river and through the woods.

Warroad Estates Golf Course (218-386-2025; www.warroadestates.com), 37293 Elm Dr., Warroad. Open Apr. 15–Oct. 15, weather permitting. This 18-hole course straddles the US–Canadian border.

Northwest Angle Country Club (218-223-8001; www.pasturegolf.com), Angle Inlet. Open May–Sept., weather permitting. When a golf course's location is described as "north of Northern Minnesota," you know you're truly going "up north." This nine-hole course may not be the most pristinely groomed you've ever played, but you may never be able to see quite so much wildlife while golfing, either.

Zippel Bay State Park (218-783-6252; www.dnr.state.mn.us/state_parks/zippel_bay/index.html), CR 8, Williams. Fishing, swimming, bird-watching, camping—Zippel Bay State Park offers these and more in its 3,000-plus acres along Lake of the Woods. Six miles of hiking trails during the summer are expanded to 11 miles in the winter for cross-country skiers.

✳ Lodging

Accommodations are open year-round unless otherwise noted.

❡ ♿ **Americinn Baudette** (218-634-3200; 800-396-5007; www.americinn .com), MN 11 W., Baudette. The nicest hotel in Baudette is the Americinn, which offers rooms and suites, an indoor pool, cold-weather hookups, a fish-cleaning area, and free high-speed Internet access. Upgraded rooms include a fireplace. Rates start at $73.

❡ ♈ **Border View Lodge** (800-776-3474; www.borderviewlodge.com), 3409 MN 172 NW, Baudette. A year-round resort north of Baudette, located where the Rainy River meets Lake of the Woods. Border View has several cabins, all of which are fully equipped and have the option of full daily maid service (bed making, dishwashing). Border View also offers ice houses, both for daily use and as an accommodation for that all-night ice-fishing getaway. There's a bar and restaurant in the lodge. Rates start at $83; packages are available.

🐾 ❡ ♿ ♈ **Wigwam Resort** (218-634-2168; 800-448-9260; www.wigwam resortlow.com), 3502 Four Mile Bay Dr. NW, Baudette. The Wigwam offers both hotel rooms in the lodge and cabins for rental. You can book accommodations only, or reserve packages that include meals at the resort's restaurant and charter fishing with a guide. Rates start at $45; packages are available.

❡ ♿ **Americinn Roseau** (218-463-1045; 800-396-5007; www.americinn .com), MN 11 W., Roseau. Like the Americinn in Baudette, this is one of the nicest hotels in the area, offering rooms and suites, an indoor pool, and cold-weather hookups. Rates start at $68.

❡ ♿ **North Country Inn and Suites** (888-300-2196; www.northcountry innandsuites.com), 902 3rd St. NW, Roseau. This motel offers 49 rooms and suites, all with refrigerator and microwave, and daily continental breakfast. There's an indoor pool and hot tub as well. Rates start at $65.

❡ **Zippel Bay Resort** (800-222-2537; www.zippelbay.com), 6080 39th St. NW, Williams. Zippel Bay has both budget cabins and deluxe log cabins, complete with fireplace and Jacuzzi; the log cabins are attractive and spacious, located on the water's edge. The resort has an outdoor pool for the summer months and a restaurant. Packages are available with or without meals; in winter, sleeper ice houses can be rented. Rates start at $35 per person, per night.

✳ Where to Eat

Because so many of the fishing and outdoor-activity resorts are located well out of city limits, many of the resorts offer restaurants or cafés themselves. Within the cities of Baudette, Roseau, and Warroad, there are several fast-food options, plus the following selections, open year-round unless otherwise noted.

ZIPPEL BAY RESORT

✏ ♿ ♈ **Ranch House** (218-634-2420), 203 W. Main St., Baudette. Three meals a day, all of them hearty. Burgers and ribs are the specialty. Entrées start at $7.

✏ ♿ **Williams Café** (218-783-3474), 2335 94th Ave. NW, Williams. Open Tues.–Sun. for breakfast and lunch. Williams Café serves plates full of home-cooked breakfasts and juicy burgers. Entrées start at $5.

✏ ♿ ♈ **Reed River Restaurant and Bar** (218-463-0993), 205 5th Ave. SE, Roseau. Open daily for lunch and dinner. A full restaurant and bar located near the Polaris Experience, Reed River has burgers, sandwiches, steaks, and ribs. Entrées start at $9.

✏ ♿ ♈ **Izzy's Lounge and Grill** (218-386-2723; www.patchmotel.com/izzys.htm), 801 State Ave. N., Warroad. Open daily for lunch and dinner. A local bar and grill; the bar is fully stocked, and the grill provides enormous meals in the form of burgers and chicken. Service is friendly, and the casual environment, with a large stone fireplace, is downright cozy. Entrées start at $7.

✏ ♿ ♈ **Lakeview Restaurant** (218-386-1225; www.sevenclanscasino.com/warroad.html), 1205 E. Lake St., Warroad. Open daily for lunch and dinner. A more upscale restaurant located at the Seven Clans Casino. Steak, shrimp, and burgers are served while diners enjoy a stellar view of the lake. Entrées start at $11.

✳ **Special Events**

✏ **Willie Walleye Day**, Baudette. Held in early June, Willie Walleye Day celebrates Baudette's claim as "Walleye Capital of the World" with a day of fun and frolic, including a 5K run/walk, lumberjack show, chain saw carving, and, of course, food.

✏ **Scandinavian Festival** (www.city.roseau.mn.us), Roseau. Held each year in mid-June, the two-day Scandinavian Festival celebrates the region's roots with events in the town of Roseau and at the Pioneer Village.

✏ **Blueberry Festival and Chili Cook-Off** (866-692-6453), Northwest Angle. An annual Aug. event celebrating the fruit of the season in a variety of cooked forms, as well as a chili cook-off among several resorts.

✏ **Pioneer Village Festival** (218-463-3052; www.roseaupioneerfarm.com), MN 11, Roseau. This event, held each year the last weekend of Aug. before Labor Day weekend, re-creates pioneer entertainment with a pancake breakfast, children's games and activities, demonstrations of pioneer skills, and a parade.

THIEF RIVER FALLS/RED RIVER VALLEY/DETROIT LAKES

✳ **To See**

Attractions are open year-round unless otherwise noted.

✏ ♿ **Peter Engelstad Pioneer Village** (218-681-5767; www.pvillage.org), 825 Oakland Park Rd., Thief River Falls. Open daily Memorial Day–Labor Day. $3 adults; free for children under 12 with a paid adult. Like the Roseau Pioneer Village, this is a collection of 19 historic buildings, each housing several artifacts from the early settler days of northwestern Minnesota. Buildings include a church, a school, log cabins, and a two-story Victorian house.

🎣 ♿ **Arctic Cat** (218-681-8558; www.arctic-cat.com), 601 Brooks Ave. S., Thief River Falls. Open Mon.–Fri. A large manufacturer of snowmobiles and ATVs, Arctic Cat offers tours of its plant at 1 PM. Call ahead for reservations.

🎣 **Digi-Key** (218-681-5703; www.digikey.com), 701 Brooks Ave. S., Thief River Falls. Open Mon.–Fri. This manufacturer of electrical components offers tours by appointment.

🍷 **Two Fools Vineyard** (218-465-4655; www.twofoolsvineyard.com), 12501 240th Ave. SE, Plummer. Open June–Oct., Sat.–Sun. Thumbing their nose at those who say grapes can't be grown in northern climates, Carol and LeRoy Stumpf grow grapes (among other fruits) and make wines such as Pinot Noir, Chardonnay, and orange Muscat.

🎣 ♿ **Heritage Village** (218-773-3952; www.egfheritage.com), MN 220 N. and 20th St. NE, East Grand Forks. Open by appointment. Festivals and events open to the public are held frequently; call or check the Web site for details. A preserved historic village re-creating life in pioneer days, including a variety of farm implements.

🎣 ♿ **Rourke Art Museum** (218-236-8861), 521 Main Ave., Moorhead. Open Fri.–Sun. A small but thoughtful collection of permanent and traveling exhibits focused on contemporary American, Hispanic, African, and Native American art.

🎣 **Comstock House** (218-291-4211; www.mnhs.org/places/sites/ch), 506 8th St. S., Moorhead. Open Memorial Day–Labor Day, Tues.–Sun. $4 adults, $3 seniors, $2 ages 6–12; free for those under 12 or with Minnesota Historical Society memberships. The 1882 home of Solomon Comstock, who founded Moorhead State University. The home has been restored and includes original furnishings.

🎣 ♿ **Hjemkmost Center** (218-299-5511; www.hjemkomst-center.com), 202 1st Ave. N., Moorhead. Open daily. $6 adults, $5 seniors and college students, $4 ages 5–17; free for those under 5. Tues. 5–8, admission is $10 per family. The Hjemkmost Center is named for the replica Viking ship built by a local man who wanted to sail her to Norway. He completed the ship and took her onto Lake Superior, but before he could journey farther, he died; family and friends rallied and sailed the ship to Norway in 1982. She's now on display as a permanent exhibit, along with a Norwegian stave church replica and a historical Red River Valley exhibit. Temporary exhibits are brought in on rotation, and the center sponsors several special events each year. Call or check the Web site for specific events.

🎣 ♿ **Log Cabin Folk Art Center** (218-299-5252), 315 4th St. S., Moorhead. Open Tues., June–Aug. A cabin built in 1859 now serves as an artist's space, with Tues. evenings open to the public. On those nights, a working folk artist is on site, along with live music; carriage rides to the Red River are offered.

🎣 ♿ 🍷 **Shooting Star Casino** (218-935-2711; 800-453-7827; www.starcasino .com), 777 Casino Rd., Mahnomen. Open daily. North of Detroit Lakes is this casino, run by the White Earth Band of Ojibwe Indians. A large, well-run establishment with slots, blackjack, bingo, and poker, Shooting Star also offers child care and a kids' arcade. Live concerts are presented regularly in the casino's main stage, and there's dining in four venues. A hotel is attached to the casino (see *Lodging*).

✳ To Do

Historical Riverwalk (800-827-1629), Thief River Falls. Over 7 miles of trail wind through Thief River Falls along Thief River and Red Lake River. The trail is open for walking, biking, and cross-country skiing, and it passes through several city parks, some historic sites, and near the dam.

Agassiz National Wildlife Refuge (218-449-4115; www.fws.gov/midwest/agassiz), 22996 220th St. NE, Middle River. Open May–Oct. during daylight hours. The headquarters is open for questions and visitor assistance Mon.–Fri. 7:30–4, excluding federal holidays. This refuge has over 60,000 acres encompassing a wide variety of environments—wetland, forest, and prairie—and is home to a diverse assortment of wildlife: Bald eagles, ducks, geese, wolves, herons, moose, and deer are just a few of the animals residing here. There's a 4-mile self-guided habitat drive as well as a 0.5-mile hiking trail; a 100-foot observation tower with a 14-foot observation deck is available during nonsnow times. Check in at headquarters to obtain the key for the tower.

Red River State Recreation Area (218-773-4950; www.dnr.state.mn.us/state_parks/red_river/index.html), 515 2nd St. NW, East Grand Forks. Open daily. One of the state's newer recreation areas was created after the disastrous 1997 floods, which destroyed homes and farms along the river. More than 500 homes and buildings were removed from the area after the floodplain was reconfigured, and a 1,200-acre recreation area was set up instead. Hiking and biking trails, fishing and boating access, and campsites are now available within easy access of both East Grand Forks and Grand Forks, North Dakota.

Tamarac National Wildlife Refuge (218-847-2641; www.fws.gov/midwest/tamarac), 35704 CR 36, Rochert. Open daily. No admission fee. Tamarac has 43,000 acres set aside for wildlife preservation. The visitor center, open weekdays 7:30–4 and weekends 10–5, has exhibits and a video presentation explaining what the refuge contains. Self-guided driving and hiking tours can lend views of bald eagles, deer, porcupine, and even the occasional black bear. In winter ice fishing, cross-country skiing, and snowshoeing are all available.

✳ Lodging

Accommodations are open year-round unless otherwise noted.

♂ ♿ **Americinn Lodge and Suites Thief River Falls** (218-681-4411; 800-634-3444; www.americinn.com), 1920 US 59 SE, Thief River Falls. This property has rooms and suites, some of the latter with fireplace and whirlpool. There's an indoor pool and a complimentary daily breakfast; for winter enthusiasts, the hotel offers cold-weather vehicle hookups. Rates start at $80.

♂ ♿ **C'mon Inn** (218-681-3000; 800-950-8111; www.cmoninn.com), 1586 US 59 S., Thief River Falls. A small but comfortable hotel with 44 rooms, an indoor pool and hot tub, and daily continental breakfast. Rates start at $65.

☀ ✍ ♿ ♈ **Americinn Lodge and Suites Moorhead** (218-287-7100; 800-287-7100; www.americinnof moorhead.com), 600 30th Ave. S., Moorhead. This is one of the larger Americinns in the state, and as such it has more amenities than most. Like most Americinns, it has an indoor pool, but this hotel also has a kiddy pool and mini golf course, both indoors. There is a hot tub for all hotel guests, and four of the suites have private hot tub. Continental breakfast is included in the rates, but unlike most Americinns, this one also has a restaurant, lounge, and comedy club on site. Rates start at $75.

✍ ♿ ♈ **Courtyard Moorhead** (218-284-1000; 800-321-2211; www .marriott.com), 1080 28th Ave. S., Moorhead. The Courtyard, a Marriott property, was designed primarily for business travelers, so the rooms are well equipped with two phone lines, free high-speed Internet access, and higher-end desks and desk chairs. The hotel also has an indoor pool; an on-site restaurant is open for breakfast and dinner. Rates start at $99.

✍ ♿ **Americinn Lodge and Suites Detroit Lakes** (218-847-8795; 877-847-8795; www.americinndl.com), 777 US 10 E., Detroit Lakes. This Americinn is in the process of redecorating its rooms and suites (the latter offer fireplace and Jacuzzi), and eventually all rooms will have HDTV. The hotel has an indoor pool and includes a full breakfast daily. Cold-weather hookups are available, and there is access from the hotel to local snowmobile trails. Rates start at $70.

✍ ♿ ♈ **The Lodge on Lake Detroit** (218-847-8439; 800-761-8439; www .thelodgeonlakedetroit.com), 1200 E. Shore Dr., Detroit Lakes. This lakefront hotel, opened in 2006, boasts rooms that all face the lake; first-floor rooms have walk-out patio, and most second- and third-floor rooms have private balcony. All are nicely appointed, with HDTV and free Internet access, and are the most luxurious in the area. Suites have additional features, such as gas fireplace or full kitchen. There's a sandy beach outside for summer, and an indoor pool and hot tub for inclement weather. A full-service spa is on site. Full breakfast is served daily, and the lounge offers drinks and appetizers in the evening, but other meals are not provided. Rates start at $109; packages available.

✍ ♿ ♈ **Holiday Inn Lakeside** (218-847-2121; www.dlinn.com), US 10 E., Detroit Lakes. Another lakeside property, the Holiday Inn isn't as upscale as the Lodge on Lake Detroit, but it has a sandy beach. The rooms are standard Holiday Inn issue, though you will find an indoor pool, whirlpool, and sauna, and—unlike the Lodge—the Holiday Inn has a full-service restaurant on site: **Ice House Bar and Grill** serves three meals daily. Rates start at $73.

✍ ♿ ♈ **Shooting Star Casino Hotel and RV Park** (218-935-2711; 800-453-7827; www.starcasino.com), 777 Casino Rd., Mahnomen. Attached to the casino (see *To See*) is a hotel with a range of accommodation options, from standard to deluxe suites. An indoor pool and hot tub and room service from the casino's restaurants are available. Behind the hotel is an RV park with water, sewer, and electricity hookups. Rates start at $49.

✳ Where to Eat

Restaurants are open year-round unless otherwise noted.

🖉 ఉ ⵂ **Evergreen Eating Emporium** (218-681-3138), 700 MN 32 S., Thief River Falls. Open daily for lunch and dinner. Housed in a large Tudor-style building, the Evergreen has two dining areas situated around a large stone fireplace as well as private dining rooms on the second floor. The cozy ambience comes with good food served in enormous portions: sandwiches and salads at lunch, heavier fare such as ribs and steaks at dinner. But the dinner menu also includes a limited selection of smaller-portion entrées for a lower price with no age restrictions, something other restaurants could emulate. Entrées start at $8.

🖉 **Johnnie's Café** (218-681-8102), 304 Main Ave. N., Thief River Falls. Open Mon.–Sat. for breakfast and lunch. A classic small-town café popular with the locals. Breakfasts are primarily eggs and pancakes, but they're plentiful and good (be sure to get the hash browns), and lunch is classic sandwiches (Reuben, grilled cheese) and burgers. Nothing fancy, but done well. Entrées start at $4.

🖉 ఉ ⵂ **Black Cat Sports Bar and Grill** (218-681-8910), 1080 MN 32 S., Thief River Falls. Open daily for lunch and dinner. A sports bar with a snowmobiling theme, thanks to the memorabilia on display from local manufacturer Arctic Cat. The food is about what you'd expect from a sports bar: heavy on burgers and appetizers. Basic and reliable. Entrées start at $7.

🖉 ఉ ⵂ **The Blue Moose Bar and Grill** (218-773-6516; www.theblue moose.net), 507 2nd St. NW, East Grand Forks. Open daily for lunch and dinner, Sun. for breakfast. Perhaps one of the few restaurants in history to have crossed a river, the Blue Moose did so following the Red River flooding in 1999. Now housed on the river in a comfortable lodge setting, this restaurant serves hearty steaks and sandwiches in huge portions. Entrées start at $14.

🖉 ఉ ⵂ **Whitey's Café Restaurant and Bar** (218-773-1831; www.whitey scafe.com), 121 Demers Ave., East

EVERGREEN EATING EMPORIUM

Grand Forks. Open daily for lunch and dinner. Whitey's, a local landmark for more than 75 years, serves traditional steak house meals (ribs, steaks, chicken) along with a few pasta options and even a couple of liver dishes. Stop by for a full meal, or just to nosh off the appetizers and late-night menu. Entrées start at $10.

✦ ঠ Ⴓ **The Broken Axe** (218-287-0080; www.thebrokenaxe.com), 700 1st Ave. N., Moorhead. Open daily for lunch and dinner. Bar food is the specialty here, with hefty appetizers, sandwiches, and burgers. Live music several times each week runs heavily to rock and alternative bands. Entrées start at $7.

ঠ Ⴓ **Sarello's** (218-287-0238), 28 Center Mall Ave., Moorhead. Open daily for dinner. If you're looking for a quiet adults night out, this is the place. The best restaurant in the area, Sarello's serves upscale Italian cuisine in an elegant environment. The wine list is extensive. Reservations are strongly recommended. Entrées start at $14.

ঠ Ⴓ **The Fireside** (218-847-8192; www.firesidedl.com), 1462 East Shore Dr., Detroit Lakes. Open daily Memorial Day–Labor Day for lunch and dinner; Sept.–May, selected days for dinner only. Call for details. One of the best choices for an upscale dining experience. Fireside serves old-fashioned retro supper-club foods with a contemporary flair; steaks are available in all sizes, and walleye comes either as a pan-fried fillet or stuffed with seafood. The meat loaf with Asiago cheese is a good bet if you're not in a steak or seafood mood. Entrées start at $17.

✦ ঠ Ⴓ **The Speakeasy** (218-844-1326; www.speakeasydl.com), 1100 North Shore Dr., Detroit Lakes. Open daily for lunch and dinner, Sun. for brunch. In this kitschy throwback to the 1920s, the servers dress as flappers, and the lounge comes complete with a Model A Ford. Pasta is the house specialty, either in a signature style or in a "design your own." Oddly for an Italian restaurant with a '20s theme, the Speakeasy has a Cinco de Mayo celebration each year, when its menu changes to Mexican. Entrées start at $11.

✦ Ⴓ **Zorbaz on the Lake** (218-847-5305; www.zorbaz.com), 402 W. Lake Dr., Detroit Lakes. Open daily; hours are limited in winter, call for specifics. A beach bar with Mexican food, pizza, pasta, and plenty of beer. Take the kids for the arcades. A dock is provided for diners arriving by boat. Entrées start at $5.

✦ ঠ Ⴓ **Shooting Star Casino** (218-935-2711; 800-453-7827; www.starcasino.com), 777 Casino Rd., Mahnomen. This casino, north of Detroit Lakes, offers four restaurants from sit-down to casual quick food, including a buffet that's plentiful. Entrées start at $6.

✳ Special Events

Festival of Birds (218-847-9202; 800-542-3992; www.visitdetroitlakes.com), Detroit Lakes. A basic event fee of $10 for the full festival or $5 per day is required, plus fees ranging $7–75 for the individual events. An annual event in May for serious birders. The Detroit Lakes area is home to more than 200 species, and the festival provides bird-watchers with three days of guided tours, presentations by experts, early-morning and evening field trips, workshops, and a dinner in the forest.

❧ **Scandinavian Hjemkomst Festival** (218-299-5452; www.scandinavian hjemkomstfestival.org), Hjemkomst Center, 202 1st Ave. N., Moorhead. An adult pass is $10; those 18 and under are free. Held each year in late June, the festival is all things Scandinavian—children's story hours, a midsummer's fest picnic, a Swedish smorbrod (smorgasbord), a banquet, dance and music performances and lessons, art exhibits, and food and craft sales.

10,000 Lakes Festival (800-493-3378; www.10klf.com), Detroit Lakes. Held each year in mid-July at the Soo Pass Ranch southeast of Detroit Lakes on US 59, the 10KLF offers more than 60 performers on four stages over four days. Acts cover rock and blues; tickets include campsites.

❧ **Heritage Days Festival** (218-773-3952; www.egfheritage.com), MN 220 N. and 20th St. NE, East Grand Forks. An annual festival held in late Aug. at the Heritage Village, Heritage Days takes visitors back in time to the beginning of the last century, with blacksmith demonstrations, threshing, broom making, and a tractor pull. A parade and bountiful food round out the celebration.

❧ **Barnesville Potato Days** (800-525-4901; www.potatodays.com), Barnesville. As you might expect, Barnesville is a major potato producer, and this annual festival, held the last weekend in Aug., reflects that heritage. It draws over 14,000 people each year, due to its good-natured view of potato activities, including mashed-potato wrestling, mashed-potato sculpting, potato-peeling and mashed-potato-eating contests, and potato car races. There's also a Miss Tater Tot Pageant, a 5K/10K race, softball, and a demolition derby. Mashed potatoes, lefse (a Scandinavian potato-based pastry), and french fries are readily available, as is—oddly—chocolate.

❧ **Greater Moorhead Days** (218-299-5296; www.ci.moorhead.mn.us), Moorhead. A 10-day celebration held in early Sept., Greater Moorhead Days includes a medallion treasure

WE Fest (800-493-3378; www.wefest.com), 25526 CR 22, Detroit Lakes. This 25-year-old festival is a three-day celebration of country music. It's held outdoors, rain or shine, in early Aug. and attracts over 50,000 of people from around the country each year. The festival is sited at the Soo Pass Ranch on US 59, southeast of Detroit Lakes. Tickets are sold at varying levels, from general admission to reserved lawn seats and reserved box seats, with prices for the three days ranging $100–300. Many attendees return year after year, and an entire subculture has built up at this festival, with some visitors setting up stores or "cafés" where they sell grilled foods and beverages off limits to drinkers under 21. Campsites are available, but reserve well in advance—this is a very popular option for WE Fest attendees. *Note:* While children are not prohibited, WE Fest tends to be an adult event; campers frequently bring in large quantities of alcohol to enjoy, and not all of the entertainment is family-friendly.

hunt, the Power Bowl Parade and Power Bowl college football game, a bocce ball tournament and golf scramble, and the "Wings & Wheels Fly-In and Car Show," a custom car show with pancake breakfast and pig roast.

✍ **Rollag Western Minnesota Steam Threshers Reunion** (218-238-5407; www.rollag.com), MN 32, Rawley. Labor Day weekend. Daily tickets are $14 for ages 15 and older; those 14 and under are free. A season pass is available for $20. This popular event is spread out over 200 acres and includes demonstrations of various generations of farm power, including horse-, gas-, and steam-powered equipment. Food and craft demonstrations are held daily, as are train (full-sized and miniature) rides, merry-go-round rides, and a parade.

✍ **First Night** (218-230-4231; www .firstnightggf.org), East Grand Forks/ Grand Forks, North Dakota. Buttons are required for admission: $8 in advance, $10 at the door. A New Year's Eve event with a wide variety of entertainment (musicians, dancers, jugglers, singers) at numerous venues across the Greater Grand Forks area. An ice sculpture garden is on display, and the evening ends with a fireworks display. No alcohol is served; shuttle buses run through the evening for participants.

Central Lake District 5

ST. CLOUD AND ENVIRONS

MILLE LACS

WILLMAR

BRAINERD

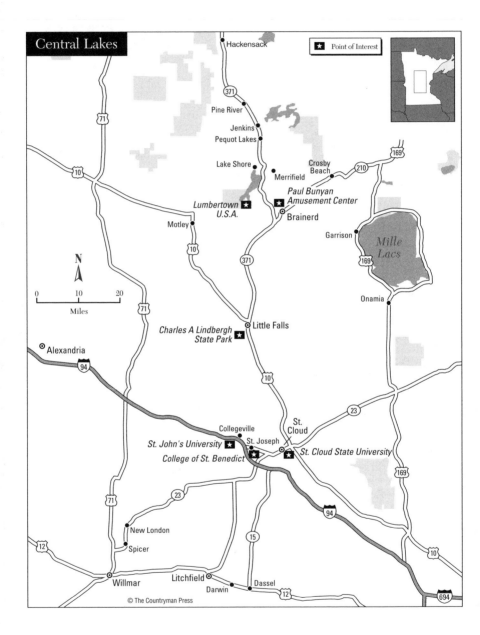

Central Lakes

Hackensack

★ Point of Interest

371

Pine River

Jenkins

Pequot Lakes

Lake Shore

Crosby
Beach

Merrifield

210

169

Lumbertown
U.S.A. ★

Paul Bunyan ★
Amusement Center

Motley

Brainerd

Garrison

Mille
Lacs

71

10

10

169

371

N

0   10   20
Miles

71

Onamia

Charles A Lindbergh ★
State Park

Little Falls

Alexandria

94

10

23

St.
Cloud

Collegeville

St. John's University ★

St. Joseph

College of St. Benedict ★

★ St. Cloud State University

169

71

23

New London

94

Spicer

15

12

Willmar

Litchfield

Dassel

10

Darwin

12

694

© The Countryman Press

CENTRAL LAKE DISTRICT

I f *lakes* are what you think of when you think of Minnesota, you're likely envisioning the Central Lake District, particularly the Brainerd area. Slightly more than two hours north of the Twin Cities, this area has long been a popular weekend getaway spot in summer; a community of mom-and-pop resorts and upscale enclaves here serves all types of interests. Brainerd and its twin city of Baxter are the most prominent communities, but they're not the only ones to consider if you're planning a lake vacation. Many of the small towns surrounding Brainerd, including Nisswa, Pequot Lakes, and Crosslake, are good bets.

Even beyond the Brainerd region are good options for water enthusiasts. Going west to the area around Willmar, you'll find rolling countryside and lakes aplenty, although those seeking higher-end accommodations may be disappointed. Minnesota's second largest lake, Lake Mille Lacs, rests east of Brainerd and is also an idyllic area to visit. Along the way, en route to both Brainerd/Mille Lacs and Willmar, are a number of historical and cultural sites of interest, particularly through the St. Cloud area.

Because these popular lake regions are close enough to the Twin Cities to allow for weekend trips, traffic can be heavy, especially on weekends. The route to Brainerd has been improved by the addition of more traffic lanes on MN 371, but Brainerd and Baxter are not towns designed for heavy traffic flow; be prepared for slow going at times.

GUIDANCE

The St. Cloud Convention and Visitors Bureau (320-251-4170; 800-264-2942; www.granitecountry.com), 525 US 10 S., Suite 1, St. Cloud. Information on St. Cloud lodgings and sightseeing.

Mille Lacs Lake Area Tourism (320-532-5626; 888-350-2692; www.millelacs .com), 204 Roosevelt Rd., Onamia.

Willmar Lakes Area Chamber of Commerce (320-235-0300; www.willmar areachamber.com), 2104 E. US 12, Willmar.

Brainerd Lakes Chamber and Convention and Visitors Bureau (218-829-2838; 800-450-2838; www.explorebrainerdlakes.com) offers extensive lodging and activity information for Brainerd/Baxter and surrounding areas.

GETTING THERE

By car: I-94 and US 10 both traverse St. Cloud. From St. Cloud, US 10 meets MN 371, which continues north to Brainerd. Willmar is served from the east and west by US 12, and from the north and south by US 71. The Mille Lacs area is ringed by US 169, MN 18, MN 27, and MN 47.

By air: Northwest Airlines and its Mesaba subsidiary serve the cities of Brainerd and St. Cloud. Willmar has a municipal airport that can handle small corporate planes. Taxis and rental cars are available from the airports into the city.

GETTING AROUND

Having a vehicle is a necessity when traveling around the Central Lakes District, unless you plan to stay solely at your resort.

WHEN TO COME

The summer months see an influx of tourists who come to enjoy the multitude of lakes and beaches, but summer isn't the only popular time. Fishing enthusiasts cast their lines into open water in summer and through holes in the ice in winter. Hunters and winter sports aficionados appreciate the fall and winter seasons as well.

MEDICAL EMERGENCY

Call **911**.

St. Cloud Hospital (320-251-2700; 800-835-6652; www.centracare.com), 1406 6th Ave. N., St. Cloud.

Mille Lacs Health System (320-532-3154; www.millelacshealth.com), 200 N. Elm St., Onamia.

Long Prairie Memorial Hospital (320-732-2414; www.centracare.com), 20 SE 9th St., Long Prairie.

Melrose Area Hospital (320-256-4231; www.centracare.com), 11 N. 5th Ave. W., Melrose.

Rice Memorial Hospital (320-235-4543; www.ricehospital.com), 301 SW Becker Ave., Willmar.

St. Joseph's Medical Center (218-829-2861; www.sjmcmn.org), 523 3rd St. N., Brainerd.

St. Cloud is home to four colleges and universities, giving it a youthful population and a wide variety of activities, both historical and cultural. Its history is
reflected in its nickname, *Granite City*, and granite is still produced and carved
in the area. It's somewhat of a gateway to the north—most travelers heading to
the Brainerd area or up to Lake of the Woods will pass through here. Consequently, traffic through the city can be quite congested, especially on summer
weekends.

✳ To See

Attractions are open year-round unless otherwise noted.

✎ ♿ **Stearns History Museum** (320-253-8424; 866-253-8424; www.stearns
-museum.org), 235 33rd Ave. S. Open daily except for holidays. $5 adults, $2
ages 5 and older; free for children under 5. $12 family rate for two adults with
children under 16 residing in the same home. Museum members receive free
admission. This county historical museum walks the fine line between education
and entertainment and succeeds on both counts. A clothing exhibit reflects the
changing attitudes toward clothes and employment over the years; the area's
agricultural history is documented, and there's a life-sized replica of a granite
quarry as well as a young children's learn-and-play area. Documents from pioneers traveling to and settling in this region are displayed.

✎ **Charles A. Lindbergh Historic Site** (320-616-5421; www.mnhs.org), 1620
Lindbergh Dr. S. Open Memorial Day–Labor Day, Tues.–Sun.; Sept.–Oct.,
Sat.–Sun. noon–4. Open some Mon. holidays; call for information. $7 adults, $6
seniors, $4 ages 6–17; free for children under 6 and for Minnesota Historical
Society members. Charles Lindbergh's childhood home, complete with original
furnishings and belongings, is on display.

✎ **Grasshopper Chapel** (320-685-3653), MN 23 and Chapel Hill Rd. Open
daily. No admission fee, although donations are welcome. A few miles west of St.
Cloud is this little chapel, built originally in 1877 in response to a grasshopper
plague that was decimating crops. The governor declared a day of prayer, and
local townsfolk pledged to build a chapel if the grasshoppers went away. The
grasshoppers did indeed disappear the next day thanks to an unusual sleet storm,
and the chapel was built as promised. The original wood building was destroyed
by a tornado in 1894, but was rebuilt in the 1950s with donated granite. Today
the tiny chapel is in a wooded, peaceful area, a beautiful spot to visit.

♿ **Saint Benedict's Monastery** (320-363-7115; www.sbm.osb.org), 104 Chapel
Ln., St. Joseph. Open daily. This 150-year-old monastery has a Spirituality Center that welcomes guests for day-, week-, or monthlong visits. Private retreats
can be customized with spiritual counseling, or visitors can simply relax in the
quiet grounds and facilities, complete with a garden labyrinth.

✎ ♿ **Saint John's Bible** (320-363-3351; www.saintjohnsbible.org), Hill Museum
and Manuscript Library, Saint John's University, Collegeville. Open Memorial
Day–Labor Day, Mon.–Sat.; Labor Day–Memorial Day, Mon.–Fri. No admission
fee. Visiting the campus of Saint John's University is worthwhile on several levels,

including the beauty of the lakeside campus itself, the Arboretum, the Pottery Studio, and the Abbey, an impressive piece of religious architecture. But the Saint John's Bible project should be included in any visit to the campus. A deeply felt homage to the days when monasteries kept literature alive by hand-transcribing texts in elaborate calligraphy, this is a newly written Bible complete with extravagant illustrations and exquisite handwritten text. Though the project will take years, parts of the completed pages are on exhibit.

& **St. Cloud State University** (320-308-0121; www.stcloudstate.edu), 720 4th Ave. S. The university has two art exhibits of note. The **Atwood Collection**, in the Atwood Memorial Center, is an ever-growing collection of contemporary American art and is open daily. The **Kiehle Gallery**, a frequently changing collection, brings in guest artists on a national level as well as promoting local and student artists. Kiehle is open Mon.–Fri.

✳ To Do

✔ & **Munsinger and Clemens Gardens** (320-255-7216; www.munsinger clemens.com), Killian Blvd. SE. Open daily spring–fall. No admission fee, although donations are requested. Two beautiful gardens along the banks of the Mississippi, Munsinger and Clemens offer both historic and contemporary gardening highlights. Munsinger Gardens was developed in the 1930s and named for the superintendent of parks; it's an informal garden space, with winding paths lined with wildflowers and pine trees. Clemens was constructed in the 1990s and is more formal, complete with rose gardens and the tallest fountain in Minnesota—the 24-foot Renaissance Fountain.

✔ & **Quarry Park and Nature Preserve** (320-255-6172; www.co.stearns.mn .us), CR 137, Waite Park. Open daily, daylight hours only. Quarry Park is land that has gradually grown back to a natural state after years of granite quarrying. A park permit is required for entrance; a one-day permit is $4, an annual permit is $14. More than 600 acres of parkland provides a wide array of experiences for visitors: open prairie, wetlands, wooded areas, a 116-foot-deep swimming hole, and 30 granite quarries. Certified scuba divers traveling with scuba buddies can dive in one of four swimming holes, and with the proper permit visitors can tackle some rock climbing. Winter brings ample cross-country skiing or snowshoeing opportunities.

✔ & **Lake Wobegon Trail** (320-255-6172; www.lakewobegontrails.com). A 46-mile paved hiking and biking trail that stretches from St. Joseph to Sauk Centre. Snowmobilers have access to it in winter. The trail is highly scenic, winding through woods, near lakes, and through several small towns.

✔ **Sinclair Lewis Boyhood Home** (320-352-5359), 820 Sinclair Lewis Ave., Sauk Centre. Open daily Memorial Day–Labor Day. Admission is $3. Talk about making lemonade out of lemons. Sinclair Lewis, the Nobel Prize–winning American novelist who skewered Sauk Centre in his novel *Main Street*, spent his formative years in this home, which is now a museum. In spite of—or perhaps because of—the attention, Sauk Centre has guarded Lewis's legacy in this carefully preserved house (a National Historic Landmark), as well as the Sinclair

Lewis Interpretive Center on I-94 coming into town. Capping things off is the annual Sinclair Lewis Days (see *Special Events*). Today the home is a beautiful piece of nostalgia, whether or not you're a fan of Lewis's work.

✳ Lodging

All accommodations are open year-round unless otherwise noted. In a category of its own is Saint Benedict's Monastery, described under *To See*.

🐾 ♿ ☿ **Radisson Suite Hotel** (320-654-1661; 888-201-1718; www.radisson.com/stcloudmn), 404 W. St. Germain. The prime choice in St. Cloud, the Radisson is an all-suite property connected by skyway to the St. Cloud Civic Center. Grand Suites are larger units, with sitting areas and Mississippi River views. The hotel has an indoor pool, whirlpool, and sauna, as well as a fine-dining restaurant (see *Where to Eat*). Rates start at $89; packages are available.

🐻 🐾 ♿ ☿ **Holiday Inn and Suites** (320-253-9000; 888-465-4329; www.holidayinn.com/stcloudmn), Division St. and 37th Ave. The Holiday Inn was fully renovated in 2007 and offers an indoor pool, whirlpool, basketball court, sauna, and fitness center. Two restaurants are on site, one a family-oriented café (kids eat free with paying adults) and one a bar and grill. Rates start at $81.

Heritage House Bed and Breakfast (320-656-5818; 888-547-4422; www.heritagehousebbmn.com), 402 6th Ave. S. This inn, built in 1904, is listed on the National Register of Historic Places. It offers four rooms, all with private bath and full breakfast by request. The rooms are themed by nationality (French, Swedish, German, and English, with the last being the most luxurious) and decorated with amenities varying from wooden floors to canopy beds. Two of the rooms have separate sitting areas as well. The public area includes a pool table and game table. Rates start at $100.

Riverside Guest Haus (320-252-2134; 888-252-2134; www.riverside guesthaus.com), 912 Riverside Dr. SE. This charmer was built in 1937 and is within walking distance of Munsinger and Clemens Gardens (see *To Do*). The inn has just two guest rooms, both with private bath and beautifully appointed with European lace, Oriental rugs, and handmade quilts. The Garden Room has access to a private second-floor patio garden balcony, while the River Room has river views, an electric fireplace, and separate sitting area. Full breakfast is included. Rates start at $115.

Dancing Bears Bed and Breakfast (320-363-7723; www.dancingbears company.com), 12822 CR 51, St. Joseph. This upscale log cabin is adjacent to Saint John's University and offers just one bedroom. A private loft overlooks the wooded area of Saint John's; full breakfast can be taken in the dining room or in the privacy of your bedroom. Rates start at $185.

Victorian Oaks Bed and Breakfast (320-202-1404; 866-842-6257; www.vicoaks.com), 404 9th Ave. S. *Victorian* is the perfect description for this inn, located walking distance of St. Cloud State University and the Civic Center. Listed on the National Register of Historic Places, Victorian Oaks was built in 1894 and now has two guest rooms and a suite. Decorated lavishly with antiques fitting the period, the rooms are on the second floor, while the first floor has a charming sitting area, dining room, and elaborate main staircase. Rates start at $89.

✳ Where to Eat

Restaurants are open year-round unless otherwise noted.

✐ ♿ ⵃ **Chanticleer** (320-654-1661; www.radisson.com/stcloudmn), 404 W. St. Germain. Open daily for breakfast and dinner. Chanticleer rises well above average hotel fare and is possibly the best fine-dining restaurant in St. Cloud. Steak, lamb, seafood, and duck are all prepared inventively and tastefully, as are several pasta dishes. Entrées start at $14.

✐ ♿ ⵃ **Ace Bar & Grill** (320-251-0232), 423 E. St. Germain. Open daily for all three meals. This cheerful bar and grill has been open for 75 years and is particularly—and justifiably—proud of its barbecued ribs. But the menu has much more than ribs, with choices varying from sandwiches to burgers to casseroles (or "hot dishes" in the Minnesota vernacular). Entrées start at $7.

✐ ♿ ⵃ **Anton's** (320-253-3611; www.antonsrestaurant.com), 2001 Frontage Rd. N., Waite Park. Open Mon.–Sat. for lunch, daily for dinner. Originally a speakeasy during the Prohibition years, Anton's is now a laidback log cabin restaurant specializing in grilled meats and sandwiches. If that's not enough to make you happy, the bar's impressive scotch list should take care of it. Entrées start at $11.

✐ ♿ ⵃ **Mexican Village** (320-252-7134), 509 W. St. Germain. Open daily for lunch and dinner. Don't go looking for authentic Mexican; instead, plan on enjoying reasonably priced Americanized Mexican served in a cheerfully (and unrepentantly) kitschy atmosphere. Entrées start at $6.

✳ Entertainment

LIVE PERFORMANCES

Probably because it's a college town, St. Cloud has a large number of live-performance venues for a city its size.

Paramount Theatre and Visual Arts Center (320-259-2463; www.paramountarts.org), 913 W. St. Germain. A vintage 1920s movie theater, the Paramount has gone through its era of neglect and emerged as a classy setting for a variety of live performances: the St. Cloud Symphony Orchestra, Chamber Music Society, St. Cloud Civic Theater, and Great River Educational Theatre all perform here regularly, and traveling performers include jazz and Broadway productions.

Fine Arts Series (320-363-5777; www.csbsju.edu/finearts), Benedicta Arts Center, College of Saint Benedict/Saint John's University. The College of Saint Benedict opened a new performing arts center in 2006, and an active schedule of artists keeps the center open and busy. Recent performers have included the Ballet Folklorico, Ladysmith Black Mambazo, BeauSoleil, and the Minnesota Orchestra.

DB Searle's (320-253-0655; www.dbsearles.com), 18 5th Ave. S. Open Mon.–Sat. Housed in a historic building first used as the "African Saloon and Barbershop." The site was bought by lawyer and Civil War veteran Dolson Bush Searle, who built a sturdy brick building that has been, through the years, everything from a bank to a funeral home. Today it's a restaurant and nightclub, with live music several nights a week and karaoke on Tues.

Bo Diddley's Pub & Deli (320-255-9811), 216 6th Ave. Open daily for lunch and dinner. A mellower-than-expected venue, with live music on Wed. and most weekends.

✳ Selective Shopping

All stores are open year-round unless otherwise noted.

Crossroads Center (320-252-2856; www.crossroadscenter.com), 4101 W. Division St. Open daily. This large mall has many of the classic national retailers, including Gap, J. Jill, Wilsons Leather, and Foot Locker. The mall itself is surrounded by smaller strip malls. *Note:* The retail area here is very popular, and the roads that surround and run through it (primarily CR 15) struggle with the traffic loads during busy times. Be prepared to spend a considerable amount of time inching along through stoplights en route to your shopping.

Downtown

Unlike some small towns, St. Cloud has managed to keep an active downtown area despite the growth of shopping centers and strip malls. Here are a few of the independent retailers worth visiting.

Books Revisited (320-259-7959; www.booksrevisited.com), 607 W. St. Germain. Open Mon.–Sat. While there's also a location at Crossroads Center, the downtown branch is the original store, and it's packed floor-to-ceiling with new and used books, including some rare items.

Electric Fetus (320-251-2569; www.electricfetus.com), 28 S. 5th Ave. Open daily. Electric Fetus has one of

the largest music inventories in the state (along with its sister locations in the Twin Cities and Duluth), as well as gifts and jewelry.

Arts Co-Op (320-252-3242), 619 St. Germain. Open Mon.–Sat. Represents local and national artists in varying media.

Loft Fine Art Gallery (320-251-8180), 819 W. St. Germain. Open Mon.–Fri. Presents works of local artists, both fine art and literary.

Antiques Gallery (320-202-9068), 619 St. Germain. Open Mon.–Sat. Fine antiques store specializing in china, glassware, pottery, and figurines.

✳ Special Events

Minnesota Homegrown Kickoff (800-635-3037; www.minnesotabluegrass.org), El Rancho Mañana, Richmond. Late May or early June. $11–35 includes camping. Old-time bluegrass, swimming, horseback riding, and camping, all in one three-day festival.

The Caramel Roll (320-356-7191; www.lakewobegontrails.com/caramelroll.htm), St. Joseph. Early June. Registering in advance costs $15 for adults, $10 for children under 16; $5 more for day-of-event registration. An annual bike-and-eat event, with your choice of 8-, 15-, or 25-mile roads, with pit stops for caramel rolls. As the Lake Wobegon Trails Association people say, "A sweet roll on a sweet trail."

Granite City Days (320-255-7295; www.granitecitydays.com), St. Cloud. A four-day festival in June, including a golf tournament, tours of historic homes and downtown St. Cloud, a parade, a block party, and a fly-in pancake breakfast, among other events.

Tour of Saints (320-363-1311; 800-651-8687; www.tourofsaints.com). Registration is $33 for adults, $20 ages 5–16. Held in early July. Not a religious event, but one for serious bikers. The tour starts and ends at the College of Saint Benedict, and riders choose either a 35- or 50-mile route through the rolling countryside and small towns in the St. Cloud area.

Sinclair Lewis Days (320-352-5201), Sauk Centre. An annual late-July celebration of the life of Sauk Centre's most famous and possibly most contentious former resident.

The week of events includes a 5K run, horseshoe and softball tournaments, a street dance, live music, and the crowning of Miss Sauk Centre.

Half-Way Jam (877-425-3526; www.halfwayjam.com), Rice. Tickets start at $30. Held the last weekend in July. Named for its location halfway between the Twin Cities and northern Minnesota, the Half-Way Jam brings in several oldies rock bands for three days of concerts. Camping can be purchased for the entire festival only. Festival organizers discourage parents from bringing children.

MILLE LACS

Minnesota's second largest lake is Lake Mille Lacs, which draws thousands of fishing and watersports lovers each year. Located on the Mille Lacs Reservation, Mille Lacs is just about as popular in winter as it is in summer, thanks to continued growing interest in ice fishing. The region has responded by adding more options for ice-house rental, including some very deluxe buildings with electricity and heat.

✳ To See

& ⍾ **Grand Casino Mille Lacs** (800-626-5825; www.grandcasinomn.com), 777 Grand Ave., Onamia. A full-scale gambling complex with slots, blackjack, and bingo. The complex also has several restaurants, a hotel, a theater with frequent live performances, a Kids Quest child-care area, and an extensive video arcade.

✐ & **Mille Lacs Indian Museum** (320-532-3632; www.mnhs.org/places/sites/mlim), 43411 Oodena Dr. Open Memorial Day–Labor Day, Wed.–Mon.; Apr., May, Sept., and Oct., Thurs.–Sat.; off-season by appointment. This museum is a joint venture between the Mille Lacs Band and the Minnesota Historical Society, and it's a thoughtful, detailed collection of exhibits showing how Native Americans of the region lived and worked centuries ago. The craft room has an especially lovely collection of beadwork and birch-bark basketry. An adjacent trading post is a re-creation of a 1930s-era trading post, and is open year-round on weekends to sell Native American gift items.

✳ To Do

The Lake Mille Lacs area is all about outdoor activities, many of which center on the massive lake. Fishing, hunting, boating, biking, hiking, cross-country skiing, snowshoeing, snowmobiling—it's all here.

Kathio State Park (320-532-3523; www.dnr.state.mn.us/state_parks/mille_lacs _kathio/index.html), 15066 Kathio State Park Rd., Onamia. Open daily. Near the Mille Lacs Indian Museum is the entrance to this park, which has year-round opportunities for recreation. The Rum River flows through the park from its source in Lake Mille Lacs, and visitors can use canoes or rowboats to explore. A swimming beach is open during summer, as is a 100-foot observation tower and a wide variety of campsites and cabins (some of which are year-round). Winter enthusiasts can cross-country ski, snowshoe, or snowmobile on groomed trails.

Mille Lacs Wildlife Management Area (320-532-3537; www.dnr.state.mn.us/ wmas/index.html), 29172 100th Ave., Onamia. Open daily. This small WMA (61 acres) is a carefully preserved area of forests and wetlands. During hunting season, camping is allowed; those with permits can hunt deer, bear, and small game.

✳ Lodging

Accommodations are open year-round unless otherwise noted.

✦ ⚐ ⌇ **Izatys Resort** (800-533-1728; www.izatys.com), 40005 85th Ave., Onamia. A luxury complex of town-homes and villas (ranging from two to four bedrooms), as well as a lodge offering hotel rooms on the shores of Lake Mille Lacs. Boat rental, two 18-hole golf courses, fishing and hunting guides, tennis courts, and indoor and outdoor pools are all available on site. Hotel rooms start at $82; homes start at $195.

✦ ⚐ ⌇ **Grand Casino Mille Lacs** (800-468-3517; www.grandcasinomn .com), 777 Grand Ave., Onamia. This huge hotel has several room types, including a number of luxurious suites with four-person Jacuzzi and separate living area. The large indoor swim-ming pool and whirlpool are in a nicely decorated wing. Rates start at $50.

✦ **Mille Lacs Lodge** (320-532-3384; www.millelacslodge.com), 8673 340th St., Onamia. This rustic, cozy lodge has just six rooms, which can be rented individually—or a group can rent the entire lodge at a discount from the individual room rate. All

rooms have private bath. The lodge grounds have a covered picnic area and a fire pit; hunting and fishing guides can be arranged, as can home-cooked meals. Rates start at $79.

🐾 ✦ ⚐ ⌇ **Twin Pines Resort** (320-692-4413; www.twinpinesmillelacs .com), 7827 US 169, Garrison. A family-friendly resort with cabins and motel rooms on Lake Mille Lacs. The property is a good value, with summer and winter fishing guides available (as well as ice-house rental in winter) and a restaurant/bar on site. Rates start at $50.

✳ Where to Eat

Restaurants are open year-round unless otherwise noted.

✦ ⚐ ⌇ **Izatys** (800-533-1728; www .izatys.com), 40005 85th Ave., Onamia. Open daily for dinner; sea-sonally for lunch; check the Web site. One of the few fine-dining restaurants in the area, Izatys has an upscale din-ner menu that includes traditional steak house foods as well as some inventive Latin American and south-western dishes. Entrées start at $14.

✏ ♿ ♉ **Grand Casino Mille Lacs** (800-626-5825; www.grandcasinomn .com), 777 Grand Ave., Onamia. The casino has four restaurants on site, one of which (Plums, a quick-service burger-and-pizza café) is open 24 hours Wed.–Sun. There's also a buffet restaurant, a casual grill restaurant, and a steak house open for dinner only. Entrées start at $4.

✏ ♿ **Svoboda's Spotlite** (320-692-4692), 111 Madison St., Garrison. Open daily for all three meals. Breakfast is served all day at this friendly café, a local institution. The home-cooked foods are simple but delicious, and prices are reasonable. Kids' and senior menus available. Entrées start at $4.

WILLMAR

The Willmar area has not seen the same kind of tourism growth experienced by Brainerd, which is not necessarily a bad thing; the rolling, forested countryside and quiet lakes here can provide the utmost in tranquility. The downside is that there's less to do for visitors who don't want to spend their entire vacation on the lake. Still, if you're looking for a restful, beautiful retreat, the Willmar area has plenty to offer.

✳ To See and Do

✏ ♿ **The Mikkelson Collection** (320-231-0384; www.fallsflyer.com), 418 Benson Ave. SE, Willmar. Call for appointment. An astonishing collection of vintage toy and full-sized boats and outboard motors, some of which are the only ones still in existence.

✏ ♿ **Schwanke's Museum** (320-231-0564), 3310 US 71 S., Willmar. Open Mon.–Sat. $5 adults, $2 for children under 12. The vehicular counterpart to the Mikkelson Collection, this museum has over 300 antique tractors, cars, and trucks.

✏ **Big Kahuna Fun Park** (320-796-2445; www.spicerfun.com), 190 Progress Way, Spicer. Open daily Memorial Day–Labor Day. Rates run $3–5. This outdoor amusement park has mini golf, bumper boats, two go-cart tracks, and a kids' Power Wheels course.

✏ ♿ **World's Largest Ball of Twine**, US 12, Darwin. Open daily. Memorialized in song by Weird Al Yankovic, the centerpiece of the little town of Darwin (east of Willmar) is the giant ball of twine, the largest to be rolled by one person. It took Francis Johnson (son of US senator Magnus Johnson) nearly 30 years to create this ball, which now stands 11 feet tall.

✏ ♿ **The Old Depot Museum** (320-275-3876; www.the olddepot.com), 651 W. US 12, Dassel. Open daily Memorial Day–Oct. 1. $2.50 adults, $1 for children under 12. East of Darwin is the little town of Dassel, which is home to this museum. The depot was built in 1913 and now houses a two-story collection of railroad artifacts. The collection is extensive, including a two-man handcar, lights, bells, whistles, railway uniforms, and spittoons.

✍ ♿ **Cokato Museum** (320-286-2427; www.cokato.mn.us/cmhs), 175 W. 4th St., Cokato. Open Tues.–Sun. Admission is free. The region's Finnish and Swedish heritage is celebrated and documented in this museum, which includes a log home and sauna, as well as a rather intimidating early dentist's office.

✳ To Do

The Willmar lakes area is really about outdoor activities. There are more than 100 lakes scattered throughout the rolling land, punctuated by farmland and forest and ringed with small resorts. Fishing, boating, biking, hiking, snowmobiling, cross-country skiing—it's a playground for the outdoors lover.

Sibley State Park (320-354-2055; www.dnr.state.mn.us/state_parks/sibley/index.html), 800 Sibley Park Rd. NE, New London. Open daily. Sibley State Park has a wide variety of activities, including hiking to the top of Mount Tom, the tallest hill for miles, and swimming, fishing, boating, and canoeing on one of the many lakes. Camping is allowed, including one camping area specifically for horse-riding campers.

✳ Lodging

Accommodations are open year-round unless otherwise noted.

✍ **Willow Bay Resort** (320-796-5517; 877-796-5517; www.willowbay resort.com), 5280 132nd Ave. NE, Spicer. Nine cabins, all either lakefront or lakeview. Cabins come with a boat; outboard motor rental is extra. A small swimming beach has plenty of plastic kayaks and paddle boats for a good playtime. Rates start at $135.

✍ ♿ **Sunset Shores Resort** (877-813-7317; www.sunsetshoresresort -mn.com), 18986 CR 5 NW, New London. This resort on Norway Lake has 10 cabins, including one with six bedrooms. The beach area has a number of toys for kids of all ages, including a water raft, paddle boats, and kayaks, and boat activities include fishing, tubing, and waterskiing. Winter visitors can prearrange ice-house rental. Rates start at $95.

🐾 ✍ ♿ **Island View Resort** (800-421-9708; www.islandviewresort -nestlake.com), 5910 132nd Ave. NE, Spicer. Several small but comfortable cabins, all with private fire rings. Island View is located on quiet Nest Lake, and the resort has a decent sandy beach with plenty of beach toys. Boat and motor rentals are available. Be sure to stop by the resort's store to meet the parrot that can whistle the Andy Griffith theme song. Rates start at $125.

Spicer Castle Bed and Breakfast (800-821-6675; http://spicercastle .com), 11600 Indian Beach Rd., Spicer. This B&B is home to the Murder Mystery Dinner Theater (see *Entertainment*). The large property has eight rooms in the main house, two in the Garden House, two in the Honey House, four in the Carriage House, and two separate cottages. The main house was built in 1895 by John Spicer, and the rooms are named for his descendants. Each has a private bath and is lovingly decorated, including artwork done by Spicer family members. Daily rates include full breakfast and an afternoon tea. Rates start at $94; packages including the Murder Mystery Dinner Theater are available.

✳ Where to Eat

The restaurant scene in Spicer hasn't evolved to the level of the Brainerd lakes, but there are still options for lake enthusiasts with an appetite. Besides some of the usual fast-food suspects (Subway, Dairy Queen), there are some local spots that serve hearty meals with friendly service.

✐ ♿ ♈ **Melvin's on the Lake** (320-796-2195; www.melvinsonthelake .com), 159 Lake Ave. S. Open daily for lunch and dinner May–Sept, Thurs.–Sat. only the rest of the year. Hearty burgers and other sandwiches, salads, plentiful appetizers, ribs and steak at dinner. Entrées start at $15.

✐ ♿ **Westwood Café** (320-796-5355), 142 Lake Ave. N. Open daily for breakfast and lunch, Mon.–Sat. for dinner. A casual café offering burgers, sandwiches, salads, and steak at dinner. Entrées start at $9.

✳ Entertainment

♿ ♈ **Spicer Castle Murder Mystery Dinner** (800-821-6675; http://spicer castle.com/mystery.html), 11600 Indian Beach Rd., Spicer. Fri. and Sat. evenings. Tickets start at $49. If you like a little mystery with your dinner, make reservations at the Spicer Castle (see *Lodging*) for an evening of food and sleuthing. The event includes a five-course dinner themed to match the locale of the murder. The dinner can be purchased separately or as part of a lodging package.

✳ Special Events

Lakes Area Studio Hop (320-231-8560; www.studiohop.org), Willmar. Taking place in late June, the hop allows guests to visit nearly 40 artists in and around the Willmar area, either in their private studios or in local art galleries.

✐ **Sonshine Festival** (800-965-9324; www.sonshinefestival.com), Willmar. Tickets start at $65 and include space for camping. Mid-July. This massive three-day Christian music festival spreads over five stages, complete with kids' activities, camping, and a skateboard park.

Arguably one of the most popular lake areas in the state, the Brainerd lakes area has undergone a shift over the last several years. The small-town community with a few large resorts and dozens of small mom-and-pop resorts is evolving into a larger-scale resort community, complete with more lodging, restaurant, and off-the-lake entertainment activities. The increased efforts to bring in more traffic year-round have succeeded, and that means this region perhaps isn't as restful as some others, particularly Willmar and Spicer. That said, for visitors wanting a wide variety of options for their vacations, the Brainerd area is hard to beat.

✳ To See

❧ **Pirate's Cove Mini-Golf and Billy Bones Raceway** (218-828-9002; www
.piratescove.net), 17992 MN 371 N., Brainerd. Open daily Memorial Day–Labor Day; weekends from the last weekend in Apr.–the third weekend of Oct. Rates start at $6.95 for adults and $6.50 for children. A fairly new and very fun pirate-themed mini golf course. You can play one of the two 18-hole courses, or play both at a discount. Next door is the Billy Bones Raceway, which has three go-cart tracks.

❧ ♿ **This Old Farm** (218-764-2524; www.thisoldfarm.net), 17553 MN 18, Brainerd. Open daily Memorial Day–Labor Day, plus selected weekends in Oct. and Dec. (for Halloween and Christmas). $12.95 ages 17 and under, $10.95 ages 18 and over, $9.95 seniors; free for children under 2. Part history village, part amusement park. Attractions include a 26-foot-tall talking Paul Bunyan, amusement rides, and the Pioneer Village, which includes an original log cabin, dentist's office, schoolhouse, and post office.

❧ ♿ **Crow Wing County Historical Museum** (218-829-3268), 320 Laurel St., Brainerd. Open Tues.–Sat. $3 adults; free for children under 12. This lively museum used to be the sheriff's office and county jail. Now it houses a wide-ranging collection of historical items detailing the region's lumber, railroad, and mining history, as well as Native American artifacts.

❧ ♿ **Brainerd International Raceway** (218-824-7220; 866-444-4455; www
.brainerdraceway.com), 5523 Birchdale Rd., Brainerd. Drag racing and road racing at their finest. Paul Newman has been among the drivers.

❧ ♿ **Nisswa Pioneer Village** (218-963-0801), Nisswa. Open mid-June–Aug., Wed.–Sat.; May–mid-June, open weekends. Admission is $1. Nisswa's Pioneer Village comprises nine buildings, including log homes and a schoolhouse, while the old caboose and train depot holds railroad relics. An annual Scandinavian festival attracts large crowds (see *Special Events*).

✳ To Do

Pequot Lakes Fire Tower, CR 11, Pequot Lakes. Admission is free. Definitely not for the faint of heart or weak of knees, but if you'd like a spectacular view of the surrounding forestland, ascend this 100-foot tower. The tower itself isn't the only climb; the walk from the parking lot is straight uphill as well.

Paul Bunyan State Trail. Starting at the site of the former Paul Bunyan Amusement Center on MN 210, this paved trail runs 48 miles to Hackensack.

Northland Arboretum (218-829-8770; http://arb.brainerd.com), 14250 Conservation Dr., Brainerd. Rather incongruously located behind the Westgate Mall, this nature preserve covers 500 acres of forest and prairie that has evolved on the site of a former landfill. The Nature Conservancy owns about 40 percent of the arboretum. Open year-round, with several miles of hiking and cross-country ski trails.

Crow Wing State Park (218-829-8022; www.dnr.state.mn.us/state_parks/crow _wing/index.html), 3124 State Park Rd., Brainerd. Not only a pristine state forest, but a remnant of the area's past as a fur-trading hotbed. The town of Crow Wing flourished during the heyday, but when the railroad decided to pass through Brainerd rather than Crow Wing, the town's fate was sealed. Today the nearly 2,100-acre park has several miles of hiking trails (some of which are groomed for cross-country skiing in winter) and excellent canoeing opportunities, including a canoe-in campsite. Within the park is the Beaulieu House, the last remaining building from the fur-trading days.

✿ **Nisswa Turtle Races**, Nisswa Trailside Information Center, Nisswa. No worries about breakneck speeds in these races, held every Wed., rain or shine, in summer months. Nevertheless, they're immensely popular with kids, and participation can rise into the hundreds. If you don't have your own turtle, it's possible to rent one. Races start at 2 PM.

✳ Lodging

Accommodations are open year-round unless otherwise noted.

✿ ⚅ ⛾ **Cragun's Resort** (800-272-4867; www.craguns.com), 11000 Craguns Dr., Brainerd. This is one of Minnesota's biggest resorts, and it's also one of the nicest. Besides the well-appointed rooms, cabins, and reunion houses, the resort has a 22,000-square-foot indoor sports complex with tennis and basketball courts, a running track, and a fitness center. The hotel itself has an indoor pool. A full-service spa is on site. Three restaurants are open year-round, two more in summer. Fifty-four holes of golf will keep golfers happy, while boaters and fishing aficionados have direct access to Gull Lake. (*Note:* Cragun's does not allow personal watercraft, or Jet Skis, to be stored on or launched from the property.) Bikes can be rented, and snowmobiles can be hired in winter. Rates start at $129; packages and off-season discounts are available.

✿ ⚅ ⛾ **Madden's** (218-829-2811; 800-642-5363; www.maddens.com), 11266 Pine Beach Peninsula, Brainerd. Open Apr.–Oct. Next door to Cragun's is Madden's, another of the state's largest and nicest resorts, offerings rooms, cabins, and reunion houses. Three 18-hole golf courses are on the property, along with one 9-hole social course. Fishing, boating, hiking, swimming, and tennis are all offered, as are trapshooting (with one week's notice) and seaplane certification. A full-service spa is on site, as is a kids' program July–mid-Aug. for ages 4–12. There are seven restaurants, three fine dining and four casual. Rates start at $137; packages and off-season discounts are available.

✄ ♿ **Train Bell Resort** (800-252-2102; www.trainbellresort.com), 21489 Train Bell Rd., Merrifield. North of Brainerd on North Long Lake, Train Bell Resort is owned and operated by Mike and Connie Bruesch, who left corporate life to run this family-friendly resort. There are several well-maintained lakeside cabins as well as a condo complex, but the resort still keeps its cozy feeling, assisted by weekly activities such as a pancake breakfast, minnow races, and Friday-night dances. Fishing boats are available for rental, and kayaks and paddle boats at the sandy beach are included with the accommodations. Rates start at $150; packages are available.

✄ ♿ ⌕ **Grand View Lodge** (218-963-2234; 866-801-2951; www.grandviewlodge.com), 23521 Nokomis Ave., Nisswa. Grand View harks back to the grand old days of lake resorts. Built in

NORTH LONG LAKE

1919, this venerable resort has maintained its historic elegance while modernizing with the amenities today's resort travelers want. Choose from lodge rooms, cabins, and suites or villas on the property's golf course. An indoor pool with waterslide shares a building with a fitness center, but in good weather swimming is done at the sandy beach. Boats can be rented, as can bikes and horses for riding. There are three 18-hole golf courses

AT THE TRAIN BELL RESORT

and one 9-hole course. The full-service spa is open year-round, as are the resort's six restaurants. Two separate kids' clubs, one for ages 3–6 and the other for ages 7–12, give parents a break from full-time child care. Lodging rates start at $140; packages and off-season discounts are available.

✐ ♿ ♈ **Breezy Point Resort** (800-432-3777; www.breezypointresort .com), 9252 Breezy Point Dr., Breezy Point. Located on Pelican Lake, this resort has a huge variety of accommodations—lodge rooms, one- and two-bedroom apartments, and a series of lodgings called the "Unique Retreats": log cabins, A-frame cabins, and full houses. The largest has 10 bedrooms and can accommodate 18 people. For recreation, there are two 18-hole golf courses, an indoor pool, and extensive sandy beach with boat rentals available. The summer months bring live musical performances. Winter brings a new round of activity, including a nine-hole golf course on the lake, skating rinks, cross-country skiing (equipment available for rental), and a snow-tubing hill adjacent to the resort. The resort has two full-service dining areas, the more attractive of which is the Antlers Dining Room, which was built with post-and-beam construction and features two large antler chandeliers. Rates start at $99; packages are available.

✐ ♿ ♈ **Lost Lake Lodge** (218-963-2681; 800-450-2681; www.lostlake .com), 7965 Lost Lake Rd., Lakeshore. Open mid-May–early Oct. This small but lovely resort has beautifully outfitted cabins in a quiet, tucked-away location on Lost Lake. Rates are all-inclusive, meaning guests have full breakfast and four-course dinners daily included in their rates, and the

food is well worth it (dinner is available to the public; see *Where to Eat*). Canoes, fishing boats, and bikes are also included in the rates, and fishing guides as well as massage therapists can be hired at an additional fee. Rates start at $132 per adult, with varying discounts for children; packages are available.

🐾 ✐ ♿ ♈ **Nordic Inn Medieval Brew and Bed** (218-546-8299; www.vikinginn.com), 210 1st Ave. NW, Crosby. Get truly into the spirit of ancient Minnesota history with a stay at this bed & breakfast. Housed in a former Methodist church, the Nordic Inn has five rooms with disparate themes, including Odin's Loft, decorated with armor and weapons, and the Locker Room, decorated for Minnesota Viking football fans. Breakfast is included in the room rates. On nights when enough rooms are occupied, guests can participate in an interactive Viking dinner theater performance, complete with Viking feast. Room rates start at $58; packages are available.

✳ Where to Eat

Restaurants are open year-round unless otherwise noted.

✐ ♿ **371 Diner** (218-829-3359), 14901 Edgewood Dr., Brainerd. Open daily for all three meals. Located on US 371 through Brainerd, the 371 Diner is a replica of a 1950s diner and has a respectable (if high-calorie) menu of burgers, sandwiches, and ice cream treats. Kids' meals are served in a cardboard racecar. Entrées start at $4.

✐ ♿ **Sawmill Inn** (218-829-5444), 601 Washington St., Brainerd. Open daily for all three meals. It doesn't look like much on the outside, but the Sawmill is the classic small-town café, complete with huge breakfasts and hearty sandwiches. Entrées start at $4.

✒ ⅋ **Zorbaz on the Lake** (218-692-4567, 36215 CR 66, Cross Lake; 218-963-4790, 8105 Lost Lake Rd., Lakeshore; www.zorbaz.com). Open daily for dinner, weekends for lunch; open daily for lunch and dinner in summer. A beach bar with Mexican food, pizza, pasta, and plenty of beer. Take the kids for the arcades. At the Cross Lake location, a dock is provided for diners arriving by boat. Entrées start at $5.

✒ ♿ ⅋ **Black Bear Lodge and Saloon** (218-828-8400; www.black bearlodgemn.com), 14819 Edgewood Dr., Baxter. Open daily for lunch and dinner; open Sunday for brunch. Standard bar-and-grill fare, including sandwiches and burgers, steaks, and seafood. Entrées start at $9.

✒ ♿ ⅋ **Brauhaus German Restaurant and Lounge** (218-652-2478; www.brauhausgerman.com), 28234 MN 34, Akeley. Open Wed.–Sun. for dinner; also for lunch on Sun. A cheerful, casual restaurant with an extensive menu of German foods, as well as American items for the finicky eaters. Entrées start at $11.

✒ ♿ ⅋ **Lost Lake Lodge** (218-963-2681; 800-450-2681; www.lostlake .com), 7965 Lost Lake Rd., Lakeshore. Open daily Memorial Day–Labor Day for dinner; weekends-only the rest of the year. One of the best fine-dining options in the Brainerd Lakes area, Lost Lake Lodge takes food staples such as walleye and chicken and turns them into unexpected and delicious offerings. Entrées start at $13.

✒ ♿ ⅋ **Prairie Bay Grill** (218-824-6444; www.prairiebay.com), 15115 Edgewood Dr., Baxter. Open daily for lunch and dinner. Pizza, pasta, sandwiches, and "meat and potato" dishes served in a casual yet upscale environment. Kids are welcome, as are vegetarians, who have several options on the menu. Entrées start at $9.

✳ **Selective Shopping**

Stores are open year-round unless otherwise noted.

CatTale's Books and Gifts (218-825-8611), 609 Laurel St., Brainerd. Open Mon.–Sat. A browser-friendly shop full of new and used books as well as cards, jewelry, and other gifts.

Itsy Bitsy (218-829-1408; www.itsy bitsyboutique.net), 604 Laurel St., Brainerd. Open Mon.–Sat. A small but charming baby shop, with clothing, gifts, and accessories for little ones.

Among the Pines (218-828-6364; www.amongthepines.com), 15670 Edgewood Dr., Baxter. Selling gifts and women's clothing, this shop is also a yarn enthusiasts' supply haven.

Rough Around the Edges (218-692-1880), 14307 Gould Street, Crosslake. Open Tues.–Sat. Country-themed gifts and home decor.

✳ **Special Events**

Brainerd Jaycees Ice Fishing Extravaganza (http://icefishing.org), Brainerd. This annual fishing tournament takes place in late Jan. Significant prizes, including ATVs and underwater cameras, are offered; competitors must purchase tickets, with the proceeds going to charity.

SHOPPING NISSWA

The little town of Nisswa, just north of Brainerd on MN 371, has become a central shopping spot with several small but fun establishments.

✎ **Rainy Days** (218-963-4891; 800-635-7809), 25491 Main St. Open daily. Bookseller for book lovers, with a wide range of reading material for grown-ups and for kids.

Sculpture Gardens (218-963-1313; 888-326-0063; www.sculpturegardens .com), 24428 Smiley Rd. Open daily. Unique home decorating items and accessories, from vases and wall hangings to iron sculptures and birdbaths.

Nordic Living (218-963-0500; 877-766-0500; www.nordicliving.us), 24463 Hazelwood Dr. N. Describing itself as a "department store for Scandinavians," Nordic Living provides gifts, home decor, clothing, and yarn supplies from and about Scandinavia.

Rebecca's Dolls and Miniatures (218-963-0165; www.rebeccasdolls.com), 541 Main St. Open May–Oct. Dolls and dollhouses and accessories, movie memorabilia, miniatures, and shadow boxes.

Totem Pole (218-963-3450; 866-506-5244; www.totempolemn.com), 25485 Main St. Open daily. All Minnetonka moccasins, all the time.

Blue Canoe Boutique (218-963-7330), 25497 Main St. Open daily. Casual and elegant clothing and jewelry.

Simpler Thymes of Nisswa (218-963-9463), 25410 Main St. Open daily. Gift shop focused on personal luxuries, including lotions and soaps, candles, gourmet foods (many locally produced), robes, and women's accessories.

✎ **Nisswa-Stämman Festival** (www .nisswastamman.org), Nisswa. This popular annual festival takes place in early June and features Scandinavian folk music, including traditional Scandinavian musical instruments. There are several live performances, dances, kids' activities, classes, and workshops.

Tour of Lakes Bicycle Ride (218-833-8122; www.paulbunyancyclists .com), Brainerd. This annual ride, held in early June, is not a race, but a way to use a bicycle to take in the spectacular scenery around the Central Lakes area. There are two routes each year, changing annually to maxi-

mize scenery possibilities. Pre-registration is recommended.

Bean Hole Days (218-568-8911), Trailside Park, Pequot Lakes. This two-day July event celebrates the traditional cooking of baked beans: They're buried in large kettles for 24 hours, then raised back up for the impatient consumers. A craft fair and Bean Hole Days coronation ceremony help make the waiting easier.

✎ **Lakes Bluegrass Festival** (218-568-7366; www.lakesbluegrassfestival .org), Pequot Lakes. Rates start at $7 for adults, $3.50 for teens (with parents); free for 12 and under (with parents). Late Aug. Four days of blue-grass concerts and workshops. Blue-grass fans can purchase a ticket for the entire series or by the day. Camping is available at the site; campsites are not prereserved, but prepurchasing a pass is recommended to guarantee a spot.

Fish House Parade, Aitkin. The day after Thanksgiving marks the official start not only to the holiday retail season, but also to this annual rite of passage into winter. Participants parade their fish houses, usually decorated to the hilt in what appears to be a one-upmanship show of hilarity.

St. Croix Valley 6

UPPER ST. CROIX

LOWER ST. CROIX

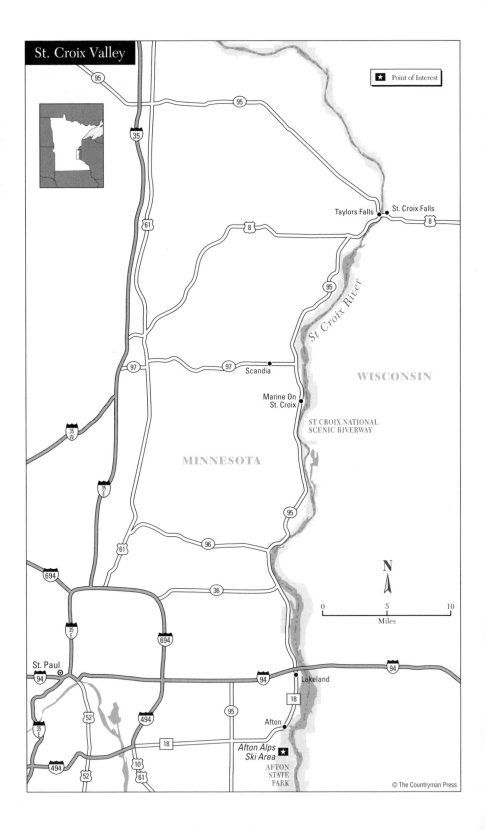

St. Croix Valley

Point of Interest

Taylors Falls   St. Croix Falls

St Croix River

WISCONSIN

Scandia

Marine On
St. Croix

ST CROIX NATIONAL
SCENIC RIVERWAY

MINNESOTA

N

0   5   10
Miles

St. Paul

Lakeland

Afton

Afton Alps
Ski Area

AFTON
STATE
PARK

© The Countryman Press

ST. CROIX VALLEY

There are lakes in this area, but the primary source of outdoor recreation in the St. Croix Valley rests along the riverbanks. This small but highly scenic region derives its beauty from the St. Croix River and surrounding landscapes, as well as the wealthy New England families who settled here more than a century ago, re-creating their home villages along the riverside; the small towns remain intact and as charming and historic as they were when they were first built. Along with the New Englanders came the Scandinavians, building tightly knit agricultural and cultural enclaves. Logging and the fur trade drove the growth of the area during the 19th century, and today's visitors can still find remnants of those industries, primarily in place-names. The small towns are quaint and wonderful to wander around, while heading upriver can provide insight into the state's Scandinavian heritage. Artists have not been immune to the area's beauty: The arts community is strong and growing throughout the valley.

GUIDANCE

Taylors Falls Chamber of Commerce (651-465-6315; 800-447-4958; http://taylorsfallschamber.org).

Stillwater Chamber of Commerce (651-439-4001; www.ilovestillwater.com), 106 S. Main St., Stillwater.

Afton Area Business Association (651-436-8883; www.aftonmnarea.com), Afton.

GETTING THERE

By car: MN 95 follows the state border along the St. Croix River from St. Croix Falls to south of Stillwater. From the Twin Cities, MN 36 goes straight into Stillwater; taking I-35 north to MN 95 will lead you into Taylors Falls. I-35 to US 8 will bring you through Franconia, while I-35 to MN 97 leads just north of Scandia. Both MN 97 and US 8 connect with MN 95.

By air: Air service is through the Minneapolis/St. Paul International Airport.

GETTING AROUND

Having a vehicle is a necessity when traveling around the St. Croix Valley region.

WHEN TO COME

Summer is the most popular time to visit, and Stillwater in particular can be quite busy and congested as shoppers and boaters converge upon the quaint little town. Fall foliage viewers come in, well, fall, but the area quiets down in winter—traffic mostly consists of shoppers.

MEDICAL EMERGENCY

Call **911**.

Lakeview Hospital (651-439-5330; 800-423-7212; www.lakeview.org), 827 Churchill St. W., Stillwater.

UPPER ST. CROIX

The upper St. Croix Valley, from Marine on St. Croix up toward Hinckley, is full of natural beauty, from rivers to woodlands to prairie to glacial trails. It's a park lover's dream. Some of Minnesota's most beautiful state parks are in this area, running along the river and offering nearly every kind of recreational opportunity, including swimming, canoeing, hiking, camping, horseback riding, cross-country skiing, and snowshoeing. The little village of Marine on St. Croix is peaceful and picturesque, and the river town of Taylors Falls includes an area—the Angel Hill District—that could have been lifted right off a New England portrait. Scandinavian culture is alive and well in Scandia, and the region's popularity among artists is demonstrated in Franconia.

✳ To See

Attractions are open year-round unless otherwise noted.

✧ **Folsom House** (651-465-3125; www.mnhs.org/places/sites/fh), 272 W. Gov-

MARINE ON ST. CROIX

also open the two weekends following Thanksgiving. $4 adults, $1 ages 6–12;
free for those under 6 and members of the Minnesota Historical Society. This
charming home looks like it was plucked out of a New England landscape, along
with several neighbors, and replanted in the Angel Hill District. Home of a lumber baron and state senator, the Folsom House gives a view of Minnesota's early
days—and of the St. Croix River.

𝒮 **Stone House Museum** (651-433-2061), 241 5th St., Marine on St. Croix.
Open Memorial Day–Labor Day, Sat.–Sun. Admission is free, but donations are
requested. This historic Scandinavian site is tucked into the small, picturesque
town of Marine on St. Croix. The Stone House, aptly named for its Scandinavian
stone architecture, was originally the town meetinghouse. Today it's a repository
for artifacts and photographs documenting Scandinavian settlers in the early
19th century.

𝒮 ⅙ **Gammelgården** (651-433-5053; www.gammelgardenmuseum.org), 20880
Olinda Trail, Scandia. Open May 1–mid-Oct., Fri.–Sun. Special events are
offered throughout the year; check the Web site for details. $4 adults; free for
children under 12. Gammelgården is a living history museum paying tribute to
the Scandinavian roots of the region. Several original immigrant homes and
other buildings, including a church, have been restored on 11 acres of farmland.
The site is open for public tours in summer, but year-round the museum offers a
vast array of special events and classes, including music festivals, sausage-making
classes, and an annual Midsommar Dag (Midsummer Day) celebration (see *Special Events*).

𝒮 **Hay Lake School Museum** (651-433-4014; http://wchsmn.org/museums/
scandia), Olinda Trail N. and Old Marine Trail, Scandia. Open June–Aug.,
Fri.–Sun.; May, Sept., and Oct., Fri. and Sun. $5 adults, $1 ages 16 and under;
free for Washington County Historical Society members. If Gammelgården isn't
enough history for you, check out the nearby Hay Lake School Museum. Listed
on the National Register of Historic Places, this museum is made up of a former
schoolhouse and a log home built in the late 1800s.

✳ To Do

Wild Mountain & Taylors Falls Recreation (651-465-6315; 800-447-4958;
www.wildmountain.com), 37200 Wild Mountain Rd., Taylors Falls. Wild Mountain takes advantage of the rolling terrain in the river area to run 25 ski and
boarding runs during winter, along with a snow-tubing course. In summer the
Recreation part of the company offers a water park with alpine slide and go-cart
tracks, as well as public and private charter river cruises, canoe and kayak rental,
and an RV park and campground.

Franconia Sculpture Park (651-257-6668; www.franconia.org), US 8 and MN
95, Franconia. Open daily. Admission is free. The Franconia Sculpture Park is,
intentionally, a work in progress. There are more than 75 exhibits in this rural
exhibition area, and each year somewhere between 15 and 25 artists are invited

AT THE FRANCONIA SCULPTURE PARK

to work and contribute art on a rotating basis. The artworks are spread across a field with flat mowed paths; guided and self-guided tours are offered.

Interstate State Park (651-465-5711; www.dnr.state.mn.us/state_parks/inter state/index.html), US 8, Taylors Falls. Open daily. This state park crosses the river from Minnesota to Wisconsin, offering visitors the best of both. River access makes kayaking and canoeing popular, and interesting geological formations, including exposed lava flows and glacial deposits, make this an intriguing area for exploration. During fall, the autumn colors provide a major draw.

Wild River State Park (651-583-2125; www.dnr.state.mn.us/state_parks/wild _river/index.html), 39797 Park Trail, Center City. Open daily. Hiking and cross-country ski trails, a guest house and camping within the park, and 18 miles of riverside beauty make this park a gem. There are also campsites for visitors with horses. Spring provides some of the most beautiful wildflower displays in the state. For those with GPS units and an itch to explore, the Minnesota DNR site listed above provides coordinates for historical searches here.

St. Croix National Scenic Riverway (715-483-3284; www.nps.gov/sacn). This is what the region is all about—252 miles of lush river scenery, starting in Wisconsin and including both the St. Croix River and the Namekagon River. The headquarters for information is the **St. Croix Visitor Center**, in St. Croix Falls, Wisconsin, which is just across the river from Taylors Falls. As the St. Croix ambles south along the Minnesota border, canoeing and camping are popular activities, but check with the visitor center before making plans—there are restrictions regarding use of campsites and boats to protect the river itself and the land on either side of it. In times of low rainfall, fire restrictions are strictly enforced.

William O'Brien State Park (651-433-0500; www.dnr.state.mn.us/state_parks/ william_obrien/index.html), 16821 O'Brien Trail N., Marine on St. Croix. Open

ST. CROIX STATE PARK

(320-384-6591; www.dnr.state.mn.us/state_parks/st_croix/index.html), 30065 St. Croix Park Rd., Hinckley. Open daily. Minnesota's largest state park was built as a Civilian Conservation Corps (CCC) project during the Depression years. More than 34,000 acres of former farmland has been redeveloped into open parkland, and the buildings constructed by the CCC helped lead to the park's designation as a National Historic Landmark.

Recreational opportunities abound. Besides the St. Croix River, the park also has the Kettle River, the first State Wild and Scenic River. There are 100 miles of trails for hiking, some of which are open to horseback riders and mountain bikers; summer visitors can rent bikes at the Adventure St. Croix Store by the campground. A swimming beach is available, and canoers and kayakers can launch on the river of their choice. Splendid views are available by climbing the park's 100-foot fire tower, or spend some time in the company of your fishing pole. A six-bedroom guest house, cabins, and rustic campsites can be reserved in advance (the guest house is open year-round). In winter, trails are groomed for cross-country skiers and snowmobilers.

daily. This small but lovely park is just north of Marine on St. Croix. Named for a lumber baron who had originally cleared the land of trees, the park is now (more than a century later) reforested and full of wildlife and river access. It's open year-round and offers trails for cross-country skiing and snowshoeing, as well as campsites with electricity for winter camping.

✳ Lodging

Accommodations are open year-round unless otherwise noted. See side bar, next page, for listings.

✳ Where to Eat

Restaurants are open year-round unless noted otherwise.

✎ ♿ **Roberta's of Marine** (651-433-9926; www.robertasofmarine.com), 41 Judd St., Marine on St. Croix. Open daily for breakfast and lunch. A tiny coffee shop with organic coffees, tasty pastries, and delicious soups. Entrées start at $3.

✎ ♿ ♈ **Tangled Up in Blue** (651-465-1000; www.tangledupinblue

THE ST. CROIX RIVER

BED & BREAKFASTS

The upper St. Croix Valley has been compared to quaint New England villages, so it's fitting that there are several charming B&Bs in the area.

The Old Jail (651-465-3112; www.oldjail.com), 349 Government St., Taylors Falls. Three suites and a cottage are offered in two buildings, one a former jail, the other having housed a wide variety of businesses: saloon, chicken-plucking factory, and mortuary. Despite its gruesome history, the suites are lovely, all including private bath, some including old-fashioned record players, one including a bathroom in a cave, and one not recommended for people over 6 feet tall. Rates include breakfast served to your room and start at $140.

The Cottage (651-465-3595; www.the-cottage.com), 950 Fox Glen Dr., Taylors Falls. Open daily Feb.–Dec. There's only one unit, but it's a suite with private dining area overlooking the St. Croix River, decorated in a cozy French country style. Rates start at $115.

Asa Parker House (651-433-5248; 888-857-9969; www.asaparkerbb.com), 17500 St. Croix Trail N., Marine on St. Croix. This lovely Greek Revival home, built in 1856, overlooks the village of Marine on St. Croix. There are four guest rooms, all with private bath; the Alice O'Brien Suite (named for the O'Brien lumber family daughter who donated land for William O'Brien State Park) has a private porch. The property is close enough to Stillwater for easy access to restaurants and shops, but just far enough to provide an idyllic, peaceful retreat. Rates start at $129; packages and extras are available.

Women's Environmental Institute at Amador Hill (651-583-0705; www .w-e-i.org), 15715 River Rd., North Branch. Located in an organic apple orchard on the edge of Wild River State Park, the WEI offers four rooms for guests or groups. Two of the rooms share a bath; the largest has a fireplace. The rooms are simple but attractive; it's the location that makes this a worthwhile getaway. Rates start at $60.

restaurant.com), 425 Bench St., Taylors Falls. Open Wed.–Sun. for dinner. A French fusion restaurant, with upscale fare and a good wine list. Entrées start at $16.

✒ ❧ **The Drive In** (651-465-7831), 572 Bench St., Taylors Falls. Open daily for lunch and dinner, Memorial Day–Labor Day. It's retro, it's got a giant rotating root beer cup on a stick, and burgers and malts are served to your vehicle by carhops. Entrées start at $4.

✒ ❧ **Scandia Café** (651-433-4054; www.scandiamn.com/scandiacafe/index.htm), 21079 Olinda Trail N., Scandia. Open daily for breakfast and lunch. The classic small-town café, often busy with locals who come in for the daily soup specials and turkey luncheon. Entrées start at $4.

✳ Special Events

Midsommar Dag (651-433-5053; www.gammelgardenmuseum.org/ midsommar.shtm), Scandia. Held each year in late June at the Gammel-gården Museum, Midsommar Dag is a celebration of the community's Scandinavian heritage. The raising of the maypole is accompanied by food, music, and dancing in traditional costumes.

🎷 **Spelmansstamma Music Festival** (651-433-5053; www.gammelgarden museum.org/spelmansstamma.shtm), Scandia. Also held each year in mid-Aug. at the Gammelgård Museum, the Spelmansstamma Music Festival provides a variety of traditional Scandinavian folk music, with a Swedish smorgasbord, craft fair, and children's activities.

LOWER ST. CROIX

Stillwater is the central attraction in the lower part of the St. Croix Valley. Calling itself the "Birthplace of Minnesota," it's one of the oldest cities in the state, built by lumber barons and transplanted New Englanders. Like any town that suffers the loss of its primary industry, Stillwater went through its slump in the early 20th century. But the natural beauty surrounding the area, combined with the charm of the downtown streets and buildings, drove a renaissance that has created thriving shops and galleries and a busy tourist trade, particularly on summer weekends, when driving down Main Street can require patience and time.

But the payoff is in the ability to stop, shop, wander along the river and watch the Stillwater Lift Bridge operate, see the sailboats and yachts dotting the water, and have almost more choices of places to dine than seems reasonable. Whether

DOWNTOWN STILLWATER

WARDEN'S HOUSE MUSEUM, STILLWATER

you're wandering on your own for a private retreat, enjoying a couple's romantic getaway, or with your family, Stillwater is a lovely place to spend a day or two. Add in the recreation and dining options south of town, and your stay could be longer.

✳ To See

Attractions are open year-round unless otherwise noted.

✐ **Warden's House Museum** (651-439-5956; http://wchsmn.org/museums/wardens_house), 602 N. Main St., Stillwater. Open Thurs.–Sun., May–Oct. $5 adults, $1 ages 16 and younger; free for members of the Washington County Historical Society. The Warden's House was built in 1853 and used as a residence for prison wardens and superintendents until 1941, when the building was sold to the Washington County Historical Society. Several of the rooms are furnished as they would have been in the late 19th century, while a few are reserved for displays relevant to the region's overall history, including the lumber industry and children's items.

✐ **Joseph Wolf Caves** (651-292-1220), 402 S. Main St., Stillwater. Open Wed.–Mon., Memorial Day–Labor Day. Open weekends Labor Day–Dec. and Mar.–Memorial Day. Admission is $5. These caves were once used for breweries, and today tours illuminate both the caverns and the history behind the brewing.

✳ To Do

St. Croix Boat & Packet Company (651-430-1234; www.andiamo-ent.com), 525 S. Main St., Stillwater. Open May–mid-Oct. Cruise the St. Croix River on

TOUR STILLWATER BY TROLLEY

THE ST. CROIX VALLEY FROM THE SKY

Given the beautiful scenery and the charming small towns, it's only logical that hot-air balloon rides would be a popular pastime in the lower St. Croix Valley. The following establishments all offer balloon service daily May–Oct., weather permitting. Contact the individual companies for off-season possibilities.

Stillwater Balloons (651-439-1800; www.stillwaterballons.com), 14791 N. 60th St., Stillwater. Morning or late-afternoon departures are offered during summer, but balloon rides (dependent on weather) can be taken year-round, and all flights conclude with a champagne celebration. Rides start at $220 per person.

Wiederkehr Balloons (651-436-8172), Lakeland. Morning and afternoon departures are available, with up to 8 passengers booked for a 12-passenger balloon. Champagne is served at the conclusion of the ride. Rates start at $250 for the first person and $200 for subsequent guests in the same party. If a couple wishes to reserve a private balloon, rates start at $795.

Aamodt's Hot Air Balloon Rides (651-351-0101; 866-546-8247; www.aamodts balloons.com), Stillwater. Aamodt's offers hot-air balloon rides with departures from its apple orchard in Stillwater. Rides are reserved for two people only and include a champagne toast. Most rides are scheduled late in the day to take advantage of the views over the St. Croix, but sunrise departures can be accommodated. Rates start at $750 per couple.

your choice of a lunch, dinner, brunch, or live-music cruise. Boats are also available for private charter. Reservations are recommended.

Gondola Romantica (651-439-1783), 425 E. Nelson St., Stillwater. Open daily May–Oct., weather permitting. Who needs Venice? This entrepreneurial effort brings romantic gondola rides right onto the St. Croix River. Options include everything from 20-minute sightseeing jaunts to a five-course dinner cruise. The company offers customized cruises as well. Gondolas hold six people; if you'd like a private excursion, reserve ahead.

Stillwater Trolley (651-430-0352; www.stillwatertrolley.com), 400 E. Nelson St., Stillwater. Open daily May–Oct., weekends Apr. and Nov. Stillwater Trolley operates enclosed, climate-controlled trolleys that take visitors on a 45-minute guided tour of the Stillwater area.

Lumberjack Sports Camps (651-439-5626), 12360 75th St., Stillwater. Takes place each year during Lumberjack Days (see *Special Events*). Got a hankering to find out what life in the lumber industry was really like? Sign up for this camp, which will put you to work learning about log rolling and cross-cut sawing.

Afton Alps (651-436-5245; 800-328-1328; www.aftonalps.com), Afton. This is one of the biggest Minnesota ski resorts, with 40 trails and 18 lifts, a snowboard park, and a tubing hill. In summer it's open to mountain bikers, and an 18-hole course is available for golfers.

Afton State Park (651-436-5391; www.dnr.state.mn.us/state_parks/afton/index.html), Afton. A beautiful nature preserve that provides a strenuous workout for visitors. There are 20 miles of hiking trails, most of which have some sharply steep inclines. The views of the St. Croix River, however, make it worth the effort. One area allows horseback riders, and several miles of trail are open for cross-country skiers in winter. Year-round camping is available.

✳ Lodging

Stillwater is blessed with a number of historic—and romantic—inns for visitors, as well as bed & breakfasts. Accommodations are open year-round unless otherwise noted.

♿ ♈ **Lowell Inn** (651-439-1100; www.lowellinn.com), 102 N. 2nd St., Stillwater. The Lowell Inn is the grand-daddy of historic hotels in Stillwater. Built in 1927 on the site of a former lumberjack hotel, this stately building has 23 impeccably decorated rooms, some with stained-glass windows, antique furnishings, and fireplace, but all with modern conveniences. Several rooms have Jacuzzi. The romance factor here is high. The hotel also has a highly regarded restaurant (see *Where to Eat*). Rates start at $75; packages are available.

♿ ♈ **Water Street Inn** (651-439-6000; www.waterstreetinn.us), 101 Water St. S. A small luxury inn with rooms and suites, most with gas fireplace. The rooms are decorated as befitting to the upscale visitors of the lumber boom days, and several pack-

ages are offered involving meals, flowers, and massages. A well-regarded restaurant and pub round out the amenities. Rates start at $129; packages are available.

🦮 ♿ ♈ **Afton House Inn** (651-436-8883; www.aftonhouseinn.com), 3291 S. St. Croix Trail, Afton. Afton House has 46 rooms, most with canopy or four-poster bed; deluxe rooms have a balcony overlooking the St. Croix River. The location near Afton Alps makes this a good choice for a ski weekend with a warm, romantic hide-away to return to at the end of the day. The inn has a restaurant and bar on site. Rates start at $79; packages are available.

BED & BREAKFASTS

Like the upper St. Croix, the Stillwater area has many choices for historic charm in bed & breakfasts.

The Elephant Walk (651-430-0528; 888-430-0359; www.elephantwalkbb.com), 801 W. Pine St. This detailed Victorian home is the residence of globe-trotting owners who have filled the interior with finds from their travels in Europe and Asia. Each of the four sumptuously decorated rooms has a theme: the Rangoon, Chiang Mai, Cadiz, and Raffles rooms are all decorated according to their geographic designation. All rooms have fireplace and refrigerator with complimentary nonalcoholic beverages; a bottle of wine and appetizers, as well as a four-course breakfast, are included in the rates. Rates start at $139.

The Ann Bean Mansion (651-430-0355; 877-837-4400; www.annbeanmansion.com), 319 W. Pine St. This whimsical home has a colorful history, complete with riches and scandal, and today it has five lovely rooms, all with fireplace and private bath. The Tower Room is a particularly cozy choice. Rooms come with plush robes, and rates include an afternoon glass of wine and full breakfast daily. Rates start at $139.

Rivertown Inn (651-430-2955; www .rivertowninn.com), 306 W. Olive St. Sitting on a hillside above Stillwater, the Rivertown provides beautiful views along with four rooms and five suites, all elaborately decorated and named for literary heavyweights (Lord Byron, Longfellow). The inn is open year-round, but summer visitors will enjoy the use of the private gardens and screened gazebo. All accommodations have luxurious bedding, plush robes, turndown service with handmade chocolates, full breakfast, and evening social hour. Rates start at $175.

Lady Goodwood (651-439-3771; 866-688-5239; www.ladygoodwood .com), 704 1st St. S. This lovingly restored 1895 Queen Anne home has several original details, include a parlor fireplace. The three guest rooms are all lavishly decorated in Victorian style and have private bath; the St. Croix Suite comes with a round king-sized bed. Rates start at $109; packages are available.

LUNA ROSSA RESTAURANT

DOCK CAFÉ

✳ Where to Eat

The lower St. Croix Valley enjoys an affluent resident population and close proximity to the Twin Cities, giving it an abundance of notable dining options, even off-season. Restaurants are open year-round unless otherwise noted.

🍴 ♿ ♉ **Luna Rossa** (651-430-0560; www.lunarossawinebar.com), 402 S. Main St., Stillwater. Open daily for lunch and dinner. Luna Rossa bills itself as an Italian steak house, but that's somewhat of a misnomer; there are plenty of steak and grilled meat options, but the restaurant also has a respectable list of Italian pasta and pizza dishes that are equally worthy of attention. Entrées start at $13.

🍴 ♿ ♉ **Savories** (651-430-0702; www .savoriesbistro.com), 108 N. Main St., Stillwater. Open Tues.–Sun. for lunch and dinner, Thurs.–Sun. for all three meals. The menu changes seasonally at this European-bistro-themed restaurant, and there's always something innovative on offer. Entrées combine Italian with Latin foods, and vegetarians are not ignored. Don't skip dessert. Entrées start at $15.

Dock Café (651-430-3770; www
.dockcafe.com), 425 S. Nelson St.
Open daily for lunch and dinner. It's
open year-round, but this is the place
to be during the warm-weather
months. Situated right on the banks
of the St. Croix, the Dock Café has
outdoor seating that gives diners full
views of river life. Not surprisingly,
the outdoor patio is popular—plan to
arrive early, or wait. However, the
indoor ambience is attractive as well,
with a fireplace and wide windows.
Menu items run heavily to meats and
seafood. Entrées start at $15.

🍴 & **Aprille's Showers Tea Room**
(651-430-2004; www.aprilleshowers
.com), 120 N. Main St., Stillwater. Tea
and luncheon served Tues.–Sun.
Walk-ins welcome, but call ahead for
special theme teas, including American Girl doll tea parties. Aprille's
Showers offers 35 kinds of tea, as well
as the traditional tea foods such as
scones and tea sandwiches. Tea with
scones is $10, while the full tea lunch-
eon is $25.

🍴 & ☿ **Stone's Restaurant** (651-269-
0612; www.stonesstillwater.com), 324
S. Main St., Stillwater. Open Mon.–
Sat. for dinner, Sat.–Sun. for lunch/
brunch. This newer steak house in an
attractive stone building offers classic

STILLWATER'S CITY CENTER

supper-club fare, including huge
steaks and seafood entrées, as well as
gourmet mac-and-cheese. For a dramatic end to your dinner, order the
baked Alaska, served tableside.
Entrées start at $17.

& ☿ **Lowell Inn** (651-439-1100; www
.lowellinn.com), 102 N. 2nd St., Stillwater. Open daily for lunch and dinner. Within the historic Lowell Inn
(see *Lodging*) are two restaurants
worth noting. The formal restaurant,
in the elegant George Washington
Room, serves classic formal dinner
foods such as duck à l'orange and
beef Wellington, while the Matter-
horn Room serves a four-course Swiss
dinner fondue each evening. Entrées
in the George Washington Room start
at $16, while the fondue is $32 per
person.

🍴 & ☿ **Lake Elmo Inn** (651-777-
8495; www.lakeelmoinn.com), 3442
Lake Elmo Ave. N., Lake Elmo.
Open daily for lunch and dinner.
Housed in a former stagecoach stop,
the Lake Elmo Inn serves upscale
fare in a "come as you are" ambience.
Seafood (local and saltwater), pork,
and pasta are the specialties, but be
sure to save room for the "Sin of the
Inn" dessert (if it's still on the periodically changing menu). Entrées start at
$19.

Bayport Cookery (651-430-1066;
www.bayportcookery.com), 328 N. 5th
Ave., Bayport. Open Wed.–Sun. for
dinner. Fixed price menus are all
that's offered, but they're all that's
needed. Relying on local and seasonal
foods, chef Jim Kyndberg offers both
a five-course and a nine-course dinner
(as well as a three-course choose-
your-own based on the nine-course
meal), with wine flights for accompa-

MILL ANTIQUES

niment. Menus might include wild boar, smoked blue cheese, or pheasant. Reservations are required and should be made at least 10 days in advance. It may not be a spontaneous stop, but it's more than worth the effort of planning. Dinners start at $35 depending on the number of courses chosen.

✳ Selective Shopping

Stillwater's main city center, along the riverfront, has developed into a visitor's shopping haven, full of small, charming shops, with hardly any chain stores to be seen. Antiques enthusiasts flock to this community for its large concentration of stores and dealers, but you'll find plenty of other kinds of retail as well.

North Main Studio (651-351-1379; www.northmainstudio.com), 402 N. Main St. Open Thurs.–Tues. (hours subject to change, call ahead to confirm; also by appointment). Local resident and artist Carl Erickson displays, sells, and creates his pottery. Visitors are welcome to watch him at work.

Tamarack House Gallery (651-439-9393; www.tamarackgalleries.com), 112 S. Main St. Open daily. Local and national artists are represented in various media, including painting, etching, sculpture, and photography.

Northern Vineyards (651-430-1032; www.northernvineyards.com), 223 Main St. N. Open daily. This award-winning winery, which uses Minnesota and Wisconsin grapes, is open daily for tastings and tours. In summer enjoy a glass of wine on the back patio, overlooking the lift bridge across the river.

Pineapple Island (651-275-0504), 402 S. Main St. Open daily. This attractive, whimsical shop with the pretty stone front specializes in gifts, including hand-painted drinkware, Thymes bath and body products, gifts for pets, and artwork and jewelry.

Art 'n' Soul/Stillwater Beads (651-275-0255), 202 S. Main St. Open daily. Upscale and humorous gifts at Art 'n' Soul, while Stillwater Beads sells a wide variety of beads, including some unusual and hard-to-find items.

Loome Antiquarian Booksellers (651-430-1092; www.loomebooks .com), 201 S. Main St. Open daily. A bookseller for serious book collectors, with hundreds of thousands of books available. There are also framed engravings for sale, as well as medieval manuscript leaves. A short walk away is the store's sister, Loome Theological Booksellers, specializing in secondhand books on theology and religion.

The Mill Antiques (651-430-1816), 410 N. Main St. Open daily. Located in a historic mill, The Mill Antiques comprises nearly 80 antiques and collectibles dealers spread over three floors. A great spot for serious antiquing or window shopping.

Midtown Antique Mall (651-430-0808; www.midtownantiques.com),

301 S. Main St. Open daily. Another good source for antiques enthusiasts, the Midtown Antique Mall has more than 100 dealers, including several furniture dealers.

✳ Special Events

Rivertown Art Festival (651-439-4001; www.rivertownartfestival.com), Stillwater. Held each year in late May, the Rivertown Art Festival takes place on the banks of the St. Croix River and brings dozens of artists in various media, some local and some national, to display their work. Food and kids' activities are available.

Afton May Fair (651-263-5159; www.aftonmnarea.com/Mayfair.htm), Afton. Complete with maypole and ribbons, the Afton May Fair takes place in late May each year, with three days of music, art shows, wine tastings from local vineyards, Native American storytelling, and Scandinavian folk dancing.

✍ **Lumberjack Days** (651-430-2306; www.lumberjackdays.com), Stillwater. A summer tradition, Lumberjack Days is held in Lowell Park on the St. Croix in mid-July and offers three days of historically themed fun and frolic. Among the events are the Lumberjack Sports Camp (see *To Do*), a chess tournament, a massive parade, an 1860 "vintage base ball" exhibition, a treasure hunt, 5K and 10K races, and lumberjack skills championships.

✍ **Fall Colors Fine Art & Jazz Festival** (651-439-4001; www.ilovestillwater.com), Stillwater. A celebration of the vivid fall colors that occurs in early Oct., the festival showcases the talents of 100 artists. You'll also find live jazz daily, a Main Street Art Crawl, and a variety of kids' activities.

Mississippi River Bluff Country

7

HASTINGS

RED WING

WABASHA

WINONA

LANESBORO

AUSTIN

ROCHESTER

NORTHFIELD

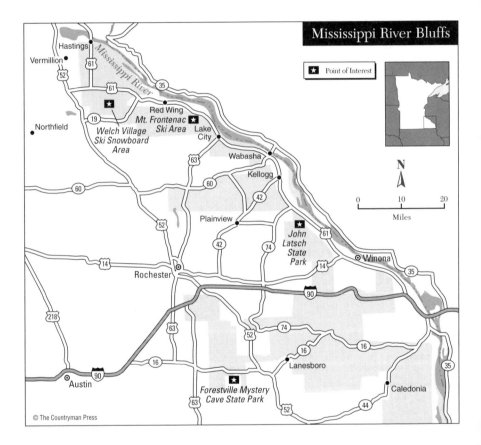

Mississippi River Bluffs

★ Point of Interest

Hastings
Vermillion
Mississippi River
61
52
61
35
Mississippi River
★
19
Red Wing
Mt. Frontenac ★
Ski Area Lake
City
Northfield
Welch Village
Ski Snowboard
Area
63
Wabasha
60
60
Kellogg
52
42
Plainview
42
John
Latsch
74
State
Park
61
14
Winona
14
Rochester
35
90
218
63
74
52
16
16
16
Lanesboro
90
16
Austin
★
Caledonia
Forestville Mystery
63 Cave State Park
52
44

N

0   10   20
              Miles

© The Countryman Press

MISSISSIPPI RIVER BLUFF COUNTRY

The southeastern corner of the state, bordered by the mighty Mississippi to the east, has some of the loveliest terrain in Minnesota: river valleys, rolling hills, woods and wildflowers in-season, and one charming small town after another, including some of the oldest towns in the state, most with many intact historic buildings and landmarks. Unlike more northern reaches, which were leveled and redesigned during the last ice age, the bluff country mostly escaped the glacial ravages and kept instead a variable terrain that includes 500-foot limestone bluffs and deep valleys. The climate here is slightly different, too, warmer and with more rainfall, leading to vegetation not seen elsewhere in the state, including black walnut trees. The region is also home to Minnesota's only poisonous snakes, the timber rattlesnake and the massasauga, which reside mostly in the bluffs themselves or in the swampy areas close to the river. But these snakes are as timid around humans as we are near them, and are slow to strike.

Bike trails abound, many of which are paved and can be used for cross-country skiing in the winter months. As you move westward from the river, clusters of tight-knit Amish communities stand in contrast with the sophistication of cities like Rochester and the tasteful attraction of SPAM in Austin.

GUIDANCE

Hastings Area Chamber of Commerce (651-437-6775; 888-612-6122; www .hastingsmn.org), 111 E. 3rd St. Hastings.

Red Wing Convention and Visitors Bureau (651-385-5934; 800-498-3444; www.redwing.org), 420 Levee St. Red Wing.

Wabasha/Kellogg Chamber of Commerce and Convention and Visitors Bureau (651-565-4158; 800-565-4158; www.wabashamn.org), 160 Main St., Wabasha.

Visit Winona (507-452-0735; 800-657-4972; www.visitwinona.com), offers extensive lodging and activity information for the Winona area.

Rochester Convention and Visitors Bureau (507-2880-4331; 800-634-8277; www.rochestercvb.org), 30 Civic Center Dr. SE, Suite 200, Rochester.

Northfield Convention and Visitors Bureau (507-645-5604; 800-658-2548; www.visitingnorthfield.com), 205 3rd St. W., Suite A, Northfield.

GETTING THERE

By car: US 52 leads south from the Twin Cities into Rochester and connects south of Rochester with I-90, which heads west to Austin or east to Wisconsin. Visitors to Northfield can use MN 19 from US 52. To visit the towns closest to the Mississippi River area, US 61 travels south along the river until it merges with I-90.

By air: Regional commercial airlines, primarily Northwest and its Mesaba branch, serve the city of Rochester. Taxis and rental cars are available from the airports into the city.

By rail: Amtrak has stops in Red Wing and Winona, crossing through from either Minneapolis/St. Paul or Chicago.

GETTING AROUND

Having a vehicle is a necessity when traveling around the Mississippi River bluffs region.

WHEN TO COME

The summer months are the most popular time to visit the river bluffs area, although fall foliage continues to draw larger numbers as well. Rochester benefits from the Mayo Clinic's presence to bring in people year-round.

MAYO CLINIC, ROCHESTER

MEDICAL EMERGENCY

Call **911**.

Regina Medical Center (651-480-4100; www.reginamedical.org), 1175 Nininger Rd., Hastings.

Fairview Red Wing Medical Center (651-267-5000; 866-297-9215; www.redwing.fairview.org), 701 Fairview Blvd., Red Wing.

St. Elizabeth's Hospital (651-565-4531; www.ministryhealth.org), 1200 Grant Blvd. W., Wabasha.

Community Memorial Hospital (651-454-3650; www.winonahealth.org), 855 Mankato Ave., Winona.

Northfield Hospital (507-646-1000; www.northfieldhospital.org), 2000 North Ave., Northfield.

Rochester Methodist Hospital (507-266-7890; www.mayoclinic

.org/methodisthospital), 201 W. Center St., Rochester. Part of the Mayo Clinic's broad range of medical services.

Saint Marys Hospital (507-255-5123; www.mayoclinic.org/saintmaryshospital), 1216 2nd St. SW, Rochester. The second of two Mayo Clinic hospitals.

HASTINGS

✳ To See

Attractions are open year-round unless otherwise noted.

❧ **The LeDuc House** (651-437-7055; www.dakotahistory.org/LeDuc/home.asp), 1629 Vermillion St., Hastings. Open mid-June–Oct., Fri.–Sun.; also for special holiday events (see the Web site). $6 adults, $5 seniors and military personnel, $3 ages 6–17, free for children 5 and under or Dakota County Historical Society members. This beautiful piece of history and architecture, built in 1866, was designed by Andrew Jackson Downing and is a rare historic building that is virtually untouched. The former home of William LeDuc, a commissioner of agriculture under President Rutherford Hayes, the building itself is a delight to visit, but the 4.5-acre grounds are lovely as well, encompassing an apple orchard and forests.

♿ ♉ **Alexis Bailly Vineyard** (651-437-1413; www.abvwines.com), 18200 Kirby Ave., Hastings. Open May–Thanksgiving, Fri.–Sun.; Thanksgiving–Christmas, Sat. only. Closed Christmas–Apr. Minnesota's first and arguably foremost vineyard, first producing a vintage in 1978. The winery works with classic and new-breed grapes that have been found to withstand extreme cold.

♿ ♉ **Treasure Island Resort and Casino** (800-222-7077; www.treasureisland casino.com), 5734 Sturgeon Lake Rd., Welch. Open daily. Slots, blackjack, poker, and bingo are all available in this massive complex southeast of Hastings. Four restaurants and several cocktail bars provide sustenance, and an attached hotel (see *Lodging*) and marina provide options besides gambling.

✳ To Do

♿ **Carpenter St. Croix Valley Nature Center** (651-437-4359; www.carpenter naturecenter.org), 12805 St. Croix Trail, Hastings. Open daily. Admission is free. This small (425 acres) but lavish nature preserve was once a private estate and apple orchard. Today it is a well-maintained natural area, the release site for the University of Minnesota's Raptor Rehabilitation Program, and offers 10 miles of trails, some of which have been adapted for visitors with limited mobility.

Hastings Trail System (651-480-6175), Hastings. The 15-mile paved bike trail winds through Hastings and along the Mississippi River.

Vermillion Falls Park, 215 21st St. E., Hastings. This park, right in the heart of Hastings, has both beautiful waterfalls and trails for hiking and biking. An oasis in the city.

✳ Lodging

Accommodations are open year-round unless otherwise noted.

Classic Rosewood Inn (651-437-3297; 888-846-7966; www.thorwood inn.com), 620 Ramsey St., Hastings. This beautiful 1880 Queen Anne home has been updated to include modern amenities in a classic B&B venue. Eight rooms and suites, all with private bath and some with fireplace and whirlpool, are richly decorated and large enough to allow massage therapists to set up tables for private sessions (reserve in advance). A full breakfast is included each day, either in the dining room or privately. Rates start at $97; packages are available.

✍ ᕕ Υ **Treasure Island Resort and Casino** (888-867-7829; www.treasure islandcasino.com), 5734 Sturgeon Lake Rd., Welch. With over 200 rooms and suites, an elaborate indoor pool and whirlpool, a fitness center, and a child-care center, Treasure Island caters to the gambling crowd but offers the additional amenities to bring in nongambling spouses and family members. Rates start at $89; packages are available.

✳ Where to Eat

Restaurants are open year-round unless otherwise noted.

✍ ᕕ Υ **Levee Café** (651-437-7577), 100 Sibley St., Hastings. Open daily for dinner; Mon.–Sat. for lunch; Sat. for breakfast, Sun. for brunch. A friendly "nice" restaurant where kids are welcome, too. Specialties are pasta and seafood. Entrées start at $7.

✍ ᕕ Υ **Mississippi Belle** (651-437-4814; www.mississippibelle.net), 101 2nd St. East, Hastings. Open Tues.–Sun. for lunch and dinner. An upscale-appearing but reasonably priced restaurant serving Italian specialties as well as steak house fare. Entrées start at $14.

✳ Selective Shopping

Stores are open year-round unless otherwise noted.

The Emporium (651-438-5444; www .theemporiumofhastings.com), 213 E. 2nd St. Open daily. A two-story antiques and consignment gallery specializing in vintage furniture, dolls, jewelry, and primitive tools and pottery.

Antiques on Main (651-480-8129), 205 2nd St. E. Open daily. Twenty dealers, many of whom buy entire estates.

The Briar Patch (651-437-4400), 103 E. 2nd St. Open Tues.–Sat. Vintage clothing, jewelry, and accessories.

Scandinavian Marketplace (651-438-9183; www.scandinavianmarket .com), 218 2nd St. E. Open daily. An extensive collection of Scandinavian home and gift items, including hand-painted furniture, tableware, clothing, books, music, and toys.

Mississippi Clayworks (651-437-5901; www.mississippiclayworks.com), 214 2nd St. E. Open Mon.–Sat. Locally made pottery, including custom orders.

✳ To See

Attractions are open year-round unless otherwise noted.

✐ ♿ **Goodhue County Historical Society** (651-388-6024; www.goodhuehistory
.mus.mn.us), 1166 Oak St. Open Tues.–Sun. $5 adults, $3 seniors, 25¢ unaccom-
panied children over 10; free for children under 16 when accompanied by an
adult and for historical society members. This sizable regional museum has
extensive collections on numerous aspects of the area's history, including archae-
ology, business, geology, immigration, and agriculture. A clothing exhibit has
samples for kids to try out, and there's a tepee to play in. *Note:* The society is
also in the process of placing signage throughout the county, noting the prior
existence of what are now known as "ghost towns."

✐ ♿ **Red Wing Shoe Museum** (651-385-1811; www.riverfrontcentreshops
.com/museum.html), 314 Main St. Open daily. Admission is free. Red Wing
Shoes are indeed manufactured in Red Wing, and this small but lively museum
in the Riverfront Centre has hands-on and historical exhibits showing how the
shoes are made and sold, including the opportunity to build your own shoe.

✐ ♿ **Red Wing Pottery Museum** (657-385-7766; www.rwcsfoundation.org/
museum.htm), Historic Pottery Place Mall, 2000 Old West Main St. Open daily.
Admission is free. Just like the shoes, Red Wing Pottery is made in Red Wing,
and it has a museum. This museum, located within a former pottery factory, has
displays illustrating the pottery process and history, along with an impressive collection of finished objects and historical pieces.

✳ To Do

Great River Road (800-657-3700), US 61. This section of the scenic byway
that runs from Canada to the Gulf of Mexico departs Red Wing and travels to La
Crescent, running along the Mississippi River. The 107-mile byway encompasses
river views, forests, small and historic river towns and villages, and countless
opportunities for natural and wildlife exploration.

Cannon Valley Trail (507-263-0508; www.cannonvalleytrail.com). A 20-mile
paved trail that runs on an old railroad track from Red River to Cannon Falls
along the Cannon River. A Wheel Pass ($3 for adults for a day, or $20 for the
season) is required. **Cannon Falls Canoe and Bike** (507-263-4657; www
.cannonfallscanoeandbike.com) rents kayaks, canoes, and bikes as well as providing shuttle services. Bike offerings include tandem and recumbent bikes, as well
as baby carts.

Frontenac State Park (651-345-3401; www.dnr.state.mn.us/state_parks/
frontenac/index.html), 29223 CR 28 Blvd., Frontenac. This state park is especially valuable for bird-watchers, with over 250 species of birds recorded here.
Camping, hiking, and a winter sliding hill are among the amenities spread across
the park's prairie, forest, and river bluff settings.

Welch Village (651-258-4567; www.welchvillage.com), 26685 CR 7 Blvd.,

Welch. Fifty runs of varying difficulty for skiers and snowboarders as well as a terrain park. The village also rents slope-side bunkhouses, which are rustic with shared baths, but offer the utmost in convenient access for devoted skiers and boarders.

✳ Lodging

Red Wing is a community full of historic inns and bed & breakfasts. As many of these inns are small and Red Wing is a popular destination, be sure to book ahead. Accommodations are open year-round unless otherwise noted.

♂ & ♈ **St. James Hotel** (800-252-1875; 800-252-1875; www.st-james-hotel.com), 406 Main St. Built in 1875, the St. James is "the" hotel in Red Wing. All rooms boast a handsome Victorian decor; larger rooms have whirlpool, and two deluxe rooms include spacious seating area. Two full-service restaurants stand on their own (The Port is a popular dinner restaurant that draws many Twin

ST. JAMES HOTEL

Cities diners; see *Where to Eat*), and there's a pub and coffee shop as well. Rates start at $129; packages are available.

🐾 ♂ **Moondance Inn** (651-388-8145; 866-388-8145; www.moondanceinn.com), 1105 W. 4th St. This beautiful stone inn has five spacious guest rooms, all with private bath and fireplace, featuring antique furniture and sumptuous decorations. Rates include daily breakfast as well as wine and cheese on weekends. Next to the Moondance is the **Guesthouse Next Door**, a 1904 Victorian home that is rented as a whole unit. It holds ten people, and children and pets are welcome. Rates at the Moondance start at $125; rates for the Guesthouse start at $350, and there is a two-night minimum. Packages are available.

Round Barn Farm (651-385-9250; 866-763-2276; www.roundbarnfarm.com), 28650 Wildwood Ln. Round Barn Farm, built in 1861 just 4 miles outside Red Wing, offers five spacious rooms beautifully decorated in vintage country style, complete with antique furniture, private bath, and fireplace or Franklin stove. Breakfast is provided daily in the dining room, which features a massive limestone fireplace. The property is located on 35 acres complete with walking trails and a gazebo. Rates start at $159; packages are available.

Candlelight Inn (651-388-8034; 800-254-9194; www.candlelightinn-redwing.com), 818 W. 3rd St. A striking Victorian home offering five rooms and suites, all with private bath and fireplace. While all the rooms are beautifully decorated, the Butternut Suite in particular is a lesson in opulence and luxury. Full breakfast and afternoon appetizers, wine, and lemonade provided for guests daily. Rates start at $119; packages are available.

Golden Lantern Inn (651-388-3315; 888-288-3315; www.goldenlantern .com), 721 East Ave. Built in 1923 by the former president of the Red Wing Shoe Company, this English Tudor has five lush rooms and suites and several public rooms available to guests. Bedrooms all have private bath; some have fireplace, sitting room, and private balcony. Full breakfast is included daily and is available in the dining room, bedroom, or (during warmer months) on the stone patio. In summer guests have access to the lavish gardens behind the inn. Rates start at $99; packages are available.

Hungry Point Inn (651-437-3660; www.hungrypointinn.com), 1 Olde Deerfield Rd., Welch. Four rooms with private bath, as well as a separate log cottage, in a New England–esque setting. Accommodations are meticulously appointed with antiques and decorations fitting to the early American feeling, although the building itself dates to 1967 (meaning the modern amenities are firmly in place). One of the rooms has a fireplace, while two others have vintage soaking tub. Full breakfast is included. Rates start at $139.

✳ Where to Eat

& ⅄ **The Port Restaurant** (651-388-2846; 800-252-1875; www.port -restaurant.com), 406 Main St. Open daily for dinner. Located in the St. James Hotel (see *Lodging*), this warmly elegant, romantic restaurant offers steak house foods (steaks, seafood, pasta) with unconventional twists. The food is excellent, and reservations are strongly recommended. Entrées start at $16.

🍴 & **The Veranda** (651-388-2846; 800-252-1875; www.port-restaurant .com), 406 Main St. Open daily for breakfast and lunch. A more casual full-service restaurant in the St. James Hotel, the Veranda overlooks the Mississippi with outdoor dining in-season. Traditional breakfast and lunch fare is served. Entrées start at $9.

🍴 & ⅄ **Liberty's** (651-388-8877; www.libertysonline.com), 303 W. 3rd St. Open daily for all three meals. There can be no complaints about access to this restaurant—not only does it deliver throughout Red Wing, but it also provides free shuttle service to and from boats and hotels. The menu aims to please with Italian, Mexican, burgers, and steaks; breakfast includes all-you-can-eat pancakes. Entrées start at $9.

🍴 & ⅄ **Oar d'oeuvre** (651-388-2155; www.greatfoodinredwing.com), 433 Main St. Open Mon.–Sat. for lunch and dinner. This nautically themed restaurant and full bar offers a menu that changes seasonally, with an emphasis on hors d'oeuvres and lighter fare. Entrées start at $7.

🍴 & **Lily's Coffee House & Flowers** (651-388-8797; www.lilyscoffee house.com), 419 W. 3rd St. Open Tues.–Sun. for breakfast and lunch. The quintessential charming small-town coffee shop and café. A surprisingly sizable menu includes sandwiches, salads, and soups, plus a wide variety of coffee drinks.

✆ ⴕ ⵙ **Blue Moon** (651-385-5799; www.bluemoonrw.net), 427 W. 3rd St. Open daily for all three meals. The Blue Moon started life as a bagel shop, then grew into a coffee shop, restaurant, and live-entertainment venue. Sandwiches, soups, and quesadillas are offered all day, and wine and beer are available. Live music is scheduled every weekend. Entrées start at $5.

✳ Entertainment

✆ ⴕ **Sheldon Theatre** (651-388-8700; 800-899-5759; www.sheldon theatre.org), 443 W. 3rd St. This lovely turn-of-the-20th-century gem acts as a live-performance venue for a wide range of performers, including all genres of music, live theater, silent films, and stage productions.

✳ Selective Shopping

Stores are open year-round unless otherwise noted.

Historic Pottery Place Mall (651-388-1428; www.rwpotteryplace.com), 2000 W. Main St. Open daily. Not all shopping malls are bland boxes. The Pottery Place Mall is located in a renovated pottery factory and houses, among other things, the Red Wing Pottery Museum. You'll also find a variety of specialty retailers, including antiques, art galleries, home furnishings, gifts, and fine chocolates.

Red Wing Pottery (651-388-3562; 800-228-0174; www.redwingpottery .com), 1920 W. Main St. Open daily. Besides offering a huge retail selection of Red Wing pottery items (as well as Fiesta Ware), the Red Wing Pottery facility also has several smaller but no less charming shops, including a Minnesota gift store, a candy shop, and a home and garden gift shop.

Red Wing Shoe Store (651-388-6233; www.redwingshoe.com), Riverfront Centre, 314 Main St. Open daily. Not surprisingly, the flagship store of the Red Wing Shoe company sells a wide variety of the high-quality work and athletic shoes.

Ruth's Germanhaus (651-388-0516;

THE SHELDON THEATRE

ANTIQUES

Red Wing has several good antiques stores that draw visitors from great distances. It helps that the antiques are sold in such a charming, historic locale.

3rd Floor Antiques (651-388-3087; www.rwpotteryplace.com), Historic Pottery Place Mall, 2000 W. Main St. Open daily.

Pottery Place Antiques (651-388-7765; www.potteryplaceantiques.com), Historic Pottery Place Mall, 2000 W. Main St. Open daily.

Memory Maker Antiques (651-385-5914), 415 Main St. Open daily.

Al's Antique Mall (651-388-0572), 512 Plum St. Open daily.

Teahouse Antiques (651-388-3669), 703 W. 4th St. Generally open daily, but call ahead.

www.ruthsgermanhaus.com), 1811 Old West Main. Open daily. German gifts, books, clothing, and food items.

Uffda Shop (651-388-8436; 800-488-3332; www.uffdashoponline.com), Bush and Main sts. Open daily. *Uffda*, which is a Norwegian exclamation, is the tongue-in-cheek name for this deeply Scandinavian store filled with specialty baking needs (krumkake irons, lefse grills), fine porcelain tableware, and other gift items.

THE UFFDA SHOP

WABASHA

✻ To See and Do

Attractions are open year-round unless otherwise noted.

🖋 ♿ **National Eagle Center** (651-565-4989; 877-332-4537; www.nationaleagle center.org), 50 Pembroke Ave. Open daily. $5 adults, $4 seniors, $3 ages 6–17, free for children 5 and under. Group discounts are available; call ahead for reservations. Located on the Mississippi River banks, the NEC has a 14,000-square-foot interpretive center with resident eagles, a viewing deck, housing for injured or sick eagles, exhibits with preserved animals and other artifacts, and demonstration and classroom areas. Every autumn the NEC holds a special "deck opening" event to mark the arrival of bald eagles for the winter; this area of the Mississippi has one of the largest concentrations of bald eagles in the contiguous United States.

✧ **Wabasha County Historical Museum** (651-345-3987), US 61, Reads Landing. Open mid-May–Sept., Fri.–Sat., or by appointment. This small museum on the second floor of a former schoolhouse is not necessarily the most comprehensive historical museum in the state, but it does have some items of interest to fans of Laura Ingalls Wilder.

✧ ♿ **Arrowhead Bluffs Museum** (651-565-3829), 17505 667th St. Open daily May–Dec. A museum for hunting enthusiasts. The museum has a large collection of mounted wildlife specimens as well as pioneer and Native American artifacts; also a complete collection of Winchester guns manufactured 1866–1982.

✧ ♿ 🍸 **Lake Pepin Paddleboat** (651-345-5188; www.pearlofthelake.com), 100 Central Point Rd., Lake City. Public cruises offered mid-May–Oct., Wed.–Sun. Private charters available. A replica of the grand old paddleboats that once dotted the local lakes and rivers. Public tours and dinner cruises are offered, with snacks and full bar available on all sailings.

✳ Lodging

Accommodations are open year-round unless otherwise noted.

✧ ♿ 🍸 **The Historic Anderson House** (651-565-2500; www.historic andersonhouse.com), 333 Main St. W. Twenty-three rooms of varying sizes and amenities, all with private bath, in this 150-year-old treasure. The Victorian decor is cozy and warm, and—unlike many B&Bs—children are welcome, as there are a few rooms large enough to accommodate more than two. Also unlike many lodgings, there are cats available by reservation for your stay. Breakfast is included, and the inn has its own public restaurant for all three meals (see *Where to Eat*). Rates start at $69.

✧ **Great River Houseboats** (651-565-3376; www.greatriverhouseboats .com), 1009 E. Main St. Open May–Oct., weather permitting. Three houseboats for rent, two of which hold up to 10 people, one that holds a maximum of 4. The smaller boat rents for a two-night minimum, while the larger ones require a week. Rates start at $600 per night for the two-night minimum.

✧ **Bridgewaters Bed and Breakfast** (651-565-4208; www.bridge watersbandb.com), 136 Bridge Ave. Five simple but tastefully decorated rooms in a turn-of-the-20th-century home with wraparound porch. Bridgewaters welcomes families, although not all rooms have private bath. Full breakfast is included. Rates start at $110; packages are available.

THE NATIONAL EAGLE CENTER

THE HISTORIC ANDERSON HOUSE

✳ Where to Eat

Restaurants are open year-round unless otherwise noted.

& ⅋ **Nosh** (651-345-2425; www .noshrestaurant.com), 310 S. Washington St., Lake City. Open Wed.–Sun. for dinner, Sat.–Sun. for lunch. The arrival of Nosh into the small town of Lake City, midway between Red Wing and Wabasha, brought an upscale, trendy cuisine to the area that was previously lacking. The food is Mediterranean-based, but whenever possible the chefs source locally for their foods, bringing in a Midwest theme as well. The main courses are spectacular, but an excellent meal can be had off the eatery's small plates menu. Save room for dessert. Entrées start at $18.

✐ & ⅋ **The Historic Anderson House** (651-565-2500; www.historic andersonhouse.com), 333 Main St. W. Open daily for all three meals. The cozy dining room at this historic inn (also a bed & breakfast) offers a solid menu—nothing flashy, but good food prepared well, with emphasis on steak, chicken, and seafood. Entrées start at $12.

✐ & ⅋ **The Olde Triangle Pub** (651-565-0256; www.oldetrianglepub .com), 219 Main St. Open daily for lunch and dinner. A casual, friendly neighborhood spot with good pub grub, including bangers and mash and Irish stew. Entrées start at $8.

✐ & ⅋ **Slippery's** (866-504-4036; www.slipperysumr.com), 10 Church Ave. Open daily for lunch and dinner. Slippery's claim to fame was being mentioned in the *Grumpy Old Men* movies, which were filmed in the Wabasha area. The restaurant also has a boat-in feature and great views of the river. Burgers, steaks, and Mexican items are served in hearty portions. Entrées start at $7.

✴ Selective Shopping

Stores are open year-round unless otherwise noted.

✧ **LARK Toys** (507-767-3387; www .larktoys.com), US 61, Kellogg. Open Mar.–Dec. daily; Jan.–Feb., open Fri.–Sun. This massive toy complex (more than 30,000 square feet) is more than just a store, it's a playground. A working carousel offers rides, and a mini golf course is available during the warmer months. *LARK* stands for "Lost Art Revival by Kreofsky," and vintage toys, many made out of wood, are produced and sold here, along with children's books. A café is on site.

WINONA

✴ To See

Attractions are open year-round unless otherwise noted.

✧ ⚹ **Downtown National Register of Historic Places District**. Winona has more than 100 buildings listed on the National Register of Historic Places, most built between 1857 and 1916 in Italianate or Queen Anne style. The best way to take in this large collection of Victorian commercial buildings (the largest concentration in Minnesota) is by foot. Free walking tour brochures of the district are available from the **Convention and Visitors Bureau** (507-452-0735, 800-657-4972, 160 Johnson St.), **visitors center** (924 Huff St.), or **Winona County Historical Society** (507-454-2723, 160 Johnson St.).

✧ ⚹ **Winona County Historical Museum** (507-454-2723; www.winonahistory .org), 160 Johnson St. Open Mar.–Dec. daily; Jan.–Feb., open Mon.–Fri. $4 adults, $2 students; free for children under 7 and Winona County Historical Society members. A large and fascinating collection of local and regional historic exhibits, covering the usual (geological history, river trade) as well as the less so (Cold War parking plans in the event of nuclear war). The museum is kid-friendly, with lots of hands-on activities, including a climb-through cave and a river steamboat.

✧ **Bunnell House** (507-452-7575; www.winonahistory.org), Homer. Open Memorial Day–Labor Day, Wed.–Sun., or by appointment. $4 adults, $2 students; free for children under 7 and Winona County Historical Society members. Built in the mid-1800s by a fur trader named Willard Bunnell, the Bunnell House is a Rural Gothic wood-framed home. Tours take visitors through all three floors, which are furnished with many pieces original to the time period.

✐ ✆ **Arches Museum** (507-523-2111; www.winonahistory.org), US 14. Open June–Aug., Wed.–Sun., or by appointment. $4 adults, $2 students; free for children under 7 and Winona County Historical Society members. A tribute to the long-lost days of roadside museums. The Arches Museum houses the collection of Walter Rahn, who was apparently fascinated with pioneer life and either collected or built items himself to illustrate their uses. The grounds also have a log cabin and a one-room schoolhouse.

✐ ✆ **Minnesota Marine Art Museum** (507-474-6626; 866-940-6626; www.minnesotamarineart.org), 800 Riverview Dr. Open Tues.–Sun. $6 adults, $3 students, $20 immediate families; free for children 4 and under. This attractive new museum, located along the Mississippi, has an extensive collection of marine art, folk art, photography, maps, and historical displays. During 2008, a newly decommissioned dredge boat will be positioned next to the museum and be open for tours.

✐ ✆ **Polish Cultural Institute** (507-454-3431; www.lacrossetribune.com/brochures/polishmuseum/polishci.htmOutdoor Activities), 102 Liberty St. Open May–Oct., Mon.–Fri.; Nov.–Apr., open by appointment. $2 per person. Group discounts are available. At one time Winona had the largest concentration of Polish immigrants in the United States, and this museum reflects that heritage with antiques, folk art, religious items, and displays detailing the immigrant experience.

✐ **Pickwick Mill** (507-457-0499; www.pickwickmill.org), 26421 CR 7, Pickwick. Open June–Aug., Tues.–Sun.; May, Sept., and Oct., weekends only; Nov.–Apr. by appointment. $3 per person or $5 per family. A Civil War–era water-powered gristmill, the Pickwick operated continuously until 1978, and many of its original components and machines are on display today.

MINNESOTA MARINE ART MUSEUM

☀ To Do

John A. Latsch State Park (507-643-6849; www.dnr.state.mn.us/state_parks/ john_latsch/index.html), 43605 Kipp Dr. One of the lesser-visited state parks, this is worth a trip if you're ready for some exercise; there's a 0.5-mile hike up a stairway that leads to outstanding views of the Mississippi and surrounding bluffs.

City parks. Winona has several city parks, two of which are of special interest. **Windom Park** (Huff and W. Broadway St.) is small—only a city block in size—but it's surrounded by several Victorian homes (some of which are listed on the National Register of Historic Places) and has a gazebo and fountain with a sculpture of Princess Wenonah. **Lake Park** (900 Huff St.), on the shores of Lake Winona, is a popular city park with an attractive rose garden (C. A. Rohrer Rose Garden), fishing piers, and a band shell with weekly live concerts in summer.

Gavin Heights City Park, Gavin Heights Rd. Nearly 600 feet above the city, this overlook is spectacular, especially on a clear day.

☀ Lodging

Accommodations are open year-round unless otherwise noted.

Alexander Mansion Bed and Breakfast (507-474-4224; www .alexandermansionbb.com), 274 E. Broadway. Four elaborately detailed Victorian rooms, all with private bath, and including five-course breakfast and evening hors d'oeuvres. The 1886 mansion also has an extensive screened porch for guests to enjoy. Rates start at $149.

Carriage House Bed and Breakfast (507-452-8256; www.chbb.com), 420 Main St. Built by lumber baron Conrad Bohn, the Carriage House was once literally that—it originally housed six carriages and several horses. Today the renovated house has four bedrooms, all with private bath, decorated in a cozy Victorian style. Breakfast is included daily, as is the use of single and tandem bicycles and, by prearrangement, a Model A Ford for local touring. Rates start at $89.

Windom Park Bed and Breakfast (507-457-9515; 866-737-1719; www .windompark.com), 369 W. Broadway. Located near Windom Park, this Colonial Revival home was built in 1900 and has four beautiful rooms in the main house, all with private bath, and two lofts in the nearby carriage house. The lofts have fireplace and two-person Jacuzzi. Breakfast is included each day, and guests are encouraged to use the other public rooms, which are also impeccably appointed. Innkeepers Craig and Karen Groth can assist with restaurant and theater recommendations and reservations. Rates start at $120.

🐾 ✿ ♿ ☂ **Holiday Inn** (507-453-0303; 888-465-4329; www.ichotels group.com), 1025 US 61 E. Of the more conventional hotels, the Holiday Inn is the nicest in Winona, with an indoor pool, sauna, and room service from the on-site Green Mill restaurant (See *Where to Eat*). Rates start at $90.

Americinn (877-946-6622; www .americinnmn.net), 60 Riverview Dr. The Americinn is located on the Mississippi River, has an indoor pool and whirlpool, and includes continental breakfast daily. Less typical of the usual Americinn, this one has a two-story Lighthouse Suite with a private hot tub and second-floor deck overlooking the river. Rates start at $86.

✳ Where to Eat

Restaurants are open year-round unless otherwise noted.

  🕭 ㅻ **Signatures** (507-454-3767; www .signatureswinona.com), 22852 CR 17, Winona. Open daily for lunch and dinner. Don't let the somewhat blah interior fool you; the food here is excellent, and you can feast on the outdoor views out of the generous windows. Working closely with local food producers has resulted in some of the region's best and most innovative cuisine. Entrées start at $15.

  🖉 🕭 ㅻ **Betty Jo Byoloski's** (507-454-2687; www.bettyjos.com), 66 Center St. Open daily for lunch and dinner. Burgers, steak, shrimp, sandwiches, salads—that's Betty Jo's. This casual neighborhood institution serves up the food in hearty portions at reasonable prices. Entrées start at $9.

  🖉 🕭 ㅻ **Green Mill** (507-452-5400; www.greenmill.com), 1025 US 61 (in the Holiday Inn). Open daily for lunch and dinner. Pizza, pasta, sandwiches, and salads. The deep-dish pizza is the chain's specialty. Entrées start at $7.

LANESBORO

✳ To See

Worth seeing is the little town itself: The entire business district is on the National Register of Historic Places. Take some time and wander at your leisure; this is arguably one of the most beautiful towns in the state.

  🖉 🕭 **Cornucopia Art Center** (507-467-2446; www.lanesboroarts.org), 103 Parkway Ave. N. Open Tues.–Sun. Mon. by appointment. An art gallery exhibiting and selling artwork by local and national artists, the center also has lofts for rent (see *Lodging*).

✳ To Do

Forestville/Mystery Cave State Park (507-352-5111; 507-935-3251; www .dnr.state.mn.us/state_parks/forestville_mystery_cave/index.html), 21071 CR 118, Preston. The park is open daily. Cave tours are offered daily mid-Apr.–Oct.; Forestville tour, Tues.–Sat. Memorial Day–Labor Day, weekends only Sept.–Oct. Cave tours are $9 adults, $6 ages 5–12, free under 5. Forestville tours are $5 adults; $4 seniors, college students, and military personnel; $3 ages 6–17; free for children under 6 and members of the Minnesota Historical Society. This state park has something for everyone. Mystery Cave takes visitors to underground pools and cave geological formations; aboveground, hikers and horse riders have 15 miles of trails that wind through the bluff areas and through wildflowers (in spring). Skiers and snowmobilers are welcome in winter. Forestville is

GUIDED TOURS

Several seasonal tour companies can guide you through the beauty and history of the area.

🖋 ♿ **Amish Tours of Harmony** (507-886-2303; 800-752-6474; www.amish-tours.com), Harmony. Apr.–Nov., Mon.–Sat. $20 adults, $6 children; free for ages 3 and under; discounts given if you use your own vehicle. Along the Minnesota–Iowa border is a small but thriving Amish community, and this tour company offers rides through the beautiful area as well as stops at selected farms and shops.

🖋 ♿ **Flaby's Amish Tours** (507-467-2577; 800-944-0099), Lanesboro. May–Oct., Mon.–Sat. $20 adults, $6 children; free for ages 3 and under. Amish country tours with planned stops at farms and shops.

🖋 ♿ **Bluff Country Jeep Tours** (507-467-2415), Deep River Rd., Lanesboro. Apr.–Oct., daily (weather permitting). $60 per ride (three people maximum). For a more adventurous ride, try this tour, which goes over rough terrain and up into the hills and bluffs overlooking the river. Tours last one hour; think hard if you get carsick easily.

AMISH TOURS IN LANESBORO

a trip back in time to a once functioning town that declined after the railroad passed it by. Today visitors cross the Carnegie Steel Bridge to visit the General Store, where costumed guides lead tours and demonstrate activities from the store's late-1800s roots, giving you the chance to work with the farm laborers in the garden.

Root River and Harmony-Preston Valley Trails (www.rootrivertrail.org). A 60-mile paved trail system that wanders along the Root River and through

LANESBORO

Lanesboro. The scenery is spectacular, and offers both level trails (along a former railroad grade) and more challenging inclines that lead to gorgeous vistas. Those adventurous enough to bike the entire trail will be rewarded with changing scenery that includes wooded areas, rivers and bluffs, and an attractive array of wildlife. The trails are open for cross-country skiers in winter (seasonal fees apply). If the riverways are what you want, local outfitters will rent canoes, kayaks, and inner tubes. Contact **Root River Outfitters** (507-467-3663; www .rootriveroutfitters.com), which offers shuttle service for one-way journeys, or **Little River General Store** (507-467-2943; www.lrgeneralstore.com), which rents boating equipment. Both outfitters rent bikes and offer shuttle service with them.

✳ Lodging

Not surprisingly, this historic town has more than its fair share of historic bed & breakfasts. Accommodations are open year-round unless otherwise noted.

Wenneson Historic Inn (507-875-2587; www.wennesonbnb.com), 425 Prospect St., Peterson. Nine rooms, all with private bath, are offered between the main house and the carriage house. Rooms are named for their color schemes, and all have pe-

riod furniture and decor. The inn is a short walk from the Root River Trail. Continental breakfast served on weekends. Rates start at $70.

The 1898 Inn (507-467-3539; www .1898inn.com), 706 Parkway Ave. S. Two rooms with private bath are available in this charming renovated Queen Anne home. Breakfast is a special event, with home-baked breads and local, organic eggs and produce. Rates start at $115.

Historic Scanlan House B&B (507-467-2158; 800-944-2158; www.scanlanhouse.com), 708 Parkway Ave. S. This 1889 Queen Anne mansion is a striking piece of architecture, and the seven rooms and suites, all with private bath, are elaborately finished and very romantic. The home itself is packed with antiques; beds and windows are dressed in linens and lace. Full breakfast is included (and if you've reserved the Safari Suite, you can have it served in your suite). Rates start at $100; packages are available.

Cady Hayes House (507-467-2621; www.cadyhayeshouse.com), 500 Calhoun Ave. Another Queen Anne charmer, this home has three guest rooms, all with private bath. The Amish Room lives up to its name with Amish furnishings, while the Norway Room as a queen-sized sleigh bed with hand-painted rosemaling. There are several common areas, including a music room with grand piano available for guests. Full breakfast is included. Rates start at $85.

Jailhouse Inn (507-765-2181; www.jailhouseinn.com), 109 Houston St. NW, Preston. This building began its history as a county jail in 1870 and now has 12 rooms and suites, all with private bath, some with dainty names like the Sun Room and other with more pointed titles: Drunk Tank, Court Room. The Cell Block Room gives you the chance to sleep behind bars. The rooms are beautifully decorated in Victorian style. Breakfast is included. Rates start at $62 (but note that the rate sheet stipulates this is for "friendly people").

Mrs. B's Historic Lanesboro Inn (507-467-2154; www.mrsbsinn.com), 101 Parkway Ave. A large and lovely limestone building on the Root River and right in downtown Lanesboro, Mrs. B's has 10 rooms with private bath (rubber ducky included), all warmly decorated with color and quilts. Full breakfast is included. Rates start at $129.

✿ **Stone Mill Suites** (507-467-8663; 866-897-8663; www.stonemillsuites.com), 100 Beacon St. E. This lime-

THE HISTORIC SCANLAN HOUSE B&B

stone mill has served as both an egg and poultry processing plant and as a grain company since it was built in 1885. In 1999 the current owners bought it and created a B&B. Each of the 10 rooms and suites is named and decorated for an aspect of the region, including the Amish Room, Grain Room, and the Egg Jacuzzi Suite. All have private bath. Continental breakfast is served daily. Kids are welcome. Rates start at $100; packages are available.

✿ **Art Lofts** (507-467-2446; www.art lofts.org), 103 Parkway Ave. N. Located above the Cornucopia Arts Center, the lofts are two simple but attractive rooms designed for guests who wish to enjoy artistic endeavors of their own; the rooms both have good access to daylight. Exposed brick walls and original artwork highlight the space's art neighbor. Rates start at $100; discounts for weeklong stays are offered.

✳ Where to Eat

Restaurants are open year-round unless otherwise noted.

✿ ♿ ♈ **Riverside at the Root** (507-467-3663; www.rootriveroutfitters .com), 109 Parkway Ave. S. Open daily for dinner, Fri.–Mon. for lunch. A casual but choice restaurant located on the Root River, with a patio and deck that takes advantage of the location. Some standard steak house items are offered, such as steak, pork, and walleye, along with pizza and pasta, and occasionally game items (elk). Riverside also offers special events, such as wine dinners. Entrées start at $13.

♿ ♈ **Old Village Hall Restaurant & Pub** (507-467-2962; www.oldvillage

hall.com), 111 Coffee St. May–Nov., open daily for dinner and Fri.–Sat. for lunch; open Wed.–Sun. for dinner the rest of the year. The former village hall and jail, on the National Register, houses Lanesboro's nicest restaurant. The menu changes seasonally and takes advantage of local, seasonal foods, including herbs from the restaurant's own herb garden. The stone building has been beautifully renovated, and the outdoor patio is a delight in summer. The creative menu might include items like lamb chops with couscous or salmon in curry sauce. Entrées start at $20.

✿ ♿ **Das Wurst Haus German Village & Deli** (507-467-2902), 117 Parkway Ave. N. Open daily for lunch Apr.–Nov. Das Wurst Haus may sound kitschy, but make no mistake— it's the real thing. Generations-old

STONE MILL SUITES

OLD VILLAGE HALL RESTAURANT & PUB

breakfast and lunch. This small diner is a place to grab a quick sandwich or burger. Entrées start at $5.

✿ & **Pedal Pushers Café** (507-467-1050; www.pedalpusherscafe.com), 121 Parkway Ave. N. Open daily for lunch and dinner. A 1950s-style restaurant with hearty breakfasts, sandwiches and burgers for lunch, and comfort food like chicken potpie and homemade meat loaf for dinner. Fountain treats and homemade pie round out the menu, which also has daily blue plate specials. Entrées start at $7.

✳ Entertainment

Commonweal Theatre (800-657-7025; www.commonwealtheatre.org), Lanesboro. The Commonweal is a national expert on the works of Henrik Ibsen, and his work is included in each season's repertoire. The theater also has a major hand in the annual Ibsen Festival (see *Special Events*). Besides Ibsen, Commonweal produces at least four other plays each year, sponsors readings of new works, and produces a live radio show every summer.

family recipes are used to prepare the restaurant's meats, breads, desserts, and even the root beer. Stop by for lunch and enjoy your hearty sandwich or soup while listening to live polka music. An adjacent shop sells the meats, mustards, and cheeses. Entrées start at $6.

✿ & **Chat 'n' Chew** (507-467-3444), 701 Parkway Ave. S. Open daily for

AUSTIN

Home of Hormel Foods, Austin proudly refers to itself as SPAM Town, USA.

✳ To See

Attractions are open year-round unless otherwise noted.

✿ & **SPAM Museum** (800-444-5713; www.spam.com/museum), I-90, Austin. Open daily May 1–Labor Day; Tues.–Sun. Labor Day–Apr. 30. Admission is free. Sure beats an art museum—at least, that's what the SPAM Museum's Web site says. This homage to canned meat manages to be both informative and irreverent. You can't fault a museum for including showings of the Monty Python SPAM skit. But besides the kitsch and humor, the museum features lively exhibits detailing the history of the Hormel Foods company, as well as films such as *SPAM: A Love Story* that give insight into SPAM's role in history, especially during WWII.

🖋 ♿ **Hormel Historic Home** (507-433-4243; www.hormelhistorichome.org), 208 4th Ave. NW. Open Mon.–Fri. $2 donation is requested but not required. This Greek Revival home was built in 1871 for then-mayor John Cook but served as the residence of the Hormel family in the early 1900s. Self-guided tours showcase the impressive building; in warmer months you can visit the Peace Gardens.

ROCHESTER

✳ To See

Attractions are open year-round unless otherwise noted.

🖋 **Mayowood** (507-282-9447; www.olmstedhistory.com), 3720 Mayowood Rd. SW. Open Tues.–Sat. May–Oct.; call for additional days during the year. $5 adults, $2 children. The 38-room mansion was home to Mayo Clinic founders and family members, and much of the architecture was designed by Dr. Charles H. Mayo himself. The home is filled with antiques from all over Europe and remains decorated as it was when occupied by the Mayos. The surrounding gardens are breathtaking, overlooking the Zumbro River with a complex plan of paths, ponds, sculptures, a pergola, teahouse, and limestone walls.

🖋 ♿ **Olmsted County History Center** (507-282-9447; www.olmstedhistory .com), 1195 West Circle Drive SW. Open Tues.–Sat. $4 adults, $1 children. More information about the Mayo family and the Mayo Clinic can be found at this small historical site, as well as information about another prominent Rochester community member, IBM. A hands-on pioneer cabin exhibit for kids and a display of artifacts from the 1883 tornado that ravaged the city are the must-sees here.

🖋 **Plummer House of the Arts** (507-281-6160; www.ci.rochester.mn.us/ departments/park/facilities/plummerhouse/index.asp), 1091 Plummer Ln. SW. Tours offered Wed., June–Aug. Private group tours can be arranged. Admission is $3. Henry Plummer, a Mayo physician and engineer, poured his design talents and money into this 49-room Tudor mansion surrounded by 11 acres of gardens and forests. House tours focus on the history and spotlight the all-original furniture. The grounds are open daily and can be visited free if no special events are in progress.

🖋 **Heritage House** (507-282-2682), 225 1st Ave. NW. Open Tues., Thurs., and Sun. 1–3:30 PM June–Aug. Admission is free. Built in 1875, this home is one of the few that survived the devastating 1883 tornado, and today it provides insight into what life was like for residents who were not blessed with the wealth of the Mayos and the Plummers. The furniture and decorations on display are largely original.

MAYO CLINIC

✈ ♿ (507-538-0440; www.mayoclinic.org/becomingpat-rst/tours.html), 200 1st St. SW. Tours are free. Mayo Clinic is Rochester's biggest claim to fame, with patients arriving from all over the world and medical experts in nearly every category. Several different tours are offered for visitors, some self-guided:

General Tour. Mon.–Fri., 10 AM. A short film about the history of the clinic is followed by a 90-minute guided tour of the campus.

Art and Architecture. Mon.–Fri., 1:30 PM. A 60-minute guided tour examining the priceless art owned by the Mayo.

Heritage Hall. Open Mon.–Fri. Visitors guide themselves through displays that detail the Mayo Clinic's history and future.

Patients and Guests Self-Guided Tours. Audio-enabled tours that visit the artwork, St. Mary's Hospital, or Mayo Historical Suites (used by the Mayo family).

High School/College Career Tours. By request at 507-284-1496. Students interested in medical careers can request tours designed to give them more insight into the field.

THE MAYO CLINIC

✳ To Do

Quarry Hill Park and Nature Center (507-281-6114; www.qhnc.org), 701 Silver Creek Rd. NE. Open daily. An urban park with extensive grounds and an active nature center offering year-round programs. Fishing ponds, paved biking trails, sandstone caves, and classes at the Nature Center are among the many amenities.

Silver Lake Park (507-281-6160; www.ci.rochester.mn.us/departments/park), 7th St. and 2nd Ave. NE. A haven for Canada geese, this lake and park just outside downtown has ample recreational opportunities in the form of bike trails and canoeing, kayaking, and paddle boating on the lake. **Silver Lake Rentals**

HERITAGE HOUSE, BUILT IN 1875

(507-261-9049; www.silverlakefun.com) rents bikes and boats during the warmer months.

✳ Lodging

Accommodations are open year-round unless otherwise noted.

🐾 ♿ 🍸 **Kahler Grand Hotel** (507-280-6200; 800-533-1655; www.kahler .com), 20 2nd Ave. SW. Across the street from the Mayo Clinic, to which it's connected by skyway, the grande dame of Rochester hotels has nearly 700 rooms and suites ranging from basic economy rooms to lavishly appointed suites. The hotel's recreation center, with pool and whirlpool, is domed to allow sky views. There are several dining options on site, both sit-down and room service, as well as a martini bar and Starbucks coffee shop. Rates start at $79 for the economy rooms and can be much higher for the luxury suites; packages are available.

🐾 ♿ **Kahler Inn and Suites** (507-285-9200; 800-533-1655; www.kahler innsuites.com), 9 3rd Ave. NW. The Kahler Grand's sister hotel is just down the street, and is smaller and less opulent but still a good choice. The inn is connected to the Mayo Clinic via a pedestrian subway. An indoor pool and whirlpool are available for guests. Lodging includes free parking and daily continental breakfast. On-site dining includes a casual café, a Jimmy Johns sandwich shop, and a Caribou Coffee shop. Rates start at $99; packages are available.

🐾 🐾 ♿ 🍸 **Marriott Rochester** (507-280-6000; 877-623-7775; www .marriott.com), 101 1st Ave. SW. Also connected to the Mayo Clinic, via skyway, the Marriott was renovated in

ROCHESTER GOES GLOBAL

Thanks to its many international visitors, Rochester is developing a strong ethnic food scene, with the Asian and Mexican standbys joining newcomers serving African and Middle Eastern cuisines.

∂ ⅋ � **Jenpachi Japanese Steak House** (507-292-1688; www.jenpachi.com), 3160 Wellner Dr. NE. Open daily for dinner, Sun. for lunch. Sushi or the drama of tabletop hibachi cooking. Entrées start at $11.

∂ ⅋ ☦ **Soriya Cuisine** (507-252-5337; www.soriyacuisine.com), 1123 Civic Center Dr. NW. Open daily for lunch and dinner. Thai, Chinese, and Cambodian dishes, and diners can request adjustments in the level of spiciness to suit their palates. Entrées start at $12.

∂ ⅋ ☦ **China Dynasty** (507-289-2333), 701 Broadway Ave. S. Open daily for lunch and dinner. Nothing fancy, but good Chinese food, including both Americanized and authentic. Entrées start at $9.

∂ ⅋ ☦ **Zorba's Greek Restaurant** (507-281-1540), 924 7th St. NW. Open daily for lunch and dinner. Hearty Greek food from a surprisingly large menu. Entrées start at $12.

∂ ⅋ ☦ **Victoria's** (507-280-6232; www.victoriasmn.com), 7 1st Ave. SW. Open daily for lunch and dinner. Victoria's prides itself, rightfully so, on making quality Italian foods from fresh ingredients (local when possible). The menu is extensive and reasonably priced. Entrées start at $10.

∂ ⅋ ☦ **The Redwood Room** (507-281-2978; www.cccrmg.com/redwood room.htm), 300 1st Ave. NW. Open daily for dinner. An Italian restaurant housed in an old warehouse, this bistro has a small menu that changes frequently, featuring homemade pastas, steaks, and pizza. Traditional Italian

2006, creating brighter, more up-to-date rooms with upgraded technology. There's an indoor pool and whirlpool, and a restaurant and bar. Rates start at $139; packages are available.

∂ ⅋ ☦ **Hilton Garden Inn** (507-285-1234; 877-782-9444; www.rochester mn.gardeninn.com), 225 S. Broadway. The Hilton has an indoor pool and on-site restaurant; all rooms have either one king or two double beds. Rates start at $129; packages are available.

∂ ⅋ ☀ **Fiksdal Hotel & Suites**

(507-288-2671; 800-366-3451; www .fiksdalhotel.com), 1215 2nd St. SW. This modest hotel has spacious rooms, recently renovated, and offers complimentary continental breakfast daily and cookies each night. Rates start at $79.

∂ ⅋ **Hampton Inn** (507-287-9050; 800-426-7866; www.hamptoninn rochester.com), 1755 S. Broadway. This attractive chain hotel offers comfortable, spacious rooms and suites, as well as full breakfast daily in its Cyber Café, which has high-speed laptop foods are tweaked, such as the spaghetti with meatballs made of lobster. Entrées start at $14.

✿ ♿ ⅋ **Fiesta Café Bar** (507-288-1116), 1645 Broadway Ave. N. Open daily for lunch and dinner. Mexican food in both Americanized and authentic incarnations. Staff are very friendly. Entrées start at $11.

♿ ⅋ **Chardonnay** (507-252-1310), 723 2nd St. SW. Open Mon.–Sat. for dinner. French cuisine, heavy on seafood and steak, and an extensive wine list. Entrées start at $25.

Internet outlets. Weeknights a soup social mixer is offered. Indoor swimming pool and whirlpool, and complimentary shuttle service to Mayo Clinic. Rates start at $109; packages are available.

✱ Where to Eat

Restaurants are open year-round unless otherwise noted.

♿ ⅋ **Avocados World Bistro** (507-282-7318; www.avocadosworld bistro.com), 1190 16th St. SW. Open daily for lunch and dinner. An inven-

tive menu fusing foods from around the world, with emphasis on the Caribbean. The jerk lamb is a specialty. For the more adventurous, try the Chef's Choice: served at the kitchen bar, and created after a visit between chef and diner. Entrées start at $14.

♿ ⅋ **Broadstreet Café & Bar** (507-281-2451; www.cccrmg.com/broad street.htm), 300 1st Ave. NW. Open daily for dinner. Possibly the best restaurant in Rochester, Broadstreet is in a cozy renovated warehouse and has an ambitious, inventive menu, including orange-crusted fresh scallops or wild mushroom and brandy ostrich, along with variations on steak and seafood. Entrées start at $19.

🍴 ♿ ⍦ **Michael's Restaurant and Lounge** (507-288-2020; www .michaelsfinedining.com), 15 Broadway Ave. S. Open Mon.–Sat. for lunch and dinner. This local staple has been around for more than 50 years and continues serving a wide array of Greek-influenced American foods, with several specials each evening. Comfort foods show up, too; try the Salisbury steak if it's offered. Entrées start at a reasonable $9.

♿ ⍦ **Sönte's** (507-292-1628; www .sontes.com), 4 3rd St. Open Mon.–Sat. for dinner. Upscale tapas-style restaurant with an extensive wine list (including 40 varietals offered by the glass). Small plates, entrées including steaks and sea bass (served as shared plates), and unique pizzas are offered, with ingredients changing seasonally. The cheese courses are nicely chosen. Entrées start at $14.

🍴 ♿ ⍦ **Roscoe's Barbecue Root Beer & Ribs** (507-285-0501, 603 4th St. SE; 507-281-4622, 4180 18th Ave. NW; www.roscoesbbq.com). Open daily for lunch and dinner. Locally owned, this award-winning barbecue joint features ribs, pork, chicken, beef, and ham in generous portions, with traditional BBQ sides (coleslaw, potatoes, baked beans). Friendly staff, quick service, mouthwatering BBQ sauce. Entrées start at $11.

🍴 ♿ ⍦ **Bilotti's Italian Village** (507-282-8668; www.bilottispizza.com), 304 1st Ave. SW. Open daily for dinner, Mon.–Fri. for dinner. It's not much to look at, but the huge menu is full of starchy Italian goodness, especially the pizzas. Entrées start at $7.

✴ Entertainment

Jon Hassler Theater (507-534-2900; 866-548-7469; www.jonhasslertheater .org), 412 W. Broadway, Plainview. Named for Minnesota novelist Jon Hassler, who spent part of his youth in the small town of Plainview. This professional regional theater produces at least four shows per season, with

---

ANTIQUING IN ROCHESTER

Rochester is an antiques shopper's paradise, with numerous shops and dealers.

Old Rooster Antique Mall (507-287-6228), 106 Broadway Ave. N.

Antique Mall on Third Street (507-287-0684), 18 SW 3rd St.

Blondell Antiques (507-282-1872; www.blondell.com/antiques), 1406 2nd St. SW.

Iridescent House (507-288-0320; www.iridescenthouse.com), 227 1st Ave. NW.

Mayowood Galleries (507-288-2695; www.kahler.com), 20 2nd Ave SW.

John Kruesel's General Merchandise (507-289-8049; www.kruesel.com), 22 3rd St. SW.

offerings as varied as Hassler adaptations, Edward Albee, Lanford Wilson, and a tribute to Frank Sinatra.

✳ Selective Shopping

Stores are open year-round unless otherwise noted.

Grand Shops (www.kahler.com), 20 2nd Ave SW. Adjacent to the Kahler Grand Hotel is this retail complex, with 60 shops including art galleries (Callaway Galleries, Kay Hoecker Gallery), Hanny's clothiers, Clever Kids toy store, Chocolate Oasis, and Mayo Clinic retailers.

Apache Mall (507-288-8056; www.apachemall.com), 333 Apache Mall. The area's largest shopping mall with 100 shops, including most of the usual chain stores: J. Jill, Abercrombie &

A CHAIN STORE RISES ABOVE
Much has been made of chain stores and big-box retailers creating soulless retail environments, but there is a spectacular exception to that in downtown Rochester. **Barnes & Noble**, the national bookseller, renovated the old Chateau Theatre (15 1st St. SW; 507-288-3848; www.bn.com), carefully retaining its charming architecture. It makes for an unusual and fun book-shopping experience.

Fitch, Champs Sports, Victoria's Secret, Gap/Gap Kids, and the Disney Store.

NORTHFIELD

Not far from the Twin Cities is this quintessential 19th-century European village, home to Carleton and St. Olaf colleges, the mill that produces Malt-O-Meal cereal, and a history involving the infamous Jesse James bank robbery.

✳ To See

Attractions are open year-round unless otherwise noted.

✐ **Northfield Historical Society Museum** (507-645-9268; www.northfield history.org), 408 Division St. Open daily Memorial Day–Labor Day, Tues.–Sun. the rest of the year. Admission is $3. The First National Bank, famous for its Jesse James connection, is part of this museum. Many of the bank's fixtures are original, and other exhibits highlight the infamous bank robbery as well as non–Jesse James parts of Northfield's history. The museum's gift shop harks back to the general-store days of the late 1800s while carrying a wide variety of local books.

✐ ♿ **Outlaw Trail Tour** (507-645-5604; 800-658-2548; www.northfieldchamber .com). Take a self-guided tour of the route the James-Younger gang took on that fateful day in 1876. Brochures and maps are available from the Northfield Chamber of Commerce; large groups and tour buses can request a tour guide.

✍ ♿ **Historic Sites and Points of Interest Tour** (507-645-5604; 800-658-2548; www.northfieldchamber.com). It's not the most exciting name for a tour, but this self-guided venture takes visitors through the beauty and charm of Northfield, with its century-old buildings and architecture. Brochures and maps are available from the Northfield Chamber of Commerce; large groups and tour buses can request a tour guide.

✍ ♿ **Goodsell Observatory** (507-646-4000; www.carleton.edu), Carleton College. Open the first Fri. evening of each month, weather permitting. Free admission. The view through the telescope is almost as beautiful as the stately architecture of the observatory building itself. Hope for clear skies—cloudy nights lead to closed observatories.

♿ **Northfield Arts Guild Gallery** (507-645-8877; www.northfieldarts guild.org), 304 Division St. Open Mon.–Sat. Free admission. The Arts Guild is part visual arts and part theater, with art classes and exhibits in the gallery. Local and national artists are displayed in a wide variety of media.

♿ **Flaten Art Museum** (507-786-3248; www.stolaf.edu/depts/art/museum), Dittmann Center, St. Olaf Ave., St. Olaf College. Open daily. Free admission. St. Olaf's art collection encompasses both US and European artists with an emphasis on textiles, ceramics, and sculpture.

✳ To Do

Cowling Arboretum (507-646-5413; http://apps.carleton.edu/campus/arb), Carleton College. Open daily. Carleton's Cowling Arboretum has 800 acres of wooded trails along the Cannon River Valley. "The arb" is open to hikers and bikers, and in winter to cross-country skiers, but be sure to stay on the trails: Protected flora and fauna that are being studied by Carleton students are off limits to visitors.

NORTHFIELD ARTS GUILD

✳ Lodging

Accommodations are open year-round unless otherwise noted.

The Archer House (507-645-5661; 800-247-2235; www.archerhouse .com), 212 Division St. This is *the* place to stay when in Northfield. This grand old inn has 36 rooms, impeccably decorated and maintained, filled with antique furniture, many with river views. Two breakfast restaurants are on site, although breakfast is not included in the surprisingly reasonable rates—which start at $75.

Magic Door Bed & Breakfast (507-581-0445; www.magicdoorbb.com), 818 Division St. S. This B&B's location, just out of the hubbub of downtown Northfield, gives it a quiet ambience, while its romantic decor makes it a wonderful getaway. The three guest rooms all have private bath and are beautifully decorated with vibrant but tasteful colors; the Summer Suite has a gas fireplace and whirlpool tub. Not only is a full breakfast included, but so is a glass of wine or beer in the afternoon—and a "bottomless" cookie jar is left out for guests as well. Rates start at $100.

✳ Where to Eat

Restaurants are open year-round unless otherwise noted.

& ♀ **Fermentations** (507-645-8345; www.fermentations-bistro.com), 236 Railway St. N., Dundas. Open Mon.–Sat. for dinner. A meticulously

planned seasonal menu that incorporates locally grown products, using them to great effect. Seasonal highlights include roasted butternut squash ravioli and pan-seared pork tenderloin, served with sweet potatoes (with marshmallows!). Entrées start at $19.

& ♀ **Chapati** (507-645-2462; www.chapati.us), 214 Division St. Open Tues.–Sun. for lunch and dinner. An Indian restaurant with a huge menu

THE ARCHER HOUSE

for both novice and experienced Indian food enthusiasts. Servers will consult with you as to your preferred level of spiciness. Entrées start at $11.

✒ ᵬ **Kurry Kabab** (507-645-9399; www.kurrykabab.com), 2018 Jefferson Rd. Open daily for lunch and dinner. Don't let the silly spelling or the strip-mall environment scare you away from this restaurant, a very respectable Indian eatery with a menu that rivals Chapati. Entrées start at $9.

✒ ᬠ ♆ **El Tequila** (507-664-9139), 1010 MN 3. Open daily for lunch and dinner. Plentiful and quality Mexican foods. This place is popular, so plan ahead. Entrées start at $9.

✒ ᬠ ♆ **Froggy Bottoms River Pub** (507-664-0260; www.froggybottoms .com), 305 Water St. S. Open Mon.– Sat. for lunch and dinner. A cheerful (sometimes boisterous) riverside pub, serving classic pub food (Irish stew, walleye, pizza) along with the beverage of your choice. Entrées start at $8.

✒ ᬠ ♆ **Tavern of Northfield** (507-663-0342), 212 Division St. Open daily for all three meals. Located at the Archer House Inn (see *Lodging*), the tavern has a wide-ranging menu including pasta, steaks, burritos, and pita sandwiches. Entrées start at $7.

✳ Entertainment

ᬠ **Northfield Arts Guild Theater** (507-645-8877; www.northfieldarts guild.org), 304 S. Division St. The theatrical arm of the Northfield Arts Guild (see *To See*), this group produces several plays each year, staged in a former church down the street from the guild's art gallery. The company also auditions new plays and conducts staged readings.

✳ Special Events

Bluff Country Studio Art Tour (800-428-2030; www.bluffcountryart tour.com), Lanesboro. Held in late Apr., this art tour spans several communities in the bluff country region, opening private studios and artist work spaces to visitors and potential art buyers.

✒ **Hastings Downtown Saturday Night Cruise-In** (651-437-4400; www.hastingsdowntown-mn.com/ cruise-in/index.html), Hastings. Summer Sat. nights in Hastings draw thousands of visitors for this annual tradition. Cars 30 or more years old are given cruising rights down the main drag, with prizes and special weekly events.

✒ ᬠ **Rochesterfest** (507-285-8769; www.rochesterfest.com), Rochester. A week in late June devoted to celebrating Rochester past and present. The festival packs a lot into seven days: lumberjack championships, a guided walk through Oakwood Cemetery, live theater and music, soccer tournaments, disk dog Frisbee championships, a street dance, a water-ski show, a hot-air balloon race, a fiddle contest, even a plane pull in which teams of 20 (humans) compete to be the fastest to pull a 727 jet 12 feet.

Great River Shakespeare Festival (507-474-7900; www.grsf.org), Winona. Held late June–late July. When Great River opened its premier season in 2003, there were plenty of skeptics: Who would drive to Winona to watch professional Shakespearean theater? Turns out plenty of people are happy to do just that, especially when it takes them into the heart of the river bluff country. Great River performs two plays each year, a tragedy and a comedy, and the festival has quickly gained national stature.

♪ ♿ Little Log House Pioneer Village and Antique Power Show (651-437-2693; www.littleloghouse show.com), 13746 220th St. E., Hastings. Held the last weekend in July. This Pioneer Village is larger than most, with 45 buildings, a replica bridge, extensive gardens, and even a dirt racetrack for vintage auto races. The only downside is that the village isn't open to the general public except during this annual event, which displays antique vehicles and machines and offers demonstrations, live music, Old West reenactments, tractor and truck pulls, and a parade. Campsites and RV sites are available for rental.

♪ ♿ Defeat of Jesse James Days (www.defeatofjessejamesday.org), Northfield. Held annually the first weekend after Labor Day. When your town has something as exciting as this in its history, it's best to have a festival, complete with dramatic reenactments. This popular event is built around the Jesse James shootout, and there's also a parade, golf tournament, antique tractor pull, vintage "base ball," rodeo, square dance, steak fry, 5K and 10K races, and a bike tour. Plan ahead and reserve hotel rooms early if you'd like to stay in the area.

Red Wing Fall Festival of Arts (651-388-7569), Red Wing. This event, taking place annually for more than 40 years, offers two days of art exhibitions, sales, and related activities.

♿ St. Olaf Christmas Festival (507-786-3811; www.stolaf.edu/christmas fest), St. Olaf College, Northfield. Held in late Nov. or early Dec., this annual tradition began in 1912 and has become a premier event for the state. Several college choral ensembles and the college orchestra put together a magnificent program of Christmas carols and hymns which are performed live (as well as broadcast on public radio and TV). Purchase tickets well in advance, as they usually sell out quickly.

♪ ♿ Ibsen Festival (800-657-7025; www.commonwealtheatre.org/ibsen _fest.html), Lanesboro. Dates vary; check the Web site or call for specifics each year. A three-day festival celebrating the life and work of Norwegian playwright Henrik Ibsen. Typical events include discussions and films about Ibsen's work, staged performances of Ibsen's plays, Scandinavian arts and crafts exhibits and classes, Scandinavian music performances, and Scandinavian meals.

Southern
Minnesota

8

MINNESOTA RIVER VALLEY

SOUTH THROUGH THE PRAIRIE

THE I-35 CORRIDOR

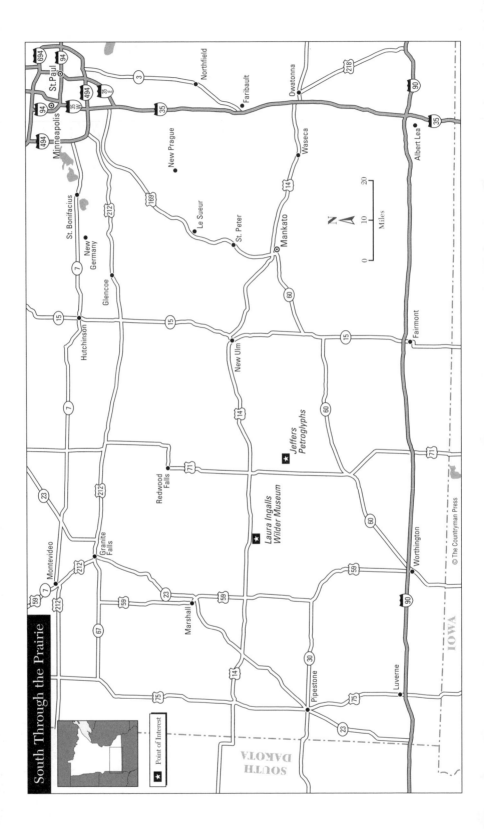

South Through the Prairie

★ Point of Interest

© The Countryman Press

MINNESOTA

Minneapolis
St. Paul
Northfield
Faribault
Owatonna
Albert Lea
New Prague
Waseca
St. Bonifacius
New Germany
Le Sueur
St. Peter
Mankato
Glencoe
Hutchinson
New Ulm
Fairmont
Montevideo
Granite Falls
Redwood Falls
Jeffers Petroglyphs
Laura Ingalls Wilder Museum
Marshall
Worthington
Pipestone
Luverne

SOUTH DAKOTA
IOWA

N
Miles
0 10 20

SOUTHERN MINNESOTA

T he southwest quadrant of the state is primarily agricultural, with miles of prairie land dotted with small towns and intriguing, even occasionally mysterious historic sites. The Minnesota River, which has its source in Ortonville on the South Dakota border, ambles southeast until Mankato provides the literal turning point for a northerly twist to the Twin Cities. It's an area of pioneers, Native Americans, wildlife, and history. The attractions may be farther apart than they are in other parts of the state, but stops like Pipestone National Monument and the Jeffers Petroglyphs, state parks like Blue Mounds, and towns entrenched in European heritage like New Ulm—and of course the pioneer appeal of Walnut Grove and the Laura Ingalls Wilder Historic Highway—have much to offer.

GUIDANCE

Albert Lea Convention and Visitors Bureau (507-373-2316; 800-345-8414; www.albertleatourism.org), 2566 N. Bridge Ave., Albert Lea.

Le Sueur Area Chamber of Commerce (507-665-2501; www.lesueurchamber .org), 500 N. Main St., Le Sueur.

New Ulm Convention and Visitors Bureau (888-463-9856; www.newulm .com), 1 N. Minnesota St., New Ulm. Offers extensive lodging and activity information for New Ulm and the Minnesota River Valley.

Worthington Area Chamber of Commerce (507-372-2919; 800-279-2919; www.worthingtonmnchamber.com), 1121 3rd Ave., Worthington.

Marshall Chamber of Commerce (507-532-4484; www.marshall-mn.org), 317 W. Main St., Marshall.

Faribault Chamber of Commerce (507-334-4481; www.visitfaribault.com), 530 Wilson Ave., Faribault.

Greater Mankato Chamber of Commerce (507-345-4519; 800-657-4733; www.greatermankato.com), 112 Riverfront Dr., Mankato.

St. Peter Area Chamber of Commerce (507-934-3400; 800-473-3404; http://tourism.stpeter.mn.us), 101 S. Front St., St. Peter.

By car: The primary routes in the southwestern part of the state, connecting Montevideo, Marshall, Pipestone, and Luverne, are MN 7 and MN 29 into Montevideo; US 212 from Montevideo to Granite Falls; and MN 23 from Granite Falls through Marshall to Pipestone, where US 75 travels south to Luverne.

From Luverne, I-90 travels directly east through Worthington, Fairmont, Blue Earth, and into Albert Lea, where it connects with I-35 heading north to Owatonna and Faribault.

West of Owatonna is Mankato, which is accessed by US 14 and US 169, as well as MN 22, MN 68, and MN 66. MN 68 travels west to New Ulm, while US 169 and MN 22 travel north to St. Peter. US 169 continues north to Belle Plaine. Before it reaches Belle Plaine, MN 19 travels east to New Prague. MN 13 travels south from New Prague to Montgomery.

By air: Commercial air service is available into Minneapolis/St. Paul; there are regional airports, such as the one in Mankato, that offer private or corporate service.

GETTING AROUND

Having a vehicle is a necessity when traveling around the southern prairie region.

WHEN TO COME

The summer months see an influx of tourists who come to enjoy the multitude of lakes and beaches, but summer isn't the only popular time, especially for fishing enthusiasts who cast their poles in open water in summer and through holes in the ice in winter. Hunters and winter sports aficionados appreciate the fall and winter seasons as well.

MEDICAL EMERGENCY

Call **911**.

Chippewa County-Montevideo Hospital (320-269-8877; www.montevideo medical.com), 824 N. 11th St., Montevideo.

Pipestone County Medical Center (507-825-5811; www.pcmhealth.org), 916 4th Ave. SW, Pipestone.

Albert Lea Medical Center (507-373-2384; 888-999-2386; www.mayohealth system.org), 404 W. Fountain St., Albert Lea.

New Ulm Medical Center (507-233-1000; www.allina.com/ahs/newulm.nsf), 1324 5th St. N., New Ulm.

Immanuel St. Joseph's Hospital (507-625-4031; 800-327-3721; www.mayo healthsystem.org), 1025 Marsh St., Mankato.

St. Peter Community Hospital (507-931-2200; www.stpeterhealth.org), 1900 N. Sunrise Dr., St. Peter.

✳ Belle Plaine

TO SEE

Hooper-Bowler-Hillstrom House (952-873-6109; www.belleplainemn.com/about/HooperHouse.php), 410 N. Cedar St., Belle Plaine. Open Sun. from Memorial Day–Labor Day; other days by appointment. Free admission. The former home of State Bank founder Samuel Bowler, this house was built in 1871, but its primary claim to fame, besides being an attractive version of a 19th-century home, is the addition Mr. Bowler added to accommodate his rather large family: a two-story outhouse. A skyway connects the second floor of the "five-holer" to the house; the upstairs facilities are situated farther back, so the waste landed behind the wall of the first floor. Souvenirs are available for sale.

✳ Le Sueur

The city of Le Sueur was named after French explorer Pierre Le Sueur, thought to be the first explorer to travel the Minnesota River, but today the community is better known as the birthplace of the founder of the Mayo Clinic and Green Giant.

TO SEE

✎ ♿ **Le Sueur City Museum** (507-655-2050), 709 N. 2nd St. Open Tues.–Thurs. year-round; Memorial Day–Labor Day, also open Fri.–Sat.; or by

HOOPER-BOWLER-HILLSTROM HOUSE

MINNESOTA RIVER VALLEY

appointment. No admission fee, but donations are welcome. A small facility in a former schoolhouse, this museum has most of what remains of the Green Giant legacy after Pillsbury bought the company and moved its headquarters out of town. The Green Giant history room has a wide variety of memorabilia and antiques. Other displays include an old-time drugstore and an antique doll collection.

☙ **W. W. Mayo House** (507-665-3250; www.mayohouse.org), 118 N. Main St. Open July–Aug., Tues.–Sat.; Apr.–June and Sept.–Nov., open Thurs.–Sat. $3 adults, $2 seniors, $1 ages 6–16; free for those under 6. This little Gothic-style home was hand built in 1859 by Dr. Mayo himself, who then set up shop on the second floor. The Civil War interrupted his practice; he traveled to New Ulm to help with wounded veterans while his wife, Louise, remained in the house to shelter 11 refugee families. By 1864 the Mayo family was reunited and moved to Rochester, where they founded the Mayo Clinic. The home's story doesn't end there; in the 1870s the Carson Nesbit Cosgrove family moved in. Cosgrove founded the Minnesota Valley Canning Company, which later became Green Giant.

WHERE TO STAY

Accommodations are open year-round unless otherwise noted.

Henderson House Bed & Breakfast (507-248-3356; www.henderson housemnbb.com), 104 N. 8th St., Henderson. A beautiful brick home on a hill overlooking the river valley,

Henderson House was built in 1875. The B&B offers four rooms, two with private bath, decorated with period antiques. Full breakfast is provided daily, sometimes including eggs from the hens kept in the backyard. Rates start at $95.

TO SEE

Attractions are open year-round unless otherwise noted.

❦ **E. St. Julien Cox House** (507-934-4309; www.nchsmn.org), 500 N. Washington Ave. Open June–Aug., Thurs.–Sat.; also selected Sat. in Dec. $3.50 adults, 50¢ ages 13–18; free for kids under 13. $5 buys a combined pass with the Treaty Site History Center (below). E. St. Julien Cox was a Civil War officer, attorney, and eventually state senator, and he built this Gothic/Italianate home in 1871. Filled with 1880s furnishings, the home is open to visitors in summer, when costumed guides explain the significance of both the home and the family.

❦ ♿ **Treaty Site History Center** (507-934-2160; www.nchsmn.org), 1851 N. Minnesota Ave. Open Tues.–Sun. $3.50 adults, 50¢ ages 13–18; free for those under 13. $5 buys a combined pass with the E. St. Julien Cox House (above). The history center has permanent and seasonal exhibitions detailing the creation of what is now southern Minnesota, along with Iowa and South Dakota, in the signing of the Traverse des Sioux Treaty in 1851. History aficionados will note that the terms of the treaty were not upheld, leading to the Dakota Conflict several years later. The center doesn't shy away from the uglier side of the history, but if you need something more peaceful and soothing, take some time to explore the restored prairie that surrounds the center.

❦ **St. Peter Regional Treatment Center** (507-931-7250), 100 Freeman Dr. Open only by appointment, this is worth calling ahead for. The treatment center is the first psychiatric hospital opened in the state, and the museum has a motley but fascinating array of artifacts from its original incarnation, including straitjackets.

HENDERSON HOUSE B&B

THE E. ST. JULIEN COX HOUSE

✳ Mankato

TO SEE

Attractions are open year-round unless otherwise noted.

✿ **The Betsy-Tacy Society** (507-345-8103; www.betsy-tacysociety.org), 322 Center St. Open Sat. 1–3 PM or by appointment. No admission fee during regular hours, although donations are requested; appointments $3 adults, $1 ages 5–16. Fans of the children's classic *Betsy-Tacy* series by Maud Hart Lovelace can visit the sites of the fictional Deep Valley in Lovelace's home city of Mankato. Tacy's home is open for tours; Betsy's house is around the corner. The society also has a brochure detailing 55 important stops in Mankato for Betsy-Tacy fans; the map was created in part by Lovelace herself. Check the society's Web site for the detailed walking map.

✿ ᕵ **R. D. Hubbard House** (507-345-5566; www.rootsweb.com/~mnbechs), 606 S. Broad St. Open Sat.–Sun. Memorial Day–Labor Day and between Thanksgiving and Christmas. $3 adults, $1 ages 6–17; under 6 free. This Victorian gem was occupied only by the Hubbard family before the Blue Earth County Historical Society acquired it, and the lack of turnover allowed the building to retain its turn-of-the-20th-century charm. Elaborate woodwork, stained glass, fabric wall coverings, and an adjacent carriage house with a collection of antique vehicles give visitors a true glimpse of the era.

✿ ᕵ **Blue Earth Heritage Center** (507-345-5566; www.rootsweb.com/ ~mnbechs), 415 Cherry St. Open Tues.–Sat. $3 adults, $1 ages 6–17; under 6 free. The museum of the Blue Earth County Historical Society has wide-ranging exhibits covering local historic events, including a Maud Hart Lovelace exhibit, displays featuring Native American artifacts, remnants from the region's early days of farming and milling, and a diorama of old Mankato.

✍ ♿ **Minnesota Vikings Training Camp** (507-389-3000; www.vikings.com), Blakeslee Field, Minnesota State University. Late July to mid-Aug. When the Vikings gear up for the season, they start out in Mankato. Practices are free, while scrimmages and games cost $10 for ages 3 and up; children under 3 are free. Get tickets in advance from the Vikings ticket office or from the Mankato Chamber of Commerce (507-345-4519; 800-657-4733).

TO DO

Sakatah Singing Hills State Trail (www.dnr.state.mn.us/state_trails/sakatah/index.html), Lime Valley Rd. A 39-mile paved trail utilizing a former railroad bed, the Sakatah winds from Mankato to Faribault through farmland and woods. The trail is multiuse, open to all forms of recreation (with the exception of snowmobiles with studded tracks—regular snowmobiles are welcome). A secondary trail is available for horseback riders only.

Minneopa State Park (507-389-5464; www.dnr.state.mn.us/state_parks/minneopa/index.html), 54497 Gadwall Rd. Open daily. In the Dakota language *minneopa* means "water falling twice," a perfect name for this park, home to Minnesota's largest waterfall. A winding trail leads to and around the falls, with a limestone stairway descending into the valley. Seppmann Mill, a wind-driven gristmill made of stone and wood, is no longer functional but continues to draw admirers. At one time there was a town here as well, but three consecutive years of grasshopper plagues in the 1870s drove the residents away. Tourists, however, continue to flock to this popular park, for the waterfalls, the hiking/cross-country skiing trails, and the bird-watching. Campsites and one cabin are available for rental.

LODGING

Accommodations are open year-round unless otherwise noted.

Butler House Bed & Breakfast (507-387-5055; www.butlerhouse.com), 704 S. Broad St. This luxurious B&B offers five lavishly decorated suites, all with private bath, some with elaborate wood or wrought-iron four-poster beds and hand-painted murals. Full breakfast is included, and mystery theme dinners can be arranged in advance for groups. Rates start at $99.

MINNEOPA STATE PARK

♂ ♿ **Americinn** (507-345-8011; www .americinnmankato.net), 240 Stadium Rd. Ninety-five rooms and suites, some of which have fireplace and whirlpool. The hotel also has an indoor pool and whirlpool, and daily continental breakfast is provided. Rates start at $99.

♂ ♿ ☿ **Country Inn and Suites** (507-388-8555; 888-201-1746; www.country inns.com/mankatomn), 1900 Premier Dr. All rooms include complimentary WiFi, microwaves, refrigerators, and full daily breakfast. Suites have whirlpools and wet bars. An indoor pool is available for guests, and a T.G.I. Friday's is attached to the hotel for lunch and dinner. Rates start at $94.

♂ ♿ ☿ **Hilton Garden Inn** (507-344-1111; www.hiltongardeninn.hilton .com), 20 Civic Center Plaza. One of the nicest hotels in Mankato. Rooms and suites include complimentary high-speed Internet access and flat-panel HDTV. There's an indoor pool and a full-service restaurant on site as well. Rates start at $139; packages are available.

WHERE TO EAT

Restaurants are open year-round unless otherwise noted.

♂ ♿ ☿ **Wine Café** (507-345-1516; www.winecafebar.com), 301 N. River-front. Open Mon.–Sat. for lunch and dinner. A charming bistro and wine shop with more than just wine. A limited bar menu is available for lunch and dinner, but there's a full bar, including 70 wines by the glass and a comparable number of beers. Live music on weekends, when the bar remains open until 2 AM. Entrées start at $6.

♂ ♿ ☿ **Whiskey River** (507-934-5600; www.riversp.com), 34166 MN 99. Open daily for lunch and dinner, Sat.–Sun. for breakfast. Congenial supper club with traditional supper club foods, including ribs, steak, and walleye. Entrées start at $11.

♿ ☿ **Contessa** (507-625-5713), 124 E. Walnut St. Open daily for lunch and dinner. Newcomers to the Mankato dining scene, the chefs at Contessa have put together an upscale menu based on high-quality ingredients, with nearly everything made in the restaurant itself (soup broths, pasta). The eclectic interior, with a copper and tile water feature and fireplaces, is warm and sophisti-cated. Entrées start at $14.

♂ ♿ ☿ **The Neighbor's Italian**

SELECTIVE SHOPPING

ANTIQUING IN MANKATO
As befits a historic region, Mankato has a thriving antiques community.
Earthly Remains (507-388-5063; www.earthlyremains.com), 731 S. Front St. Open Mon.–Sat. One of the largest antiques dealers in the city.
Old Town Antiques (507-388-0600), 521 N. Riverfront Dr. Open Mon.–Sat.
Antique Mart (507-345-3393), 529 S. Front St. Open Mon.–Sat.
Riverfront Antiques (507-388-5152), 1027 N. Riverfront Dr. Open Mon.–Sat.
Generations Antiques (507-345-7551), 615 S. Front St. Open Mon.–Sat.

Bistro (507-625-6776; www.neighbors
italianbistro.com), 1812 S. Riverfront
Dr. Open daily for lunch and dinner.
An excellent Italian bistro with homemade pastas and a thoughtful menu.
When available, try the butternut
squash ravioli with maple sage butter
and bacon. Entrées start at $14.

✔ ♿ ♀ **Dino's Pizzeria** (507-385-
3466; www.dinospizzeria.com), 239
Belgrade Ave. A New York–style
pizzeria using fresh ingredients for its
pizzas, pastas, and sandwiches.
Entrées start at $9.

ENTERTAINMENT

Highland Summer Theatre (507-
389-2118; www.msutheatre.com), 210
Performing Arts Center, Minnesota
State University. A professional
summer-stock theater for over 40
years, Highland presents four productions each season (June and July), two
of which are musicals.

✳ New Ulm

Minnesota's German heritage is alive and well in this small town packed with
historic sites and ethnic festivals.

TO SEE

Attractions are open year-round unless otherwise noted.

✔ ♿ **Glockenspiel**, Minnesota St. and 4th St. N. New Ulm is home to one of
the world's few freestanding carillons. The 45-foot glockenspiel puts on its show
three times a day, more often during
festivals; when the bells chime, 3-
foot-tall polka figures dance out—
except at Christmas, when a nativity
scene appears instead.

✔ ♿ **August Schell Brewery** (507-
354-5528; 800-770-5020; www.schell
brewery.com), Schell's Rd. Schell is
the second oldest family brewing
company in the United States, having
opened in 1860. Today the brewery
offers tours, a museum, and a gift
shop. Brewery tours ($2) are offered
daily Memorial Day–Labor Day,
Fri.–Sun. the rest of the year. The
museum does not charge an admission fee. The surrounding gardens
and deer park are open daily, no
admission.

✔ **Hermann Monument**, Center St.
and Monument St. Open daily
Memorial Day–Labor Day, weekends

NEW ULM'S GLOCKENSPIEL

through Oct. Admission $1.25. This towering monument was built in 1897 in honor of Hermann of Cherusci, who is recognized for liberating Germany from Rome in AD 9 and is considered the liberator of the German people. The memorial stands 102 feet tall and, for those willing to climb the stairs, provides an excellent view of greater New Ulm. Bring a picnic lunch to enjoy in the park grounds.

SCHELL BREWERY GIFT SHOP

✒ **Wanda Gag House** (507-359-2632), 226 N. Washington St. Open Sat.–Sun. June–Aug., Dec., and festival weekends; year-round by appointment. Admission $2. Children's author Wanda Gag, author and illustrator of such classics as *Millions of Cats*, was born and raised in this home in New Ulm. The compact home with turrets and skylights makes for an interesting afternoon's exploration.

✒ ♿ **Brown County Historical Museum** (507-233-2616; www.browncounty historymnusa.org), 2 N. Broadway St. Open Mon.–Sat. $3 adults; students and children are free. Housed in a 1910 post office, the museum is a surprisingly diverse and comprehensive of historic and cultural artifacts and displays. German heritage, Native American presence, and the economic mainstays of the area (known as "beer, brats, and bricks") are all detailed in various exhibits. The Dakota Conflict is especially well covered.

✒ **John Lind House** (507-354-8802; www.lindhouse.org), 622 Center St. Open June–Aug., daily; Apr., May, Sept., Oct., open Fri.–Sun. By appointment the rest of the year. Admission $2. Built in 1887, this Victorian beauty served as both home and host for state functions for Governor John Lind. The house had fallen into serious disrepair before being listed on the National Register and being purchased by the newly formed Lind House Association, which restored it and operates it today. While tours are available, this is still a working building, home to the local United Way.

🍷 **Morgan Creek Vineyards** (507-947-3547; www.morgancreekvineyards.com), 23707 478th Ave. Open May–Nov., Fri.–Sun. Morgan Creek celebrates 10 years of vintages in 2008, and it's still the only Minnesota vineyard with an underground winery. Stop by during regular business hours for tours and tastings, or check the Web site for one of the numerous special events.

✒ **Harkin Store** (507-354-8666; www.mnhs.org/places/sites/hs), CR 21. Open Memorial Day–Labor Day, Tues.–Sun.; weekends in May and Sept.–mid-Oct. $2 adults, free for those under 13. Eight miles northwest of New Ulm is this classic store, a piece of history still vibrant today. The Harkin Store was a community general store until the day the railroad decided to bypass it. The store was forced to close, and today much of the merchandise seen on the shelves has been there since the closing. Costumed guides provide historical background and explain what some of the products, common in their day but unknown today, were for.

TO DO

Flandrau State Park (507-233-9800; www.dnr.state.mn.us/state_parks/flandrau/index.html), 1300 Summit Ave. Open daily. At only 800 acres, this is a smaller park, but it's popular nonetheless due in no small part to the fact that it's within walking distance of downtown New Ulm. The sand-bottomed swimming pond and extensive campgrounds are a big draw here, as are the hiking trails. The trails are groomed for cross-country skiing in winter, and ski and snowshoe rentals are available.

LODGING

Accommodations are open year-round unless otherwise noted.

✐ ♿ 🍸 **Holiday Inn** (507-359-2941; 888-465-4329; www.ichotelsgroup.com), 2101 S. Broadway. Even the Holiday Inn gets into the spirit of things with its Ye Olde Germany exterior. Otherwise it's a standard Holiday Inn, with an indoor pool and an on-site restaurant (Otto's Bierstube). Rates start at $81.

Deutsche Strasse Bed & Breakfast (507-354-2005; 866-226-9856; www.deutschestrasse.com), 404 S. German St. Built in 1884, this congenial home has five rooms, all with private bath and most with fireplace. Full breakfast is served in the cheerful sunroom. Rates start at $104; packages are available.

Beyer Haus Bed & Breakfast (507-354-3180; www.beyerhaus.com), 224 S. Broadway. This stately Queen Anne mansion has four rooms, all with fireplaces and private bath, and all located in remote corners of the home, allowing extra privacy for guests. The rooms are beautifully decorated with a full range of amenities, including cable TV with DVD player. Guests receive full breakfast daily and evening snacks. Rates start at $129; packages are available.

✐ ♿ **The Bohemian Bed & Breakfast** (507-354-2268; www.the-bohemian.com), 304 S. German St. A unique "stick-style" Victorian mansion, the Bohemian has seven rooms, all with private bath, and some with two-person whirlpool tub. The rooms are full of both antiques and contemporary art, fitting the *Bohemian* part of its name. Rates start at $89; packages are available.

Bingham Hall Bed & Breakfast (507-354-6766; 800-486-3514; www.bingham-hall.com), 500 S. German. This luxurious B&B has four rooms, all with private bath and queen-sized bed with down comforter. Most of the rooms have fireplace or whirlpool bath, and one room (Elijah) has an air massage chair. Rates start at $99.

WHERE TO EAT

Restaurants are open year-round unless otherwise noted.

✐ ♿ 🍸 **George's Fine Steaks and Spirits** (507-354-7440; www.georgessteaks.biz), 301 N. Minnesota St. Open daily for lunch and dinner. A congenial steak house in a pretty bistro building. Steaks, ribs, walleye, and some pasta options. Entrées start at $13.

✐ ♿ 🍸 **Kaiserhoff** (507-359-2071), 221 N. Minnesota St. Open daily for lunch and dinner. New Ulm's oldest German restaurant, this place is a local stalwart, serving up heaping por-

GEORGE'S IN NEW ULM

tions of German and American foods. The ribs are their proudest moment. Entrées start at $12.

🖉 ♿ **Ulmer Café** (507-354-8122), 115 N. Minnesota St. Open daily for breakfast and lunch. The local diner with plentiful breakfasts and lunches. Entrées start at $6.

🖉 ♿ **Backerei and Coffee Shop** (507-354-6011), 27 S. Minnesota St.

WEEDS & REEDS

Open daily for breakfast. This longtime local bakery still knows how to produce pastries, and the prices are very reasonable. Pastries start at $1.

🖉 ♿ **Olde World Deli** (507-354-8400; www.oldeworlddeli.com), 26 S. Minnesota St. Open Mon.–Sat. for lunch. This little café and catering company offers daily specials of soups, salads, sandwiches, and entrées, including several German foods. Entrées start at $7.

🖉 ♿ **Larkspur Market** (507-359-2500; www.larkspurmarket.com), 16 N. Minnesota St. Open Mon.–Sat. for breakfast and lunch, Sun. for lunch. Sumptuous baked goods and a changing-daily menu of lunch specials. The café is located within a gift shop full of kitchen and gourmet food products as well as bath and body gifts. Entrées start at $6.

SELECTIVE SHOPPING

Stores are open year-round unless otherwise noted.

Domeier's German Store (507-354-4231), 1020 S. Minnesota St. Open Mon.–Sat. Domeier's is packed full of German imports from the kitschy to the classic to the collector's dreams.

Guten Tag Haus (507-233-4287; www.gutentaghaus.com), 127 N. Minnesota St. Open daily. Importer of German gifts, including a large array of Christmas items.

Sausage Shop (507-354-3300; www .newulmtel.net/~lendon), 301 N. Broadway St. Open Mon.–Sat. All kinds of meats—especially sausage— and baked goods, too.

Weeds & Reeds (507-359-1147), 500 N. Broadway St. Open Mon.–Sat. A fun home-and-garden gift store built into a renovated 1926 gas station.

Silk Purse (507-276-2973), 2 N. Minnesota St. Open the first Fri.–Sat. of each month, during selected New Ulm festivals, and by appointment.

Silk Purse sells vintage and antique home and accessory items, recycled and refurnished.

✳ Montevideo to Ortonville

TO SEE

Attractions are open year-round unless otherwise noted.

✄ ♿ **Olof Swensson Farm** (320-269-7636), CR 6. Open Sun. Memorial Day–Labor Day. Admission $3. Olof Swensson was a Norwegian immigrant who settled in this area in 1872. He was a highly active resident, a builder who worked on his 22-room farmhouse and timber-framed barn, a Lutheran minister, and a political activist. The farm has been restored, including a gristmill with hand-cut granite grist stones.

✄ ♿ **Historic Chippewa City** (320-269-7636), 151 Arne Anderson Dr. Open daily Memorial Day–Labor Day. $4 adults, $2 ages 6–18; free under age 6. Chippewa City was originally the county seat, but as a town it declined after Montevideo took over the governmental role. Today 24 restored buildings have been preserved as a living history museum, including a buggy shop (containing a horse-drawn hearse), the village hall, and a log cabin.

LAC QUI PARLE STATE PARK

(320-734-4450; www.dnr.state.mn.us/state_parks/lac_qui_parle/index.html), 14047 20th St. NW, Watson. Open daily. *Lac Qui Parle*, which translates into "lake that speaks," was also the name of the band of Wahpeton Dakota who built a small village here centuries ago. In 1826 a trading post was built by explorer Joseph Renville, and a mission soon followed, which saw the translation of the Bible into Dakota. Today all that remains of the trading post is an interpretive sign, but the mission is marked by a chapel that was rebuilt by the WPA in the 1940s.

Besides Native American and trade history, Lac Qui Parle has 6 miles of trails for hiking and horseback riding, and the trails are groomed in winter for cross-country skiing. Canoers can watch for wildlife while canoeing on the Lack Qui Parle and Minnesota rivers. There are several campsites and a small sandy beach. The park is adjacent to the 27,000-acre Lac Qui Parle Wildlife Management Area, which is home to geese, deer, and bald eagles. The lake itself is a migratory stopping point for thousands of Canada geese each spring and fall.

Big Stone National Wildlife Refuge (320-273-2191; www.fws.gov/midwest/ bigstone), 44843 CR 19, Odessa. Open daily. An 11,500-acre wildlife refuge southeast of Ortonville, Big Stone counts more than 260 bird species, including bald eagles, and bison can be seen wandering in the 1,700 acres of prairie grasses. A 9-mile paved auto trail is open in summer, and hiking trails and canoe routes provide more intimate access.

Big Stone Lake State Park (320-839-3663; www.dnr.state.mn.us/state_parks/ big_stone_lake/index.html), 35889 Meadowbrook State Park Rd., Ortonville. Open daily. Big Stone Lake is the source for the Minnesota River. The southern part of the park is known as the Meadowbrook Area, which is the most user-friendly in terms of amenities: campground, beach, canoe rental, good fishing, and hiking trails (noted for views of wildflowers in spring). The northern area is the Bonanza Area, a designated Scientific and Natural Area for its 80 acres of native oak savanna and glacial till prairie habitat. There is a hiking trail here also, but be sure not to disturb the protected habitat.

LODGING

Accommodations are open year-round unless otherwise noted.

★ ✎ ᕁ Country Inns and Suites (320-269-8000; 877-269-8001; www .countryinns.com/montevideomn), 1805 E. MN 7. Rooms and suites in the Carlson Country Inns style, as well as an indoor pool and whirlpool. Full breakfast included in the rates, which start at $75.

The Broodio at Moonstone Farm (320-269-8971; www.prairiefare.com/ moonstone/farmstay.html), 9060 40th St. SW. A one-room cottage that used to be a chicken "brooding" house, the Broodio is a charming and idyllic get-away for the visitor looking for peace and quiet. Moonstone Farm is an organic, sustainable agriculture farm, and guests have access to a canoe, beach, and sauna. Continental break-fast is delivered to the cottage. Rates start at $75.

WHERE TO EAT

Restaurants are open year-round unless otherwise noted.

✎ ᕁ **Valentino's** (320-269-5106), 110 S. 1st St. Open Mon.–Thurs. for all three meals, Fri.–Sat. for breakfast and lunch. A surprisingly elegant yet casual restaurant, Valentino's has tasteful wood decor and artwork, and a simple but delectable menu of soups, sandwiches, and daily specials. Entrées start at $8.

✎ ᕁ **Java River Café** (320-269-7106; www.javarivercafe.com), 210 S. 1st St. Open Mon.–Sat. for breakfast and lunch. Not just coffee drinks— although the coffee is top notch—but well-made sandwiches, soups, and pastries, frequently incorporating locally grown and raised food sources. Live music and book discussions are regularly scheduled. Entrées start at $7.

✎ ᕁ **Art's Dairy Freeze** (320-269-6282), 1307 Black Oak Ave. Open daily in summer. It's all about the ice cream at this local summer landmark. Ice cream treats start at $2.

✳ Pipestone

In the far southeastern corner of the state is Pipestone, a town rich in Native American and quarrying history.

TO DO

✦ **Pipestone National Monument** (507-825-5464; www.nps.gov/pipe), US 75, Pipestone. Open daily. $3 adults, free for children 15 and under. $5 per car. Pipestone National Monument is a significant historic and cultural site. The red pipestone, so called because its primary use is to be carved into ceremonial pipe bowls, has been quarried by Native Americans since at least the 17th century, and the quarry is viewed as a sacred site. The pipes from this quarry were highly

---

TO SEE: THE PIPESTONE COMMERCIAL HISTORIC DISTRICT
(www.pipestoneminnesota.com). This two-block stretch in the downtown area of Pipestone contains 30 buildings and is listed on the National Register of Historic Places. Most of the building took place in the 1890s, after railroad service was established. Of particular note is the use of Sioux quartzite in 17 of the structures. Specific buildings of interest are listed below:

&. ♈ **Calumet Inn** (507-825-5871; 800-535-7610; www.calumetinn.com), 104 W. Main St. Built in direct response to the needs of travelers arriving with the new railroad, the Calumet has suffered its share of tragedies (fire on more than one occasion) over the decades. At one point the hotel was in such disrepair that it was closed, but in 1979 it was purchased and renovated. Today it offers 38 guest rooms, furnished with period antiques, as well as a lounge and pub. Rates start at $85.

✦ &. **Pipestone County Museum** (507-825-2563; www.pipestoneminnesota .com), 113 S. Hiawatha Ave. Open daily Memorial Day–Labor Day, Mon.–Sat. the rest of the year. $3; children under 12 are free. This lovely, elaborate building was once the imposing city hall and now houses the historical museum. Besides regular hours for the exhibits, check with the museum for its special events.

✦ &. **Syndicate Block** (www.pipestoneminnesota.com), 201–205 W. Main St. This block comprises the oldest and largest of the Sioux quartzite buildings. Originally a post office and meat market, the block is now mostly retail and offices.

✦ &. **Moore Block** (www.pipestoneminnesota.com), 102 E. Main St. This smaller Sioux quartzite building is distinguished by the work of Leon Moore, an amateur sculptor who sculpted several gargoyles and biblical scenes onto the building's exterior.

acclaimed across the United States, and the land that produced it was, for the most part, neutral territory for different tribes because of the symbolic power of the site. Today the only quarrying allowed is by Native Americans, a right they retained when they sold the land to the US government in 1937. A comprehensive visitor center details the significance and history of the area, and there are locally made pipestone products in the gift shop. During the summer months, visitors can watch as quarrying takes place. Hiking the Circle Trail, a 0.75-mile walk from the visitor center, provides beautiful views of quartzite, as well as native prairie grasses. Other points of interest include Winnewissa Falls and the Oracle, a naturally occurring stone "face" that Native Americans believed to be a sentient being.

Blue Mounds State Park (507-283-1307; www.dnr.state.mn.us), US 75, Luverne. Open daily. It's a bit out of the way for many visitors to Minnesota, but Blue Mounds offers natural opportunities not easily available elsewhere. The 1,800-acre park sits above surrounding farmland by virtue of a natural pedestal of Sioux quartzite. There are 13 miles of hiking trails, and campsites are available for reservation. The Blue Mounds were named for their appearance to westward-moving settlers; a stretch of rock 1,250 feet long runs in an east–west direction and corresponds to the rising and setting of the sun. It is thought to have been placed by early Dakota. Deer, coyote, numerous birds, and even bison live here and can be seen by visitors.

LODGING

✐ ♿ ♟ **Calumet Inn**. See the sidebar on previous page.

WHERE TO EAT

Restaurants are open year-round unless otherwise noted.

✐ ♿ **Lange's Café and Bakery** (507-825-4488), 110 8th Ave. SE. Open 24/7, serving home-cooked meals including the usual sandwiches and soups as well as some more inventive pastas and meat dishes. Be sure to have the pie for dessert. Entrées start at $7.

✐ ♿ ♟ **Glass House Restaurant** (507-348-7651), 711 MN 23. Open daily for lunch and dinner. Steak house menu, including seafood and chicken, and a Sunday smorgasbord. Entrées start at $10.

✐ ♿ ♟ **Calumet Inn**. See the sidebar on previous page.

TO SEE

✂ ♿ **Pioneer Village** (507-376-3125; www.noblespioneervillage.com), Stower Dr. Open daily Memorial Day–Labor Day. $6 adults, $1 ages 6–15; free for those ages 90 and over or 5 and under. Located on the county fairgrounds, this village is one of the largest collections of pioneer buildings in the state and a fascinating place to visit. There are nearly 50 items of interest, including an early hospital, millinery shop, gas station, farmhouse, and sod house (the latter constructed in the 1970s as a replica). Guided tours can be arranged, but brochures allow easy self-guiding. Picnic tables are available for a nice summer's day.

LODGING

Historic Dayton House Bed & Breakfast (507-727-1311; www.daytonhouse.org), 1311 4th Ave. This grand home in Worthington was owned by three prominent families in succession, including the Dayton family, eventually of department-store fame (the chain eventually was sold to Marshall Fields, then to Macy's). A local historic group took over the restoration of the building, with excellent results, and there are now two plush suites available. Both have private bath, sitting area, antique furnishings, high-speed Internet and flat-screen TV, and a better-than-average continental breakfast daily. Rates start at $110.

✳ Laura Ingalls Wilder Historic Highway

No question about it, one of the biggest draws in southwestern Minnesota is the connection to Laura Ingalls Wilder and her pioneer family and friends.

TO SEE

Attractions are open year-round unless otherwise noted.

✂ ♿ **Laura Ingalls Wilder Museum** (507-859-2358; 800-528-7280; www.walnutgrove.org), US 14, Walnut Grove. Open daily Apr.–Oct.; Mon.–Sat. in Mar., Nov., and Dec.; Mon.–Fri. in Jan.–Feb. $5 adults, $2 ages 6–12, free for those 5 and under. The museum covers two different eras in Wilder's life: that of her family's stay in the region back in the 1800s, and that of the popular TV series during the 1970s. The displays are fun and informative for visitors who are either history buffs or fans of the *Little House* books; there are several items (including photos and a quilt sewn by Laura and her daughter Rose) that either belonged to Laura herself or to friends and family, and several exhibits related to the time period itself. Artifacts from the TV series are also on display.

✂ **Ingalls Dugout Site** (507-859-2358; 800-528-7280; www.walnutgrove.org), US 14, Walnut Grove. Open daily May–Oct., weather permitting. $4 per car or $20 per tour bus. Along the banks of Plum Creek is this dugout home, where the

Ingalls family lived 1874–1876 before selling it after several crop failures and moving to Iowa. The Ingallses' ownership was discovered by the books' illustrator, Garth Williams, who informed the current owners of the historic nature of their property. There's not much to see anymore; the original sod house disappeared long ago, leaving behind a depression in the ground, but true *Little House* fans will want to visit. The site is scenic, and picnic tables are available to make a pleasant stop.

✒ **Sod House on the Prairie** (507-723-5138; www.sodhouse.org), 12598 Magnolia Ave, Sanborn. Open daily Apr.–Oct. $4; free for ages 6 and under. Laura Ingalls Wilder may not have lived here, but this is a nice accompaniment to the Dugout Site (see above). This replica homesite includes a sod home, dugout, and log cabin; the "soddie" was built in the style of Laura's day, with 2-foot-thick walls and lumber roof and floor, as opposed to the dugout, which has a dirt floor and roof. In previous years the soddie was available as a bed & breakfast, but at least temporarily, only tours are offered.

✒ ♿ **Wheels Across the Prairie Museum** (507-629-3661; www.wheelsacross theprairie.org), 3297 US 14, Tracy. Open daily mid-May mid-Sept. $3 adults; free for ages 12 and under. Essentially a pioneer museum, Wheels Across the

---

TO DO

✒ **Jeffers Petroglyphs** (507-628-5591, www.mnhs.org/places/sites/jp; http://jefferspetroglyphs.com), US 71. Open Memorial Day–Labor Day, daily; May and Sept., open Fri.–Sun. Also by appointment Oct.–Nov. $5 adults, $4 seniors, $3 ages 6–17; free for those ages 5 and under and Minnesota Historical Society members. The petroglyphs are southwest of the Laura Ingalls Highway, but they're well worth the slight detour. Thought to date from 3000 BC to possibly as recently as the mid-1700s, there are over 2,000 Native American carvings found across the islands of rock that appear throughout the prairie grasses. Two separate trails visit the glyphs, both starting at the visitor center, one only 0.5 mile round trip, the other slightly over a mile. Interpreters are available to explain the significance of the glyphs, which have a wide range of subject matter and meaning: Humans, arrows, elk, buffalo, deer, and turtles are just some of the identifiable figures. The images detail the history of the region and the people, identifying significant events and sacred ceremonies. Native Americans still come today for religious visits.

But it's not just the historic or spiritual aspects that make this a worthy visit. The landscape is striking: pink quartzite, prairie grasses, prickly pear cactus, and dozens of wildflowers. In the northern reaches, areas of buffalo rubs can be seen, where migrating bison would stop to rub their coats against the rocks, eventually leaving a glossy surface. Take some time after visiting the glyphs to admire the rest of the scenery.

Prairie includes several vintage buildings, such as a one-room schoolhouse, Episcopal church, log cabin, and train depot. Tracy is the small town Laura Ingalls Wilder visited on her first train trip, so the railway exhibit is of particular interest.

LODGING

Accommodations are open year-round unless otherwise noted.

✎ **Valentine Inn** (507-629-3827), 385 Emory St., Tracy. Four rooms, all with private bath, in this Victorian home that began its life as a hospital. Two rooms have walkout porch. Rates start at $85.

🐾 ✎ ♿ **Wilder Inn** (507-629-3350), 1000 Craig Ave., Tracy. A small motel a few miles from Walnut Grove. Each room has a microwave and mini fridge; daily continental breakfast is included. Rates start at $72.

WHERE TO EAT

✎ ♿ **Nellie's Café** (507-859-2384), US 14, Walnut Grove. Open daily for breakfast and lunch, Mon.–Fri. for dinner. Basic but good small-town café, with breakfast specials and sandwiches. Entrées start at $4.

THE I-35 CORRIDOR

✳ Albert Lea

TO DO

Attractions are open year-round unless otherwise noted.

✎ ♿ **Story Lady Doll & Toy Museum** (507-377-1820; www.storylady museum.com), 131 N. Broadway. Open Tues.–Sat. $2 adults, $1 ages 12 and under. More than 1,500 dolls are found in this amazing collection, from antique to current day. The adjacent gift shop has plenty of doll adoption opportunities.

✎ ♿ **Freeborn County Historical Museum** (507-373-8003; www.smig.net/fchm), 1031 Bridge St. The museum is open Tues.–Fri. year-round; also the first and third Sat. in June–Aug. The village is open Tues.–Fri. in May–Sept., as well as the first and third Sat. in June–Aug. $5 adults, $1 ages 12–18; free for kids under 12. An extensive and eclectic collection of memorabilia and historical exhibits make this a worthwhile visit. Pop-culture icons Eddie Cochran (an early rock–and-roll singer) and Marion Ross (of TV's *Happy Days*) both spent part of their childhoods here, and accordingly earned exhibits. But beyond celebrities, the museum has artifacts and displays from the Civil War and both world wars; stagecoaches and railroads; farm implements; formal clothing; and antique appliances, to name just a few. The adjacent village has several buildings, including a furnished parsonage, barbershop, and general store.

Myre-Big Island State Park (507-379-3403; www.dnr.state.mn.us/state _parks/myre_big_island/index.html), 19499 780th Ave. Migrating waterfowl, evidence of possibly permanent Native American settlements that date back 9,000 years, 16 miles of hiking trails through oak savanna and prairie (several of which are groomed for winter sports), and campsites make this park a favorite of locals and visitors alike.

LODGING

✍ **1858 Log Cabin Bed & Breakfast** (507-448-0089; www.1858log cabin.com), 11859 755th Ave., Glenville. This pre–Civil War log cabin has been retrofitted for today's travelers (electricity and indoor plumbing, anyone?) but still offers a glimpse into living quarters of days past. Kids are welcome. Antique furniture with hand-painted Norwegian rosemaling and patchwork quilts strengthen the pioneer experience. Daily breakfast included. Rates start at $110.

✳ Owatonna

TO SEE

Attractions are open year-round unless otherwise noted.

✍ ৬ **Cabela's** (507-451-4545; www.cabelas.com), 3900 Cabela Dr. Open daily. Yes, it's a big store, but it's more than just a shopping experience. The 150,000-square-foot hunting and fishing giant has been elevated to major tourist attrac-

CABELA'S

STATE SCHOOL ORPHANAGE MUSEUM

tion, including the arrival of tour buses. Hundreds of animal mounts are posted around the store, and not just of the Minnesota variety; African animals
including elephants and baboons are represented. A 60,000-gallon freshwater
aquarium has examples of Minnesota fish. You can shop, or you can sightsee,
or you can do both. There's also a restaurant.

✍ ♿ **Village of Yesteryear** (507-451-1420; www.steelecohistoricalsociety.org/
village.php), 1448 Austin Rd. Open May–Oct., Tues.–Sun.; other times by
appointment. $5 adults, $3 ages 7–16; free for those ages 6 and under with an
adult. A collection of 15 pioneer buildings, many with original or period-
appropriate furnishings.

✍ ♿ **State School Orphanage Museum** (507-444-4315; 800-423-6466; www
.orphanagemuseum.com), 540 West Hills Circle. Open daily. No admission
fee, though donations are welcome. The former home to more than 10,000
Minnesota orphans between 1886 and 1945. The large main building is
impressive, but it must have been imposing for the children being sent here.
There's video footage of the orphans from the 1930s, and visitors are welcome
to explore the building and grounds, right down to the underground root cellar. Most poignant is the Children's Cemetery. The former dining room now
houses the **Owatonna Arts Center** (507-451-0533; www.owatonnaartscen-
ter.org), which features local artists.

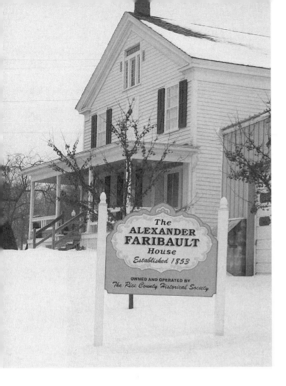

The ALEXANDER FARIBAULT House Established 1853

OWNED AND OPERATED BY The Rice County Historical Society

✴ Faribault

TO SEE

Attractions are open year-round unless otherwise noted.

✎ **Faribault Woolen Mills** (507-334-1644; 800-448-9665; www.faribault mills.com), 1819 2nd Ave. NW. Tours offered Mon.–Fri. at 10 AM or 2 PM. Admission free. This is the last woolen mill in the United States to process wool from sheep to final product. The company produces more than half of all the nation's wool blankets. The tour takes visitors through most of the process and provides shopping opportunities at the gift shop and outlet center.

✎ **Alexander Faribault House** (507-334-7913; www.rchistory.org/afarb house.html), 12 1st Ave. NE. Open May–Sept., Mon.–Fri., and by appointment. $2 adults; free for ages 5 and under. Built in 1853 by Faribault founding father Alexander Faribault, this Greek Revival home is one of Minnesota's oldest surviving buildings. The Rice County Historical Society took over the daunting task of restoration in 1945, with the end result a beautifully preserved piece of Minnesota history. Furnishings aren't original, but they accurately reflect the period.

✴ Special Events

✎ **Worthington Windsurfing Regatta and Unvarnished Music Festival** (www.worthingtonwindsurf ing.com), Worthington. June. Windsurfing championships and an indie music festival make for a great combination of interests. Beachfront waveboarding, an art fair, and possibly even fire eaters round out the entertainment.

✎ **Heritage Fest** (www.visitfaribault .com), Faribault. June. Food, music, carnival rides, dances, and a parade celebrating Faribault's rich ethnic history.

✎ **Sauerkraut Days** (www.hender sonmn.com), Henderson. Late June. Parades, tournaments, food, music, and a kraut-eating contest.

✎ **Laura Ingalls Wilder Pageant** (888-859-3102; www.walnutgrove .org), Walnut Grove. Held the last three weekends in July. This annual homage to Laura Ingalls Wilder is held on the banks of Plum Creek and covers some of the significant points of the *Little House* books. Note: This is a very popular event, and tickets sell out well in advance. Local lodging options are limited, so book ahead (see the "Laura Ingalls Memorial Highway" section).

Kolacky Days Czech Festival
(www.montgomerymn.org/events.html),
Montgomery. Late July. A three-day
festival that's occurred every year for
almost 80 years, focusing on the
town's Czech heritage. Kolacky is a
Czech fruit-filled bun, and that's just
one of the many ethnic foods that can
be found during the festival. Other
events include softball, volleyball, and
horseshoe tournaments, the Bun Run
foot race, Tour de Bun bike race, contemporary and classic Czech music,
and dancing.

Pipestone Civil War Days (www
.pipestoneminnesota.com), Pipestone.
Held in mid-Aug. in even-numbered
years (2008, 2010). Life during the
Civil War is brought back to life in
various components: battle reenactments, church services, children's
games, etiquette and dancing lessons,
a Grand Ball, and camp tours.

**Faribault Airfest and Balloon
Rally and Tree Frog Music Festival** (www.faribaultairfest.com; www
.treefrogmusic.com), Faribault. Sept.
It may seem like an odd combination,
but this way there's something for
everyone. Hot-air balloon races, air-
craft displays, and helicopter rides
take place along with performances by
several live bands, an art exhibit, children's activities, and food (and a beer
garden) for everyone.

King Turkey Days (507-372-2919;
www.worthingtonmnchamber.com),
Worthington. Held the second Sat.

after Labor Day. For nearly 70 years
man has raced turkey in an attempt to
win the coveted title of King Turkey.
That's the premise at the heart of this
tongue-in-cheek festival, which features pancake breakfasts, volleyball
tournaments, and a parade. But the
crowning event is the Great Gobbler
Gallop, in which teams of wild racing
turkeys take to the streets.

Mahkato Traditional Pow Wow
(www.greatermankato.com), Mankato.
Sept. The Land of Memories Park in
Mankato is home to this annual event
in which thousands of Native Americans of many tribes gather to reenact
ceremonial dance in traditional garb.
Displays of Native American costumes, traditional foods, and crafts
are offered.

Octoberfest (www.newulm.com),
New Ulm. Held the first two weekends in Oct. German food and beer,
live music, trolley tours, and children's games.

**River Crossings: an Art Fair in
Motion** (www.rivercrossingsart.org),
St. Peter, Mankato. Early Oct. Juried
art show, along with live music and
spoken word performances.

**South Central Minnesota Studio
Art Tour** (www.southcentralarttour
.com), Faribault, Northfield, and
Owatonna. Late Oct. These three
communities join forces to sponsor
this art tour, in which local artists
open their galleries and studios for
the public.

INDEX